THE

MEDAL YEARBOOK
1998

Edited by
James Mackay, MA, DLitt
John W. Mussell
and
the Editorial Team of MEDAL NEWS

ISBN 1 870 192 14 1
(Hardback edition 1 870 192 17 6)

Published by
TOKEN PUBLISHING LIMITED
PO Box 14, HONITON, Devon EX14 9YP, UK
Telephone: 01404 831 878   Fax: 01404 831 895

Printed in Great Britain by Friary Press, Bridport Road, Dorchester, Dorset.

CONTENTS

INDEX TO ADVERTISERS

PREFACE

THIS is the fourth annual edition of the MEDAL YEARBOOK, and the fact that we are not content to sit back and rest on our laurels can be seen by the extensive revision of the text, and especially the prices, which appears in each edition. Last year we incorporated prices for miniatures, a move which has been warmly welcomed by collectors and in particular the Miniature Medals Branch of the Orders and Medals Research Society. This information, like all of the other data which appears in this volume, depends to a large extent on the input of the experts. The field of medals is such a vast one explored on different levels, that no one person can possibly know everything. We at Token Publishing regard ourselves as a clearing-house for information which is supplied to us, and we will ensure that it is incorporated in the next edition.

In the course of the past year we have had much more feedback from readers than in the previous three years combined. This is extremely heartening. We hope that we have taken on board all of the criticism (which has invariably been constructive) and made the necessary adjustments or revisions to the text. As a result we have added no fewer than 15 entirely new medals to the main body of the text, and made substantial revisions in many of the existing entries. Of these, only two are actually new issues, the NATO Medal (206A) and the Ambulance Service (Emergency Duties) Long Service and Good Conduct Medal (264A). Significantly, the greatest improvements to our listing have been made in the sections dealing with jubilee, royal visit and police medals—all areas on the periphery of mainstream medal studies, but now attracting increasing interest. Doubtless there are other medals in these categories, especially from the colonies and Commonwealth countries. We therefore appeal to readers having specialised knowledge in any area to submit data for inclusion in a future edition.

We are also looking carefully at the matter of honours and awards, medals and decorations from Canada, Australia, New Zealand and other Commonwealth countries. This is a substantial field and its inclusion would necessitate a major expansion of the Yearbook. We would welcome the view of readers as to whether this development would be considered desirable.

Among the many other improvements that are immediately obvious in this year's edition we are delighted to include a completely up-dated photographic medal ribbon section. The ribbons for this important part of the book have been painstakingly put together by Ray Holdich to whom we owe a debt of gratitude.

As always, we are indebted to those of our readers who have taken the trouble to give us corrections, amendments or additional material. In particular we should like to thank the following for their assistance in making this edition as up-to-date as possible: Ivor F. Bush, David Deptford, Norman Gooding, John R. Hailey, Colin Hole, David Martin, Denis J. Poole, Malcolm Rouse, Alan Stevenson, John Tamplin, Major Noel W. Taylor, Kerry Tabrett and John Wilson.

Our special thanks are due to a number of dealers and collectors but particularly Chris Dixon, Andrew Litherland and Mark Cline for checking the prices of medals and miniatures, in light of auction results in the course of the past year, as well as prices given in dealers' lists for material which seldom passes through the saleroom.

THAT WAS THE YEAR THAT WAS!

An at-a-glance résumé of the main events and occurrences that affected the medal hobby during the past months, as reported in MEDAL NEWS . . .

August 1996

The Gallantry Medallists' League is formed from the former DCM League and CGM Association. This change was brought about by the review of the Armed Forces Gallantry Awards in 1993 which resulted in both the DCM and CGM being discontinued and their place taken by the Conspicuous Gallantry Cross awarded to all ranks of all three services.

Expresso TV launch an Aviation Video Series in association with the Imperial War Museum. The first videos deal with the Messerschmitt BT109 and the nine-year epic to salvage Hurricane Z7015 from the sea and restore it to flying condition.

A collection of memorabilia, medals and decorations pertaining to the Cambridgeshire Regiment is inaugurated at the Imperial War Museum, Duxford on August 27.

A shop entitled Welsh Medals and Militaria opens at 1A Pontcanna Street, Cardiff, catering to collectors of badges, bayonets, uniforms and other military collectables as well as medals and decorations especially of Welsh interest.

September 1996

The annual convention of the Orders and Medals Research Society takes place on September 21 at the New Connaught Rooms, London, with Major General Andrew Keeling, CB, CBE, as guest of honour. At this event MEDAL YEARBOOK was launched with a change of name.

The Muster of the Gallantry Medallists League takes place at Lancing College on September 24. Members were inspected by Field Marshall the Lord Bramall, accompanied by Rear Admiral H. W. E. Hollins.

The National Maritime Museum launches an appeal to raise £4 million to top up the £11.8 million awarded by the Heritage Lottery Fund. The money will go towards the Neptune Court Project, to open up a large area behind the Museum's main entrance and reveal a spectacular courtyard with a 2500 square metre roof, which will provide new reception facilities and 11 galleries. As part of the fund-raising activities, supporters are encouraged to have their name, or that of a loved one, engraved on slate for display in the atrium.

The George Medal awarded to Dover fire officer Alex Campbell in respect of the fire aboard HMS *Sandhurst* in July 1940 is acquired by the Dover Museum and goes on permanent display.

Malcolm Gordon enters into partnership with Mike Couzens to form Gordons Medals Ltd, trading at the Grays in the Mews Antique Centre, London.

Field Marshal the Lord Bramall, KG, GCB, OBE, MC, JP, accompanied by Rear Admiral H. W. E. Hollins, CB, inspects members of the Gallantry Medallists League, September 24, 1996.

October 1996

The first part of the collection of Naval Medals formed by the late Captain K. J. Douglas-Morris comes under the hammer at Dix Noonan Webb and realises a total of just over £310,000.

Imperial Auctions is established at Accrington, the first sale of coins, medals and militaria being scheduled to take place in February 1997.

The National Maritime Museum at Greenwich opens a new Picture Research Room to provide greater public access to its collections. The room is equipped with microfilm, photographs, illustrated catalogues and printing facilities. In addition, users have access to a database containing images of over 47,000 items in the Museum's care. The Picture Research Room is open 10am–1pm and 2pm–5pm Monday to Friday.

November 1996

The 40th anniversary of the Suez campaign is marked by the publication of *Wings Over Suez*, launched at a special ceremony at the Fleet Air Arm Museum, Yeovilton. The book, published by Grub Street and written by Brian Cull, David Nicolle and Shlomo Aloni, covers the military expansion of both Egypt and Israel, the Sinai campaign, the Anglo-French build-up and the air and seaborne operations of November 1956. Several veterans of the war attended the launch and were on hand to sign copies of the book.

The latest Operational Honours List is published on November 8 naming 97 recipients of military honours, including 13 for gallantry in action in Northern Ireland and Bosnia.

Sotheby's at Billingshurst sell a Spitfire which had been salvaged from the Humber estuary and painstakingly rebuilt over 13 years by Stephen Arnold and Julian Mitchell of space, time and funds forced them to sell the aircraft before restoration was completed, but it fetched £73,000 nonetheless. It was bought by an American oilman, Patrick F. Taylor, on behalf of the New Orleans National D-Day Museum. The fighter was piloted by a Belgian, killed when the plane crashed in 1944. The wreck was recovered from the riverbed 40 years later.

December 1996

A new permanent gallery at the National Army Museum opens on December 3, devoted to "The Rise of the Redcoat: the British Army from Henry V to George III". The display tells the story of the British Army from the archers of Agincourt to the Redcoats of the American Revolution. This new gallery complements the existing displays which now take the story of the British Army from 1415 right down to the present day.

January 1997

The Public Record Office at Kew opens the first batch of soldiers' papers relating to those who served in the First World War. Among the first batch are the service records of film star Ronald Colman, mass-murderer Reginald Christie and Private John Williams, who won his VC at Rorke's Drift in 1879 and re-enlisted in 1914 at the age of 57 to serve throughout the First World War.

Five years after the Gulf War, the Royal Mint, in conjunction with Gold Investments Ltd, sells the original gold sovereigns carried by military

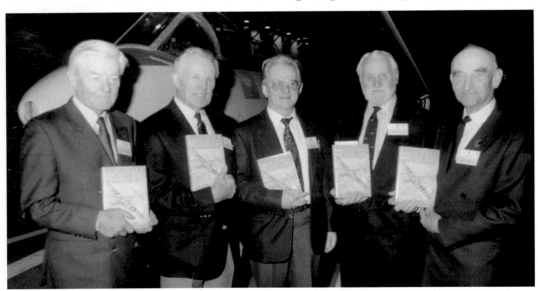

Captain Bruce Clark, Rear Admiral Ray Rawbone, CB, AFC, Brian Cull (author), Commander W. H. Cowling, Vice Admiral Sir Edward Anson, KCB, signed copies of Wings Over Suez, *at the Fleet Air Arm Museum on November 1.*

The Royal Mint offers collectors the chance to own sovereigns carried by troops in the Gulf war.

personnel who took part in Operation Granby. The sovereigns were part of the escape kit issued to servicemen and secreted in their uniforms for use as barter in the event of being shot down behind enemy lines. The Mint offers one of the actual sovereigns carried, in a special descriptive pack, together with miniature replicas of the two medals issued to all British servicemen who took part in the war.

David Erskine-Hill, formerly of Sotheby's, joins Spink and Son as Director of the Medal Collectors' Department. His position at Sotheby's Medal Department in Billingshurst is taken by Edward Playfair. Nicholas Watts, formerly a cataloguer in Bonham's Numismatic Department, also joins the staff of Spink's.

On Sunday January 25, the 118th anniversary of the epic defence of Rorke's Drift, Brigadier David Bromhead, great-great-nephew of Lieut Gonville Bromhead VC, exchanges greetings with officers and men of 121 Infantry Battalion, South African Defence Force, a Zulu unit consisting of men whose ancestors also took part in the battle. Brigadier Bromhead is the Colonel of the Royal Regiment of Wales, successors to the South Wales Borderers, the regiment which won 11 Victoria Crosses at Rorke's Drift.

MEDAL NEWS expands from quarto to A4 page size. With an increase in the number of pages as well, the change is warmly welcomed by readers and advertisers alike.

February 1997

Well-known medal dealer Trevor Davies, Director of Roberts Medals, dies on February 3 at the age of 59. Roberts Medals was formed in 1983 and specialised in medals and decorations pertaining to Africa.

The second part of the Douglas-Morris Collection is sold at Dix Noonan Webb on February 12, bringing the grand total to just under £600,000.

The Napoleonic Fair takes place at the Royal National Hotel, Russell Square, London. Over 80 dealers take part, offering everything from medals and badges to uniforms, equipment, models, militaria, books, videos and battlefield tours.

March 1997

The group of medals and decorations awarded to Air Chief Marshal Lord Dowding which was to have been the highlight of the Spink sale on March 18 is withdrawn and sold privately to the RAF Museum, Hendon prior to the auction. The price paid was £60,000, being the upper end of the pre-sale estimate. The medals have already gone on permanent display, alongside the medals and decorations of Reichsmarschall Hermann Goering, commander of the Luftwaffe.

Brian Clark, the well-known Middlesbrough medal dealer, died on March 25 at the age of 55.

April 1997

The West Country Militaria and Medal Fair moves to a new venue. Based at Bristol since its inception in 1989, it is held on April 27 this year at the Yate Leisure Centre near Chipping Sodbury.

The New Zealand Minister of Defence announces that Her Majesty the Queen has approved the award of the New Zealand General Service Medal to the Armed Forces involved in operations on the Malay-Thai border between 1960 and 1964. A silver clasp to the NZGSM is to be inscribed *Malaya 1960–64*. This assuages a long-standing grievance from those involved who had not previously received medallic recognition as their service had fallen into a gap between the entitlement dates of British awards. This retrospective award has required an amendment to the Royal Warrant. The NZGSM itself was instituted as a retrospective award to personnel who served in Japan at the end of the Second World War, 1946–9.

An exhibition at the National Army Museum opens on April 2 and runs to May 18 devoted to unpublished stories from the Ohio University collection of the papers of Cornelius Ryan, the war correspondent who later wrote the best-selling books *The Last Battle* and *A Bridge Too Far.*

May 1997

Command Paper 3526 introduces the Northern Ireland Home Service Medal which will replace the Ulster Defence Regiment Medal. Unlike the UDR Medal, the new medal will not give officers post-nominal letters. It is expected that this medal will establish a precedent for new medals for all the reserve forces to be introduced in due course. Full details of this medal will be given in the 1999 edition of MEDAL YEARBOOK.

Members of the British Forces (mostly Royal Lincolnshire Regiment and Cameronians) who served with the special "O Force" in Aqaba, Jordan in the early 1950s are eligible for a new medal being produced with the sanction of King Hussein. The deployment of the Force forestalled an Egyptian-backed coup to topple the Hashemite dynasty, but no medal or clasp was ever authorised. The new medal, designed by G. E. Harris, has the profile of King Hussein on the obverse.

La Coupole (the Cupola) opens on May 9 at the Pas de Calais. Originally built by the Nazis in 1943 as the launch site for the V2 rockets, the gigantic underground base has been converted into a history Centre of War and Rockets at a cost of 69 million francs.

June 1997

Bonhams' sale of medals on June 5 includes the impressive James R. Barracks Collection, comprising every Japanese order in all classes including the rare Collar of the Supreme Order of the Chrysanthemum. The sale also features the William Long Collection of gallantry awards and campaign medals to Irish regiments.

The annual Victorian Military Society Fair takes place over the weekend of June 28–29 at the Historic Dockyard, Chatham. The theme of the event is the Diamond Jubilee of Queen Victoria, celebrated exactly a century earlier.

July 1997

The celebrated collection of coins, tokens and medals relating to the First World War, formed by Raoul Van Trappen of Ghent, forms the centrepiece of the two-part sale at Spink and Son on July 9 and 17.

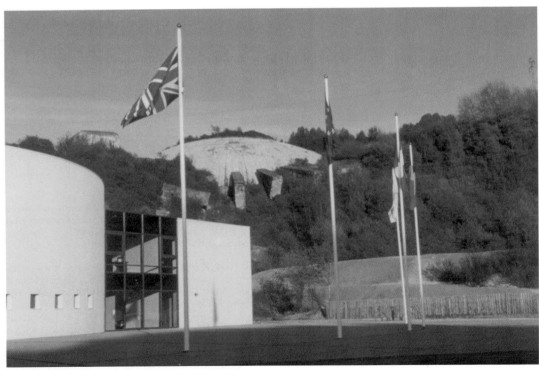

Hitler's V2 rocket base, La Coupole, Pas de Calais, is opened to the public.

13

MARKET TRENDS

In the period under review (mid-1996 to mid-1997) the economic trends of the previous twelve months continued, inflation was low and interest rates stable. In the second half of the current period there was a change of government, followed in short order by three increases in interest rates to curb inflationary tendencies. The first budget of the new Chancellor, Gordon Brown, was not sufficiently stringent to dampen down spending, while the sudden influx of windfall cash arising from the conversion of the leading building societies to banks was expected to trigger a boom in consumer spending. The pound was at an 80 year high against the US dollar and the Deutschemark, but while the strong pound was a boon to British tourists abroad it made life difficult for exporters and manufacturers in general, and the fear that tougher conditions in industry would add to belt-tightening and the loss of jobs also tended to curb windfall spending. That other barometer of the economy, the housing market, continued to perform erratically; and while there was talk of a recovery in London and the Home Counties, the housing market remained stagnant in other parts of the country.

These economic factors have inevitably had their knock-on effect on the medal market. The most noticeable result of the strong pound has been to make British bidders at auction more competitive. Conversely this has tended to deter all but the most determined American and European bidders at the London sales, although those of us who were disappointed by the crazy bids in, say, the recent Van Trappen sale at Spink's might be forgiven for thinking that the world has gone mad. The plain truth is that so much of the material in the Van Trappen Collection was completely new to the market that it was probably a case of the estimates erring on the low side. So much of this material was unrepeatable and in a spirit of "now-or-never" both private collectors and the trade had to go well above estimate to secure the lots they wanted.

The undoubted highlight of the past year has been the dispersal of the fabulous collection of naval medals formed by the late Captain K. J. Douglas-Morris, RN, which Dix Noonan Webb disposed of in two sales, on October 16 and February 12, yielding a total of just under £600,000 in all. This collection was remarkable not only for its extent and comprehensiveness but also for the depth of research evident, and it was the latter aspect which played a notable part in many of the realisations. The two-part catalogue, bound into a single volume, will be regarded as required reading for anyone researching naval medals from now on.

The late Captain Douglas Morris whose collection was sold in two memorable auctions by Dix Noonan Webb.

The dispersal of the collection of long service and efficiency medals formed by the late J. Hobbs (Glendining, July 3, 1996) was quite an eye-opener, in view of the prices realised for Efficiency Medals with elusive country suspension bars. As a result, we have completely revised our listing for this medal, and now provide a table showing the various permutations and combinations of obverse and suspension bar. Obviously there is a vast difference between the rarity of EMs from Australia or Canada and those from Nigeria or Rhodesia and Nyasaland. In the Hobbs sale, for example, two medals from Southern Rhodesia and Rhodesia and Nyasaland suspensions fetched £640—five times the estimate.

Interest in individual campaign medals continued to be extremely buoyant. Inevitably personal factors often came into the reckoning. Thus the Waterloo Medal to Dr Arthur Stewart of 71 Regiment and Inspector General of Hospitals excited more than usual interest, with regimental and medical themes playing a vital part. In addition, the owner of Stewart's Military GSM was also a contestant, anxious to reunite the two medals. As a consequence this medal was bid up to £1,900, against an estimate of £750–£800). Similarly three groups of medals to the Babbington family spanning a century from South Africa (1829) to the First World War were keenly fought over by a dealer wanting them for a client and a family member who had to pay £3,600 (estimate £600–£700) to secure them. When several themes of interests combine in a single group it is difficult to predict the outcome. The Victorian Royal Red Cross group of seven to Superintending Nursing Sister Joan Gray (Sotheby's, July 29, 1996) was a case in point, attracting bids from collectors of medical, nursing and women's awards. In the end the lot was knocked down for £9,000, twice estimate.

The personal factor always looms large, especially when it comes to groups of orders and decorations. The Order of Merit and CBE group awarded to the aircraft designer Sir Geoffrey de Havilland was purchased by the Royal Air Force Museum at Sotheby's in November for £14,000 (estimate £8,000–£12,000).

Other factors can also influence the outcome. A Constabulary Medal for Ireland, 1921 awarded to Temporary Cadet George Gash fetched £1,700 at Spink's on November 6 against an estimate of £800–£900, but no doubt interest in the notorious Auxiliaries and Black and Tans has been heightened by the recent film about Michael Collins. Conversely the relative lack of interest in the former Soviet Union probably explains the poor performance of two interesting lots at Spink's last November. The Military Medal awarded to Senior Sergeant Shashio, one of only four MMs awarded to the Red Army, was bought in at £1,200, having failed to reach its estimate of £1,900–£2,000, while the group of 12 to fighter ace Major Deuchik sold for £2,400, rather below the estimate of £2,500–£3,000.

Usual combinations continued to excite considerable interest. Among the more exotic may be mentioned the CB, KH, both naval and military GSM and Sultan's Gold Medal for Egypt 1801 awarded to Colonel Sir John Morillyon Wilson, 1st Foot, who was wounded 13 times during service in the Peninsula and North America. Estimated at £6,000–£8,000, this group realised £11,200 at Dix Noonan Webb on November 29.

Below we itemise the results achieved by the major decorations and campaign groups, with the pre-sale estimates (where known) in parentheses, during the 1996/97 auction season.

GALLANTRY MEDALS AND GROUPS
Victoria Cross

Indian Mutiny group of five to Lieutenant Colonel T. B. Hackett, Royal Welch Fusiliers. **£58,700** (£18,000–£20,000). *Sotheby, March 25.*

Delhi 1857 award to Captain George Forrest. **£38,000** (£25,000–£30,000). *Glendining, March 19.*

Bhootan group to Captain J. Dundas, RE. **£38,000** (25,000–£28,000). *Spink, March 18.*

Crimean group, including the CGM and Legion d'Honneur, to Seaman Joseph Trewavas. **£29,000** (£24,000–£28,000). *Dix Noonan Webb, October 16.*

Indian Mutiny Victoria Cross group to Lt Col. T. B. Hackett, sold by Sotheby's for £58,000.

WWI group to Private George Peachment, KRRC, Loos. **£27,000** (£18,000–£20,000). *Spink, November 6.*

WWI group to Private G. McIntosh, Gordon Highlanders. **£32,000** (£18,000–£20,000). *Spink, November 6.*

Gallipoli group to Lieutenant Colonel Richard Willis, Lancashire Fusiliers. **£54,000** (£30,000–£35,000). *Dix Noonan Webb, November 29.*

VC and DSM group to Petty Officer Pitcher, Q Ships. **£28,000** (£30,000–£35,000). *Dix Noonan Webb, February 12.*

Distinguished Service Order

DSO and bar group, Q Ships. **£3,900** (£2,000–£3,000). *Dix Noonan Webb, October 16.*

DSO and CMG group to Air Commodore E. L. Gerrard, RAF (formerly RM and RNAS). **£8,500** (£3,000–£5,000). *Sotheby, November 27.*

DSO and bar and WWI AFC group of six to Group Captain Gaskell-Blackburn. **£6,200** (£3,000–£4,000). *Dix Noonan Webb, November 29.*

DSO, OBE, DSC and two bars group of nine to Group Captain B. D. Hobbs. **£5,300** (£3,000–£4,000). *Glendining, March 20.*

Distinguished Service Cross

DSC group for Gallipoli 1915 with CGM for Somaliland 1904. **£7,800** (£7,000–£9,000). *Dix Noonan Webb, October 16.*

DSC group for St Nazaire. **£2,500** (£3,000–£4,000). *Sotheby, July 29.*

DSC, DFC and AFC group to Group Captain Edward Burling. **£9,200** (£6,000–£8,000). *Dix Noonan Webb, October 16.*

Military Cross

Ypres group of five. **£1,350** (£400–£500). *Spink, November 6.*

MC, DCM and MM group of seven to Sub Lieutenant C. B. Wheeler, RNVR. **£5,200** (£3,000–£4,000). *Dix Noonan Webb, February 12.*

Distinguished Conduct Medal

Group to 21st Lancers, for a charger at Omdurman. **£5,200** (£3,000–£4,000). *Sotheby, July 29.*

Dongola group of seven. **£4,500** (£3,000–£3,500). *Dix Noonan Webb, November 29.*

DCM with MM and bar and Medaille Militaire in a WWI group of six to Corporal F. Palmer. **£1,400.** *Dix Noonan Webb, March 25.*

Distinguished Service Medal

WWI group with diary of the Tanganyika campaign. **£3,300** (£1,500–£2,000). *Dix Noonan Webb, October 16.*

Royal Naval Armoured Cars, Austria 1917. **£850** (£400–£500). *Dix Noonan Webb, February 12.*

Army Gold Cross with five bars sold by Spink for £18,500.

CAMPAIGN MEDALS AND GROUPS
Army Gold Cross

With five bars to Lieutenant Colonel Henry Hardinge, one of only seven such awards. **£18,500** (£18,000–£22,000). *Spink, March 18.*

With two bars to Lieutenant General Sir Joseph Carncross, one of 18 such awards. **£11,500** (£10,000–£12,000). *Spink, March 18.*

Small Naval Gold Medal

To Admiral Sir William Parker for action against the French fleet in the three days before the Glorious First of June, 1794. **£10,000** (£10,000–£12,000). *Dix Noonan Webb, November 29.*

Naval General Service Medal

With *Trafalgar* clasp. **£1,800** (£1,300–£2,000). *Glendining, July 3.*

With military GSM, CB, KH and Sultan's Gold Medal for Egypt, to Colonel Sir John M. Wilson. **£11,200** (£6,000–£8,000). *Dix Noonan Webb, November 29.*

With clasp for *Yangtse 1949* with Korea and UN medals, to Stoker Mechanic Bannister. **£1,800** (£500–£700). *Dix Noonan Webb, October 16.*

Military General Service Medal

With 12 bars (Waterloo medal missing). **£2,200** (£1,200–£1,400). *Glendining, July 3.*

DATES FOR YOUR DIARY

Military Cross group to 2 Lt H. A. Somerville who shot down WWI German air ace Max Muller—sold in our April 30, 1997 sale for £4,750.

The following dates have been arranged for our
1998 AUCTION SALES

SALE DAYS

416 January 6th
417 February 10th
418 March 17th
419 April 28th
Spring Connoisseur Collectiors Sale April 29th
420 June 9th
421 July 14th
422 August 25th
423 October 6th
Autumn Connoisseur Collectors Sale October 7th
424 November 17th

Final entries 9am–1pm on dates listed below:

November 15th
January 10th
February 14th
March 21st
March 17th
May 2nd
June 13th
July18th
August 29th
August 25th
October 10th

• All sales comprise Military Medals, Militaria, Arms, Armour, Coins and Collectors Items
• Fine illustrated catalogues £6.00 (post Free UK) Overseas Airmail £7.00
• Connoisseur Sale Catalogues £12.00 (post free worldwide)
• All Catalogues contain a "prices realised list" of the previous Sale.

WALLIS & WALLIS
West Street Auction Galleries, Lewes, Sussex, England
Tel: 01273 (Lewes) 480208   Fax: (01273) 476562

INTO THE NEXT MILLENNIUM

While the premier gallantry awards, the Victoria Cross and the George Cross, have, since their inception, been made regardless of rank, this has not been the case with other honours and awards, where distinctions between commissioned and other ranks as well as the separate branches of the armed forces have been rigidly maintained.

Interestingly, it was King George V who, during the First World War, first raised the matter of replacing this caste system for bravery and distinguished service by an all-ranks system, but when he broached the subject with the Prime Minister, David Lloyd George shied away because he was afraid that any suggestion of the sort would upset the admirals and the generals.

In the 1930s the notion of identical gallantry awards for officers and men was proposed by Arnold Wilson, MP, himself the holder of a DSO won in 1916. Unfortunately Wilson, despite his age, volunteered for active service with the RAF on the outbreak of the Second World War and was killed in action as an airgunner at the age of 55. His egalitarian ideas died with him, and it was not until 1964 that the proposal was revived.

This time the prime-mover was HRH Prince Philip, himself the recipient of an all-ranks decoration, the French Croix de Guerre, for services with the Royal Navy in the Second World War. The Duke of Edinburgh wrote to the Chiefs of Staff recommending that "all gallantry awards should be open to all ranks". The Chiefs of Staff felt obliged to heed this recommendation, and in time-honoured fashion set up a review committee. This, however, was biased from the outset; in the words of the senior Army adviser, "with respect to HRH the Duke of Edinburgh, it seems to me that the only people who are likely to welcome change would be the lunatic fringe who are anxious to level anything and everything down to suit their own dreary principles". This reactionary viewpoint won the argument and no action was taken.

In the aftermath of the South Atlantic campaign,

William Waldegrave MP wrote to Margaret Thatcher proposing that gallantry awards should be available to all ranks. The Prime Minister endorsed this view and she pressed the Chiefs of Staff to rethink their policy. Another review committee was set up, but this was one battle the Iron Lady did not win. The entrenched views of the senior generals and admirals remained quite unchanged.

John Major, however, set the ball rolling with sweeping changes in civil honours, in line with his policy of advancing the classless society. This provoked a leader in *The Times* (January 11, 1991) which questioned why "the Armed Forces had not followed the lead given by the Civil system in abandoning the obsolete distinction between the gallantry awards appropriate for officers and those for other ranks". Once more the Chiefs of Staff reacted swiftly by setting up yet another review committee in the hopes of deflecting such dangerous notions. This time, however, they had to deal with the Prime Minister who intervened personally and bluntly told the Chiefs of Staff that no recommendations would be acceptable unless rank-related awards were abolished. The Chiefs of Staff finally gave way, and Malcom Rifkind, the Minister of Defence, was able to announce on October 18, 1993 that henceforward all gallantry awards would be available to servicemen and women regardless of rank. This revolution may well be regarded in years to come as John Major's most important achievement.

Since then, therefore, the old-fashioned system has been considerably streamlined. The Victoria Cross remains as the sole award at the top level of gallantry. At the second level, however, four decorations (DSO, CGM, DCM and CGM Flying) have been replaced by the Conspicuous Gallantry Cross, while at the third level the Distinguished Service Medal, Military Medal and Distinguished Flying Medal have been abolished. Lower down the scale, there is the Mention in Despatches (in action with the enemy) and the Queen's Commendations (for bravery not in action, for bravery in the air and for valuable service), distinguished by different emblems worn on the medal ribbon.

These distinctions were set out in tabular form in the 1997 MEDAL YEARBOOK. Since that time the half-yearly Operational Honours Lists have demonstrated the new system very clearly. Nevertheless, this does throw up some anomalies. The Air Force Cross, hitherto recognising not only non-operational gallantry in the air but also meritorious service while flying, is now confined to the first of these roles, while the latter has been transferred to the Order of the British Empire. It would seem logical, in the interests of rationalising awards, to scrap the Air Force Cross altogether and replace it with the George Cross, George Medal or Queen's Gallantry Medal, depending on the level of bravery involved. As it is, the three "civilian"

gallantry awards have often in the past been awarded to service personnel for bravery though not in the presence of the enemy, e.g. on bomb-disposal duties. The award of the QGM recently to Sergeant Iain Andrew Harris of the Royal Marines In Northern Ireland presumably comes into this category, although no details were given in view of the continuing sensitivity regarding security of operations in that troubled province.

The newly instituted Queen's Commendation for Valuable Services has been lavishly awarded in the latest list, with 37 to those serving in Northern Ireland and 23 to personnel in Bosnia. At the same time, meritorious service in these two hot-spots has resulted in 24 awards of the Order of the British Empire: three CBEs, four OBEs and two MBEs for service in Bosnia, and two OBEs and 13 MBEs in Northern Ireland. Despite the classless principle, however, no one below the rank of warrant officer was awarded the MBE in Northern Ireland, while the lowest rank to be recognised in Bosnia was a Staff Sergeant, Christopher Mark Williams. The sergeants, corporals and privates who, in the good old days, would have qualified for the British Empire Medal, seem to have lost out entirely.

STORAGE OF MEDALS

The vexing question of storing medals is one which crops up regularly. Just what are the problems . . . and what are the solutions? This article, by *L. R. Lee, Senior Scientific Officer at the Department of Conservation, The British Museum*, helps to provide the final answer

Metals can corrode in the presence of certain volatile materials. These substances are present in the atmosphere, but generally at low concentrations. However, materials such as wood, fabric and adhesives, used in a storage system, may emit these substances causing higher concentrations which can cause deterioration of objects in the storage area.

Silver is tarnished by reducible sulphides, commonly hydrogen sulphide and carbonyl sulphide, which can be emitted by fabrics, especially those made of wool, and by some adhesives.

Copper and its alloys are corroded by chlorides, sulphides and organic acids. The source of these may again be fabrics, but also certain plastics. For example, polyvinyl chloride (PVC) can give off chlorine-containing gases.

Acidic papers and boards, wood, wood composites and some adhesives can give off organic acids. The corrosion of lead is initiated by acetic acid and basic lead carbonate is formed. Woood and wood composites may emit formic acid and formaldehyde. Formic acid will cause lead, and sometimes copper alloys, to corrode, producing a formate salt; formaldehyde may cause similar problems at high concentrations.

The following recommendations for the storage of coins and medals are based on tests carried out in the Conservation Research Group of the Department of Conservation in The British Museum to evaluate the suitability of materials for use with metals.

Materials recommended for use

Wood and wood-composite cabinets and trays

These are usually suitable for the storage of silver artefacts. However, in our tests, lead almost always corroded, and copper occasionally corroded in the presence of wood, especially oak. In general, when any wood is to be used, it should be well seasoned and dried. Tropical hardwoods, e.g. mahogany, appear to be less corrosive, but should not be used for storage of lead.

Wood-composites, such as plywood, fibreboard and blockboard, are generally unsuitable for use with lead, and often unsuitable for use with copper. This is due to harmful, volatile materials emitted by both the wood component and the adhesive or binder component. Manufacturers are becoming aware of problems associated with volatile gases, and some types of fibreboards, e.g. Medite, are designed to have low level emissions of formaldehyde. However, these fibreboards are still a source of organic acids; evidence suggests that these acids are more corrosive than formaldehyde.

Plastic cabinets and trays

Plastic cabinets and trays are an alternative to using wood and specialist ranges are available from a number of manufacturers and have been found to be suitable for use with all metals.

Metal cabinets

Stove-enamelled metal cabinets are generally suitable for storage of all types of materials. A wide variety of these are available, but they are not designed specifically for the storage of medals. Again, it is advisable to ensure the suitability of a plastic material by testing.

Adhesives

Cascamite (a powdered urea formaldehyde adhesive) is a general woodwork glue which may be used for construction of cabinets and inserts. Other glues which have passed our tests include Evostik Impact II, UHU All Purpose glue, Thixofix non-drip adhesive and Devcon 5 minute epoxy. However, the tests on these adhesives evaluated their suitability for use in construction of storage units, not for use on a medal itself. Glues base on polyvinyl acetate emulsions should be avoided, as they can degrade with time, producing harmful acetic acid. Some silicone sealants also emit acetic acid, but "non-corrosive" products are now available.

Lining materials

Drawers or trays within the cabinets are often lined. Plastazote, a polyethylene foam, available in a variety of colours, may be used as an insert with suitably sized profiles cut out to accommodate the coins. The foam will afford protection to the medals, as it will prevent them moving around and suffering mechanical damage when the drawers or trays are opened and closed.

Textiles may be used to line drawers and trays. The use of felt should be avoided since it causes silver to tarnish. Other fabrics can also cause problems. The Conservation Research Section has a large collection of fabrics which have been tested and will undertake tests on any sample on a commercial basis.

Paper envelopes

Many envelopes are made of poor quality paper, which will become acidic and unsuitable for use in storage. Therefore envelopes should be made from archival quality paper on board.

Plastic envelopes and boxes

Some plastics may degrade and produce harmful vapours or droplets of plasticiser. Therefore, archival quality plastic envelopes should be used. These are made of polyester or high quality polythene. The medals can be stored individually in plastic boxes such as clear, colourless polystyrene boxes. These may be lined with Plastazoate foam to avoid mechanical damage.

Fabric and paper discs

Woollen felt discs should not be used in proximity with silver, as they emit sulphide gases which will cause rapid tarnishing. A loop nylon fabric may be a suitable alternative, as it has similar qualities to felt. It will not fray when cut, acts as a "cushion", and is available in a variety of colours.

Paper discs should be made of archival quality paper or board.

Inks

Inks used for annotating paper discs should have a permanent colour, and be tested for acidity prior to use. Several pens have been tested by scientists in Glasgow. The following were found to be suitable for archival purposes: Artline Calligraphy Pen black EK 243; Edding Profipen 0.1 1800; Pentel Document pens permanent MR 205 (black or blue); GPO standard ballpoint pen PO SP15.

Other Considerations

Absorbents

Should an artefact be particularly prone to corrosion, an absorbent material may be incorporated into its storage container. Charcoal cloth, a fabric made of activated carbon may be used to absorb all types of gases. However, this cloth should not be paced in direct contact with silver, copper or iron medals, as it contains non-volatile chlorides which can cause corrosion. Zinc oxide pellets, Puraspec catalyst, which react with hydrogen sulphide and hence reduce the rate at which silver tarnishes, can also be used.

Light

On occasions, whilst on display, silver items have acquired a white "bloom". This has been shown to be a result of photochemical degradation of the original silver chloride patina forming powdery metallic silver.

It is unlikely that medals would be continually exposed to bright light whilst in storage, but this potential hazard should be borne in mind.

Conclusions

Care must be taken when selecting material for use in the storage of medals, as corrosive gases can be emitted by a variety of substances. As an extra precaution, an absorbent material may be incorporated into the storage system.

In addition to the information given in this article, advice on the selection of materials can be obtained from the author at the Conservation Research Group of the Department of Conservation, The British Museum, London WC1B 3DG. An occasional Paper, OP111, entitled "Selection of Materials for the Storage or Display of Museum Objects" written by the author and D. Thickett, is also available; this contains further information on the subject—contact British Museum Press, telephone 0171 323 1234.

PITFALLS FOR THE UNWARY

Medal collecting has its fair share of pitfalls to trap the unwary. Your best guarantee always is to purchase medals only from reputable dealers who will gladly refund your money should the medal turn out to be not quite what it seems. The main problem arises when you buy medals from general antique shops, street market stalls, swapmeets and collectors' fairs. Despite the Trades Descriptions Act and other legislation in recent years, in practice it is very difficult and expensive to win restitution. It is one thing to study a medal critically in the comfort of one's own home, with all the right tools and reference books at hand; and quite another matter to spot a fake or outright forgery while browsing in a dealer's stock. But a little care, and a better idea of the potential problems, may prevent you from making a costly mistake. In this short article *Harold Dane* points out a few of the pitfalls for the beginner.

OUTRIGHT FORGERY

The traditional method of producing an outright forgery of a medal was to make moulds from a genuine example and then take casts from it. The most obvious telltale sign of forgery is the metal itself, for forgers seldom took the trouble to get exactly the right composition of alloy. A good example of this is the forgery of the India General Service Medal of 1854 which has a leaden appearance and a peculiarly soapy texture to the touch. On checking the diameter of the suspect medals, using callipers and a half-millimetre scale, it will invariably be found that the diameter is slightly smaller than the genuine medal. This is due to the fact that the plaster used in the mould shrinks slightly as it dries, with the result that any cast made subsequently will be correspondingly smaller and thinner.

Whether the alloy is suspect or not, it is strongly advised that you get into the habit of checking the dimensions of medals, suspension bars and clasps accurately. Both the thickness and diameter of medals should be measured as precisely as possible, the latter being checked at several points—for a reason which will become obvious later.

Apart from alloy and dimensions, the other telltale sign of forgery is the surface condition. Is every detail of the design sharp, or is there evidence of blurring? There are quite fundamental differences in the techniques of production, between a genuinely struck medal and a cast forgery. The latter will usually show some signs of microscopic surface pitting, caused by tiny air bubbles in the molten metal as it cools down. Some forgeries we have examined are actually unbelievably crude, and the wonder is that anyone could be deceived by them—but they frequently are! These forgeries were produced in simple sand moulds which, although lacking the shrinkage factor inherent in plaster moulds, have a grainy quality. Sometimes attempts will be made to remove this grainy characteristic as well as other surface blemishes, by chasing—an ancient technique of metalsmiths which involves filing and scraping with fine chisels and burins. This technique inevitably leaves very fine marks which are absent in genuinely struck medals. Casts also exhibit fine lines on the rim, where the two halves of the mould join, and although they are invariably filed off this often leaves a slight ridge, often visible by holding the medal with the rim to the light and rotating it slowly.

In more recent years, as the value of medals has soared, forgers have been taking infinitely greater pains, even going to the length of having new dies made (by hubbing from a genuine original) and then striking them. Such struck forgeries are more difficult to detect, but usually there is some subtle difference in the design which betrays their true character. The Air Crew Europe Star, for example, has been a frequent target of the forger, and several counterfeits of varying quality have been recorded. These range from the easily detectable type, with three pearls instead of five on the central arch of the crown, to a very accurate design albeit slightly thinner than the genuine star and having the points noticeably rounded instead of cut square.

Unfortunately with today's computer-aided technology, forgeries are becoming more and more difficult to detect but hopefully the same technology will help us to combat the problem by making simple methods of detection available to everyone.

COPIES

Under this heading come all manner of reproductions and imitations, which are often much harder to detect, especially if their provenance leads you to believe them to be genuine—or at least to be not so wary. It was not uncommon in years gone by, when the wearing of medals was much more frequent than it is today, for generals, admirals, ambassadors and other high officials to have a second set of medals mounted for everyday wear. These copies were often produce by the firms who held the government contracts to manufacture the originals, and they were struck from the same dies, using the same materials. In this case, however, as a precaution, these medals were clearly marked COPY. Where this was stamped in incuse lettering there was little fear of erasure, but where raised capitals were employed these could be filed off. Again, it is advisable to check medals for any evidence of file-marks or erasure on the rim or in the field.

This problem becomes especially acute where gallantry medals and decorations are concerned. It has sometimes been the case that the recipient of a gallantry medal has been compelled, through straitened circumstances, to sell the medal while retaining the campaign medals which made up the rest of the group. Subsequently he obtains an official copy or duplicate medal to complete the set, and in the fulness of time this group comes on the market. In extreme cases the copy decoration may even be detached from the group and sold separately. Thus we have instances of gallantry awards appearing to sell twice over, when in fact only one was the genuine original and the second one was the replacement. This is a potential minefield, for there are also other reasons for replacement medals supplied by the official contractors for legitimate reasons. Gallantry awards, notably the Victoria Cross, have been replaced due to accidental loss or theft, and have then been worn just as proudly by the recipient. At the end of the day, however, the status of these replacements is somewhat less than that of the original medals, and is usually reflected in the market value. The question of status is something of a grey area which only the individual collector can decide for himself.

Campaign and general service medals, issued to serving soldiers to replace those lost or stolen are clearly marked "Replacement" at the time of issue and, as such, are not highly regarded by dealers or collectors. Unfortunately there have been numerous examples in recent years of these replacements having their true identity concealed by erasure. Be on your guard against such medals which appear to have been filed, rubbed or disfigured along the rim where the naming is found, as this could imply that the word "Replacement" has been removed for fraudulent purposes.

FAKES

These are genuine medals which have been tampered with in some way in order to convert a common (and relatively cheap) item into a rarity commanding a greatly enhanced price. Fakery is much harder to detect than forgery and each case has to be examined on its individual merits, but below (*and in more depth, with regard to renaming, on pages 25–26*) we give a few pointers to look out for.

One common practice is to take a perfectly genuine medal and replace a common campaign clasp by one which is rare. Apart from the fact that the substitute will probably be an out and out forgery, detectable by the factors outlined above, a high-powered magnifier will usually show up evidence of tampering with the rivets securing the clasp to the medal. This in itself is not proof positive of substitution, for clasps can work loose for various reasons; but any sign of tampering with the rivets, or their replacement, should put you immediately on your guard. Examine the rivets closely for signs of file marks, soldering or any other form of tampering.

The chief ploy to improve the value of a medal, however, stems from the British practice of naming campaign medals to their recipients. This has given rise to a form of faking in which a medal named to someone in a plentiful regiment, or to a non-combatant, has had the original name erased by careful filing, and a new name, rank, number and regiment substituted. Some of these fakes were relatively crude in that the original name might be left intact and only the regiment altered; but as medal rolls and regimental muster rolls became more widely available to collectors and military historians, and fakers were forced to give closer attention to adding the name of a serviceman who would theoretically have been awarded such a medal.

This is where a careful measurement of the diameter, from several angles, is vital. Medals should be perfectly round and regular, so that any variation in diameter measured from different points will almost certainly indicate that the rim has been slightly shaved to remove the original impressed lettering. In some cases the original letteing may have been raised; filing this off may not materially affect the diameter, but the substitution of incuse or engraved lettering may be a dead giveaway. It is very important, therefore, to study the detailed catalogues of individual medals, and compare the method of naming with that found on your specimen. Even this is not always fool proof, for replacement medals issued to serving soldiers to make up for lost medals may be named in a manner which differed from the original issue. 19th century campaign medals were not always marked as clearly as they are nowadays to indicate that they were replacements, but the use of different lettering may provide a clue.

Of course, renaming or altering a medal in some way has not always been done to fool the collector; serving servicemen have been guilty of such practices over the years for a variety of reasons!

Any aspect of a medal which appears to differ from the norm should immediately put the collector on his guard. However, it is only fair to point out that many long-running general service medals differed in some subtle way in the fastenings of the clasps over a long period. In this case it is necessary to become fully acquainted with the different styles, including different shapes and sizes of rivets, types of solder and even twisted wire—all of which have been used quite legitimately at various times for the same medal.

Similarly differences in the lettering and numerals inscribed on campaign clasps may not betray the handiwork of the forger or faker, for such subtle variations may merely denote that the clasps were the work of one of the Royal Mint's sub-contractors. For example, India General Service Medals may be found with clasps manufactured at the branch mint in Calcutta, rather than in London. Once again, it is necessary for the collector to study all the available literature in his chosen field and thoroughly familiarise himself with the variants which may quite legitimately arise, as well as the difference between genuine and fake which have been recorded over the years.

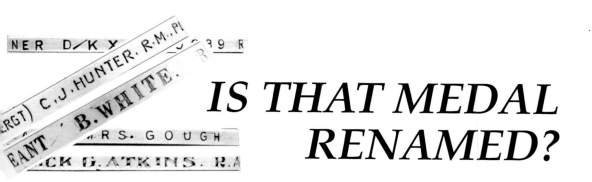

IS THAT MEDAL RENAMED?

Trying to determine whether a medal is correctly named is a problem that every collector has to face at some time or another. R. J. Scarlett offers advice and a few simple guidelines for the inexperienced collector. This advice can only be a general guide, but such guidelines can be helpful provided that readers remember that there are always exceptions to the rule.

When checking for evidence of renaming always examine the medal with the aid of a magnifying glass. It is useful to bear in mind the following points:

1. Generally speaking, it is easier to re-name engraved medals than those that bear impressed namings. An engraved medal is relatively quick and easy to rename as it is necessary to remove less metal to erase the original naming.

   To rename a medal with an impressed naming requires special tools which are not easy to obtain.

   This having been said, it should be pointed out that many of the most notorious cases of renaming (especially with more expensive medals), done with the intention to deceive, have involved impressed medals.

2. Always consider whether the style of naming is correct for the particular medal under consideration, also for the particular clasp(s) concerned and for the regiment, etc. Sometimes medals issued for the same campaign are named in different styles depending on the unit involved and the clasp(s). A good example of this is the India General Service medal 1854–95. Such information can be acquired in part from books and articles, but these can be inaccurate or not sufficently specialised. The best way to acquire knowledge is by examining as many medals as possible. Always take full advantage of medal fairs, auction viewings, visits to dealers' premises and chances to look at friends' medal collections to enhance your knowledge.

3. Before a medal can be renamed, the original naming must be removed and one can usually see some evidence of this, such as in the form of file marks. Figure 1 shows the results of an attempt to remove a

Figure 1

Figure 2

Figure 3

recipient's name from a medal—notice the many scratch marks caused by the file.

Unless the removal of the original naming has been done extremely carefully the edge of the medal may have a "rounded" appearance, instead of being square and flat. Figure 2 shows a renamed medal with edge view silhouette. See how "rounded" the edge is when compared with the flat edge of a correctly named medal in *Figure 3*.

4. If the suspender on the medal is assumed to be the 12 o'clock position, the naming on most medals appears on the edge between 9 o'clock and 3 o'clock. When the original naming is removed this thins down the rim between these two points. This is well illustrated in Figures 4 and 5. The former (4) shows a renamed medal with a thin rim while the naming has been removed and the latter (5) shows a correct medal with an even rim all round. The removal of the original naming will also reduce the size of the medal and this can be checked by using either a micrometer or a vernier calliper. The diameter of the medal should be measured across the 9 o'clock to 3 o'clock position and then across the 1 o'clock to 7 o'clock position. If the medal is not renamed, the two measurements should be the same. A "suspect" medal can also be checked for size against a known genuine medal, although it should be noted that a random check of say 10 similar medals will show variations in size.

5. Traces of an original naming may be visible under the new naming. Figures 6, 7 and 8 show examples of this. In Figure 6, traces are seen under the new naming and also beyond the end of it. Figure 7 shows

Figure 4

Figure 5

the outline of an impressed letter "A" under the new "S" and also shows traces of file marks. Figure 8 has a small impressed "T" appearing between the "L" and "A" of the new naming.

To recap, always check a medal for the following points

a. Is it named in the correct style.
b. Does the edge show file marks?
c. Is the edge flat?
d. Is the rim thinned at any point?
e. Is the diameter the same all round?
f. Are there traces of the original naming?
g. Has the medal been checked in all respects with a known correct medal?

A term which often appears in auction house and dealers' lists is "officially corrected" and "corrrected". Normally these expressions refer to instances where a single letter in the naming has been corrected by the issuing authority or by the recipient in order to rectify spelling mistakes, etc. Figures 9 and 10 show examples of "official" corrections. In both cases, traces of file marks can be seen and the corrected letter is impressed more heavily than the other letters.

Examples of privately corrected errors can be seen in Figures 11 and 12, here the new letters have been engraved rather than impressed and so do not match the rest of the naming. Traces of file marks are also visible. Figure 13 shows an example of where the correction is an "addition" due to the recipient's naming being incorrectly spelt. It is corrected by the addition of the letter "E", which is engraved and hence does not match the rest of the impressed naming. The engraved full-stop after the "K" can just be seen beneath the new "E". Figure 14 shows a Naval General Service medal 1793–1840, where the recipient has had his original rank removed and his later rank of "Lieut" added. Again this is engraved and does not match the rest of the naming, which is correctly impressed. Once more, notice the traces of file marks and the original impressed full-stop some way beyond the "Lieut".

These kinds of corrections to namings were necessary because of human error and hence cannot really be classified as renamings.

Why do renamed medals exist on the market? The majority were not produced to deceive medal collectors, but are the result of officers and men losing their own medals and having to find replacements. The obvious and easiest remedy was to buy someone else's medals and have them renamed. Servicemen out to impress their friends and family were not above adding an extra medal to their rows and what better proof of entitlement than to see that the medal had their name on it. Many such medals were renamed by local jewellers.

Most collectors shun renamed medals and they are not usually offered for sale. An "official" correction unfortunately mars the appeal of a medal and hence affects the price. However some medals are very skillfully renamed with the sole intention of deceiving the unwary collector and dealer. This is especially so with rare and, therefore more expensive medals. The best advice is to use the check list given in this article and then, if still in doubt, consult a competent authority.

Figure 6

Figure 7

Figure 8

Figure 9

Figure 10

Figure 11

Figure 12

Figure 13

Figure 14

MINIATURE MEDALS AND DECORATIONS

The collecting of miniature medals has gained in popularity over the past few years and as a result groups and single miniatures that were once sold with their full-size counterparts, as an added extra, are now being traded in their own right. Consequently it has been decided to include the market prices for these attractive and often superbly-produced little pieces in the catalogue section. Collectors wishing to learn more about miniature medals are invited to contact the Miniature Medals Branch of the Orders & Medals Research Society whose address can be found opposite.

Miniatures are small versions of orders, decorations and medals designed for formal evening wear. The custom appears to have developed in Continental Europe in the early years of the 18th century, but is now more or less universal, although the actual practice varies from country to country. In the United Kingdom, for example, miniatures are confined to mess kit and evening dress (white tie and tails), whereas in the United States it is quite common to see miniatures worn with dinner jackets. In Europe, miniatures are often worn without ribbons, suspended from a tiny chain, but in Britain and elsewhere miniatures are worn with exact replicas of the appropriate ribbons correspondingly reduced in size.

The scale of miniatures likewise varies from country to country. In Britain miniatures are usually half the size of the full-sized medals, but the Scandinavian countries use a 17mm size, while France and the Low Countries prefer a 14mm size, calculated from the diameter of medals or the badges of orders.

In the 18th and early 19th centuries the breast stars of orders were also worn in miniature, but nowadays only the badges of the orders are miniaturised. In Europe the higher classes of orders are designated by placing wings in silver, gold and silver, or gold, according to the class, below the rosette on the riband of the Officer Class. In Britain, however, miniatures are exact replicas of the badges they represent, and no additional rosettes or emblems are added to the ribands to denote a particular class.

Miniatures differ in one major respect from the full-scale; whereas the latter were produced by specific contractors, the former have been manufactured by many jewellers and goldsmiths. Consequently, the quality may vary considerably, from a very faithful replica (doubtless produced by the same firm that made the originals and using scaled-down dies for the purpose), to quite crude imitations that differs in many details from the full sized version. In many instances, miniature medal groups may be found with the original case as supplied by the jeweller, so that identification is not a problem. Many other groups, however, have long since parted company from their presentation cases, and identification is then only possible from other factors, either stylistic or from marks. Some miniatures are hallmarked (i.e. they bear the punches of an assay office and the mark of the manufacturer), and in such cases the miniature can not only be identified, but even the date of manufacture adduced from the year letter. Not all miniatures by any means are hallmarked, especially if they fall below the statutory minimum weight, so that this aid to identification is not always present.

The value placed on miniatures is governed by condition, of course, but other factors that must be taken into consideration are the provenance and authenticity of the medal or group. Miniatures which are contemporary with the original award are rated more highly than replacements procured many years later. And miniature groups which can definitely be assigned to a particular recipient are worth a premium over those whose original owner cannot be determined. Unlike the full-scale originals, miniatures very seldom bear the name of the recipient. Nevertheless, this is a fascinating aspect of medal collecting, much less expensive than the full-size medals but often as rewarding for the human interest which miniatures represent.

A NOTE ON THE PRICING OF MINIATURES

As explained on page 28, miniature medals, unlike their full size counterparts, come in a bewildering spread of quality and variety as they were produced by numerous manufacturers, none of which were strictly controlled, if controlled at all, by HM Mint or any Government Department. Therefore, the pricing of a miniature can be more complex than its parent medal which, after all, is either genuine or not. For example, a miniature that should have a straight bar suspender can be found with all manner of suspensions, a miniature for a particular campaign can come in a variety of forms, viz. wording on one can be misspelt, differ from another or be omitted altogether. Consequently as quite a few Victorian war and campaign miniatures, and almost all miniature orders and decorations, have been reproduced at a later date, in some cases, a much later date, pricing them can be a problem.

To help the collector, especially the newcomer, the prices for 19th century miniatures in this YEARBOOK are for contemporary, quality pieces nearest to the full size in all respects. For 20th century miniatures, I have given the price for the most common variety and as almost all campaign miniatures from the 1960s onwards are plated base metal with slip on clasps, it is for these that the price is shown.

The pricing of any collectable can never be an exact science, so the prices given here are not to be taken as definitive, but merely a guide and, if used as such with a sprinkling of common sense and that indefinable "feel" for a medal, should help you build a collection that gives you more pleasure than pain.

Mark Cline
President
Miniature Medals Branch of the OMRS

For further information on the collecting of miniature medals, readers are invited to contact:

**The Honorary Secretary
The Miniature Medals Branch
Orders and Medals Research Society
31 Gatcombe
Great Holm
Milton Keynes
Bucks MK8 9EA**

WEARING AWARDS

The wearing of Orders, Decorations and Medals is a complex subject too complicated to cover in a publication such as this. However, there a number of questions that collectors frequently ask, so we have attempted to deal with these as fully as possible.

Full-size Awards Mounted for Wear

Orders, decorations and medals are worn on the left breast in a line suspended from a single brooch mount or a rectangular frame (court mounted), the latter gives a firmer grip which occasions less damage than medals hanging more loosely from a brooch. The brooch/frame is covered by the medal ribbons. The most senior medal (see the following Order of Precedence) is furthest from the left shoulder. The obverse of the medals should show (this will usually be the sovereign's head, coat of arms, cypher, etc.).

If more than five medals are worn (three for the Navy), they should not be suspended side by side, but overlapped, the senior medal and ribbon is the one to be positioned so it can be seen completely. Medals should be lined up straight by the bottom rim/point, the length of ribbon should be one and a quarter inches (33mm) from the top of the mount to the first clasp or the suspension, which ever is appropriate (one and three quarters (45mm) for the Navy). Where the awards differ in size then a ribbon adjustment will be necessary to ensure a straight line.

Mentions-in-Despatches emblems should be worn on the relevant campaign medal, for example on the Victory Medal for the First World War and the War Medal 1939–45 for the Second World War. Where a recipient has no relevant campaign medal,

the MID emblem is worn directly on the coat after any medal ribbons, or if no ribbons then in the position of a single ribbon.

There are a number of awards for which the sovereign has granted permission that they be worn on the right breast:

Royal Humane Society Medals
Stanhope Gold Medal
Royal National Lifeboat Institution Medal
Order of St John of Jerusalem Life Saving Medal.

Foreign Order, Decorations and Medals

The British sovereign's subjects are not permitted to accept and wear the orders, decorations and medals of a foreign country of which the sovereign is not head of state. Application can be made for wear and permission is of two types: (a) restricted, that is instructions are given as to the exact occasions on which the award(s) may be worn; (b) unrestricted which allows the item(s) to be worn on all occasions according to the Order of Precedence, that is, generally speaking, arranged after British awards by date—first orders, then decorations, followed by medals (there are exceptions for the members of the armed services serving in an overseas force and receive that country's awards).

Awards are worn on a variety of State, evening or other occasions and the rules governing the wearing of orders according to dress are quite detailed. The subject is covered fully in Spink's Guide to the Wearing of Orders, Decorations and Medals, *available from the Book Department, Spink & Son Ltd, 5–7 King Street, St James's, London SW1Y 6QS.*

THE ORDER OF PRECEDENCE

The Order of Precedence, or the order in which decorations and medals should be worn in the United Kingdom and the Commonwealth, is set out below, as announced by the Central Chancery of the Orders of Knighthood.

Victoria Cross
George Cross
Conspicuous Gallantry Cross
Most Noble Order of the Garter
Most Ancient and Most Noble Order of the Thistle
Most Illustrious Order of St. Patrick
Knights Grand Cross, The Most Honourable Order of the Bath (GCB)
Order of Merit
Baronet's Badge
Knight Grand Commander, The Most Exalted Order of the Star of India (GCSI)
Knights Grand Cross, The Most Distinguished Order of St. Michael and St. George (GCMG)
Knight Grand Commander, The Most Eminent Order of the Indian Empire (GCIE)
The Order of the Crown of India
Knights Grand Cross, The Royal Victorian Order (GCVO)
Knights Grand Cross, The Most Excellent Order of the British Empire (GBE)
Order of the Companions of Honour (CH)
Knight Commander, The Most Honourable Order of the Bath (KCB)
Knight Commander, The Most Exalted Order of the Star of India (KCSI)
Knight Commander, The Most Distinguished Order of St. Michael and St. George (KCMG)
Knight Commander, The Most Eminent Order of the Indian Empire (KCIE)
Knight Commander, The Royal Victorian Order (KCVO)
Knight Commander, The Most Excellent Order of the British Empire (KBE)
Knight Bachelor's Badge
Companion, The Most Honourable Order of the Bath (CB)
Companion, The Most Exalted Order of the Star of India (CSI)
Companion, The Most Distinguished Order of St. Michael and St. George (CMG)
Companion, The Most Eminent Order of the Indian Empire (CIE)
Commander, The Royal Victorian Order (CVO)
Commander, The Most Excellent Order of the British Empire (CBE)
Distinguished Service Order (DSO)
Lieutenant, The Royal Victorian Order (LVO)

Officer, The Most Excellent Order of the British Empire (OBE)
Imperial Service Order (ISO)
Member, The Royal Victorian Order (MVO)
Member, The Most Excellent Order of the British Empire (MBE)
Indian Order of Merit—Military

DECORATIONS
Royal Red Cross, Class 1
Distinguished Service Cross
Military Cross
Distinguished Flying Cross
Air Force Cross
Royal Red Cross, Class II
Order of British India
Kaisar-I-Hind Medal
Order of St John

GALLANTRY AND DISTINGUISHED CONDUCT MEDALS
Union of South Africa Queen's Medal for Bravery in gold
Distinguished Conduct Medal
Conspicuous Gallantry Medal
Conspicuous Gallantry Medal (Flying)
George Medal
Queen's Police Medal for Gallantry
Queen's Fire Service Medal for Gallantry
Royal West African Frontier Force Distinguished Conduct Medal
King's African Rifles Distinguished Conduct Medal
Indian Distinguished Service Medal
Union of South Africa Queen's Medal for Bravery in silver
Distinguished Service Medal
Military Medal
Distinguished Flying Medal
Air Force Medal
Royal Ulster Constabulary Medal
Medal for Saving Life at Sea
Indian Order of Merit (Civil)
Indian Police Medal for Gallantry
Ceylon Police Medal for Gallantry
Sierra Leone Police Medal for Gallantry
Sierra Leone Fire Brigades Medal for Gallantry
Colonial Police Medal for Gallantry
Queen's Gallantry Medal

Royal Victorian Medal (gold, silver and bronze)
British Empire Medal
Canada Medal
Queen's Police Medal for Distinguished Service
Queen's Fire Service Medal for Distinguished Service
Queen's Medal for Chiefs
War Medals, including the UN Medals—in order of
    date of campaign for which awarded
Polar Medals—in order of date of award
Imperial Service Medal

POLICE MEDALS FOR VALUABLE SERVICE

Indian Police Medal for Meritorious Service
Ceylon Police Medal for Merit
Sierra Leone Police Medal for Meritorious Service
Sierra Leone Fire Brigades Medal for Meritorious
    Service
Colonial Police Medal for Meritorious Service
Badge of Honour

JUBILEE, CORONATION, DURBAR MEDALS

Queen Victoria's Jubilee Medal 1887 (gold, silver and
    bronze)
Queen Victoria's Police Jubilee Medal 1887
Queen Victoria's Jubilee Medal 1897 (gold, silver and
    bronze)
Queen Victoria's Police Jubilee Medal 1897
Queen Victoria's Commemoration Medal 1900
    (Ireland)
King Edward VII's Coronation 1902
King Edward VII's Police Coronation 1902
King Edward VII's Durbar 1903 (gold, silver and
    bronze)
King Edward VII's Police Medal 1903 (Scotland)
King's Visit Commemoration Medal 1903 (Ireland)
King George V's Coronation Medal 1911
King George V's Police Coronation Medal 1911
King George V's Visit Police Commemoration Medal
    1911 (Ireland)
King George V's Durbar Medal 1911 (gold, silver and
    bronze)
King George V's Silver Jubilee Medal 1935
King George VI's Coronation Medal 1937
Queen Elizabeth II's Coronation Medal 1953
Queen Elizabeth II's Silver Jubilee Medal 1977
King George V's Long and Faithful Service Medal
King George VI's Long and Faithful Service Medal
Queen Elizabeth II's Long and Faithful Service Medal

EFFICIENCY AND LONG SERVICE
DECORATIONS AND MEDALS

Medal for Meritorious Service
Accumulated Campaign Service Medal
The Medal for Long Service and Good Conduct,
    Army
Naval Long Service and Good Conduct Medal
Medal for Meritorious Service (Royal Navy 1918–28)
Indian Long Service and Good Conduct Medal (for
    Europeans of Indian Army)
Indian Meritorious Service Medal (for Europeans of
    Indian Army)
Royal Marines Meritorious Service Medal (1849–1947)
Royal Air Force Meritorious Service Medal 1918–28
Royal Air Force Long Service and Good Conduct
    Medal

Ulster Defence Regiment Long Service and Good
    Conduct Medal
Indian Long Service and Good Conduct Medal
    (Indian Army)
Royal West African Frontier Force Long Service and
    Good Conduct Medal
Royal Sierra Leone Military Forces Long Service and
    Good Conduct Medal
King's African Rifles Long Service and Good Conduct
    Medal
Indian Meritorious Service Medal (for Indian Army)
Police Long Service and Good Conduct Medal
Fire Brigade Long Service and Good Conduct Medal
African Police Medal for Meritorious Service
Royal Canadian Mounted Police Long Service Medal
Ceylon Police Long Service Medal
Ceylon Fire Services Long Service Medal
Sierra Leone Police Long Service Medal
Colonial Police Long Service Medal
Sierra Leone Fire Brigade Long Service Medal
Mauritius Police Long Service and Good Conduct
    Medal
Mauritius Fire Service Long Service and Good
    Conduct Medal
Mauritius Prisons Service Long Service and Good
    Conduct Medal
Colonial Fire Brigades Long Service Medal
Colonial Prison Service Medal
Army Emergency Reserve Decoration
Volunteer Officers' Decoration
Volunteer Long Service Medal
Volunteer Officers' Decoration (for India and the
    Colonies)
Volunteer Long Service Medal (for India and the
    Colonies)
Colonial Auxiliary Forces Officers' Decoration
Colonial Auxiliary Forces Long Service Medal
Medal for Good Shooting (Naval)
Militia Long Service Medal
Imperial Yeomanry Long Service Medal
Territorial Decoration
Ceylon Armed Service Long Service Medal
Efficiency Decoration
Territorial Efficiency Medal
Efficiency Medal
Special Reserve Long Service and Good Conduct Medal
Decoration for Officers of the Royal Naval Reserve
Decoration for Officers of the Royal Naval Volunteer
    Reserve
Royal Naval Reserve Long Service and Good
    Conduct Medal
Royal Naval Volunteer Reserve Long Service and
    Good Conduct Medal
Royal Naval Auxiliary Sick Berth Reserve Long
    Service and Good Conduct Medal
Royal Fleet Reserve Long Service and Good Conduct
    Medal
Royal Naval Wireless Auxiliary Reserve Long Service
    and Good Conduct Medal
Royal Naval Auxiliary Service Medal
Air Efficiency Award
Ulster Defence Regiment Medal
Queen's Medal (for Champion Shots of the Royal
    Navy and Royal Marines)
Queen's Medal (for Champion Shots of the New
    Zealand Naval Forces)

Queen's Medal (for Champion Shots in the Military Forces)
Queen's Medal (for Champion Shots of the Air Force)
Cadet Forces Medal
Coast Guard Auxiliary Service Long Service Medal
Special Constabulary Long Service Medal
Canadian Forces Decoration
Royal Observer Corps Medal
Civil Defence Long Service Medal
Rhodesia Medal
Royal Ulster Constabulary Service Medal
Union of South Africa Commemoration Medal
Indian Independence Medal
Pakistan Medal
Ceylon Armed Services Inauguration Medal
Ceylon Police Independence Medal (1948)
Sierra Leone Independence Medal
Jamaica Independence Medal
Uganda Independence Medal

Malawi Independence Medal
Fiji Independence Medal
Papua New Guinea Independence Medal
Solomon Islands Independence Medal
Service Medal of the Order of St. John
Badge of the Order of the League of Mercy
Voluntary medical Service Medal
Women's Voluntary Service Medal
South African Medal for War Services
Colonial Special Constabulary Medal
Honorary Membership of Commonwealth Orders (instituted by the Sovereign, in order of date of award)
Other Commonwealth Members, orders, Decorations and Medals (instituted since 1949 otherwise than by the Sovereign, and awards by States of Malaysia and Brunei in order of date of award)
Foreign Orders in order of date of award
Foreign Decorations in order of date of award
Foreign Medals in order of date of award

THE ORDER IN WHICH CAMPAIGN STARS AND MEDALS AWARDED FOR SERVICE DURING WORLD WAR I AND II ARE WORN

1914 Star with dated "Mons" clasp "15th AUGUST– 22nd NOVEMBER 1914"
1914 Star
1914/15 Star
British War Medal
Mercantile Marine Medal
Victory Medal
Territorial Force War Medal

1939/45 Star
Atlantic Star
Air Crew Europe Star
Africa Star

Pacific Star
Burma Star
Italy Star
France and Germany Star
Defence Medal
Canadian/Newfoundland Volunteer Service Medal
1939/45 War Medal
1939/45 Africa Service Medal of the Union of South Africa
India Service Medal
New Zealand War Service Medal
Southern Rhodesia Service Medal
Australian Service Medal

POST-NOMINAL LETTERS

Recipients of some awards are entitled to use post-nominal letters including the following:

VC	KCVO	AFC	IOM—*Civil*
CGC	DCVO	ARRC	CPM—*gallantry*
GC	KBE	OBI	QGM
KG *(not used by ladies)*	DBE	OB—*distinguished service*	QSM
KT *(not used by ladies)*	CB		RVM
KP	CSI	AM	BEM
GCB *(also used by ladies)*	CMG	DCM	CM or MdeC
OM	CIE	CGM	QPM—*distinguished service*
GCSI	CVO	GM	
GCMG *(also used by ladies)*	CBE	QPM—*gallantry*	QFSM—*distinguished service*
GCIE	DSO	QFSM—*gallantry*	
CI *(ladies only)*	LVO	EM	CPMSM
GCVO *(also used by ladies)*	OBE	DCM—*West Africa Frontier Force*	MSM—*only awarded in Navy prior to 29/7/28*
	QSO		
GBE *(also used by ladies)*	ISO	DCM—*Kings African Rifles*	ERD
CH	MVO	IDSM	VD
KCB	MBE	BGM	TD
DCB	IOM—*military*	DSM	ED
KCSI	OB—*gallantry*	MM	RD
KCMG	RRC	DFM	VRD
DCMG	DSC	AFM	AEA *(officers only)*
KCIE	MC	SGM	UDR *(officers only)*
	DFC		CD

AWARDS OF THE BRITISH COMMONWEALTH

In recent years many countries of the British Commonwealth have created their own individual systems of Honours and Awards. However, some British awards are still recognised within these systems. The medals and awards of these countries instituted prior to their own systems being introduced, are included in the main section of this book. In this edition of the YEARBOOK we include the Orders of Precedence encompassing their own and former British honours and awards of three of the countries most commonly encountered by collectors. The lists are as supplied by the appropriate authorities. In future editions we will be looking more closely at some of these awards.

THE ORDER OF PRECEDENCE IN AUSTRALIA

Victoria Cross
George Cross
Cross of Valour
Most Noble Order of the Garter
Most Ancient and Most Noble Order of the Thistle
Knight Grand Cross, the Most Honourable Order of the Bath
Order of Merit
Knight, the Order of Australia
Knight Grand Cross, the Most Distinguished Order of St Michael & St George
Knight Grand Cross, the Royal Victorian Order
Knight Grand Cross, the Order of the British Empire
Companion, the Order of Australia
Companion of Honour
Knight Commander, the Most Honourable Order of the Bath
Knight Commander, the Most Distinguished Order of St Michael & St George
Knight Commander, the Royal Victorian Order
Knight Commander, the Order of the British Empire
Knight Bachelor
Officer, the Order of Australia
Companion, the Most Honourable Order of the Bath
Companion, the Most Distinguished Order of St Michael & St George
Commander, the Royal Victorian Order
Commander, the Order of the British Empire
Star of Gallantry

Star of Courage
Distinguished Service Order
Distinguished Service Cross (Australian)
Member, the Order of Australia
Lieutenant, the Royal Victorian Order
Officer, the Order of the British Empire
Companion, the Imperial Service Order
Member, the Royal Victorian Order
Member, the Order of the British Empire
Conspicuous Service Cross
Nursing Service Cross
Royal Red Cross 1st Class
Distinguished Service Cross (British)
Military Cross
Distinguished Flying Cross
Air Force Cross
Royal Red Cross 2nd Class
Medal for Gallantry
Distinguished Service Medal (Australian)
Public Service Medal
Australian Police Medal
Australian Fire Service Medal
Member of the Order of Australia
Order of St John
Distinguished Conduct Medal
Conspicuous Gallantry Medal
George Medal
Bravery Medal
Conspicuous Service Medal

Antarctic Medal
Queen's Police Medal for Gallantry
Queen's Fire Service Medal for Gallantry
Distinguished Service Medal (British)
Military Medal
Distinguished Flying Medal
Air Force Medal
Queen's Gallantry Medal
Royal Victorian Medal
British Empire Medal
Queen's Police Medal for Distinguished Service
Queen's Fire Service Medal for Distinguished Service
Commendation for Gallantry

Commendation for Brave Conduct
Queen's Commendation for Brave Conduct
Commendation for Distinguished Service
War Medals in order of campaign
Australian Active Service Medal
Australian Service Medal
Australian Service Medal 1945–75
Police Overseas Service Medal
Civilian Service Medal
Polar Medal
Imperial Service Medal
Coronation/Jubilee Medals
Defence Force Service Medal
Reserve Force Decoration
Reserve Force Medal
National Medal
Champion Shots Medal
Long Service Medals
Independece/Anniversary Medals
Approved Foreign Orders, Medals and Decorations
    in order of date of award.

Order of Australia.

Star of Courage—Australia.

THE ORDER OF PRECEDENCE IN CANADA

Victoria Cross
George Cross
Cross of Valour
Order of Merit
Order of the Companions of Honour
Companion, the Order of Canada
Commander, the Order of Military Merit
Officer, the Order of Canada
Companion, The Most Honourable Order of the
    Bath
Companion, The Most Distinguished Order of St
    Michael and St George
Commander, The Royal Victorian Order
Commander, The Most Excellent Order of the
    British Empire

Distinguished Service Order
Officer, the Order of Military Merit
Lieutenant, The Royal Victoria Order
Officer, The Most Excellent Order of the British
    Empire
Imperial Service Order
Member, the Order of Canada
Member, the Order of Military Merit
Member, The Royal Victorian Order
Member, The Most Excellent Order of the British
    Empire
Member of the Royal Red Cross
Distinguished Service Cross
Military Cross
Distinguished Flying Cross

Air Force Cross
Star of Courage
Medal of Bravery
Associate of the Royal Red Cross
The Most Venerable Order of the Hospital of St John
    of Jerusalem (all grades) (no post-nominals)
Distinguished Conduct Medal
Conspicuous Gallantry Medal
George Medal
Distinguished Service Medal
Military Medal
Distinguished Flying Medal
Air Force Medal
Queen's Gallantry Medal
Royal Victorian Medal
British Empire Medal
War Medals in order of campaign
United Nations Medals in order of campaign
Polar Medals
Coronation and Jubilee medals in date order

125th Anniversary of the Confederation of Canada
    Medal (1992)
Army Long Service and Good Conduct Medal
Naval Long Service and Good Conduct Medal
Air Force Long Service and Good Conduct Medal
RCMP Long Service Medal
Volunteer Officer's Decoration
Volunteer Long Service Medal
Colonial Auxiliary Forces Officer's Decoration
Colonial Auxiliary Forces Long Service Medal
Efficiency Decoration
Efficiency Medal
Naval Volunteer Reserve Decoration
Naval Volunteer Reserve Long Service and Good
    Conduct Medal
Air Efficiency Award
The Queen's Medal for Champion Shot
Canadian Forces Decoration
Service Medal of the Most Venerable order of the
    Hospital of St John of Jerusalem
Approved Foreign Orders, Medals and Decorations
    in order of date of award.

Order of Canada.

Medal of Bravery—Canada.

THE ORDER OF PRECEDENCE IN NEW ZEALAND

Victoria Cross
George Cross
Order of the Garter
Knights Grand Cross, The Most Honourable Order
    of the Bath
Order of Merit
New Zealand Cross
Baronets Badge
Knights Grand Cross, The Most Distinguished Order
    of St Michael and St George (GCMG)
Knights Grand Cross, The Royal Victorian Order
Knights Grand Cross, The Most Excellent Order of
    the British Empire
Order of Companions of Honour
Order of New Zealand

Knight Commander, The Most Honourable Order
    of the Bath
Knight Commander, The Most Distinguished Order
    of St Michael and St George
Knight Commander, The Royal Victorian Order
Knight Commander, The Most Excellent Order of
    the British Empire
Knight Bachelors badge
Companion, The Most Honourable Order of the Bath
Companion, The Most Distinguished Order of St
    Michael and St George
Commander, The Royal Victorian Order
Commander, The Most Excellent Order of the British
    Empire
Distinguished Service Order

Queen's Service Medal—New Zealand.

Lieutenant, The Royal Victorian Order
Officer, The Most Excellent Order of the British
    Empire
Queen's Service Order
Imperial Service Order
Member, The Royal Victorian Order
Member, The Most Excellent Order of the British
    Empire
Royal Red Cross (Member)
Distinguished Service Cross
Military Cross
Distinguished Flying Cross
Air Force Cross
Royal Red Cross (Associate)
Order of St John (All classes)
Albert Medal
Distinguished Conduct Medal
Conspicuous Gallantry Medal
George Medal
Queen's Police Medal for Gallantry
Distinguished Service Medal
Military Medal
Distinguished Flying Medal
Air Force Medal
Empire Gallantry Medal
Queen's Gallantry Medal
Royal Victorian Medals
Queen's Service Medal

British Empire Medal
Queen's Police Medal for Distinguished Service
Queen's Fire Service Medal for Distinguished Service
War Medals in order of campaign
New Zealand General Service Medal
Polar Medal
Imperial Service Medal
Coronation and Jubilee Medals in date order
New Zealand 1990 Commemoration Medal
New Zealand Suffrage Centenial Medal 1993
New Zealand Meritorious Service Medal
New Zealand Armed Forces Award
New Zealand Army Long Service and Good
    Conduct Medal
Royal New Zealand Navy Long Service and Good
    Conduct Medal
Royal New Zealand Air Force Long Service and
    Good Conduct Medal
New Zealand Police Long Service and Good
    Conduct Medal
New Zealand Fire Brigades Long Service and Good
    Conduct Medal
New Zealand Prison Service Medal
New Zealand Traffic Service Medal
Colonial Auxiliary Forces Decoration
Colonial Auxiliary Forces Long Service Medal
New Zealand Efficiency Decoration
New Zealand Efficiency Medal
Royal New Zealand Naval Volunteer Reserve
    Decoration
Royal Naval Reserve Decoration
Royal New Zealand Naval Volunteer Reserve Long
    Service and Good Conduct Medal
Royal Naval Reserve Long Service and Good
    Conduct Medal
Air Efficiency Award
Queen's Medal for Champion Shots of the New
    Zealand Naval Forces
Queen's Medal for Champion Shots of the Military
    Forces
Queen's Medal for Champion Shots of the Air Forces
Cadet Forces Medal
Rhodesia Medal 1980
Service Medal of the Order of St John
Other Commonwealth Members' Orders,
    Decorations and Medals in date of award
Approved Foreign Orders, Decorations and Medals
    in order of date of award

ORDERS OF CHIVALRY

The most colourful and romantic of all awards are those connected with the orders of chivalry. Many of them have their origins in the Middle Ages, when knights in armour formed the elite fighting force in every European country. This was the period when knights jousted in tournaments as a pastime, between going off to the Holy Land on the wars of Christendom known as the Crusades. This was the era of such popular heroes as Richard the Lionheart, William the Lion, Robert the Bruce, the Black Prince, Pepin of Herstal and John the Blind King of Bohemia. Their exploits have passed into the folklore of Europe, together with the legends of Roland and his Paladins or King Arthur and the Knights of the Round Table.

From the idea of a select band of knights, pledged to the support of a king or an ideal (usually religious), sprang the orders of chivalry. Many of these existed in the Middle Ages but most of them died out as feudalism went into decline. In some cases they survived; in others they disappeared for centuries, only to be resurrected at a later date. Still others were devised and instituted in relatively modern times, and indeed, continue to evolve. For example, Canada instituted the Order of Canada in 1967 and both Australia and New Zealand introduced their own orders in 1975.

In their original form membership of the orders of chivalry were just as highly coveted as they are today, but the insignia was usually simple or even non-existent. The complicated system of insignia which now surrounds these orders is fairly modern, dating from the 16th century or later. Nowadays most orders also exist in several classes, with the insignia becoming increasingly elaborate with each higher class.

Britain's senior order is the Garter, and although it consists of one class only it provides a good example of the pomp and ceremony which often surrounds these awards. It was founded by King Edward III and is said to derive its name from the fact that the King was attending a dance one day, when a lady's garter slipped from her leg and fell to the floor. To save her the embarrassment of retrieving her garter—and thus letting everyone know it was hers—the King himself picked it up and tied it round his own leg. Lest anyone should doubt that it was his garter he said, in court French, "Let evil be to him who evil thinks". From this curious incident came the idea of a very exclusive order of knighthood, consisting of the sovereign and 26 knights.

The insignia of this order consists of a Garter, a mantle of blue velvet lined with taffeta with the star of the Order embroidered on the left breast, a hood of crimson velvet, a surcoat of crimson velvet lined with white taffeta, a hat of black velvet lined with white taffeta, with a plume of white ostrich and black heron feathers fastened by a band of diamonds, a collar of gold composed of buckled garters and lovers' knots with red roses, the George (an enamelled figure of St George slaying the dragon) suspended from the collar, the

Lesser George or badge, worn from a broad blue sash passing over the left shoulder to the right hip, and the star, a silver eight-pointed decoration bearing the red cross of St George surrounded by the garter and motto.

The insignia is exceptionally elaborate, the other orders of chivalry varying considerably in their complexity according to the class of the order. The full insignia is only worn on special occasions. In the case of the Garter usually the Lesser George and the breast star are worn on their own.

On the death of a Knight of the Garter the insignia must be returned to the Central Chancery of Orders of Knighthood, and therefore few examples of the Garter ever come on to the market. Those that do are usually examples from the 17th and 18th centuries when regulations regarding the return of insignia were not so strict. In the case of the lesser orders, insignia is returnable on promotion to a higher class. All collar chains are returnable, although that of the Order of St Michael and St George could be retained prior to 1948.

British orders are manufactured by firms holding contracts from the Central Chancery of Orders of Knighthood, and the values quoted in this Yearbook are for the official issues. It should be noted, however, that holders of orders frequently have replicas of breast stars made for use on different uniforms and it is sometimes difficult to tell these replicas from the originals as in many cases the replicas were made by the court jewellers responsible for making the originals. In addition, many jewellers in such European capitals as Vienna, Berlin and Paris have a long tradition of manufacturing the insignia of orders for sale to collectors.

The badges and breast stars of orders of chivalry are very seldom named to the recipient and therefore lack the personal interest of campaign medals and many gallantry awards. For this reason they do not command the same interest or respect of collectors. Nevertheless, in cases where the insignia of orders can be definitely proved to have belonged to some famous person, the interest and value are enhanced. In any case, these orders are invariably very attractive examples of the jeweller's art, and they often possess titles and stories as colourful and romantic as their appearance.

1. THE MOST NOBLE ORDER OF THE GARTER

KG Star
(a Victorian example)

Instituted: 1348.

Ribbon: 100mm plain dark blue. Not worn in undress uniform.

Garter: Dark blue velvet. Two versions may be encountered, with embroidered lettering and other details, or with gold lettering, buckle and tab. Worn on the left leg by gentlemen and on the left forearm by laides.

Collar Chain: Gold composed of alternate buckled garters, each encircling a red enamelled rose, and lovers' knots in gold although sometimes enamelled white.

Collar badge: An enamelled figure of St George fighting the dragon.

Star: Originally always embroidered in metal thread, a style which continues in the mantle to this day. Prior to 1858 knights often purchased metal stars in addition and since that date metal stars have been officially issued. These consist of a silver eight-pointed radiate star bearing in its centre and red cross of St George on a white ground, surrounded by the garter and motto HONI SOIT QUI MAL Y PENSE (evil be who evil thinks).

Sash Badge: The Lesser George, similar to the collar badge but encircled by an oval garter bearing the motto.

Comments: *Membership of the Order of the Garter is confined to the reigning sovereign, the Prince of Wales and 25 other Knights, and is the personal gift of the monarch. In addition to the 25 Knights there have, from time to time, been extra Knights, invariably non-Christians such as the Sultans of Turkey or the Emperor of Japan. The Emperor Hirohito, incidentally had the dubious distinction of being the only person awarded the Garter twice: in 1922 and again in 1971, having forfieted the original award as a result of the Japanese entry into the Second World War in 1941. Sir Winston Churchill was invested with the insignia originally presented in 1702 to his illustrious ancestor, the Duke of Marlborough. All official insignia is returnable to the Central Chancery of Knighthood on the death of the holder.*

VALUE:

Collar chain   Rare
Collar badge (the George)   £50,000–100,000
Star (in metal)   £1500–5000
Star (embroidered)   £400–1000
Sash badge (Lesser George) £3000–40,000
Garter (embroidered) £300–500
Garter (gold lettering
    and buckle)   £1200–2500

Miniature
    Star (metal)   £100–150

Lesser George
(this early example has the
garter enamelled in blue)

*Prices are for privately made examples many of which are
    jewelled and enamelled.

49

2. THE MOST ANCIENT AND MOST NOBLE ORDER OF THE THISTLE

KT Star

Instituted: 1687.

Ribbon: 100mm plain dark green. Not worn in undress uniform.

Collar Chain: Gold of alternate thistles and sprigs of rue enamelled in proper colours.

Collar Badge: The jewel is a gold and enamelled figure of St Andrew in a green gown and purple surcoat, bearing before him a white saltire cross, the whole surrounded by rays of gold.

Star: Silver, consisting of a St Andrew's cross, with other rays issuing between the points of the cross and, in the centre, on a gold background, a thistle enamelled in proper colours surrounded by a green circle bearing the Latin motto NEMO ME IMPUNE LACESSIT (no one assails me with impunity).

Sash Badge: The medal of the Order is a gold figure of St Andrew bearing before him a saltire cross, surrounded by an oval collar bearing the motto, surmounted by a gold cord fitted with a ring for suspension. Examples are found in plain gold, or with enamelling and/or set with jewels.

Comments: *This order is said to have been founded in AD 787, alluding to barefoot enemy soldiers who cried out when they trod on thistles and thus alerted the Scots of an imminent attack. The order had long been defunct when it was revived by King James VII and II and re-established in December 1703 by Queen Anne. It now consists of the sovereign and 16 Knights, making it the most exclusive of the orders of chivalry. At death, the official insignia is returned to the Central Chancery.*

VALUE:

Collar chain	Rare
Collar badge	Rare
Star (metal)	£1500–4000
Star (embroidered)	£400–600
Sash badge	£5000–8000

Miniature

Star (metal)	£250–300

Examples of Sash Badges

3. THE MOST ILLUSTRIOUS ORDER OF ST PATRICK

KP Star

Sash Badge

Instituted: February 5, 1783.

Ribbon: 100 mm sky-blue. Not worn in undress uniform.

Collar Chain: Gold, composed of five roses and six harps alternating, each tied together with a gold knot. The roses are enamelled alternately white petals within red and red within white.

Collar Badge: An imperial crown enamelled in proper colours from which is suspended by two rings a gold harp and from this a circular badge with a white enamelled centre embellished with the red saltire cross on which is surmounted a green three-petalled shamrock its leaves decorated with gold crowns, the whole surrounded by a gold collar bearing the Latin motto QUIS SEPARABIT (who shall separate us?) with the date of foundation in roman numerals round the foot MDCCLXXXII.

Star: A silver eight-pointed star, having in its centre, on a white field, the saltire cross of St Parick in red enamel charged with a green trefoil bearing a gold crown on each leaf.

Sash Badge: The saltire cross in red enamel surmounted by a green shamrock with gold crowns as above, surrounded by an oval collar of pale blue with the Latin motto round the top and the date of foundation round the foot, the whole enclosed by a gold and white enamel surround charged with 32 shamrocks.

Comments: *Founded by King George III to reward the loyalty of Irish peers during the American War of Independence, it originally comprised the monarch and 15 Knights. In 1833 it was extended to include the Lord-Lieutenant of Ireland and 22 Knights, with certain extra and honorary knights. Appointments of non-royal Knights to the Order ceased with the partition of Ireland in 1922,although three of the sons of King George V were appointed after that date—the Prince of Wales (1927), the Duke of York (1936) and the Duke of Gloucester (1934). It became obsolete in 1974 with the death of the last holder. All items of official insignia were returned at death. Unlike the other two great orders, the sash for this Order is worn in the manner of the lesser orders, over the right shoulder.*

VALUE:

Collar chain	Rare
Collar badge	£8000–12,000
Star (metal)	£1500–3000
Star (embroidered)	£400–600
Sash badge	£5000–7000
Miniature	
Star (metal)	£200–250

4. THE MOST HONOURABLE ORDER OF THE BATH

GCB Star (Military)

Instituted: 1725.

Ribbon: 38mm.

Collar Chain: Gold composed of nine crowns and eight devices, each consisting of a rose, a thistle and a shamrock issuing from a sceptre all enamelled in their proper colours. The crowns and devices are joined by gold, white-enamelled knots.

Collar Badge: A skeletal gold badge with an oval collar inscribed TRIA JUNCTA IN UNO (three joined in one) in white enamelled letters, enclosing a thistle, rose and shamrock issuing from a sceptre, with a crown above the sceptre and two crowns below, at the sides.

Star: A silver flaming star surmounted by a circular gold band enamelled red bearing the motto round the top and having a laurel spray round the foot, enclosing three gold crowns enamelled in red.

Sash Badge: As the Collar Badge but smaller and without white enamelling.

Comments: *Established by King George I, this was a single-class Order comprising the monarch, a prince of the blood royal, a Great Master and 35 Knights of Companions (KB). It was re-organised at the conclusion of the Napoleonic Wars (see below).*

VALUE:

Collar chain	£18,000–25,000
Collar badge	Rare
Star (metal)	£2000–3500
Star (embroidered)	£400–800
Sash badge	£2000–3000

KNIGHT GRAND CROSS

The Order was re-organised in 1815 in two divisions, Military and Civil. The Military Division had three classes: Knight Grand Cross (GCB), Knight Commander (KCB) and Companion (CB), while the Civil Division continued with the single class of Knight Grand Cross. In 1847 the Civil Division came into line with the Military, and divided into three classes.

Metal: Gold (1815–87): silver-gilt (since 1887).

Collar Badge: The Military Badge is a gold Maltese cross of eight points, each point tipped with a small gold ball, and in each angle between the arms of the cross is a gold lion. In the centre of the cross is a device comprising a rose, thistle and shamrock issuing from a sceptre, and three imperial crowns . This device is surrounded by a red enamelled circle on which appears the Latin motto TRIA JUNCTA IN UNO (three joined in one) in gold lettering. The circle is surrounded by two branches of laurel, enamelled green, and below is a blue enamelled scroll with the German motto ICH DIEN (I serve) in gold.

The Civil Badge is of gold filigree work, and oval in shape. It consists of a bandlet bearing the motto, and in the centre is the usual device of the rose, thistle and shamrock issuing from a sceptre, together with the three crowns.

Star: A gold Maltese cross of the same pattern as the Military Badge, mounted on a silver flaming star (Military); or a silver eight-pointed star with a central device of three crowns on a silver ground, encircled by the motto on a red enamelled ribbon (Civil).

Sash Badges: Similar to the Collar Badges, they were originally made in gold but since 1887 silver-gilt has been substituted.

VALUE:	Military	Civil
Collar chain (gold)	£18,000–25,000	£18,000–25,000
Collar chain (silver gilt)	£8000–10,000	£8000–10,000
Collar badge (gold)	£2000–3500	£800–1000
Star (metal)	£500–1000	£300–400
Star (embroidered)	£300–500	£200–300
Sash badge (gold)	£1800–3000	£800–1000
Sash badge (gilt)	£800–1000	£400–600

4. THE MOST HONOURABLE ORDER OF THE BATH *continued*

KCB Star (Civil)

GCB Sash Badge (Civil)   *KCB Neck Badge (Military)*

KNIGHTS COMMANDERS (KCB) AND COMPANIONS (CB)

Holders of the KCB wear a neck badge suspended by a ribbon as well as a breast star. Prior to 1917 Companions wore a breast badge, the same way as a medal: but in that year it was converted into a neck badge.

Star: (KCB): (Military) a star with the gold Maltese cross omitted, and in the shape of a cross pattée, the three crowns and motto in the centre surrounded by a green enamelled laurel wreath. (Civil) similar but omitting the laurel wreath.

Breast Badge (CB): Similar to the Star but smaller.

Neck Badge (KCB): Similar to the Collar badges of the GCB but smaller, in Military and Civil versions as above.

Neck Badge (CB): Similar to the above, but smaller.

VALUE:

	Military	Miniature	Civil	Miniature
Knight Commander				
Star (metal)	£300–500		£200–400	
Star (embroidered)	£150–400		£100–250	
Neck badge (gold)	£700–1200		£ 400–500	
Neck badge (gilt)	£350–450		£200–250	
Companion				
Breast badge (gold)	£600–1200	£100–150	£350–400	£80–100
Breast badge (gilt)	£350–450	£30–50	£180–220	£20–40
Neck badge (gilt)	£300–400		£140–180	

5. THE ROYAL GUELPHIC ORDER

Instituted: 1815.
Ribbon: 44mm light blue watered silk.

KNIGHTS GRAND CROSS (GCH)

KCH Star (Military)

Collar Chain: Gold, with lions and crowns alternating, linked by scrolled royal cyphers.
Collar Badge: An eight-pointed Maltese cross with balls on each point and a lion passant gardant in each angle. (Obverse) in the centre, on a ground of red enamel, is a white horse of Hanover surrounded by a circle of light blue enamel with the motto in gold lettering NEC ASPERA TERRENT (difficulties do not terrify). Surrounding this circle is a green enamelled laurel wreath. (Reverse) the monogram GR in gold letters on a red ground, surmounted by the British crown and surrounded by a gold circle with the date of the institution MDCCCXV. In the Military version two crossed swords are mounted above the cross and below a Hanoverian crown. In the Civil version the swords are omited, and the wreath is of oak-leaves instead of laurel.
Star: A radiate star with rays grouped into eight points, the centre being similar to the Collar Badge. Behind the laurel wreathed centre are two crossed swords (Military); in the Civil version the swords are omitted and the wreath is of oak leaves.
Sash Badge: Similar to the Collar Badge but smaller.

Comments: *Founded by HRH the Prince Regent (later King George IV), it took its name from the family surname of the British sovereigns from George I onwards and was awarded by the crown of Hanover to both British and Hanverian subjects for distinguished services to Hanover. Under Salic Law, a woman could not succeed to the Hanoverian throne, so on the death of King William IV in 1837 Hanover passed to Prince Augustus, Duke of Cumberland, and thereafter the Guelphic Order became a purely Hanoverian award.*

VALUE:

	Military	Civil
Collar chain (gold)	£7000–9000	£7000–9000
Collar chain (silver gilt)	£4000–5000	£4000–5000
Collar Chain (copper gilt)	£2000–5000	£2000–3000
Collar badge	£5000–6000	£2500–3500
Star	£1000–2000	£500–1000
Sash badge	£6000–8000	£3000–4000

KNIGHTS COMMANDERS (KCH) AND KNIGHTS (KH)

Knights Commanders wore a neck badge suspended by a ribbon, and a breast star, while Knights wore a breast badge only.
Star: As above, but smaller.
Neck Badge: Similar to the Collar Badge but smaller.
Breast Badge: Two versions, in gold and enamel or silver and enamel.

VALUE:

	Military	Miniature	Civil	Miniature
Star	£600–1000		£400–600	
Neck badge	£1500–2000		£800–1200	
Breast badge (gold)	£800–1200	£250–300	£500–700	£200–250

KH Breast Badge (Military)

6. THE MOST DISTINGUISHED ORDER OF ST MICHAEL AND ST GEORGE

Instituted: 1818.
Ribbon: 38mm three equal bands of Saxon blue, scarlet and Saxon blue.

KNIGHTS GRAND CROSS (GCMG)

Knights Grand Cross wear a mantle of Saxon blue lined with scarlet silk tied with cords of blue and scarlet silk and gold, and having on the left side the star of the Order. The chapeau or hat is of blue satin, lined with scarlet and surmounted by black and white ostrich feathers. The collar, mantle and chapeau are only worn on special occasions or when commanded by the sovereign, but in ordinary full dress the badge is worn on the left hip from a broad ribbon passing over the right shoulder and the star on the left breast.

Collar Chain: Silver gilt formed alternately on lions of England, Maltese crosses enamelled in white, and the cyphers SM and SG with, in the centre, two winged lions of St Mark each holding a book and seven arrows.

Star: A silver star of seven groups of rays, with a gold ray between each group, surmounted overall by the cross of St George in red enamel. In the centre is a representation of St Michael encountering Satan within a blue circular riband bearing the motto AUSPICIUM MELIORIS AEVI (A token of a better age).

Sash Badge: A gold seven-pointed star with V-shaped extremities, enamelled white and edged with gold, surmounted by an imperial crown. In the centre on one side is a representation in enamel of St Michael encountering Satan and on the other St George on horseback fighting the dragon. This device is surrounded by a circle of blue enamel bearing the Latin motto in gold lettering. Silver-gilt was substituted for gold in 1887.

Comments: *Founded by HRH the Prince Regent and awarded originally to citizens of Malta and the Ionian Islands in the Adriatic Sea, both of which had been ceded to Britain during the Napoleonic Wars. The Ionian Islands were transferred to Greece in 1859. Towards the end of the 19th century, however, the Order was awarded to those who had performed distinguished service in the colonies and protectorates of the British Empire and in more recent times it has been widely used as an award to ambassadors and senior diplomats as well as colonial governors.*

VALUE:

Collar chain	£1400–1800
Star	£500–600
Sash badge (gold)	£3000–4000
Sash badge (gilt)	£600–800

GCMG Star

6. THE MOST DISTINGUISHED ORDER OF ST MICHAEL AND ST GEORGE *continued*

KCMG Star

KNIGHTS COMMANDERS (KCMG) AND COMPANIONS (CMG)

Knights Commanders wear the badge suspended round the neck from a narrower ribbon of the same colours, and a breast star; Companions wear a neck badge. In undress uniform Knights Grand Cross and Knights Commanders wear the ribbon of Companions of the Order. Prior to 1917 Companions wore a breast badge, worn the same way as a medal, but this was then changed to a neck badge.

Star: A silver eight-pointed star charged with the red St George's cross and having the same central device as the GCMG Star. This was introduced in 1859.

Neck Badge: Similar to the sash badge of the GCMG but smaller. Those worn by KCMG were of gold and enamel until 1887 but silver-gilt and enamel thereafter. The CMG neck badges are invariably of enamel and silver-gilt.

Breast Badge: Similar to the star of the KCMG but smaller and made of gold and enamel till 1887, and silver gilt and enamel from then till 1917.

VALUE:		Miniature
Knight Commander		
Star	£300–400	
Neck badge (gold)	£800–900	
Neck badge (gilt)	£350–450	
Companion		
Breast badge (gold)	£500–600	£80–100
Breast badge (gilt)	£350–400	£30–50
Neck badge (gilt)	£250–350	

7. THE MOST EXALTED ORDER OF THE STAR OF INDIA

Instituted: 1861.
Ribbon: Broad light blue with white edges (GCSI); 50mm plain white (KCSI); 38mm plain white (CSI).

KNIGHTS GRAND COMMANDERS (GCSI)

KCSI Neck Badge

The insignia consisted of a gold collar and badge, a mantle of light blue satin with a representation of the star on the left side and tied with a white silk cord with blue and silver tassels. The collar and mantle were only worn on special occasions and in ordinary full dress uniform a GCSI wore the star on the left breast and the badge on the left hip from a broad sash of light blue edged in white.

Collar Chain: Gold formed of lotus flowers, palm branches and united red and white roses.

Badge: An onyx cameo bearing the left-facing bust of Queen Victoria wearing an imperial crown, set in a gold ornamental oval containing the motto of the Order HEAVEN'S LIGHT OUR GUIDE in diamonds, on a pale blue ground surmounted by a five-pointed star in chased silver.

Star: A five-pointed star in diamonds resting on a circular riband of light blue enamel bearing the motto in diamonds, the whole set on a circular star of golden rays.

Comments: *Founded by Queen Victoria a few years after the British Crown took over the administration of India from the Honourable East India Company, it was intended primarily as an award to loyal Indian princes. The highest class was designated Knight Grand Commander, rather than Cross, because the majority of recipient were not Christians (either Hindus or Muslims). The Order at first consisted of the sovereign, a Grand Master (the Viceroy of India), 36 Knights Grand Commanders (18 British and 18 Indian), 85 Knights Commanders and 170 Companions. The GCSI was the most lavish of all British orders. It lapsed in 1947 when the sub-continent attained independence. Until then all insignia of this Order was returnable on the death of recipients. After 1947, however, recipients or their heirs were allowed in certain cases to purchase the star and badges of any of the three applicable classes, but not the collar chain of the Knight Grand Commander.*

VALUE:

Collar chain	Rare
Star and badge	£25,000–30,000

KNIGHTS COMMANDERS (KCSI) AND COMPANIONS (CSI)

Knights Commanders wore a badge round the neck and a star on the left breast, while Companions originally had a breast badge which was transmuted into a neck badge from 1917 onwards.

Star: Similar to that of the GCSI but in silver.

Neck Badge: Similar to the collar badge of the GCSI but smaller and less ornate.

Breast Badge: Similar to the above but smaller and less ornate and fitted with a straight bar suspender. Subtle differences in the ornament at the foot of the blue border and the external ornament at the sides and foot of the oval.

Comments: *The second and third classes of the Order were awarded to Indian and British subjectsof the armed forces and Indian Civil Service for distinguished service of not less than 30 years' duration.*

VALUE:		*Miniature*
Star and Neck badge (KCSI)	£4000–6000	
Breast badge (CSI)	£2500–3000	£150–200 (gold), £80–100 (gilt)
Neck badge (CSI)	£1400–1600	

8. THE MOST EMINENT ORDER OF THE INDIAN EMPIRE

Instituted: 1878.
Ribbon: Broad of imperial purple (GCIE); 50mm imperial purple (KCIE); 38mm imperial purple (CIE).

KNIGHTS GRAND COMMANDERS (GCIE)

KCIE Neck Badge

The insignia consisted of a collar, badge and mantle of imperial purple or dark blue satin lined with white silk and fastened with a white silk cord with gold tassels, and having on the left side a representation of the Star of the Order. On ordinary full-dress occasions, however, Knights Grand Commanders wore the badge on the left hip from a broad sash, and a star on the left breast.

Collar Chain: Silver-gilt, composed of elephants, lotus flowers, peacocks in their pride and Indian roses with, in the centre, the imperial crown, the whole linked together by chains.

Badge: A gold five-petalled rose, enamelled crimson and with a green barb between each petal. In the centre is an effigy of Queen Victoria on a gold ground, surrounded by a purple riband originally inscribed VICTORIA IMPERATRIX but from 1901 onwards inscribed IMPERATRICIS AUSPICIIS (under the auspices of the Empress).

Star: Composed of fine silver rays with smaller gold rays between them, the whole alternately plain and scaled. In the centre, within a purple circle bearing the motto and surmounted by the imperial crown in gold, is the effigy of Queen Victoria on a gold ground.

Comments: *Founded by Queen Victoria after assuming the title of Empress of India, it was originally confined to Companions only, together with the Sovereign and Grand Master. Members of the Council of the Governor-General were admitted ex officio as Companions. It was intended for award in respect of meritorious services in India but from the outset it was regarded as a junior alternative to the Star of India. In 1886 the Order was expanded to two classes by the addition of Knights Commanders up to a maximum of 50 in number. In 1887, however, it was again re-organised into three classes: up to 25 Knights Grand Commanders (GCIE), up to 50 Knights Commanders (KCIE) and an unlimited number of Companions (CIE). The Order has been in abeyance since 1947.*

VALUE:

Collar chain	Rare
Star and badge	£4000–5000

KNIGHTS COMMANDERS (KCIE) AND COMPANIONS (CIE)

The insignia of Knights Commanders consisted of a neck badge and a breast star, while that of Companions was originally a breast badge, converted to a neck badge in 1917.

Star: Similar to that of the GCIE but fashioned entirely in silver.

Neck badge: Similar to the collar or sash badge of the GCIE but in correspondingly smaller sizes and differing in minor details.

Breast badge: Similar to the sash badge of the GCIE but differing in minor details, notably the spacing ornament at the foot of the blue circle. Two versions exist, with or without INDIA on the petals of the lotus flower.

VALUE:		Miniature
Knights Commanders		
Star and Neck badge	£1400–2000	
Companions		
Breast badge (INDIA)	£800–1000	£150–200 (gold)
Breast badge (smaller, without INDIA)	£400–450	£100–150 (gold), £30–80 (gilt)
Neck badge	£300–350	

9. THE ROYAL FAMILY ORDER

Instituted: 1820.

Ribbon: 50mm sky blue moire (1820); 38mm dark blue bordered by narrow stripes of yellow and broader stripes of crimson with narrow black edges (1902); 50mm pale blue moire (1911); 50mm pink moire (1937); 50mm pale yellow silk moire (1953). These ribbons are tied in a bow and worn on the left shoulder.

Descriptions: An upright oval heavily bordered by diamonds and surmounted by a crown, also embellished in diamonds. The oval contains a miniature portrait of the sovereign in enamels.

Comments: *Awarded to the Queen and female relatives of the reigning monarch. It was instituted by King George IV who conferred such orders on his sister, Princess Charlotte Augusta, wife of Frederick William, King of Wurttemberg, and his niece Princess Augusta Caroline, who married the Grand Duke of Mecklenburg-Strelitz. Queen Victoria instituted a separate Order (see next entry), but this Order was revived by King Edward VII in 1902 and continued by successive sovereigns ever since. Special badges are given to ladies-in-waiting. The insignia of these Family Orders very seldom appear on the market and on account of their immense rarity they are unpriced here.*

VALUE:
George IV	Rare
Edward VIII	Rare
George V	Rare
George VI	Rare
Elizabeth II	Rare
Ladies-in-waiting badges	From £1000

10. THE ROYAL ORDER OF VICTORIA AND ALBERT

Instituted: 1862.

Ribbon: 38mm white moire, in the form of a bow worn on the left shoulder.

Description: An upright oval onyx cameo bearing conjoined profiles of HRH Prince Albert, the Prince Consort and Queen Victoria. The badges of the First and Second Classes are set in diamonds and surmounted by an imperial crown similarly embellished, the badge of the Second Class being rather smaller. The badge of the Third Class is set in pearls, while that of the Fourth Class takes the form of a monogram "V & A" set with pearls and surmounted by an imperial crown.

VALUE:
First Class	£24,000–26,000
Second Class	£16,000–18,000
Third Class	£10,000–12,000
Fourth Class	£ 4000–5000

11. THE IMPERIAL ORDER OF THE CROWN OF INDIA

Instituted: January 1, 1878.

Ribbon: 38mm light blue watered silk with narrow white stripes towards the edges, formed in a bow worn on the left shoulder.

Description: A badge consisting of the royal and imperial monogram VRI in diamonds, turquoises and pearls, surrounded by an oval frame and surmounted by a jewelled imperial crown.

Comments: *Awarded by Queen Victoria to the princesses of the royal and imperial house, the wives or other female relatives of Indian princes and other Indian ladies, and of the wives or other female relatives of any of the persons who had held or were holding the offices of Viceroy and Governor-General of India, Governors of Madras or Bombay, or of Principal Secretary of State for India, as the sovereign might think fit to appoint. This order, conferred on females only, became obsolete in 1947.*

VALUE:
Breast badge	£6000–10,000

12. THE ROYAL VICTORIAN ORDER

Instituted: April 1896.
Ribbon: Dark blue with borders of narrow red, white and red stripes on either side.

KNIGHTS GRAND CROSS AND DAMES GRAND CROSS (GCVO)

The insignia consists of a mantle of dark blue silk, edged with red satin, lined with white silk, and fastened by a cordon of dark blue silk and gold; a gold collar and a badge, worn only on special occasions. Knights wear the badge on the left hip from a broad ribbon worn over the right shoulder, with a star on the left breast, while Dames wear a somewhat narrower ribbon over the right shoulder with the badge, and a star similar to that of the Knights. Dames' insignia are smaller than those of the Knights.

Collar: Silver gilt composed of octagonal pieces and oblong perforated and ornamental frames alternately linked together with gold. The pieces are edged and ornamented with gold, and each contains on a blue-enamelled ground a gold rose jewellerd with a carbuncle. The frames are gold and each contains a portion of inscription VICTORIA BRITT. DEF. FID. IND. IMP. in letters of white enamel. In the centre of the collar, within a perforated and ornamental frame of gold, is an octagonal piece enamelled blue, edged with red, and charged with a white saltire, superimposed by a gold medallion of Queen Victoria's effigy fromwhich is suspended the badge.

Badge: A white-enamelled Maltese cross of eight points, in the centre of which is an oval of crimson enamel bearing the cypher VRI in gold letters. Encircling this is a blue enamel riband with the name VICTORIA in gold letters, and above this is the imperial crown enamelled in proper colours.

Star: Of chipped silver of eight points on which is mounted a white-enamelled Maltese cross with VRI in an oval at the centre.

Comments: *Awarded for extraordinary, important or personal services to the sovereign of the Royal Family. Ladies became eligible for the Order in 1936. Most of the badges of the Royal Victorian Order are numbered on the reverse and are returnable on promotion. Honourary awards are unnumbered.*

VALUE:

	Knights	Dames
Collar	£5000–6000	£6000–7000
Star and Badge	£900–1200	£1000–1200

GCVO star

KNIGHTS COMMANDERS (KCVO), DAMES COMMANDERS (DCVO), COMMANDERS (CVO), LIEUTENANTS (LVO) AND MEMBERS (MVO)

The insignia of the Second, Third, Fourth and Fifth Classes follows the usual pattern. Knights wear a neck badge and a breast star, Dames a breast star and a badge on the left shoulder from a ribbon tied in a bow, Commanders the same neck badge (men) or shoulder badge (women), Lieutenants a somewhat smaller breast badge worn in line with other medals and decorations (men) or a shoulder badge (women) and Members breast or shoulder badges in frosted silver instead of white enamel. The two lowest classes of the Order were originally designated member Fourth Class or member Fifth Class (MVO), but in 1988 the Fourth Class was renamed Lieutenant (LVO) and the Fifth Class simply Member (MVO).

VALUE:

	Gentlemen	*Miniature*	Ladies
Neck badge and breast star	£400–600		£500–600
Neck badge (CVO)	£300–350	£30–50	£400–450
Breast or shoulder badge (LVO)	£200–250	£30–50	£250–300
Breast or shoulder badge (MVO)	£180–220	£15–25	£220–250

13. ROYAL VICTORIAN MEDAL

Instituted: April 1896.

Ribbon: As for the Royal Victorian Order (above); foreign Associates, however, wear a ribbon with a central white stripe added.

Metal: Silver-gilt, silver or bronze.

Size: 36mm.

Description: (Obverse) the effigy of the reigning sovereign; (reverse) the royal cypher on an ornamental shield within a laurel wreath.

Comments: *Awarded to those below the rank of officers who perform personal services to the sovereign or to members of the Royal Family. Originally awarded in silver or bronze, a higher class, in silver-gilt, was instituted by King George V. Only two medals (both silver) were issued in the brief reign of King Edward VIII (1936) and only four bronze medals were issued in the reign of King George VI. Any person in possession of the bronze medal to whom a silver medal is awarded, can wear both, and the silver-gilt medal in addition if such be conferred upon him or her. Clasps are awarded for further services to each class of the medal, while the medals may be worn in addition to the insignia of the Order if the latter is subsequently conferred. To distinguish between British and foreign recipients, King George VI decreed in 1951 that the ribbon worn by the latter should have an additional stripe, these recipients to be designated Associates. In 1983 the order for wearing this medal was altered, and it was no longer to be worn after campaign medals but took precedence over them.*

VALUE:

	Silver-gilt	Miniature	Silver	Miniature	Bronze	Miniature
Victoria	—	£45–50	£100–120	£25–35	£80–100	£25–35
Edward VII	£250–300		£120–150	£15–20	£80–100	£20–30
George V	—		£80–90	£10–15	£250–300	£15–20
Edward VIII	—		Rare		—	
George VI	£100–120		£80–120	£10–15	Rare	£10–15
Elizabeth II	£140–160		£120–130	£10–15	£100–120	£10–15

14. THE ROYAL VICTORIAN CHAIN

Instituted: 1902.

Ribbon: None.

Metal: Silver gilt

Description: A chain consisting of three Tudor roses, two thistles, two shamrocks and two lotus flowers (the heraldic flowers of England, Scotland, Ireland and India respectively), connected by a slender double trace of gold chain. At the bottom of the front loop is a centre piece consisting of the royal cypher in enamel surrounded by a wreath and surmounted by a crown. From this centrepiece hangs a replica of the badge of a Knight Grand Cross of the Royal Victorian order. Ladies were the insignia in the form of a shoulder badge suspended from a miniature chain with links leading to a rose, thistle, shamrock and lotus. An even more elaborate collar, with diamonds encrusting the crown and cypher, was adopted in 1921 and there is a ladies' version of this as well.

Comments: *Sometimes regarded as the highest grade of the Royal Victorian Order, it is actually a quite separate Order and was introduced by King Edward VII for conferment as a special mark of the sovereign's favour, and then only very rarely, upon Royalty, or other especially distinguished personages, both foreign and British.*

VALUE

	Gentlemen	Ladies
Chain (1902–21)	Rare	Rare
Chain with diamonds	Rare	Rare

15. ORDER OF MERIT

Order of Merit obverse

Instituted: 1902.
Ribbon: 50mm half blue, half crimson.
Metal: Gold.
Size: Height 50mm; max. width 35mm.
Description: A pattée convexed cross, enamelled red, edged blue. (Obverse) FOR MERIT in the centre surrounded by a white band and a laurel wreath enamelled in proper colours. (Reverse) the royal cypher in gold on a blue ground with a white surround and a laurel wreath as above. The cross is surmounted by a Tudor crown to which is attached a ring for suspension. Naval and military recipients have crossed swords in the angles of the cross.
Comments: *This highly prestigious Order consists of the sovereign and a maximum of 24 members in one class only. There is, however, no limit on the number of foreign honorary members, although only ten have so far been admitted to the Order. It was intended for award to those whose achievements in the fields of art, music and literature were outstanding, but it was later extended to naval and military leaders in wartime. To date, fewer than 160 awards have been made, including a mere five ladies, from Florence Nightingale (1907) to Baroness Thatcher. The insignia of those appointed since 1991 have to be returned on the death of the recipient. The insignia of members appointed prior to that date is retained, but understandably few items have come on to the market.*

VALUE:

	Military	Civil
Edward VII	£5000–6000	£3500–4500
George V	£5000–6000	£3000–4000
George VI	Rare	£4000–5000
Elizabeth II	Rare	£3500–4500

Order of Merit reverse

16. THE MOST EXCELLENT ORDER OF THE BRITISH EMPIRE

GBE Star (2nd type)

CBE Badge (2nd type)

Instituted: June 1917.

Ribbon: 38mm originally purple, with a narrow central scarlet stripe for the Military Division; rose-pink edged with pearl grey, with a narrow central stripe of pearl-grey for the Military Division (since 1936). A silver crossed oakleaf emblem for gallantry was instituted in 1957.

Comments: *Founded by King George V during the First World War for services to the Empire at home, in India and in the overseas dominions and colonies, other than those rendered by the Navy and Army, although it could be conferred upon officers of the armed forces for services of a non-combatant character. A Military Division was created in December 1918 and awards made to commissioned officers and warrant officers in respect of distinguished service in action. The insignia of the Civil and Military Divisions is identical, distinguished only by the respective ribbons.*

KNIGHTS AND DAMES GRAND CROSS (GBE)

The insignia includes a mantle of rose-pink satin lined with pearl-grey silk, tied by a cord of pearl-grey silk, with two rose-pink and silver tassels attached. On the left side of the mantle is a representation of the star of the First Class of the Order. The mantle, collar and collar badge are only worn on special occasions. In dress uniform, however, the badge is worn over the left hip from a broad (96mm) riband passing over the right shoulder, while Dames wear the badge from a narrower (57mm) ribbon in a bow on the left shoulder; both with the breast star of the Order.

Collar: Silver-gilt with medallions of the royal arms and of the royal and imperial cypher of King George V alternately linked together with cables. In the centre is the imperial crown between two sea lions. The collar for Dames is somewhat narrower than that for Knights.

Badge: A cross patonce in silver-gilt the arms enamelled pearl-grey. In the centre, within a circle enamelled crimson, the figure of Britannia, replaced since 1936 by the conjoined left-facing crowned busts of King George V and Queen Mary, surrounded by a circle inscribed FOR GOD AND THE EMPIRE.

Star: An eight-pointed star of silver chips on which is superimposed the enamelled medallion as for the badge (Britannia or George V and Queen Mary). The star worn by Dames is smaller.

VALUE:

	Britannia	King and Queen
Knights Grand Cross		
Collar	£5000–6000	£5000–6000
Badge and star	£900–1000	£1000–1200
Dames Grand Cross		
Collar	£6000–7000	£6000–7000
Badge and star	£1000–1200	£1200–1400

16. THE MOST EXCELLENT ORDER OF THE BRITISH EMPIRE *continued*

KNIGHTS COMMANDERS (KBE), DAMES COMMANDERS (DBE), COMMANDERS (CBE) AND MEMBERS (MBE)

KBE Star

The insignia of these four Classes follows the same pattern as other Orders. Both Britannia and King and Queen medallion types have been issued.

Star: A star of four large points and four minor points in chipped silver, with the enamelled medallion superimposed. The star worn by Dames is smaller.

Neck Badge: Similar to the badge of the GBE but smaller and worn from a 44mm ribbon round the neck (men) or from a shoulder bow (ladies). Worn by KBE, DBE and CBE.

Breast Badge: As above, but in silver-gilt (OBE) or frosted silver (MBE), with shoulder versions for ladies, worn with a 38mm ribbon.

VALUE:	Britannia	*Miniature*	King and Queen	*Miniature*
Badge and Star (KBE,)	£380–450		£380–450	
Badge and Star (DBE)	£380–450		£450–550	
Neck badge (CBE)	£120–130	£15–20	£150–180	£15–20
Shoulder badge (CBE)	£140–160		£180–220	
Breast badge (OBE)	£45–55	£10–15	£55–65	£10–15
Shoulder badge (OBE)	£45–55		£55–65	
Breast badge (MBE)	£45–55	£8–10	£55–65	£8–10
Shoulder badge (MBE)	£45–55		£55–65	

OBE badge (silver-gilt) and reverse of the MBE badge (frosted silver).

Ribbons: (top to bottom) OBE (Civil) 1st type, OBE (Civil) 2nd type, OBE (Military) 1st type and OBE (Military) 2nd type.

17. MEDAL OF THE ORDER OF THE BRITISH EMPIRE

Instituted: June 1917.
Ribbon: 32mm plain purple (Civil), with a narrow scarlet central stripe (Military).
Medal: Silver.
Size: 30mm.
Description: (Obverse) a seated figure of Britannia facing right, her left arm extended and her right holding a trident, with the inscription FOR GOD AND THE EMPIRE round the upper part of the circumference; (reverse) the royal and imperial cypher GRI surmounted by a Tudor crown, the whole enclosed in a cable circle. Fitted with a plain ring for suspension.
Comments: *Instituted as a lower award connected with the Order, it consisted originally of a Civil Division, but a Military Division, distinguishable solely by the ribbon, was added in December 1918. This medal was issued unnamed but many were subsequently engraved or impressed on the rim privately. Fewer than 2000 medals were awarded before they were discontinued in 1922.*

VALUE:

		Miniature
Medal unnamed as issued	£80–90	£30–40
Military award with named medal group	£150–200	
Civil award with supporting documents	£100–150	

18. EMPIRE GALLANTRY MEDAL

1st type rev.

Instituted: December 29, 1922.
Ribbon: Originally plain purple (Civil), with a thin scarlet central stripe (Military; from July 1937 rose-pink with pearl-grey edges (Civil) and a central pearl-grey stripe (Military). A silver laurel branch was added to the ribbon (1933), with a smaller version for wear on the ribbon alone.
Metal: Silver.
Size: 36mm.
Description: (Obverse) the seated figure of Britannia, her left hand resting on a shield and her right holding a trident, with a blazing sun upper right. The words FOR GOD AND THE EMPIRE inscribed round the upper part of the circumference, with FOR in the wave lower left above the exergue which bears the word GALLANTRY. (Reverse) 1st type has six lions passant gardant, with the Royal cypher in the centre surmounted by an imperial crown. The George VI issue has four lions, two either side and round the foot, in two concentric arcs, the words INSTITUTED BY KING GEORGE V. It is suspended from a straight bar ornamented with laurel leaves. Named in seriffed capitals engraved round the rim.
Comments: *This medal, officially known as the Medal of the Order of the British Empire for Gallantry, replaced the Medal of the Order of the British Empire and was awarded for specific acts of gallantry. It was abolished on the institution of the George Cross in September 1940, while it was announced in the London Gazette of April 22, 1941 that a recipient still living on September 24, 1940 should return it to the Central Chancery of the Orders of Knighthood and become a holder of the George Cross instead. Not all EGMs, however, were exchanged or returned. Only 130 medals were issued, 64 being civil, 62 military and 4 honorary.*

VALUE:

		Miniature
George V	£3000–3500	£20–25
George VI	£3000–3500	£25–30

19. BRITISH EMPIRE MEDAL

BEM (Military) 2nd type

Instituted: December 1922.
Ribbon: As above, but without the silver laurel branch.
Metal: Silver.
Size: 36mm.
Description: As above, but with the words MERITORIOUS SERVICE in the exergue. Suspended from a straight bar ornamented with oak leaves. A silver bar decorated with oak leaves was introduced in March 1941 for further acts, and is denoted by a silver rosette on the ribbon worn on its own. An emblem of crossed silver oak leaves was introduced in December 1957 to denote a gallantry award, a smaller version being worn on the ribbon alone. Named in engraved capitals round the rim.
Comments: *Formally entitled the Medal of the Order of the British Empire for Meritorious Service, it is generally known simply as the British Empire Medal. It is awarded for meritorious service by both civil and military personnel. The medal may be worn even if the recipient is promoted to a higher grade of the Order. The gallantry awards, instituted in December 1957, ceased in 1974 on the introduction of the Queen's Gallantry Medal.*

VALUE

	Military	Civil	Miniature
George V	£150–180	£100–120	£10–15
George VI GRI cypher	£100–150	£70–80	£10–15
George VI GVIR cypher	£100–150	£70–80	£10–15
Elizabeth II	£100–150	£80–100	£10–15
Elizabeth II with gallantry emblem	£300–600	£200–300	

20. THE ORDER OF THE COMPANIONS OF HONOUR

Instituted: June 1917
Ribbon: 38mm carmine with borders of gold thread.
Metal: Silver gilt.
Size: Height 48mm; max. width 29mm.
Description: An oval badge consisting of a medallion with an oak tree, a shield bearing the royal arms hanging from one branch, and on the left a knight armed and in armour, mounted on a horse. The badge has a blue border with the motto IN ACTION FAITHFUL AND IN HONOUR CLEAR in gold letters. The oval is surmounted by an imperial crown. Gentlemen wear the badge round their necks, while ladies wear it from a bow at the left shoulder.
Comments: Instituted at the same time as the Order of the British Empire, it carries no title or precedence although the post-nominal letters CH are used. The Order consists of the sovereign and one class of members. Not more than 50 men or women who have rendered conspicuous service of national importance were admitted, but in 1943 this was increased to 65. The Order is awarded in Britain and the Commonwealth on a quota basis: UK (45), Australia (7), New Zealand (2), other countries (11). It is awarded for outstanding achievements in the arts, literature, music, science, politics, industry and religion.

VALUE

Gentlemen	£1800–2000
Ladies	£1800–2000

21. THE BARONET'S BADGE

Instituted: 1629
Ribbon: 30mm orange watered silk (Nova Scotia); 44mm orange bordered with narrow blue edges (other Baronets).
Metal: Gold or silver-gilt.
Size: Height 55mm; max. width 41mm(Nova Scotia) or 44mm (later badges).
Description: An upright oval badge with a plain ring suspension. The badge of the Baronets of Nova Scotia was originally skeletal, with a shield bearing the lion rempant of Scotland, decorated with pearls and enamels, surmounted by a Scottish crown and surrounded by a blue border inscribed in gold FAX MENTIS HONESTAE GLORIA. The remaining badges (authorised in 1929) have a solid ground and a central shield with the red hand of Ulster surmounted by a crown and a border of gold and blue enamel decorated with roses (England), shamrocks (Ireland), roses and thistles combined (Great Britain) or roses, thistles and shamrocks combined (United Kingdom). Engraved on the reverse with the recipient's title and date of creation.
Comments: *In an ingenious attempt to raise money without recourse to Parliament, King James I sold grants of land in Nova Scotia. Five years later King Charles I conferred on holders of this land the dignity and rank of Baronets of Nava Scotia, with the title Sir, and decreed that such baronets should wear round their necks "an orange tawny ribbon whereon shall be pendent an escutcheon". After the Union of 1707 Baronets of Scotland properly charged their arms with the badge of Ulster, the red hand, being created Baronets of the United Kingdom. No Baronets of Scotland have been created since 1707, or of Ireland since 1801. Later baronets are of Great Britain, or of the United Kingdom. Badges for the latter were not introduced until 1929, the tercentenary year of the original institution.*

Baronet's badge—United Kingdom

VALUE:	Gold	Silver-gilt
Nova Scotia, 18th–early 19th centuries	£1500–3000	£500–800
Nova Scotia, late 19th and 20th centuries	£1400–1600	£400–600
England (rose surround)	£800–1000	£400–600
Ireland (shamrock surround)	£800–1000	£400–600
Great Britain (roses and thistles)	£800–1000	£400–600
United Kingdom (roses, thistles and shamrocks)	£800–1000	£400–600

22. THE KNIGHT BACHELOR'S BADGE

Instituted: 1929.
Ribbon: 38mm scarlet with broad yellow borders.
Metal: Silver-gilt and enamels.
Size: Height 81mm; max. width 60mm. Reduced in 1933 and 1974.
Description: An upright oval medallion enclosed by a scroll, bearing a cross-hilted sword, belted and sheathed, pommel upwards, between two spurs, rowels upwards, the whole set about with the sword-belt.
Comments: *The title Knight Bachelor (KB) was introduced by King Henry III to signify that the title would die with the holder, and not be transmited to the holder's heir. The badge was authorised by King George V at the same time as the Baronet's Badge, in response to a request from the Imperial Society of Knights Bachelors who wished to have a distinctive badge denoting their rank. The original badge was of the dimensions given above and affixed to the breast by means of a pin on the reverse. This badge was reduced in size in 1933 and again in 1974 when it was fitted with a ring for suspension by a ribbon round the neck.*

Knight Bachelor's badge

VALUE:		Miniature
First type (1929)	£180–220	£20–30
Smaller type (1933)	£160–200	**Skeletal type**
Neck badge (1974)	£180–220	£10–20

23. THE ORDER OF ST JOHN OF JERUSALEM

Instituted: May 14, 1888.
Ribbon: Plain black watered silk. Sash ribbons for Bailiffs, 100mm; Dames Grand Cross, 65mm. Ribbons for Knights, 50mm; Dames of Justice 32mm in a bow. Ribbons for Commanders, Officers and Serving Brothers, 38mm for men and 32mm for ladies.
Metal: Gold, silver-gilt and silver, or base metal.
Sash Badge: An eight-pointed gold Maltese cross in white enamel with two lions and two unicorns in the angles. Confined to Bailiffs and Dames Grand Cross.
Neck Badge: Worn by Knights of Justice and Chaplains in gold and Knights of Grace and Commanders (Brothers) in silver. These neck badges are all of the same size.
Star: The eight-pointed Maltese cross in white enamel without the lions and unicorns (Grand Cross and Justice) or with lions and unicorns (Grace and Sub-Prelate). A sub-Prelate is an Order Chaplain (so his badge is included above) who holds high rank in the Church as distinct from the Order.
Shoulder Badge: Worn by Dames of Justice in gold and Dames of Grace, Commanders (Sisters) and Officers (Sisters) in silver. The badge is the same size for Dame and Commander but smaller for Officers.
Breast Badges: Officers (Brothers) is the Order badge with animals, in silver (1926–36) and in silver and enamel subsequently. Those worn by Serving Brothers, and as shoulder badges by Serving Sisters, have undergone six main phases:
1892–1939: a circular badge with crosses and animals raised above the surface of the medal.
1939–1949: circular skeletal badge with ring suspension and the eight-point cross set in a silver rim.
1949–1974: the first badge resumed.
1974–1984: a badge of the same design but with the cross and animals flush with their background.
1984–1991: the cross and animals in white metal, slightly smaller than the Officer (Brother) cross and the whole convex on the obverse.
Since 1991: Cross and animals thicker, with each arm raised and shaped on both sides of a central channel, the whole in rhodium.
Donats' Badges: God, silver or bronze, consisting of the badge of the Order with the upper arm of the cross replaced by an ornamental piece of metal for suspension.
Comments: *The Most Venerable Order of St John of Jerusalem was incorporated by Royal Charter of Queen Victoria and granted the epithet Venerable in 1926; despite its title, it has no connection with the Knights Hospitallers of Jerusalem, who were subsequently based at Rhodes and Malta and are now located at Rome. In 1926 the Order was reorganised into five Classes like certain other Orders. Both men and women are eligible for membership. Her Majesty the Queen is the Sovereign Head of the Order. Next in authority is the Grand Prior, followed by Bailiffs and Dames Grand Cross, Knights and Dames of Justice, Knights and Dames of Grace, Commanders, Officers and Serving Brothers and Sisters. Associates are people who are not citizens of the United Kingdom, the British Commonwealth or the Republic of Ireland, or are non-Christians, who have rendered conspicuous service to the Order and may be attached to any grade of the Order. They wear the insignia of that grade, at one time distinguished only by a central narrow white stripe on the ribbon, but now all ribbons are identical. Donats are people who have made generous contributions to the funds of the Order. They are not enrolled as members of the Order but receive badges in gold, silver or bronze.*

VALUE:

	Gold	Silver/Gilt	Bronze	Miniature
Bailiff badge and star	£1500–2200	£800–1000	—	
Dame Grand Cross	£1500–2000	£500–600	—	
Knight of Justice neck badge and star	£800–900	£400–500	£150–250	
Dame of Justice shoulder badge and star	£800–900	£400–500	£200–300	
Knight of Grace neck badge and star	—	£350–400	£150–250	
Dame of Grace shoulder badge and star	—	£350–400	£150–250	
Commander (Brother) neck badge	—	£130–180	£60–80	
Commander (Sister) shoulder badge	—	£35–50	£30–50	
Officer breast badge, plain silver	—	£35–50	—	£10–15
Office breast badge, enamelled	—	£40–60	£30–50	£15–20
Officer (Sister) enamelled badge	—	£40–60	£30–50	
Serving Brother/Sister 1926–39	—	£50–60	£30–50	£10–12
Serving Brother/Sister 1939–49	—	£40–60	£40–60	£10–12
Serving Brother/Sister 1949–	—	—	£30–50	
Donat's medals	£80–100	£40–50	£30–40	£25–30

DECORATIONS

The award of decorations for distinguished military service is an ancient institution. In his *Antiquities of the Jews*, the historian Josephus relates that, in the third century BC, King Alexander was so pleased with Jonathan the High Priest that he sent him a gold button as a mark of favour for his skill in leading the Jews in battle. Subsequently Jonathan was presented with a second gold button for his gallant conduct in the field, making these incidents among the earliest recorded for which specific military awards were granted. The award of jewels, gold buttons and badges for valour was carried on in most European countries on a sporadic basis but the present system of decorations is essentially a modern one dating back no farther than the middle of the seventeenth century. Earlier medals were quasi-commemorative and include the famous Armada Medal of 1588. A few medals in silver or gold were awarded to officers for distinguished service during the English Civil War, although the first "official" rewards in Britain were probably those issued by Parliament to naval officers following their victories over the Dutch fleet in 1653.

Decorations may be divided into those awarded for individual acts of heroism and those conferred in recognition of distinguished military, political or social service. In general terms collectors prefer a decoration awarded for bravery in the field rather than a political honour given automatically to a civil servant, just because he happens to have been in a particular grade for a certain number of years. The debasement of civil awards, such as the OBE and MBE, is reflected in the relative lack of interest shown by collectors.

It is generally true to say that military decorations are more desirable, but it is important to note that one decoration may be more highly prized than another, while the same decoration may well be more valuable to collectors when issued in one period rather than in another. At one extreme is the greatly coveted Victoria Cross, only 1354 of which (including three bars) have been awarded since its inception. VCs won during the Crimean War (111 awarded) are usually less highly regarded than Crosses awarded during the First World War, where, although numerically greater (633) they were far more dearly won. Second World War Crosses are correspondingly more expensive as only 182 were awarded and even now comparatively few of them have ever come on to the market. Today, while pre-1914 Crosses would rate at least £10,000 and those from the First World War slightly more, Second World War Crosses start around £20,000 but have been known to fetch several times as much, depending on the precise circumstances and the branch of the services.

At the other extreme is the Military Medal, of which no fewer than 115,589 were awarded during the First World War alone. For this reason a MM from this period can still be picked up for under £100, whereas one from the Second World War would usually fetch about four times as much, and awards made during the minor campaigns of the 1930s or the Korean War often rate at least ten times as much.

The value of a decoration, where its provenance can be unquestionably established, depends largely on the decoration itself, whether awarded to an officer or an enlisted man, the individual circumstances of the award, the campaign or action concerned, the regiment, unit or ship involved, and the often very personal details of the act or acts of bravery. These factors are extraordinarily difficult to quantify, hence the frequent large discrepancies in the prices fetched by decorations at auction.

The addition of even relatively common decorations, such as the Military Cross or the Military Medal to the average First World War campaign medal group, invariably enhances its value very considerably while the addition of bars for subsequent awards likewise rates a good premium. Decorations awarded to officers tend to fetch more than those awarded to other ranks, mainly because they are proportionately rarer but also because it is usually easier to trace the career details of an officer.

Sometimes the rank of the recipient may have a bearing on the demand for a particular decoration: e.g. Military Crosses awarded to warrant officers are scarcer than those awarded to subalterns and captains. The branch of the armed services may also have some bearing. Thus a Military Medal awarded to a member of the RAF rates far higher than one awarded to a soldier, while a medal awarded to a seaman in one of the naval battalions which fought on the Western Front is also equally desirable.

Initially the Distinguished Service Order could be won by commissioned officers of any rank but after 1914, when the Military Cross was instituted, it was usually restricted to officers of field rank. DSOs awarded to lieutenants and captains in the Army in both World Wars are therefore comparatively rare and invariably expensive, usually as they were awarded for acts of heroism which in earlier campaigns might have merited the VC.

The opportunity for individual acts of bravery varied

from service to service, and in different conflicts. Thus sailors in the Second World War generally had less scope than air crew. Consequently specifically naval awards, such as the Conspicuous Gallantry Medal and the Distinguished Service Cross, are much more scarce than the corresponding RAF awards for Conspicuous Gallantry and the Distinguished Flying Cross.

The addition of bars to gallantry decorations greatly enhances the scarcity and value of such medals. The VC, for example, has been won by only three men on two occasions; none of these VC and bar combinations has ever come on the market, but should one come up for sale, it is certain that the price would be spectacular. The average First World War MM is today worth around £60, but with a bar for second award its value immediately jumps to about three times as much, while MMs with two or more bars are very much more expensive.

It is important to note that in some cases (the DSO for example) decorations were issued unnamed; for this reason the citation or any other supporting documents relevant to the award should be kept with the decoration wherever possible to confirm its attribution.

Engraving of Gallantry Decorations

After the special investiture for the South Atlantic campaign held on February 8, 1983, the question as to why certain awards were engraved with the date only was raised within the Ministry of Defence. A joint service working party considered the matter and recommended that procedures for all decorations and medals for gallantry in the face of the enemy and for the Air Force Cross when awarded for a specific act of gallantry should be brought into line. A submission was accordingly made to the Queen by the Committee on the Grant of Honours, Decorations and Medals and in April 1984 Her Majesty approved the following:

(i)   That the Distinguished Service Cross, Military Cross, Distinguished Flying Cross and Air Force Cross when awarded for gallantry should be engraved with the personal details of the recipient with effect from January 1, 1984.
(ii) That there should be no retrospection;
(iii) That the badge of a Companion of the Distinguished Service Order should not be engraved (in common with the badges of other orders); and
(iv) That the Royal Red Cross (RRC and ARRC) and the Air Force Cross when awarded for meritorious service should not be engraved.

Condition

The same terms are applied to describe the condition of medals and decorations as apply to coins, although the wear to which they are put is caused by other factors. In modern times, when the number of occasions on which medals are worn are relatively few and far between, the condition of most items will be found to be Very Fine (VF) to Extremely Fine (EF). Indeed, in many cases, the medals may never have been worn at all. A good proportion of Second World War medals and decorations are found in almost mint condition as they were not issued till long after the war, by which time their recipients had been demobilised. In some cases they even turn up still in the original cardboard box in which they were posted to the recipients or their next-of-kin.

Before the First World War, however, the wearing of medals was customary on all but the most informal occasions and when actually serving on active duty. Thus medals could be, and often were, subject to a great deal of wear. Medals worn by cavalrymen are often found in poor condition, with scratches and edge knocks occasioned by the constant jangling of one medal against another while on horseback. Often the medals in a group have an abrasive effect on each other. For this reason the Queen's Medal for Egypt (1882) is comparatively rare in excellent condition, as it was usually worn in juxtaposition to the bronze Khedive's Star whose points were capable of doing considerable damage to its silver companion. Apart from these factors it should also be remembered that part of the ritual of 'spit and polish' involved cleaning one's medals and they were therefore submitted to vigorous cleaning with metal polish over long periods of service.

For these reasons medals are often sold by dealers "as worn"—a euphemism which conceals a lifetime of hardy service on the chest of some grizzled veteran. Because of the strong personal element involved in medal-collecting, however, genuine wear does not affect the value of a medal to the same degree that it would in other branches of numismatics. There is a school of thought which considers that such signs enhance the interest and value of a medal or group.

This line of thinking also explains the controversy over medal ribbons. Some military outfitters still carry extensive stocks of medal ribbons covering every campaign from Waterloo onwards, so that it is a very easy matter to obtain a fresh length of ribbon for any medal requiring it, and there is no doubt that the appearance of a piece is greatly improved by a clean, bright new ribbon. On the other hand, that ribbon was not the one actually worn by Corporal Bloggs on parade and, to the purist, it would spoil the total effect of the medal. Some collectors therefore retain the original ribbon, even though it may be faded and frayed. As ribbons are things which one cannot authenticate, however, there seems to be little material benefit to be gained from clinging rigidly to a tattered strip of silk when an identical piece can be obtained relatively cheaply. In reality, most collectors compromise by obtaining new ribbons while preserving the old lengths out of sentiment.

Pricing

The prices quoted are *average* figures for medals and decorations as individual items. Combinations with other decorations and campaign medals will produce a value usually well in excess of the aggregate of the individual items. Value will depend to a large extent on the personal factors and circumstances of the award, but where general factors are involved (e.g. the design of the medal, the period of issue or the campaign concerned, or in some cases the branch of the services) these are itemised separately. "—" indicates that either no examples have come onto the market or no examples have been issued. The figure in brackets (where available) is the *approximate* number awarded.

In the lists which follow, it should be assumed that decorations were instituted by Royal Warrant, unless otherwise stated.

24. THE VICTORIA CROSS

Instituted: January 1856.
Ribbon: Crimson. Originally naval crosses used a blue ribbon, but since 1918 the crimson (Army) ribbon has been used for all awards. A miniature cross emblem is worn on the ribbon alone in undress uniform.
Metal: Bronze, originally from Russian guns captured in the Crimea. Modern research, however, reveals that guns captured in other conflicts, e.g. China, have also been used at various periods.
Size: Height 41mm; max. width 36mm.
Description: A cross pattée. (Obverse) a lion statant gardant on the royal crown, with the words FOR VALOUR on a semi-circular scroll. (Reverse) a circular panel on which is engraved the date of the act for which the decoration was awarded. The Cross is suspended by a ring from a seriffed "V" attached to a suspension bar decorated with laurel leaves. The reverse of the suspension bar is engraved with the name, rank and ship, regiment or squadron of the recipient.
Comments: *Introduced as the premier award for gallantry, available for all ranks, to cover all actions since the outbreak of the Crimean War in 1854, it was allegedly created on the suggestion of Prince Albert, the Prince Consort. Of the 1354 awards since 1856, 832 have gone to the Army, 107 to the Navy, 31 to the RAF, ten to the Royal Marines and four to civilians. Second award bars have been awarded three times. The facility for posthumous awards, made retrospective to 1856, began in 1902 and was confirmed in 1907, while the early practice of forfeitures (eight between 1863 and 1908) was discontinued after the First World War.*

VALUE:	Royal Navy	Army	RFC/RAF	Miniature
1856–1914 (522)	£22,000–28,000	£20,000–25,000	—	
1914–18 (633)	£23,000–28,000	£22,000–28,000	£80,000–120,000	
1920–45 (187)	£30,000–40,000	£28,000–40,000	£40,000–60,000	
post-1945 (12)	—	From £50,000	—	£10–20

NB These prices can only be construed as a general guide. Quite a few awards would exceed these price ranges, particularly Commonwealth examples or those appertaining to well known actions.

24A. CONSPICUOUS GALLANTRY CROSS

Instituted: October 1993.
Ribbon: White with blue edges and a red central stripe.
Metal: Silver.
Size: Max. width 36mm
Description: A cross pattée imposed on a wreath of laurel, with the royal crown in a circular panel in the centre. Suspended by a ring from a plain suspension bar.
Comments: *As part of the decision to remove distinctions of rank in awards for bravery this decoration replaced the DSO for gallantry as well as the Conspicuous Gallantry Medal and the Distinguished Conduct Medal. It was first awarded in 1995 to Corporal Wayne Mills of the Duke of Wellington's Regiment for gallantry in action during service with the UN Peacekeeping Forces in Bosnia.*

VALUE: — *Miniature* £15–18

25. NEW ZEALAND CROSS

Instituted: 10 March 1869 (by an Order in Council, Wellington).
Ribbon: 38mm crimson.
Metal: Silver with gold appliqué.
Size: Height 52mm; max. width 38mm.
Description: A silver cross pattée with a six-pointed gold star on each limb. In the centre are the words NEW ZEALAND within a gold laurel wreath. The cross is surmounted by a gold Tudor crown which is attached by a ring and a seriffed "V" to a silver bar ornamented with gold laurel leaves, through which the ribbon passes. The recipient's name and details are engraved on the reverse.
Comments: *The rarest of all gallantry awards, it was conferred for bravery during the second series of Maori Wars (1860-72). Only 23 Crosses were awarded, the last being authorised in 1910. This medal was called into being solely because local volunteer forces were not eligible for the VC. Replicas of the Cross have been authorised by the New Zealand government.*

VALUE: £15,000–20,000   *Miniature* £250–750
          Official copy £350–450   (depending on the quality which is extremely varied)

26. GEORGE CROSS

Instituted: 24 September 1940.

Ribbon: 38mm dark blue. A silver miniature cross emblem is worn on the ribbon alone.

Metal: Silver.

Size: Height 48mm; max. width 45mm.

Description: A plain bordered cross with a circular medallion in the centre depicting the effigy of St George and the Dragon after Benedetto Pistrucci, surrounded by the words FOR GALLANTRY. In the angle of each limb is the Royal cypher GVI. The plain reverse bears in the centre the name of the recipient and date of the award. The Cross hangs by a ring from a bar adorned with laurel leaves.

Comments: *The highest gallantry award for civilians, as well as for members of the armed forces in actions for which purely military honours would not normally be granted. It superseded the Empire Gallantry Medal whose holders were then required to return it and receive the GC in exchange. By Warrant of December 1971 suviving recipients of the Albert and Edward Medals were also invited to exchange their awards for the GC—a move which created a controversy which is still continuing, particularly among those who received the Albert Medal. Perhaps the most famous Cross was that conferred on the island of Malta in recognition of its gallantry during the Second World War. Apart from exchange awards, between 1940 and 1947 the GC was awarded to 102 men and four women; since 1947 a further 40 awards have been made. To date no second award bars have been awarded.*

VALUE:

Service awards 1940 to date	£5000–8000
Civilian awards 1940 to date	£2500–3500
Service exchange pre-1940	£2500–3000
Civilian exchange pre-1940	£2000–3000
Miniature	£10-15

27. DISTINGUISHED SERVICE ORDER

Instituted: 1886.

Ribbon: 29mm crimson with dark blue edges.

Metal: Originally gold; silver-gilt (since 1889).

Size: Height 44mm; max. width 41.5mm.

Description: A cross with curved ends, overlaid with white enamel. (Obverse) a green enamel laurel wreath enclosing an imperial crown; (reverse) the royal monogram within a similar wreath. It is suspended from its ribbon by a swivel ring and a straight laureated bar. Additional awards are denoted by bars ornamented by a crown. Silver rosettes on the ribbon alone are worn in undress uniform. Since its inception, the DSO has been issued unnamed, but since 1938 the year of award has been engraved on the reverse of the lower suspension bar as well as the reverse of the bars for second or subsequent awards.

Comments: *Intended to reward commissioned officers below field rank for distinguished service in time of war, and for which the VC would not be appropriate. Previously the CB had sometimes been awarded to junior officers, although intended mainly for those of field rank. It was also available to officers in both the other armed services. In September 1942 the regulations were relaxed to permit award of the DSO to officers of the Merchant Navy who performed acts of gallantry in the presence of the enemy. As a result of the 1993 Review of gallantry awards and resultant changes to the operational gallantry award system, the DSO is now awarded for "Leadership" only— theoretically to all ranks (it is not awarded posthumously). It has been replaced by the Conspicuous Gallantry Cross as the reward for gallantry.*

VALUE:

	Unnamed single	Attributable group	*Miniature*
Victoria, gold (153)	£1500–2000	£2800–4000	£60
Victoria, silver-gilt (1170)	£700–800	£1250–1750	£40
Edward VII (78)	£900–1100	£2500–3500	£60 (gold)
George V (9900)	£425–475	£650–950	£25 (gilt), £50 (gold)
George VI 1st type 1938–48 (4880)	£550–650	£1500–1800	£40 (gilt)
George VI 2nd type 1948–52 (63)	£800–1200	£2500–3500	£40 (gilt)
Elizabeth II (110)	£800–1200	£2500–4500	£30

28. IMPERIAL SERVICE ORDER

Instituted: August 1902.
Ribbon: 38mm three equal sections of blue, crimson and blue.
Metal: Silver with gold overlay.
Size: Height 61mm; max. width 55mm.
Description: The badge consists of a circular gold plaque bearing the royal cypher and surrounded by the words FOR FAITHFUL SERVICE. This plaque is then superimposed on a seven-pointed silver star surmounted by a crown and ring for suspension. The badge of the ISO awarded to women is similar but has a laurel wreath instead of the star-shaped base.
Comments: *Instituted by King Edward VII as a means of rewarding long and faithful service in the Administration and Clerical grades of the Civil Service at home and overseas. Women were admitted to the order in 1908. The order was awarded after at least 25 years service at home, 20 years and 6 months (India) and 16 years in the tropics, but in exceptional cases awards were made for "eminently meritorious service" irrespective of qualifiying period.*

VALUE:			*Miniature*
Edward VII	Gentleman (489)	£100–120	£25–30
	Lady (3)	£280–350	£50–60
George V	Gentleman (909)	£110–120	£20–25
	Lady (2)	£280–350	£45–50
George VI	Gentleman (608)	£110–120	£15–20
	Lady (8)	£280–350	£30–35
Elizabeth II	Gentleman (2,153)*	£120–150	£10–15
	Lady (114)*	£280–350	£20–25

*1953–94

29. IMPERIAL SERVICE MEDAL

Instituted: August 1902.
Ribbon: Same as above.
Metal: Silver and bronze.
Description: Originally similar to the ISO but with a silver plaque and bronze star or wreath. In 1920 the ISM was transformed into a circular medal of silver with the sovereign's effigy on the obverse and a reverse depicting a naked man resting from his labours, with FOR FAITHFUL SERVICE in the exergue.
Comments: *Instituted at the same time as the ISO but intended for junior grades of the Civil Service.*

VALUE:			*Miniature*
Edward VII (4,525)	Gentleman	£40–50	£15–20
	Lady	£180–200	£30–40
George V Star (Gentlemen) (6,386)		£30–40	£12–15
George V Wreath (Ladies)		£180–200	£30–40
George V Circular type			
Crowned bust (19,519)		£12–15	£10–12
Coinage profile (15,517)		£12–15	£10–12
George VI			
Crowned bust INDIAE:IMP (38,857)		£12–15	£8–10
Crowned bust FID:DEF (15,893)		£12–15	£8–10
Elizabeth II			
Tudor crown BRITT:OMN (7,835)		£12–15	£8–10
Tudor crown DEI:GRATIA (122,262)		£12–15	£8–10
Imperial crown (33,497 up to 1994)		£12–15	£8–10

30. INDIAN ORDER OF MERIT

Instituted: 1837 (by the Honourable East India Company).

Ribbon: Dark blue with crimson edges (military) or crimson with dark blue edges (civil).

Metal: Silver and gold.

Size: Height 41mm; max. width 40mm.

Description: An eight-pointed star with a circular centre surrounded by a laurel wreath and containing crossed sabres and the relevant inscription. The star is suspended by a curvilinear suspension bar. The different classes were denoted by the composition of the star, noted below.

Comments: *The oldest gallantry award of the British Empire, it was founded in 1837 by the Honourable East India Company. Twenty years later it became an official British award when the administration of India passed to the Crown after the Sepoy Mutiny. Originally known simply as the Order of Merit, it was renamed in 1902 following the introduction of the prestigious British order of that name. There were three classes of the order, promotion from one class to the next being the reward for further acts of bravery. A civil division (also in three classes) was introduced in 1902. Ten years later the military division was reduced to two classes, when troops of the Indian Army became eligible for the VC. The civil division became a single class in 1939 and the military in 1945. Both divisions came to an end with the British Raj in 1947.*

VALUE:

Military Division

1837-1912 Reward of Valor

1st class in gold (42)	£1400–1600
2nd class in silver and gold (130)	£400–500
3rd class in silver (2740)	£200–150

1912-1939 Reward of Valor

1st class in silver and gold (26)	£400–500
2nd class in silver (1215)	£200–150

1939-1944 Reward for Gallantry

1st class in silver and gold (2)	Rare
2nd class in silver (332)	£250–350
1945-1947 Reward for Gallantry (44mm diameter)	Rare

Civil Division

1902-1939 For Bravery (35mm diameter)

1st class in gold (0)	—
2nd class in silver and gold (0)	—
3rd class in silver (39)	£600–800

1939-1947 For Bravery (26mm diameter)

Single class (10)	Rare

Miniature	£100–150

NB These prices represent unattributable pieces. Values can climb rapidly when in company with related campaign medals, particularly for the Victorian era.

31. ROYAL RED CROSS

First Class obverse

2nd Class reverse

Instituted: 27 April 1883.
Ribbon: 25mm dark blue edged with crimson, in a bow.
Metal: Gold (later silver-gilt) and silver.
Size: Height 41mm; max. width 35mm.
Description: (Obverse) The *1st class* badge was originally a gold cross
pattée, enamelled red with gold edges, but from 1889 silver-gilt was
substituted for gold. At the centre was a crowned and veiled
portrait, with the words FAITH, HOPE and CHARITY inscribed on
three arms, and the date 1883 on the lower arm. Subsequently the
effigy of the reigning monarch was substituted for the allegorical
profile; (reverse) crowned royal cypher. *2nd Class:* in silver, design
as the 1st class but the inscriptions on the arms appear on the
reverse. Awards from 1938 have the year of issue engraved on the
reverse of the lower arm.
Comments: *This decoration had the distinction of being confined to females
until 1976. It is conferred on members of the nursing services regardless of
rank. A second class award was introduced in November 1915. Bars for the
first class were introduced in 1917. Holders of the second class are
promoted to the first class on second awards. Holders of the first class
decoration are known as Members (RRC) while recipients of the second
class are Associates (ARRC).*

VALUE:	First class (RRC)	Miniature	Second class (ARRC)	Miniature
Victoria, gold	£800–1000		—	£90–100
Victoria, silver-gilt	£400–500		—	£60–70
Edward VII	£500–550		—	£90–100
George V	£100–150	£20–30	£40–50	£10–20
George V, with bar	£300–350		—	
George VI GRI	£150–200	£20–30	£80–100	£10–20
George VI GVIR	£200–300	£20–30	£150–180	£10–20
Elizabeth II	£200–250	£20–30	£100–150	£10–20

32. DISTINGUISHED SERVICE CROSS

Instituted: June 1901.
Ribbon: 36mm three equal parts of dark blue, white and dark blue.
Metal: Silver.
Size: Height 43mm; max. width 43mm.
Description: A plain cross with rounded ends. (Obverse) crowned
royal cypher in the centre, suspended by a ring; (reverse) plain apart
from the hallmark. From 1940 onwards the year of issue was
engraved on the reverse of the lower limb.
Comments: *Known as the Conspicuous Service Cross when instituted, it was
awarded to warrant and subordinate officers of the Royal Navy who were
ineligible for the DSO. In October 1914 it was renamed the Distinguished
Service Cross and thrown open to all naval officers below the rank of
lieutenant-commander. Bars for second awards were authorised in 1916
and in 1931 eligibility for the award was enlarged to include officers of the
Merchant Navy. In 1940 Army and RAF officers serving aboard naval
vessels also became eligible for the award. Since 1945 fewer than 100 DSCs
have been awarded. As a result of the 1993 Review of gallantry awards and
resultant changes to the operational gallantry award system, this award is
now available to both officers and other ranks, the DSM having been
discontinued.*

VALUE:	Unnamed single	Attributable group	Miniature
Edward VII	Rare	£5000–7000	£150–200
George V	£325–375	£450–550	£10–12
George VI GRI	£350–380	£450–600	£10–12
George VI GVIR	Rare	£2000–2500	£30–50
Elizabeth II	Rare	£2000–3000	£10–12

33. MILITARY CROSS

Instituted: 31 December 1914.
Ribbon: 38mm three equal bars of white, deep purple and white.
Metal: Silver.
Size: Height 46mm; max. width 44mm.
Description: An ornamental cross with straight arms terminating in broad finials decorated with imperial crowns. The royal cypher appears at the centre and the cross is suspended from a plain silver suspension bar.
Comments: *There was no gallantry award, lesser than the VC and DSO, for junior Army officers and warrant officers until shortly after the outbreak of the First World War when the MC was instituted. Originally awarded to captains, lieutenants and warrant officers of the Army (including RFC), it was subsequently extended to include equivalent ranks of the RAF when performing acts of bravery on the ground and there was even provision for the Royal Naval Division and the Royal Marines during the First World War. Awards were extended to majors by an amending warrant of 1931. Bars for second and subsequent awards have a crown at the centre. The MC is always issued unnamed, although since about 1938 the reverse of the cross or bar is officially dated with the year of issue. As a result of the 1993 Review of gallantry awards and resultant changes to the operational gallantry award system, this award is now available to both officers and other ranks, the Military Medal having been discontinued.*

VALUE:	Unnamed single	Attributable group	*Miniature*
George V 1914-1920 (37,000)	£200–250	£300–350	£8–10
George V 1914-1920 one bar (3000)	£350–380	£800–1000	
George V 1914-1920 two bars (170)	£400–450	£2500–3500	
George V 1914-1920 three bars (4)	—	—	
George V 1921-1936 (350)	—	£400–800	
George V 1921-1936 one bar (31)	—	£800–1200	
George VI GRI 1939-1945 (11,000)	£250–3500	£600–800	£8–10
George VI GRI one bar (500)	£350–400	£600–800	
George VI GVIR (158)	Rare	£1500–200	£10–15
Elizabeth II	£500–600	£2000–3000	£8–10
Elizabeth II one bar	Rare	Rare	

34. DISTINGUISHED FLYING CROSS

Instituted: June 1918.
Ribbon: 30mm diagonal alternate stripes of white and deep purple.
Metal: Silver.
Size: Height 60mm; max. width 54mm.
Description: (Obverse) a cross flory terminating with a rose, surmounted by another cross made of propeller blades charged in the centre with a roundel within a laurel wreath. The horizontal arms bear wings and the crowned RAF monogram at the centre; (reverse) the royal cypher above the date 1918. The cross is suspended from a bar decorated with a sprig of laurel.
Comments: *Established for officers and warrant officers of the RAF in respect of acts of valour while flying in active operations against the enemy. The DFC is issued unnamed, but Second World War crosses usually have the year of issue engraved on the reverse of the lower limb.As a result of the 1993 Review of gallantry awards and resultant changes to the operational gallantry award system, this award is now available to both officers and other ranks, the Distinguished Flying Medal having been discontinued.*

VALUE:	Unnamed single	Attributable group	*Miniature*
George V 1918-20 (1100)	£450–550	£700–900	£15–20
George V 1918-20 one bar (70)	£600–700	£1000–1500	
George V 1918-20 two bars (3)	—	Rare	
George V 1920-36 (130)	—	£800–1000	
George V 1920-36 one bar (20)	—	£1400–1800	
George V 1920-36 two bars (4)	—	Rare	
George VI GRI 1939-45 (20,000)	£375–450	£500–2500	£15–20
George VI 1939-45 one bar (1550)	£450–520	£650–3500	
George VI 1939-45 two bars (42)	—	£1600–5000	
George VI GVIR 1948-52 (65)	Rare	£800–2000	£15–20
Elizabeth II (260)	Rare	£1200–3000	£12–15

35. AIR FORCE CROSS

Instituted: June 1918.

Ribbon: 30mm originally horizontal but since June 1919 diagonal alternate stripes of white and crimson.

Metal: Silver.

Size: eight 60mm; max. width 54mm.

Description: (Obverse) the cross consists of a thunderbolt, the arms conjoined by wings, base bar terminating in a bomb, surmounted by another cross of aeroplane propellers, the finials inscribed with the royal cypher. A central roundel depicts Hermes mounted on a hawk bestowing a wreath; (reverse) the royal cypher and the date 1918.

Comments: *This decoration, awarded to officers and warrant officers of the RAF, was instituted in June 1918 for gallantry on non-operational misions and for meritorious service on flying duties. Since the 1993 Review of gallantry awards it is now available to all ranks (the Air Force Medal having been discontinued) for non-operational gallantry in the air only (no longer for meritorious service also).*

VALUE:	Unnamed single	Attributable group	Miniature
George V 1918-20 (680)	£500–550	£700–900	£15–20
George V 1918-20 one bar (12)	—	Rare	
George V 1918-20 two bars (3)	—	Rare	
George V 1920-36 (160)	—	£700–800	
George VI GRI (2000)	£500–550	£600–700	£15–20
George VI one bar (26)	£550–600	£1000–1200	
George VI two bars (1)	—	—	
George VI GVIR (980)	£550–650	£800–1000	£15–20
Elizabeth II	£550–650	£800–1000	£10–12

36. ORDER OF BRITISH INDIA

Instituted: 1837 by the Honourable East India Company.

Ribbon: Worn around the neck, the base colour of the ribbon was originally sky blue but this was altered to crimson in 1838, allegedly because the hair oil favoured by Indians of all classes would soon have soiled a light ribbon. From 1939 onwards the first class ribbon had two thin vertical lines of light blue at the centre, while the second class ribbon had a single vertical line. Originally these distinctive ribbons were only worn in undress uniform (without the insignia itself), but from 1945 they replaced the plain crimson ribbons when worn with the decoration.

Metal: Gold.

Size: Height 42mm; max. width 38mm.

Description: The first class badge consists of a gold star with a crown between the upper two points and a blue enamelled centre bearing a lion surrounded by the words ORDER OF BRITISH INDIA enclosed in a laurel wreath. The second class badge is smaller, with dark blue enamel in the centre and with no crown.

Comments: *Intended for long and faithful service by native officers of the Indian Army, it was thrown open in 1939 to officers of the armed forces, frontier guards, military police and officers of the Indian native states. There were two classes, promotion to the first being made from the second. Recipients of both classes were entitled to the letters OBI after their names, but holders of the first class had the rank of Sardar Bahadur, while those of the second were merely Bahadur. A few awards were made by Pakistan to British officers seconded to the Pakistani forces at the time of independence.*

VALUE:		Miniature
1st class, light blue centre and dark blue surround	£400–500	£150–200
1st class, sky blue centre and surround (1939)	£400–500	£150–200
2nd class	£400–450	£150–200

NB The prices quoted are for unattributable awards.

37. ORDER OF BURMA

Instituted 1940.
Ribbon: 38mm dark green with light blue edges.
Metal: Gold.
Size: Height 52mm; max. width 38mm.
Description: The badge consists of a gold-rayed circle with a central roundel charged with a peacock in his pride azure, surmounted by an imperial crown.
Comments: *Instituted by King George VI, three years after Burma became independent of British India. Only 24 awards were made, to Governor's Commissioned Officers for long, faithful and honourable service in the army, frontier force and military police of Burma. By an amendment of 1945 the order could also be awarded for individual acts of heroism or particularly meritorious service. It was abolished in 1947.*

VALUE: Rare

38. KAISAR-I-HIND MEDAL

Instituted: May 1900.
Ribbon: 37mm bluish green.
Metal: Gold, silver or bronze.
Size: Height 61mm; max. width 34mm.
Description: An oval badge surmounted by the imperial crown. (Obverse) the royal cypher set within a wreath; (reverse) FOR PUBLIC SERVICE IN INDIA round the edge and KAISAR-I-HIND (Emperor of India) on a scroll across the centre against a floral background.
Comments: *Queen Victoria founded this medal for award to those, regardless of colour, creed or sex, who had performed public service in India. Originally in two classes George V introduced a 3rd Class in bronze. The medals were originally large and hollow but were changed to smaller in diameter and solid during the reign of George V.*

Victoria obv.

VALUE:	1st class (gold)	*Miniature*	2nd class (silver)	*Miniature*	3rd class (bronze)
Victoria	£600–700	£120–150	£200–250	£80–100	–
Edward VII	£600–650	£120–150	£180–220	£80–100	–
George V 1st	£500–600	£50–100	£150–180	£25–50	–
George V 2nd	£450–500	£50–100	£100–120	£25–50	£80–100
George VI	£500–600	£120–150	£100–120	£50–80	£80–100

Victoria rev.   *George VI*   *obv.*   *rev.*

39. ALBERT MEDAL

Instituted: 7 March 1866.

Ribbons: Originally 16mm blue with two white stripes (gold 1st class), changed on introduction of the 2nd class to 35mm blue with four white stripes. The 2nd class remained 16mm blue with two white stripes until 1904 when it was changed to 35mm blue with two white stripes. For the gold 1st class medal the ribbon was 35mm crimson with four white stripes, that for the 2nd class originally 16mm crimson with two white stripes, changing in 1904 to a 35mm ribbon.

Metal: Gold (early issues gold and bronze); bronze.

Size: Height 57mm; max. width 30mm.

Description: The badge consists of an oval enclosing the entwined initials V and A. The sea medals have, in addition, an anchor. The oval is enclosed by a bronze garter with the words FOR GALLANTRY IN SAVING LIFE, with AT SEA or ON LAND as appropriate, and enamelled in blue or crimson respectively. The whole is surmounted by a crown pierced by a ring for suspension. The first class medal was originally worked in gold and bronze and later in gold alone, the second class in bronze alone.

Comments: *Named in memory of the Prince Consort who died in 1861, this series of medals was instituted for gallantry in saving life at sea. An amendment of 1867 created two classes of medal and ten years later awards were extended to gallantry in saving life on land. In 1917 the title of the awards was altered, the first class becoming the Albert Medal in Gold and the second class merely the Albert Medal. It was last awarded to a living recipient in April 1943, the last posthumous award being in May 1945. The last bronze medal awarded to a living recipient was in January 1949, and posthumous in August 1970. In 1949 the Medal in Gold was abolished and replaced by the George Cross and henceforward the Albert Medal (second class) was only awarded posthumously. In 1971 the award of the medal ceased and holders were invited to exchange their medals for the George Cross. Of the 64 eligible to exchange, 49 did so.*

VALUE:

	Civilian	Service	Miniature
Gold Sea (25)	£3500–4500	£4500–5500	£40–60*
Bronze Sea (216)	£2200–2500	£2500–3000	£30–50
Gold Land (45)	£2500–3000	£3000–4000	£40–60*
Bronze Land (282)	£1800–2000	£2000–2500	£30–50

*assumed gilt

40. UNION OF SOUTH AFRICA QUEEN'S MEDAL FOR BRAVERY (WOLTEMADE MEDAL)

Instituted: 1939 by the Government of the Union of South Africa.

Ribbon: Royal blue with narrow orange edges.

Metal: Gold or silver.

Size: 37mm.

Description: (Obverse) an effigy of the reigning sovereign; (reverse) a celebrated act of heroism by Wolraad Woltemade who rescued sailors from the wreck of the East Indiaman *De Jong Thomas* which ran aground in Table Bay on 17 June 1773. Seven times Woltemade rode into the raging surf to save fourteen seamen from drowning, but on the eighth attempt both rider and horse perished.

Comments: *This medal was awarded to citizens of the Union of South Africa and dependent territories who endangered their lives in saving the lives of others. It was awarded very sparingly, in gold or silver.*

VALUE:

George VI Gold (1)	—
George VI Silver (34)	Rare
Elizabeth II Silver (1)	—

41. DISTINGUISHED CONDUCT MEDAL

1st type obv.

Instituted: 1854.
Ribbon: 32mm crimson with a dark blue central stripe.
Metal: Silver.
Size: 36mm.
Description: (Obverse) originally a trophy of arms but, since 1902, the effigy of the reigning sovereign; (reverse) a four-line inscription across the field FOR DISTINGUISHED CONDUCT IN THE FIELD.
Comments: *The need for a gallantry medal for other ranks was first recognised during the Crimean War, although previously the Meritorious Service Medal (qv) had very occasionally been awarded for gallantry in the field. The medals have always been issued named, and carry the number, rank and name of the recipient on the rim, together with the date of the act of gallantry from 1881 until about 1901. Bars are given for subsequent awards and these too were dated from the first issued in 1881 until 1916 when the more usual laurelled bars were adopted. Since 1916 it has ranked as a superior decoration to the Military Medal. As a result of the 1993 Review of gallantry awards and resultant changes to the operational gallantry award system, the decoration has been replaced by the Conspicuous Gallantry Cross.*

VALUE:

Crimea (800)	£600–4000
Indian Mutiny (17)	£5500–7000
India general service 1854-95	£1500–3000
Abyssinia 1867-8 (7)	£2000–3000
Ashantee 1873-4 (33)	£1800–2000
Zulu War 1877-9 (16)	£3000–7000
Afghanistan 1878-80 (61)	£1800–2500
First Boer War 1880-1 (20)	£2500–5000
Egypt & Sudan 1882-9 (134)	£2500–3000
India 1895-1901	£1500–2200
Sudan 1896-7	£1500–5500
Second Boer War 1899-1902 (2090)	£450–1200
Boxer Rebellion 1900	£3000–7000
Edward VII	Many rarities
George V 1st type (25,000)	£280–1000
George V 2nd type 1930-7 (14)	£800–2000
George VI, IND IMP 1937-47	£1100–2000
George VI, 2nd type 1948-52 (25)	£1500–3000
Elizabeth II, BR: OMN:	£2500–4000
Elizabeth II, DEI GRATIA	£2500–6000
Miniature	
Victoria	£25–30
Edward VII	£25–30
George V	£10–15
George VI	£10–15
Elizabeth II	£10–15

42. DISTINGUISHED CONDUCT MEDAL (DOMINION & COLONIAL)

Instituted: 31 May 1895.
Ribbon: 32mm crimson with a dark blue central stripe.
Metal: Silver.
Size: 36mm.
Description: As above, but the reverse bears the name of the issuing country or colony round the top.
Comments: *A separate DCM for warrant officers, NCOs and men of the colonial forces. Medals were struck for the Cape of Good Hope, New Zealand, New South Wales, Queensland, Tasmania, Natal and Canada, but only the last two actually issued them and the others are known only as specimens.*

VALUE:

Victoria Canada (1)	Rare
Victoria Natal (1)	Rare
Edward VII Natal (9)	Rare

43. DISTINGUISHED CONDUCT MEDAL (KAR & WAFF)

Instituted: early 1900s.
Ribbon: As above.
Metal: Silver.
Size: 3mm.
Description: As no. 40, with either King's African Rifles or West Africa Frontier Force around the top of the reverse.
Comments: *Separate awards for gallantry were instituted in respect of the King's African Rifles (East Africa) and the West Africa Frontier Force (Nigeria, Sierra Leone, Gambia and the Gold Coast). These were issued until 1942 when they were superseded by the British DCM.*

VALUE:	Attributable groups
Edward VII KAR (2)	—
Edward VII WAFF (55)	Rare
George V KAR (190)	£300–450
George V WAFF (165)	£400–500

44. CONSPICUOUS GALLANTRY MEDAL

Instituted: 1855.
Ribbon: 31mm white (RN) or sky blue (RAF) with dark blue edges.
Metal: Silver.
Size: 36mm.
Description: (Obverse) the effigy of the reigning monarch; (reverse) the words FOR CONSPICUOUS GALLANTRY in three lines within a crowned laurel wreath.
Comments: *Conceived as the naval counterpart to the DCM, it was instituted for award to petty officers and seamen of the Royal Navy and to NCOs and other ranks of the Royal Marines. Originally awarded only for gallantry during the Crimean War, it was revived in 1874 to recognise heroism during the Ashantee War and has since been awarded, albeit sparingly, for other wars and campaigns. The Crimean issue utilised the dies of the Meritorious Service Medal which had the date 1848 below the truncation of the Queen's neck on the obverse. The raised relief inscription MERITORIOUS SERVICE on the reverse was erased and the words CONSPICUOUS GALLANTRY engraved in their place. When the decoration was revived in 1874 a new obverse was designed without a date while a new die, with the entire inscription in raised relief, was employed for the reverse. In 1943 the CGM was extended to NCOs and other ranks of the RAF. Both naval and RAF medals are identical, but the naval medal has a white ribbon with dark blue edges, whereas the RAF award has a pale blue ribbon with dark blue edges. It ranks as one of the rarest decorations: the only two medals issued in the present reign were awarded to an airman in the RAAF for gallantry in Vietnam (1968) and to a seaman during the South Atlantic War (1982). As a result of the 1993 Review and resultant changes to the operational gallantry award system, the decoration has been replaced by the Conspicuous Gallantry Cross.*

VALUE:	Attributable groups
Victoria 1st type (11)	£2500–3000
Victoria 2nd type (51)	£2000–5000
Edward VII (2)	£8000–9000
George V (110)	£1800–2500
George VI Navy (72)	£3000–10,000
George VI RAF (111)	£2500–4500
Elizabeth II Navy (1)	—
Elizabeth II RAF (1)	—
Miniature	
Victoria	£50–80
Edward VII	£50–80
George V	£20–30
George VI	£15–20
Elizabeth II	£15–20

45. GEORGE MEDAL

Instituted: 1940.

Ribbon: 32mm crimson with five narrow blue stripes.

Metal: Silver.

Size: 36mm.

Description: (Obverse) the effigy of the reigning monarch; (reverse) St George and the Dragon, modelled by George Kruger Gray, after the bookplate by Stephen Gooden for the Royal Library, Windsor.

Comments: *Awarded for acts of bravery where the services were not so outstanding as to merit the George Cross. Though primarily a civilian award, it has also been given to service personnel for heroism not in the face of the enemy. Of the approximately 2000 medals awarded, 1030 have been to civilians.*

VALUE:	Civilian	Service
George VI 1st type 1940-47	£600–750	£700–900
George VI 2nd type 1948-52	£600–750	£800–900
Elizabeth II 1st type 1953	£600–800	£1000–1500
Elizabeth II 2nd type	£800–900	£1200–1600
Miniature		
George VI	£10–15	
Elizabeth II	£10–15	

46. KING'S POLICE MEDAL

Instituted: 7 July 1909.

Ribbons: 36mm Originally deep blue with silver edges, but in 1916 a central silver stripe was added. Gallantry awards have thin crimson stripes superimposed on the silver stripes.

Metal: Silver.

Size: 36mm.

Description: (Obverse) the monarch's effigy; (reverse) a standing figure with sword and shield inscribed TO GUARD MY PEOPLE. The first issue had a laurel spray in the exergue, but in 1933 two separate reverses were introduced and the words FOR GALLANTRY or FOR DISTINGUISHED SERVICE were placed in the exergue.

Comments: *Instituted to reward "courage and devotion to duty" in the police and fire services of the UK and overseas dominions. Recognising the bravery of the firemen during the Blitz, the medal was retitled the King's Police and Fire Services Medal in 1940, but no change was made in the design of the medal itself. From 1950, the gallantry medals were only awarded posthumously and all medals were discontinued in 1954 when seperate awards were established for the two services (see numbers 47 and 48).*

VALUE:		Miniature
Edward VII (100)	£600–800	£25–30
George V 1st type coinage head (1900)	£150–300	£20–25
George V 2nd type crowned head	£200–300	£20–25
George V for Gallantry (350)	£350–450	£15–20
George V for Distinguished Service	£180–220	£15–20
George VI 1st type for Gallantry (440)	£450–550	£10–15
George VI 2nd type for Gallantry (50)	£500–700	£10–15
George VI 1st type for Distinguished Service	£180–220	£10–15
George VI 2nd type for Distinguished Service	£180–220	£10–15

47. QUEEN'S POLICE MEDAL

Instituted: 19 May 1954.
Ribbon: Three silver stripes and two broad dark blue stripes.
Metal: Silver.
Size: 36mm.
Description: (Obverse) effigy of the reigning sovereign; (reverse) a standing figure (as on the KPM) but the laurel spray has been restored to the exergue and the words FOR GALLANTRY or FOR DISTINGUISHED POLICE SERVICE are inscribed round the circumference.

VALUE:

Elizabeth II for Gallantry (23)	£500–600
Elizabeth II for Distinguished Service (1100)	£250–350
Miniature	£10–15

48. QUEEN'S FIRE SERVICE MEDAL

Instituted: 19 May 1954.
Ribbon: Red with three yellow stripes (distiguished service) or similar, with thin dark blue stripes bisecting the yellow stripes (gallantry).
Metal: Silver.
Size: 36mm
Description: (Obverse) effigy of the reigning monarch; (reverse) standing figure with sword and shield (as on KPM), laurel spray in the exergue, and inscription round the circumference FOR GALLANTRY or FOR DISTINGUISHED FIRE SERVICE.

VALUE:

Elizabeth II for Gallantry	Rare
Elizabeth II for Distinguished Service	£350–450
Miniature	£10–12

49. KING'S POLICE MEDAL (SOUTH AFRICA)

Instituted: 24 September 1937.
Ribbon: Silver with two broad dark blue stripes.
Metal: Silver.
Size: 36mm.
Description: (Obverse) effigy of George VI and title including the words ET IMPERATOR (1937-49), George VI minus IMPERATOR (1950-52) and Queen Elizabeth II (1953-60). (Reverse) as UK but inscribed in English and Afrikaans. Inscribed FOR BRAVERY VIR DAPPERHEID or FOR DISTINGUISHED SERVICE VIR VOORTREFLIKE DIENS.
Comments: *Awarded to members of the South Africa Police for courage and devotion to duty. In 1938 it was extended to cover the constabulary of South West Africa.*

VALUE:

George VI 1st type 1937-49	
for Gallantry (10)	Rare
for Distinguished Service (13)	Rare
George VI 2nd type 1950-52	
for Distinguished Service (13)	Rare
Elizabeth II 1953-60	
for Gallantry (20)	Rare
Elizabeth II 1953-69	
for Distinguished Service (3)	Rare

50. EDWARD MEDAL (MINES)

Instituted: July 1907.
Ribbon: Dark blue edged with yellow.
Metal: Silver or bronze.
Size: 33mm.
Description: (Obverse) the monarch's effigy; (reverse) a miner rescuing a stricken comrade, with the caption FOR COURAGE across the top (designed by W. Reynolds-Stephens).
Comments: *Awarded for life-saving in mines and quarries, in two grades: first class (silver) and second class (bronze). Interestingly, the cost of these medals was borne not by the State but from a fund created by a group of philanthropic individuals led by A. Hewlett, a leading mine-owner. Medals were engraved with the names of the recipient from the outset, but since the 1930s the date and sometimes the place of the action have also been inscribed. The medal is now only granted posthumously, living recipients having been invited to exchange their medals for the GC, under Royal Warrant of 1971. Two silver and seven bronze medallists elected not to do so. This is one of the rarest gallantry awards, only 77 silver and 318 bronze medals having been granted since its inception. The last awards to living recipients were made in 1949.*

VALUE:	Silver	Bronze
Edward VII	£600–800	£500–600
George V 1st type	£600–800	£500–600
George V 2nd type	£1200–1500	£600–800
George VI 1st type	£1500–1800	£1200–1400
George VI 2nd type	—	Rare
Elizabeth II	Not issued	From £1800
Miniature		
Edward VII	£60–80	
George V	£50–60	
George VI	£70–80	

51. EDWARD MEDAL (INDUSTRY)

1st type rev.

2nd type rev.

Instituted: December 1909.
Ribbon: As above.
Metal: Silver or bronze.
Size: 33mm.
Description: (Obverse) effigy of the reigning monarch; (reverse) originally a worker helping an injured workmate with a factory in the background and the words FOR COURAGE inscribed diagonally across the top. A second reverse, depicting a standing female figure with a laurel branch and a factory skyline in the background, was introduced in 1912.
Comments: *Awarded for acts of bravery in factory accidents and disasters. Like the Mines medal it was also available in two classes, but no first class medals have been awarded since 1948. This medal is now only awarded posthumously, living recipients having been invited to exchange their medals for the GC, under Royal Warrant of 1971. A total of 25 silver and 163 bronze awards have been issued.*

VALUE:	Silver	Bronze
Edward VII	Rare	Rare
George V 1st Obv, 1st Rev	—	£1500–1800
George V 1st Obv, 2nd Rev	£1400–1500	£500–600
George V 2nd Obv, 2nd Rev	Rare	£1200–1400
George VI 1st type	—	£1000–1200
George VI 2nd type	Not issued	Rare
Elizabeth II 1st type	Not issued	Rare
Elizabeth II 2nd type	Not issued	Rare
Miniature		
George V	£60–80	
George VI (modern)	£15–20	

52. INDIAN DISTINGUISHED SERVICE MEDAL

Instituted: 25 June 1907.
Ribbon: Crimson with broad dark blue edges.
Metal: Silver.
Size: 36mm.
Description: (Obverse) the sovereign's effigy; (reverse) the words FOR DISTINGUISHED SERVICE in a laurel wreath.
Comments: *Awarded for distinguished service in the field by Indian commissioned and non-commissioned officers and men of the Indian Army, the reserve forces, border militia and levies, military police and troops employed by the Indian Government. An amendment of 1917 extended the award to Indian non-combatants engaged on field service, bars for subsequent awards being authorised at the same time. It was formally extended to the Royal Indian Marine in 1929 and members of the Indian Air Force in 1940. Finally it was extended in 1944 to include non-European personnel of the Hong Kong and Singapore Royal Artillery although it became obsolete in 1947.*

VALUE:

		Miniature
Edward VII (140)	£450–500	£40–50
George V KAISAR-I-HIND (3800)	£100–200	£30–40
George V 2nd type (140)	£300–400	£30–40
George VI (1190)	£150–250	

53. BURMA GALLANTRY MEDAL

Instituted: 10 May 1940.
Ribbon: Jungle green with a broad crimson stripe in the centre.
Metal: Silver.
Size: 36mm.
Description: (Obverse) the effigy of King George VI; (reverse) the words BURMA at the top and FOR GALLANTRY in a laurel wreath.
Comments: *As Burma ceased to be part of the Indian Empire in April 1937 a separate gallantry award was required for its armed services. The Burma Gallantry Medal was awarded by the Governor to officers and men of the Burma Army, frontier forces, military police, Burma RNVR and Burma AAF, although by an amendment of 1945 subsequent awards were restricted to NCOs and men. The medal became obsolete in 1947 when Burma became an independent republic and left the Commonwealth. Just over 200 medals and three bars were awarded, mainly for heroism in operations behind the Japanese lines.*

VALUE:	Miniature
£2000–3000	£30–35

54. DISTINGUISHED SERVICE MEDAL

Instituted: 14 October 1914.

Ribbon: Dark blue with two white stripes towards the centre.

Metal: Silver.

Size: 36mm.

Description: (Obverse) the sovereign's effigy; (reverse) a crowned wreath inscribed FOR DISTINGUISHED SERVICE.

Comments: *Awarded to petty officers and ratings of the Royal Navy, NCOs and other ranks of the Royal Marines and all other persons holding corresponding ranks or positions in the naval forces, for acts of bravery in face of the enemy not sufficiently meritorious to make them eligible for the CGM. It was later extended to cover the Merchant Navy and Army, the WRNS and RAF personnel serving aboard ships in the Second World War. Of particular interest and desirability are medals awarded for outstanding actions, e.g. Jutland, Q-Ships, the Murmansk convoys, the Yangtze incident and the Falklands War. First World War bars for subsequent awards are dated on the reverse, but Second World War bars are undated. As a result of the 1993 Review of gallantry awards and resultant changes to the operational gallantry award system, this award has been replaced by the DSC which is now available* both *to officers and other ranks.*

VALUE:

		Miniature
George V uncrowned head 1914-30 (4100)	£150–1000	£15–18
George VI IND IMP 1938-49 (7100)	£200–500	£10–15
George VI 2nd type 1949-53	£800–2000	£10–15
Elizabeth II BR OMN 1953-7	£2000–3000	£8–10
Elizabeth II 2nd type	£2000–4000	£8–10

55. MILITARY MEDAL

Instituted: 25 March 1916.

Ribbon: Broad dark blue edges flanking a central section of three narrow white and two narrow crimson stripes.

Metal: Silver.

Size: 36mm.

Description: (Obverse) the sovereign's effigy—six types to date; (reverse) the crowned royal cypher above the inscription FOR BRAVERY IN THE FIELD, enclosed in a wreath.

Comments: *Awarded to NCOs and men of the Army (including RFC and RND) for individual or associated acts of bravery not of sufficient heroism as to merit the DCM. In June 1916 it was extended to women, two of the earliest awards being to civilian ladies for their conduct during the Easter Rising in Dublin that year. Some 115,600 medals were awarded during the First World War alone, together with 5796 first bars, 180 second bars and 1 third bar. Over 15,000 medals were conferred during the Second World War, with 177 first bars and 1 second bar. About 300 medals and 4 first bars were awarded for bravery in minor campaigns between the two world wars, while some 932 medals and 8 first bars have been conferred since 1947. As a result of the 1993 Review of gallantry awards and resultant changes to the operational gallantry award system, this award has been replaced by the MC which is now available* both *to officers and other ranks.*

VALUE:

		Miniature
George V uncrowned head 1916-30	£90–180*	£10–12
named to a woman	£800–1500	
George V crowned head 1930-38	£2500–4000	£15–20
George VI IND IMP 1938-48	£350–1000	£8–10
George VI 2nd type 1948-53	£800–2000	£8–10
Elizabeth II BR: OMN 1953-8	£1800–3000	£8–10
Elizabeth II 2nd type	£1800–4000	£8–10

Groups to RFC and RND will be considerably higher.

56. DISTINGUISHED FLYING MEDAL

Instituted: 1918.

Ribbon: Originally purple and white horizontal stripes but since 1919 thirteen narrow diagonal stripes alternationg white and purple.

Metal: Silver.

Size: 42mm tall; 34mm wide.

Description: An oval medal, (obverse) the sovereign's effigy; (reverse) Athena Nike seated on an aeroplane, with a hawk rising from her hand. Originally undated, but the date 1918 was added to the reverse with the advent of the George VI obverse. The medal is suspended by a pair of wings from a straight bar.

Comments: *Introduced at the same time as the DFC, it was awarded to NCOs and men of the RAF for courage or devotion to duty while flying on active operations against the enemy. During the Second World War it was extended to the equivalent ranks of the Army and Fleet Air Arm personnel engaged in similar operations. First World War medals have the names of recipients impressed in large seriffed lettering, whereas Second World War medals are rather coarsely engraved. Approximately 150 medals have been awarded since 1945. As a result of the 1993 Review of gallantry awards and resultant changes to the operational gallantry award system, this award has been replaced by the DFC which is now available both to officers and other ranks.*

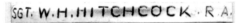

Example of WWI impressed naming

WWII engraved naming

VALUE:		Miniature
George V uncrowned head 1918-30 (105)	£700–2000	£15–18
George V crowned head 1930-38	£2000–3500	£25–30
George VI IND IMP 1938-49 (6500)	£450–2000	£8–10
George VI 2nd type 1949-53	£1000–2000	£8–10
Elizabeth II	£1200–2000	£8–10

57. AIR FORCE MEDAL

Instituted: 1918.

Ribbon: Originally horizontal narrow stripes of white and crimson but since July 1919 diagonal narrow stripes of the same colours.

Metal: Silver.

Size: 42mm tall; 32mm wide.

Description: An oval medal with a laurel border. (Obverse) the sovereign's effigy; (reverse) Hermes mounted on a hawk bestowing a laurel wreath. The medal is suspended by a pair of wings from a straight bar, like the DFM.

Comments: *Instituted at the same time as the AFC, it was awarded to NCOs and men of the RAF for courage or devotion to duty while flying, but not on active operations against the enemy. About 100 medals and 2 first bars were awarded during the First World War, 106 medals and 3 bars between the wars and 259 medals during the Second World War. After the 1993 Review of gallantry awards the AFM was discontinued; the AFC is now available both to officers and other ranks.*

VALUE:		Miniature
George V uncrowned head 1918-30	£750–1000	£12–15
George V crowned head 1930-38	£2000–3000	£20–25
George VI IND IMP 1939-49	£500–800	£8–10
George VI 2nd type 1949-53	£500–800	£8–10
Elizabeth II	£500–800	£8–10

58. CONSTABULARY MEDAL (IRELAND)

1st type obv.

Instituted: 1842.
Ribbon: Originally light blue, but changed to green in 1872.
Metal: Silver.
Size: 36mm.
Description: (Obverse) a crowned harp within a wreath of oak leaves and shamrocks, with REWARD OF MERIT round the top and IRISH CONSTABULARY round the foot. In the first version the front of the harp took the form of a female figure but later variants had a plain harp and the shape of the crown and details of the wreath were also altered. These changes theoretically came in 1867 when the Constabulary acquired the epithet Royal, which was then added to the inscription round the top, although some medals issued as late as 1921 had the pre-1867 title. (Reverse) a wreath of laurel and shamrock, within which are engraved the recipient's name, rank, number, date and sometimes the location of the action.
Comments: *Originally awarded for gallantry and meritorious service by members of the Irish Constabulary. From 1872, however, it was awarded only for gallantry. It was first conferred in 1848 and became obsolete in 1922 when the Irish Free State was established. Bars for second awards were authorised in 1920. About 315 medals and 7 bars were awarded (or, in some cases, second medals—the records are inconclusive), mostly for actions in connection with the Easter Rising of 1916 (23) or the subsequent Anglo-Irish War of 1920 (180) and 1921 (55).*

2nd type obv.

VALUE:

First type	Rare
Second type	£800–1200

59. INDIAN POLICE MEDAL

1st type

Instituted: 23 February 1932.
Ribbon: Crimson flanked by bands of dark blue and silver grey. From 1942 onwards an additional silver stripe appeared in the centre of the ribbon intended for the gallantry medal.
Metal: Bronze.
Size: 36mm.
Description: (Obverse) the King Emperor; (reverse) a crowned wreath inscribed INDIAN POLICE, with the words FOR DISTINGUISHED CONDUCT across the centre. In December 1944 the reverse was re-designed in two types, with the words FOR GALLANTRY or FOR MERITORIOUS SERVICE in place of the previous legend.
Comments: *Intended for members of the Indian police forces and fire brigades as a reward for gallantry or meritorious service. The medal became obsolete in 1950 when India became a republic.*

VALUE:

		Miniature
George V	£200–300	£20–25
George VI Distinguished Conduct	£250–300	£20–25
George VI for Gallantry	£300–400	£20–25
George VI for Meritorious Service	£200–300	£20–25

2nd type (after 1944)

60. BURMA POLICE MEDAL

Instituted: 14 December 1937.
Ribbon: A wide central blue stripe flanked by broad black stripes and white edges.
Metal: Bronze.
Size: 36mm.
Description: (Obverse) the effigy of George VI; (reverse) similar to the Indian medal (first type)and inscribed FOR DISTINGUISHED CONDUCT, irrespective of whether awarded for gallantry or distinguished service.
Comments: *Introduced following the separation of Burma from India, it was abolished in 1948. All ranks of the police, frontier force and fire brigades, both European and Burmese, were eligible.*

VALUE:		MIniature
For Gallantry (53)	£700–800	£20–25
For Meritorious Service (80)	£400–500	£10–15

61. COLONIAL POLICE MEDAL

Instituted: 10 May 1938.
Ribbon: Blue with green edges and a thin silver stripe separating the colours, but the gallantry award had an additional thin red line through the centre of each green edge stripe.
Metal: Silver.
Size: 36mm.
Description: (Obverse) the sovereign's effigy; (reverse) a policeman's truncheon superimposed on a laurel wreath. The left side of the circumference is inscribed COLONIAL POLICE FORCES and the right either FOR GALLANTRY or FOR MERITORIOUS SERVICE.
Comments: *Intended to reward all ranks of the police throughout the Empire for acts of conspicuous bravery or for meritorious service. The number to be issued was limited to 150 in any one year. Only 450 were awarded for gallantry, whilst almost 3000 were issued for meritorious service.*

VALUE:		Miniature
George VI GRI for Gallantry	£500–1200	£10–12
George VI GRI for Meritorious Service	£200–350	£12–15
George VI GVIR for Gallantry	£500–1000	£12–15
George VI GVIR for Meritorious Service	£200–350	£12–15
Elizabeth II 1st type for Gallantry	£500–1000	£15–20
Elizabeth II 1st type for Meritorious Service	£200–300	£15–20
Elizabeth II 2nd type for Gallantry	£500–1000	£15–20
Elizabeth II 2nd type for Meritorious Service	£200–300	£15–20

62. COLONIAL FIRE BRIGADE MEDAL

Instituted: 10 May 1938.
Ribbon: As above.
Metal: Silver.
Size: 36mm.
Description: (Obverse) the effigy of the reigning sovereign; (reverse) a fireman's helmet and axe, with the inscription COLONIAL FIRE BRIGADES FOR GALLANTRY or FOR MERITORIOUS SERVICE.
Comments: *As No. 59 this medal was intended to reward all ranks of the Colonial fire brigades but very few were awarded for gallantry.*

VALUE:		Miniature
George VI GRI for Gallantry	Rare	£12–15
George VI GRI for Meritorious Service	Rare	£12–15
George VI GVIR for Gallantry	Rare	£12–15
George VI GVIR for Meritorious Service	£200–300	£12–15
Elizabeth II 1st type for Gallantry	From £750	£10–12
Elizabeth II 1st type for Meritorious Service	£200–300	£10–12
Elizabeth II 2nd type for Gallantry	£400–600	£10–12
Elizabeth II 2nd type for Meritorious Service	£150–250	£10–12

63. QUEEN'S GALLANTRY MEDAL

Instituted: 20 June 1974.
Ribbon: Dark blue with a central pearl-grey stripe bisected by a narrow rose-pink stripe.
Metal: Silver.
Size: 36mm.
Description: (Obverse) the Queen's effigy; (reverse) an imperial crown above THE QUEEN'S GALLANTRY MEDAL flanked by laurel sprigs.
Comments: *Awarded for exemplary acts of bravery. Although intended primarily for civilians, it is also awarded to members of the armed forces for actions which would not be deemed suitable for a military decoration. With the introduction of the QGM the gallantry awards of the MBE and BEM came to an end. A bar is added for a second award. Fewer than 400 medals have been awarded.*

VALUE:

		Miniature
Service award	£1400–2000	£10
Civilian award	£600–800	

64. ALLIED SUBJECTS' MEDAL

Instituted: November 1920.
Ribbon: Bright red with a light blue centre, flanked by narrow stripes of yellow, black and white (thus incorporating the Belgian and French national colours).
Metal: Silver or bronze.
Size: 36mm.
Description: (Obverse) the effigy of King George V; (reverse) designed by Edmund Dulac, the female allegory of Humanity offering a cup to a British soldier resting on the ground, with ruined buildings in the background.
Comment: *Shortly after the cessation of the First World War it was proposed that services rendered to the Allied cause, specifically by those who had helped British prisoners of war to escape, should be rewarded by a medal. The decision to go ahead was delayed on account of disagreement between the War Office and the Foreign Office, but eventually the first awards were announced in November 1920, with supplementary lists in 1921 and 1922. Medals were issued unnamed and almost half of the total issue, namely 56 silver and 247 bronze medals, were issued to women.*

VALUE:

		Miniature
Silver (134)	£500–700	£35–40
Bronze (574)	£300–400	£40–45

NB These prices are for unattributable awards.

65. KING'S MEDAL FOR COURAGE IN THE CAUSE OF FREEDOM

Instituted: 23 August 1945
Ribbon: White with two narrow dark blue stripes in the centre and broad red stripes at the edges.
Metal: Silver.
Size: 36mm.
Description: (Obverse) the crowned profile of King George VI; (reverse) inscribed, within a chain link, THE KING'S MEDAL FOR COURAGE IN THE CAUSE OF FREEDOM.
Comments: *Introduced to acknowledge acts of courage by foreign civilians or members of the armed services "in the furtherance of the British Commonwealth in the Allied cause" during the Second World War. Like its First World War counterpart, it was intended mainly to reward those who had assisted British escapees in enemy-occupied territories. About 3200 medals were issued, commencing in 1947.*

VALUE: £250–300 (unattributable) *Miniature* £10–20

66. KING'S MEDAL FOR SERVICE IN THE CAUSE OF FREEDOM

Instituted: 23 August 1945.
Ribbon: White with a central red bar flanked by dark blue stripes.
Metal: Silver.
Size: 36mm.
Description: (Obverse) effigy of King George VI; (reverse) a medieval warrior in armour carrying a broken lance, receiving nourishment from a female.
Comments: *Introduced at the same time as the foregoing, it was intended for foreign civilians who had helped the Allied cause in other less dangerous ways, such as fund-raising and organising ambulance services. 2490 medals were issued.*

VALUE: £200–250 (unattributable)   *Miniature* £10–15

67. SEA GALLANTRY MEDAL

Instituted: 1855, under the Merchant Shipping Acts of 1854 and 1894.
Ribbon: Bright red with narrow white stripes towards the edges.
Metal: Silver or bronze.
Size: 58mm or 33mm.
Description: (Obverse) Profile of Queen Victoria; (reverse) a family on a storm-tossed shore reviving a drowning sailor. Both obverse and reverse were sculpted by Bernard Wyon.
Comments: *Exceptionally, this group of medals was authorised not by Royal Warrant but by Parliamentary legislation, under the terms of the Merchant Shipping Acts of 1854 and 1894. The 1854 Act made provision for monetary rewards for life saving at sea, but in 1855 this was transmuted into medals, in gold, silver or bronze, in two categories, for gallantry (where the rescuer placed his own life at risk) and for humanity (where the risks were minimal). The gold medal, if ever awarded, must have been of the greatest rarity. These medals, issued by the Board of Trade, were 58mm in diameter and not intended for wearing. The only difference between the medals lay in the wording of the inscription round the circumference of the obverse. Later medals were issued by the Ministry of Transport. In 1903 Edward VII ordered that the medal be reduced to 1.27 inches (33mm) in diameter and fitted with a suspension bar and ribbon for wearing. Both large and small medals were always issued with the recipient's name round the rim.*

VALUE:

	Silver	Bronze	*Miniature*
Victoria Gallantry	£400–500	£250–350	£100–150
Victoria Humanity	Rare	Rare	
Edward VII Gallantry (large)	£1400–1800	£1200–1400	
Edward VII Gallantry (small)	£450–500	£400–450	£100–150
Edward VII Humanity (small)	£450–500	£400–450	
George V	£350–450	£300–400	£50–75
George VI 1st type	Rare	Rare	
George VI 2nd type	—	Rare	
Elizabeth II	Rare	Rare	

68. SEA GALLANTRY MEDAL (FOREIGN SERVICES)

Type 4 rev.

Instituted: 1841.
Ribbon: Plain crimson till 1922; thereafter the same ribbon as the SGM above.
Metal: Gold, silver or bronze.
Size: 36mm or 33mm.
Description: The large medal had Victoria's effigy (young head) on the obverse, but there were five reverse types showing a crowned wreath with PRESENTED BY (or FROM) THE BRITISH GOVERNMENT inside the wreath. Outside the wreath were the following variants:
1. Individually struck inscriptions (1841-49 but sometimes later).
2. FOR SAVING THE LIFE OF A BRITISH SUBJECT (1849-54)
3. FOR ASSISTING A BRITISH VESSEL IN DISTRESS (1849-54)
4. FOR SAVING THE LIVES OF BRITISH SUBJECTS (1850-54)
There are also unissued specimens or patterns with a Latin inscription within the wreath VICTORIA REGINA CUDI JUSSIT MDCCCXLI.
The small medal, intended for wear, has five obverse types combined with four reverse types: as 2 above (1854-1906), as 3 above (1854-1896), as 4 above (1854-1926), or FOR GALLANTRY AND HUMANITY (1858 to the present day).
Comments: *Although intended to reward foreigners who rendered assistance to British subjects in distress some early awards were actually made for rescues on dry land. Originally a special reverse was struck for each incident, but this was found to be unnecessarily expensive, so a standard reverse was devised in 1849. Medals before 1854 had a diameter of 45mm and were not fitted with suspension. After 1854 the diameter was reduced to 33mm and scrolled suspension bars were fitted. Of the large medals about 100 gold, 120 silver and 14 bronze were issued, while some 10 gold and 24 bronze specimens have been recorded.*

VALUE:

	Gold	Silver	Bronze
Victoria large	£1400–1800	£400–500	£400–500
Victoria small	£1000–1200	£250–350	—
Edward VII	£1000–1500	£400–500	—
George V	£1000–1200	£250–350	—
George VI	—	Rare	—
Elizabeth II	Rare	Rare	—

69. BRITISH NORTH BORNEO COMPANY'S BRAVERY CROSS

Instituted: 1890 by the British North Borneo Company.
Ribbon: Yellow watered silk.
Metal: Silver or bronze.
Size: 36mm.
Description: The cross pattée has a central medallion bearing a lion passant gardant with the Company motto PERGO ET PERAGO (I carry on and accomplish) within a garter. The arms of the cross are inscribed BRITISH NORTH BORNEO with FOR BRAVERY in the lower limb.
Comments: *Both silver and bronze crosses were manufactured by Joseph Moore of Birmingham. Both silver and bronze medals were issued unnamed. The only genuine striking of silver medals bears the Birmingham hallmark for 1890. Examples with the word STERLING on the reverse are modern copies. The reverse of the bronze medal is smooth, with no marks.*

VALUE:
Silver	£300–350
Bronze	£150–200

70. NATIVE CHIEFS' MEDAL

Instituted: 1920.
Ribbon: Yellow with two white central stripes (silver-gilt) or a single white stripe (silver).
Metal: Silver or silver-gilt.
Size: 40mm x 34mm (oval) or 36mm (circular).
Description: Originally an oval badge with collar. (Obverse) the crowned effigy of the monarch; (reverse) a warship, symbolic of imperial power. The Queen's Medal for Chiefs is circular with a beaded frame and has a crowned effigy of Elizabeth II entitled QUEEN ELIZABETH THE SECOND. It is fitted with a plain ring for suspension.

Comments: *Various large silver medals were struck for award to native chiefs in various parts of the world, from the eighteenth century onwards, and of these the awards to American Indian chiefs are probably the best known. In 1920, however, a standard King's Medal for Chiefs was instituted. It was awarded exceptionally in silver-gilt (first class), and usually in silver (second class). The oval medal was worn round the neck from a silver collar. The more modern issues, however, are intended for wear with a ribbon from the breast.*

VALUE:		Silver-gilt	Silver
	George V	£800–1000	£700–800
	George VI	£800–1000	£500–600
	Elizabeth II	£800–1000	£600–700

MENTIONS AND COMMENDATIONS

Below are illustrated the emblems denoting Mentions and Commendations introduced on August 12, 1994. These emblems are to be worn on the appropriate medal ribbon.

FOR GALLANTRY			FOR VALUABLE SERVICE
IN ACTION WITH THE ENEMY (ALL ENVIRONMENTS)	NOT IN ACTION WITH THE ENEMY or OUT OF THEATRE (EXCEPT FLYING)	NOT IN ACTION WITH THE ENEMY or OUT OF THEATRE (FLYING)	IN-THEATRE BUT NOT IN ACTION WITH THE ENEMY
MENTION IN DESPATCHES	QUEEN'S COMMENDATION FOR BRAVERY	QUEEN'S COMMENDATION FOR BRAVERY IN THE AIR	QUEEN'S COMMENDATION FOR VALUABLE SERVICE
A single oak leaf in SILVER	A spray of laurel leaves in SILVER	A new emblem in SILVER	A spray of oak leaves in SILVER

CAMPAIGN MEDALS

The evolution of medals struck to commemorate, and later to reward participants in, a battle or campaign was a very gradual process. The forerunner of the modern campaign medal was the Armada Medal, cast in gold or silver, which appears to have been awarded to naval officers and distinguished persons after the abortive Spanish invasion of 1588. The obverse bears a flattering portrait of Queen Elizabeth (thought to have been designed by Nicholas Hilliard, the celebrated miniaturist) with a Latin inscription signifying "enclosing the most precious treasure in the world" (i.e. the Queen herself). On the reverse, the safety of the kingdom is represented by a bay tree growing on a little island, immune from the flashes of lightning which seem to strike it. This medal, and a similar type depicting the Ark floating calmly on a stormy sea, bore loops at the top so that a chain or cord could be passed through it for suspension from the neck of the recipient.

The Civil War produced a number of gallantry medals, mentioned in the previous section; but in 1650 Parliament authorised a medal which was struck in silver, bronze or lead to celebrate Cromwell's miraculous victory over the Scots at Dunbar. This was the first medal granted to all the participants on the Parliamentary side, and not restricted to high-ranking officers, or given for individual acts of heroism.

The Dunbar Medal thus established several useful precedents, which were eventually to form the criteria of the campaign medal as we know it today. After this promising start, however, the pattern of medals and their issue were much more restrictive. Naval medals were struck in gold for award to admirals and captains during the First Dutch War (1650–53), while the battle of Culloden (1746) was marked by a medal portraying the "Butcher" Duke of Cumberland, and granted to officers who took part in the defeat of the Jacobites.

In the second half of the eighteenth century there were a number of medals, but these were of a private or semi-official nature. The Honourable East India Company took the lead in awarding medals to its troops. These medals were often struck in two sizes and in gold as well as silver, for award to different ranks. The siege of Gibraltar (1779–83) was marked by an issue of medals to the defenders, but this was made on the initiative (and at the expense) of the garrison commanders, Generals Eliott and Picton, themselves.

During the French Revolutionary and Napoleonic Wars several medals were produced by private individuals for issue to combatants. Alexander Davison and Matthew Boulton were responsible for the medals granted to the officers and men who fought the battles of the Nile (1798) and Trafalgar (1805). Davison also produced a Trafalgar medal in pewter surrounded by a copper rim; it is recorded that the seamen who received it were so disgusted at the base metal that they threw it into the sea! At the same time, however, Government recognition was given to senior officers who had distinguished themselves in certain battles and engagements and a number of gold medals were awarded. The events thus marked included the capture of Ceylon (1795–96) and the battles of Maida, Bagur and Palamos.

Towards the end of the Napoleonic Wars an Army Gold Medal was instituted in two sizes—large (generals) and small (field officers). Clasps for second and third battles and campaigns were added to the medal, but when an officer became eligible for a third clasp the medal was exchanged for a Gold Cross with the names of the four battles engraved on its arms. Clasps for subsequent campaigns were then added to the cross (the Duke of Wellington receiving the Gold Cross with nine clasps). A total of 163 crosses, 85 large and 599 small medals was awarded, so that, apart from their intrinsic value, these decorations command very high prices when they appear in the saleroom.

The first medal awarded to all ranks of the Army was the Waterloo Medal, issued in 1816 shortly after the battle which brought the Napoleonic Wars to an end. No action was taken to grant medals for the other campaigns in the Napoleonic Wars until 1847 when Military and Naval General Service Medals were awarded retrospectively to veterans who were then still alive. As applications were made, in some cases, in respect of campaigns more than fifty years earlier, it is hardly surprising that the number of medals awarded was comparatively small, while the number of clasps awarded for certain engagements was quite minute. The Military General Service Medal was restricted to land campaigns during the Peninsular War (1808–13), the American War (1812–14) and isolated actions in the West Indies, Egypt and Java, whereas the Naval GSM covered a far longer period, ranging from the capture of the French frigate *La Cleopatra* by HMS *Nymphe* in June 1793, to the naval blockade of the Syrian coast in 1840, during the British operations against Mehemet Ali. Thus Naval Medals with the clasp for Syria are relatively plentiful (7057 awarded) while in several cases clasps were awarded to one man alone, and in seven cases there were no claimants for clasps at all. It is worth bearing in mind that applications for the medals and clasps resulted mainly from the publicity given by printed advertisements and notices posted up all over the country. With the poor general standard of literacy prevalent at the time, many people who were entitled to the medals would have been quite unaware of their existence.

The Naming of Medals

The Military and Naval GSMs, with their multitudinous combinations of clasps, have long been popular with collectors, but the other campaign medals of the past century and a half have a strong following as well. With the exception of the stars and medals awarded during the Second World War, all British campaign medals have usually borne the name of the recipient and usually his (or her) number, rank and regiment, unit or ship as well. This brings a personal element into the study of medals which is lacking in most other branches of numismatics. The name on a medal is very important for two reasons. It is a means of testing the genuineness, not only of the medal itself, but its bar combination, and secondly it enables the collector to link the medal not only with the man who earned it, but with his unit or formation, and thus plays a vital part in the development of naval or military history, if only a small part in most cases.

Much of the potential value of a medal depends on the man who won it, or the unit to which he belonged. To form a coherent collection as opposed to a random accumulation of medals, the collector would be well advised to specialise in some aspect of the subject, restricting his interests perhaps to one medal (the Naval GSM) or a single group (British campaigns in India), or to medals awarded to the men of a particular regiment. The information given on the rim or back of a medal is therefore important in helping to identify it and assign it to its correct place. Even this has to be qualified to some extent. Some regiments are more popular than others with collectors and much depends on the part, active or passive, played by a unit in a particular battle or campaign for which the medal was awarded. Then again, the combination of event with the corps or regiment of the recipient must also be considered.

At one extreme we find the Royal Regiment of Artillery living up to its motto *Ubique* (everywhere) by being represented in virtually every land action (and not a few naval actions, as witness the Atlantic Star worn by former Maritime Gunners), so that a comprehensive collection of medals awarded to the RA would be a formidable feat.

At the other extreme one finds odd detachments, sometimes consisting of one or two men only, seconded from a regiment for service with another unit. The Indian GSM, with bar for Hazara (1891), is usually found named to personnel of the 11th Bengal Lancers and various battalions of the Bengal Infantry, but according to the medal rolls it was also given to six men of the 2nd Manchester Regiment, two men of the Queen's Regiment and one each to troopers of the 2nd and 7th

Dragoon Guards. Whereas a specimen of the IGS medal with this bar is not hard to find named to a soldier in one of the Bengal units, it constitutes a major rarity when awarded to one of the "odd men" and its value is correspondingly high.

As the personal details given on a medal regarding the recipient are so important, it is necessary for the collector to verify two facts—that the person whose name is on the medal was actually present at the action for which either the medal or its bars were awarded, and secondly, that the naming of the bar and the attachment of the bars is correct and not tampered with in any way. As regards the first, the Public Record Office at Kew, London is a goldmine of information for all naval and military campaigns. Apart from despatches, reports and muster rolls covering the actions, there are the medal rolls compiled from the applications for medals and bars. Transcriptions of the medal rolls are held by regimental museums and also by such bodies as the Military Historical Association and the Orders and Medals Research Society. Details of these and other clubs and societies devoted to medal collecting are given on page 250.

The presence of a name on the roll does not mean that a medal or clasp was inevitably awarded; conversely authenticated medals are known to exist named to persons not listed on the medal roll. There are often divergences between the muster and medal rolls. Moreover, discrepancies in the spelling of recipients' names are not uncommon and bars are sometimes found listed for regiments which were not even in existence when the battle was fought! This is explained, however, by the fact that a man may have been serving with one unit which took part in the campaign and subsequently transferred to another regiment. When claiming his medal he probably gave his *present* unit, rather than the one in which he was serving at the time of the action.

Unfortunately cases of medals having been tampered with are by no means rare, so it is necessary to be able to recognise evidence of fakery. A favourite device of the faker is to alter the name and personal details of the recipient and to substitute another name in order to enhance the medal's value. This is done simply by filing the inscription off the rim and adding a new one. In order to check for such alterations a similar medal of proven genuineness should be compared with a pair of fine callipers. Take the measurements at several points round the rim so that any unevenness should soon be apparent (see pages 25–27).

We cannot stress too much the importance of being closely familiar with the various styles of naming medals. Over the past 150 years an incredible variety of lettering— roman, italic, script, sans-serif, seriffed in all shapes and sizes—has been used at one time or another. In some cases the inscription was applied by impressing in raised relief; in others the inscription was punched in or engraved by hand. If a medal is normally impressed and you come across an engraved example you should immediately be on your guard. This is not an infallible test, however, as medals have been known with more than one style of naming, particularly if duplicates were issued at a much later date to replace medals lost or destroyed.

A rather more subtle approach was adopted by some fakers in respect of the Naval GSM. The three commonest clasps—*Algiers* (1362), *Navarino* (1137) and *Syria* (7057)— were awarded to many recipients possessing common names such as Jones or Smith which can be matched with recipients of some very rare clasps. In the case of the Naval GSM the ship on which the recipient served is not given, thus aiding the fraudulent substitution of clasps. It is necessary, therefore, to check the condition of clasps, even if the naming appears to be correct. Points to watch for are file or solder marks on the rivets which secure the clasps to each other and to the suspender of the medal. This test is not infallible as clasps *do* occasionally work loose if subject to constant wear (particularly if the recipient was a cavalryman, for obvious reasons). But clasps whose rivets appear to have been hammered should automatically be suspect, until a check of the medal rolls pass them as authentic. Examples of the earlier medals, particularly those awarded to officers, may be found with unorthodox coupling. Major L. L. Gordon, in his definitive work *British Battles and Medals*, mentions a Naval GSM awarded to one of his ancestors, with clasps for *Guadaloupe* and *Anse la Barque* in a large rectangular style which must have been unofficial. The medal is quite authentic, so it must be presumed that officers were allowed a certain degree of latitude in the manner in which they altered their medals.

Medals with clasps awarded for participation in subsequent engagements are invariably worth much more than the basic medal. In general, the greater number of clasps, the more valuable the medal, although, conversely, there are a few instances in which single-clasp medals are scarcer than twin-clasp medals. There is no short answer to this and individual rare clasps can enhance the value of an otherwise common medal out of all proportion. Thus the Naval GSM with clasp for *Syria* currently rates £180–220, but one of the two medals known to have been issued with the *Acheron* clasp of 1805 would easily rate twelve times as much. Again, relative value can only be determined by reference to all the circumstances of the award.

The person to whom a medal was issued has considerable bearing on its value. If the recipient belonged to a regiment which played a spectacular part in a battle, this generally rates a premium. The rank of the recipient also has some bearing; in general the higher the rank, the more valuable the medal. Medals to commissioned officers rate more than those awarded to NCOs and other ranks, and the medals of British servicemen rate more as a rule than those awarded to native troops. Medals granted to women usually command a relatively good premium. Another grim aspect is that medals issued to personnel who were wounded or killed in the campaign also rate more highly than those issued to servicemen who came through unscathed.

With the collector of British campaign medals the person to whom the medal was awarded tends to become almost as important as the medal itself. It is often not sufficient to collect the medal and leave it at that. The collector feels that he must investigate it and delve into

the archives to find out all that he can about the recipient. The Public Record Office and regimental museums have already been mentioned, but do not overlook the usefulness of such reference tools as the monumental Mormon International Genealogical Index (now on microfiche and available in good public libraries and county record offices). All of these should help you to flesh out the bare bones of the details given in the muster and medal rolls.

Medal Groups

Apart from the combination of clasps on a medal and the significance of the recipient, there is a third factor to be considered in assessing the value of medals, namely the relationship of one medal to another in a group awarded to one person. Just as the number of clasps on a medal is not in itself a significant factor, so also the number of medals in a group is not necessarily important *per se*. Groups of five or more medals, whose recipient can be identified, are by no means uncommon. For example, a fairly common five medal group would consist of 1914–15 Medal, War Medal and Victory Medal (for the First World War) and the Defence Medal and War Medal (for the Second World War). Thousands of men served throughout the first war to do duty, in a less active role, during a part at least of the second, long enough to qualify for the latter pair of medals.

It should be noted that none of the medals awarded for service in the Second World War was named to the recipient, so that groups comprising such medals alone cannot be readily identified and are thus lacking in the interest possessed by those containing named medals. Six-medal groups for service in the Second World War are not uncommon, particularly the combination of 1939–45 Star, Africa Star, Italy Star, France and Germany Star, Defence Medal and War Medal awarded to Army personnel who served from any time up to late 1942 and took part in the campaigns of North Africa and Europe.

Conversely it would be possible for troops to have served over a longer period and seen more action, and only been awarded the 1939–45 Star, Burma Star (with Pacific bar) and the War Medal. Naval groups consisting of the 1939–45 Star, Atlantic Star (with bar for France and Germany), Italy Star and War Medal are less common and therefore more desirable (with, of course, the rider that it must be possible to identify the recipient), while the most desirable of all is the three-medal group of 1939–45 Star (with Battle of Britain bar), Air Crew Europe Star (with bar for France and Germany) and the War Medal. Such a group, together with a Distinguished Flying Cross awarded to one of The Few, is a highly coveted set indeed, providing, as always, that one can prove its authenticity. In any event, the addition of a named medal to a Second World War group (e.g. a long service award, a gallantry medal, or some other category of medal named to the recipient), together with supporting collateral material (citations, log-books, pay-books, service records, newspaper cuttings, etc), should help to establish the provenance of the group.

71. LOUISBURG MEDAL

Date: 1758.
Campaign: Canada (Seven Years War).
Branch of Service: British Army and Navy.
Ribbon: 32mm half yellow, half black.
Metals: Gold, silver or bronze.
Size: 42mm.
Description: (Obverse) the globe surrounded by allegorical figures of victory and flanked by servicemen; (reverse) burning ships in the harbour.
Comments: *More in the nature of a decoration, this medal was only given to certain recipients for acts of bravery or distinguished service in the capture in July 1758 of Louisburg in Canada during the Seven Years War. James Wolfe and Jeffrey Amherst commanded the land forces and Edward Boscawen the fleet.*

VALUE:

Gold	Rare
Silver	£2000–4000
Bronze	£600–800

72. CARIB WAR MEDAL

Date: 1773.
Campaign: Carib rebellion, St Vincent.
Branch of Service: Local militia or volunteers.
Ribbon: None.
Metal: Silver.
Size: 52mm.
Description: (Obverse) bust of George III in armour; (reverse) Britannia offering an olive branch to a defeated Carib, the date MDCCLXXIII in the exergue.
Comments: *The Legislative Assembly of St Vincent in the West Indies instituted this award to members of the militia and volunteers who served in the campaign of 1773 which put down a native rebellion that had been fomented by the French.*

VALUE:

Silver	£800–900

73. DECCAN MEDAL

Date: 1784.
Campaign: Western India and Gujerat 1778-84.
Branch of Service: HEIC forces.
Ribbon: Yellow cord.
Metals: Gold or silver.
Size: 40.5mm or 32mm.
Description: (Obverse) a rather languid Britannia with a trophy of arms, thrusting a laurel wreath towards a distant fort. (Reverse) an inscription in Farsi signifying "As coins are current in the world, so shall be the bravery and exploits of these heroes by whom the name of the victorious English nation was carried from Bengal to the Deccan. Presented in AH 1199 [1784] by the East India Company's Calcutta Government".
Comments: *The first medals struck by order of the Honourable East India Company were conferred on Indian troops for service in western India and Gujerat under the command of Warren Hastings. They were struck at Calcutta in two sizes; both gold and silver exist in the larger size but only silver medals in the smaller diameter.*

VALUE:

40.5mm gold	£4000–6000
40.5mm silver	£800–1000
32mm silver	£450–550

74. DEFENCE OF GIBRALTAR

Date: 1783.

Eliott's medal   Picton's medal

Campaign: Siege of Gibraltar 1779-83.
Branch of Service: British and Hanoverian forces.
Ribbon: None.
Metal: Silver.
Size: 59mm (Picton) and 49mm (Eliott).
Description: Eliott's medal was confined to the Hanoverian troops, hence the reverse inscribed
   BRUDERSCHAFT (German for "brotherhood") above a wreath containing the names of the three
   Hanoverian commanders and General Eliott. The obverse, by Lewis Pingo, shows a view of the Rock and
   the naval attack of 13 September 1782 which was the climax of the siege. Picton's medal, awarded to the
   British forces, has a larger than usual diameter, with a map of the Rock on the obverse and a 22-line text—the
   most verbose British medal—above a recumbent lion clutching a shield bearing the castle and key emblem of
   Gibraltar on the reverse.
Comments: *Several medals of a private nature were struck to commemorate the defence of Gibraltar during the Franco-*
   Spanish siege of 1779–83, but those most commonly encountered are the silver medals which were provided by George
   Augustus Eliott and Sir Thomas Picton, the military commanders.

VALUE:

Picton medal	£450–550
Eliott medal	£400–500

75. MYSORE MEDAL

Date: 1792.
Campaign: Mysore 1790-92.
Branch of Service: HEIC forces.
Ribbon: Yellow cord.
Metal: Gold or silver.
Size: 43mm or 38mm.
Description: (Obverse) a sepoy of the HEIC Army holding British and Company flags over a trophy of arms with the fortress of Seringapatam in the background; (reverse) a bilingual inscription (in English and Farsi). The medal has a ring for suspension round the neck by a cord.
Comments: *Indian officers and men who served under Marquis Cornwallis and Generals Abercromby and Meadows received this medal for service in the campaign which brought about the downfall of Tippoo Sultan of Mysore.*

VALUE:

43mm gold (subadars)	£5000–7000
43mm silver (jemadars)	£800–1200
38mm silver (other ranks)	£550–600

76. ST VINCENT'S BLACK CORPS MEDAL

Date: 1795.
Campaign: Carib rebellion 1795.
Branch of Service: Local militia volunteers.
Ribbon: None.
Metal: Bronze.
Size: 48.5mm.
Description: (Obverse) the winged figure of Victory brandishing a sword over a fallen foe who has abandoned his musket; (reverse) native holding musket and bayonet, BOLD LOYAL OBEDIENT around and H.G.FEC. in exergue.
Comments: *Awarded to the officers and NCOs of the Corps of Natives raised by Major Seton from among the island's slaves for service against the rebellious Caribs and French forces.*

VALUE:

Bronze	£600–700

77. CAPTURE OF CEYLON MEDAL

Date: 1796.
Campaign: Ceylon 1795.
Branch of Service: HEIC forces.
Ribbon: Yellow cord.
Metal: Gold or silver.
Size: 50mm.
Description: The plain design has an English inscription on the obverse, and the Farsi equivalent on the reverse.
Comments: *Awarded for service in the capture of Ceylon (Sri Lanka) from the Dutch during the French Revolutionary Wars. It is generally believed that the gold medals were awarded to Captains Barton and Clarke while the silver medals went to the native gunners of the Bengal Artillery.*

VALUE:

Gold (2)	—
Silver (121)	£650–750

78. DAVISON'S NILE MEDAL

Date: 1798.   **Campaign:** Battle of the Nile 1798.
Branch of Service: Royal Navy.
Ribbon: 32mm, deep navy blue.
Metal: Gold, silver, gilt-bronze and bronze.   **Size:** 47mm.
Description: (Obverse) Peace caressing a shield decorated with the portrait of Horatio Nelson; (reverse) the
British fleet at Aboukir Bay.
Comments: *Nelson's victory at the mouth of the Nile on 1 August 1798 was celebrated in a novel manner by his prize
agent, Alexander Davison, whose name and London address appear in the edge inscription of the medal designed by
Kuchler. Originally issued without a suspender, many recipients added a ring to enable the medal to be worn.*

VALUE:

Gold (admirals and captains)	£4000–6000	Gilt-bronze (petty officers)	£200–250
Silver (junior officers)	£400–500	Bronze (ratings)	£80–120

79. SERINGAPATAM MEDAL

Date: 1808.   **Campaign:** Seringapatam, India, 1799.
Branch of Service: HEIC forces.
Ribbon: 38mm gold.
Metal: Gold, silver-gilt, silver, bronze and pewter.   **Size:** 48mm or 45mm.
Description: (Obverse) the British lion fighting a Bengal tiger with the date of the capture of the fortress IV
MAY MDCCXCIX (1799) in the exergue; (reverse) the assault on Seringapatam.
Comments: *The British and native troops who took part in the renewed campaign against Tippoo Sultan were awarded
this medal in 1808 in various metals without suspension (a number of different types of suspenders and rings were
subsequently fitted by individual recipients). The medal was designed by Kuchler and struck in England and Calcutta,
the latter version being slightly smaller. There are several different strikings of these medals.*

VALUE:

Gold 48mm (113)	£3000–4000	Silver 45mm	£280–300
Gold 45mm	£2500–3000	Bronze 48mm (5000)	£180–220
Silver-gilt 48mm (185)	£400–500	Pewter 48mm (45,000)	£140–170
Silver 48mm (3636)	£350–450		

80. EARL ST. VINCENT'S MEDAL

Date: 1800.   **Campaign:** Mediterranean.
Branch of Service: Royal Navy.
Ribbon: None.
Metal: Gold or silver.   **Size:** 48mm
Description: (Obverse) left-facing bust of the Earl in Admiral's uniform; (reverse) a sailor and marine.
Comments: *A private medal presented by Admiral Earl St Vincent to the petty officers and men of HMS* Ville de Paris *who remained loyal during the mutiny of the Mediterranean fleet. The gold medals are believed to have been presented by Earl St Vincent to friends and senior naval colleagues.*

VALUE:

Gold	£3000–4000
Silver	£350–400

81. EGYPT MEDAL

Date: 1801.   **Campaign:** Egypt 1801.
Branch of Service: HEIC forces.
Ribbon: Yellow cord.
Metal: Gold or silver.   **Size:** 48mm.
Description: (Obverse) a sepoy holding a Union Jack, with an encampment in the background. A four-line Farsi text occupies the exergue; (reverse) a warship and the Pyramids.
Comments: *Issued by the Honourable East India Company to British and Indian troops in the Company's service who took part in the conquest of Egypt under Generals Baird and Abercromby.*

VALUE:

Gold (16)	Rare
Silver (2200)	£500–600

82. SULTAN'S MEDAL FOR EGYPT

Date: 1801.
Campaign: Egypt 1801.
Branch of Service: British forces.
Ribbon: None. Originally suspended by gold hook and chain.
Metals: Gold or silver.
Size: Various (see below).
Description: The very thin discs have an elaborate arabesque border enclosing the *toughra* or sign manual of the Sultan.
Comments: *This medal was conferred by Sultan Selim III of Turkey on the British officers and NCOs who took part in the campaign against the French. It was produced in five gold versions for award to different ranks of commissioned officers, as well as one in silver for award to sergeants and corporals.*

VALUE:

Gold 54mm studded with jewels	Rare
Gold 54mm plain	£2000–2500
Gold 48mm	£1500–1800
Gold 43mm	£1100–1300
Gold 36mm	£500–550
Silver 36mm	£450–500
Miniature	
Gold	£100–150
Silver	£50–80

83. HIGHLAND SOCIETY'S MEDAL FOR EGYPT

Date: 1801.
Campaign: Egypt 1801.
Branch of Service: British forces.
Ribbon: None.
Metals: Gold, silver and bronze.
Size: 49mm.
Description: The medal was designed by Pidgeon. (Obverse) the right-facing bust of General Sir Ralph Abercromby, with a Latin inscription alluding to his death in Egypt; (reverse) a Highlander and the date 21 MAR. 1801 with the Gaelic inscription NA FIR A CHOISIN BUAIDH (These are the heroes who achieved victory in Egypt).
Comments: *The Highland and Agricultural Society (now Royal) was founded in 1784 to promote the development of agriculture in Scotland generally and the Highlands in particular. General Abercromby (born at Tullibody, 1734) commanded the British expedition to Egypt, and the landing at Aboukir Bay on 2 March 1801 in the face of strenuous French opposition, is justly regarded as one of the most brilliant and daring exploits of all time. The French made a surprise attack on the British camp on the night of 21 March and Abercromby was struck by a ricochet; he died aboard the flagship seven days later. Medals in gold were presented to the Prince Regent and Abercromby's sons, but silver and bronze medals were later struck and awarded to senior officers of the expedition as well as soldiers who had distinguished themselves in the campaign.*

VALUE:

Gold	—
Silver	£600–800
Bronze	£250–300

84. BOULTON'S TRAFALGAR MEDAL

Date: 1805.
Campaign: Battle of Trafalgar 1805.
Branch of Service: Royal Navy.
Ribbon: 32mm navy blue (originally issued without suspension).
Metals: Gold, silver, white metal, gilt-bronze or bronze.   **Size:** 48mm.
Description: (Obverse) bust of Nelson; (reverse) a battle scene.
Comments: *Matthew Boulton of the Soho Mint, Birmingham, struck this medal on his own initiative for presentation to the survivors of the battle of Trafalgar. It was awarded in gold, silver and white metal, but bronze and gilt-bronze specimens also exist. The edge bears an incuse inscription "From M. Boulton to the Heroes of Trafalgar".*

VALUE:

Gold	£6000–10,000	Gilt-bronze	£400–600
Silver	£500–800	Bronze	£150–220
White metal	£120–300	*NB These prices are dependent on attribution.*	

85. DAVISON'S TRAFALGAR MEDAL

Date: 1805.
Campaign: Battle of Trafalgar 1805.
Branch of Service: Royal Navy.
Ribbon: 32mm navy blue.
Metal: Pewter with a copper rim.   **Size:** 52mm.
Description: (Obverse) bust of Nelson; (reverse) a man-of-war with an appropriate biblical quotation from Exodus "The Lord is a Man-of-War".
Comments: *Alexander Davison, Nelson's prize agent, had this medal struck for award to the ratings who took part in the battle.*

VALUE: £600–800

86. CAPTURE OF RODRIGUEZ, ISLE OF BOURBON AND ISLE OF FRANCE

Date: 1810.
Campaign: Indian Ocean 1809-10.
Branch of Service: HEIC forces.
Ribbon: Yellow cord.
Metal: Gold or silver.
Size: 49mm.
Description: (Obverse) a sepoy in front of a cannon with the Union Jack; (reverse) a wreath with inscriptions in English and Farsi.
Comments: *The East India Company awarded this medal to native troops of the Bengal and Bombay Armies for the capture of three French islands in the Indian Ocean (the latter two being better known today as Mauritius and Reunion) between July 1809 and December 1810.*

VALUE:

Gold (50)	£4000–6000
Silver (2200)	£550–650

87. BAGUR AND PALAMOS MEDAL

Date: 1811.
Campaign: Peninsular War 1810.
Branch of Service: Royal Navy.
Ribbon: Red with yellow edges.
Metal: Gold or silver.
Size: 45mm.
Description: (Obverse) the conjoined crowned shields of Britain and Spain in a wreath with ALIANZA ETERNA (eternal alliance) round the foot; (reverse) inscription in Spanish GRATITUDE OF SPAIN TO THE BRAVE BRITISH AT BAGUR 10 SEPT. 1810, PALAMOS 14 SEPT. 1810.
Comments: *Awarded by the Spanish government to the crews of the British warships* Ajax, Cambrian *and* Kent *who landed at Bagur and Palamos to seize French ships. The British force was, in fact, driven back with very heavy losses.*

VALUE:

Gold (8)	£3000–4000
Silver (600)	£600–800

88. JAVA MEDAL

Date: 1811.
Campaign: Java 1811.
Branch of Service: HEIC forces.
Ribbon: Yellow cord.
Metals: Gold or silver.
Size: 49mm.
Description: (Obverse) the assault on Fort Cornelis; (reverse) inscriptions in English and Farsi.
Comments: *Awarded by the HEIC for the seizure of Java from the Dutch. The 750 British officers and men who took part in the operation were not only awarded this medal but were eligible for the Military GSM with Java clasp, issued 38 years later. Senior officers of the Company were given the gold medal, while junior officers, NCOs and sepoys received the silver version.*

VALUE:

Gold (133)	£3000–4000
Silver (6519)	£450–550

89. NEPAUL MEDAL

Date: 1816.
Campaign: Nepal 1814-16.
Branch of Service: HEIC native troops.
Ribbon: Yellow cord.
Metal: Silver.
Size: 51mm.
Description: (Obverse) a fortified mountain-top with a cannon in the foreground; (reverse) Farsi inscription.
Comments: *This medal marked the campaign to pacify Nepal led by Generals Marley, Ochterlony and Gillespie (the last named being killed in action). At the conclusion of the war Ochterlony began recruiting Gurkha mercenaries, a policy which has continued in the British Army to this day. The clasp "Nepaul" was granted with the Army of India Medal to British forces in 1851.*

VALUE: £500–600

90. CEYLON MEDAL

Date: 1818.
Campaign: Ceylon (Sri Lanka) 1818.
Branch of Service: British and HEIC forces.
Ribbon: 38mm deep navy blue.
Metal: Gold or silver.
Size: 35mm.
Description: The very plain design has "Ceylon 1818" within a wreath (obverse) and REWARD OF MERIT at top and bottom of the reverse, the personal details being engraved in the centre.
Comments: *Awarded by the Ceylon government for gallant conduct during the Kandian rebellion. Only selected officers and men of the 19th, 73rd and 83rd Foot, the 1st and 2nd Ceylon Regiments and 7th, 15th and 18th Madras Native Infantry received this medal.*

VALUE:

Gold (2)	—	
Silver (45)	£1500–2000	

91. BURMA MEDAL

Date: 1826.
Campaign: Burma 1824-26.
Branch of Service: HEIC native forces.
Ribbon: 38mm crimson edged with navy blue.
Metals: Gold or silver.
Size: 39mm.
Description: (Obverse) the Burmese elephant kneeling in submission before the British lion; (reverse) the epic assault on Rangoon by the Irrawaddy Flotilla.
Comments: *Granted to native officers and men who participated in the campaign for the subjugation of Burma. This was the first of the HEIC campaign medals in what was to become a standard 1.5 inch (38mm) diameter. The medal was fitted with a large steel ring for suspension and issued unnamed. British troops in this campaign were belatedly (1851) given the clasp "Ava" to the Army of India Medal.*

VALUE: *Miniature*

Gold (750)	£2000–2500	
Silver (24,000)	£400–500	£250–300

92. COORG MEDAL

Date: 1837.
Campaign: Coorg rebellion 1837.
Branch of Service: HEIC loyal Coorg forces.
Ribbon: Yellow cord.
Metals: Gold, silver or bronze.
Size: 50mm.
Description: (Obverse) a Coorg holding a musket, with kukri upraised; (reverse) weapons in a wreath with the inscription FOR DISTINGUISHED CONDUCT AND LOYALTY TO THE BRITISH GOVERNMENT COORG APRIL 1837, the equivalent in Canarese appearing on the obverse.
Comments: *Native troops who remained loyal during the Canara rebellion of April-May 1837 were awarded this medal by the HEIC the following August. Bronze specimens were also struck but not officially issued and may have been restrikes or later copies. Bronzed and silvered electrotype copies are also known.*

VALUE:

Gold (44)	£4000–6000
Silver (300)	£550–650
Bronze	£200–300

93. NAVAL GOLD MEDAL

Date: 1795.
Campaign: Naval actions 1795-1815.
Branch of Service: Royal Navy.
Ribbon: 44mm white with broad dark blue edges.
Metal: Gold.
Size: 51mm and 38mm.
Description: The medals were glazed on both sides and individually engraved on the reverse with the name of the recipient and details of the engagement in a wreath of laurel and oak leaves. (Obverse) the winged figure of Victory bestowing a laurel wreath on the head of Britannia standing in the prow of a galley with a Union Jack shield behind her, her right foot on a helmet, her left hand holding a spear.
Comments: *Instituted in 1795, a year after Lord Howe's naval victory on "the glorious First of June", this medal was awarded continually till 1815 when the Order of the Bath was expanded into three classes. Large medals were awarded to admirals and small medals went to captains. As medals were awarded for separate actions it was possible for officers to wear more than one, and Lord Nelson himself had three.*

VALUE:

Large medal (23)	From £25,000
Small medal (116)	From £8,000

94. NAVAL GENERAL SERVICE MEDAL

Date: 1847.
Campaign: Naval battles and boat actions 1793-1840.
Branch of Service: Royal Navy.
Ribbon: 32mm white with dark blue edges.
Metal: Silver.
Size: 36mm.
Description: (Obverse) the Young Head profile of Queen Victoria by William Wyon; (reverse) Britannia with her trident seated on a sea horse.
Clasps: No fewer than 230 different clasps for major battles, minor engagements, cutting-out operations and boat service were authorised. These either have the name or date of the action, the name of a ship capturing or defeating an enemy vessel, or the words BOAT SERVICE followed by a date. No fewer than 20,933 medals were awarded but most of them had a single clasp. Multi-clasp medals are worth very considerably more. The greatest number of clasps to a single medal was seven (two awards made); four medals had six clasps and fourteen medals had five clasps. For reasons of space only those clasps which are met with fairly often in the salerooms are listed below. At the other end of the scale it should be noted that only one recipient claimed the clasps for *Hussar* (17 May 1795), *Dido* (24 June 1795), *Spider* (25 August 1795), *Espoir* (7 August 1798), *Viper* (26 December 1799), *Loire* (5 February 1800), *Louisa* (28 October 1807), *Carrier* (4 November 1807), *Superieure* (10 February 1809), *Growler* (22 May 1812) and the boat actions of 15 March 1793, 4 November 1803, 4 November 1810 and 3-6 September 1814. In several cases no claimants came forward at all. The numbers of clasps awarded are not an accurate guide to value, as some actions are rated more highly than others, and clasps associated with actions in the War of 1812 have a very strong following in the USA as well as Britain. Clasps for famous battles, such as Trafalgar, likewise command a high premium out of all proportion to the number of clasps awarded.
Comments: *Instituted in 1847 and issued to* **surviving** *claimants in 1848, this medal was originally intended to cover naval engagements of the French Revolutionary and Napoleonic Wars (1793-1815) but was almost immediately extended to cover all naval actions of a more recent date, down to the expedition to Syria in 1840. It was fitted with a straight suspender.*

VALUE:

Fleet Actions		Ship Actions	
1 June 1794 (540)	£500–600	Mars 21 April 1798 (26)	£1000–1200
14 March 1795 (95)	£600–700	Lion 15 July 1798 (23)	£1000–1200
23 June 1795 (177)	£500–600	Acre 30 May 1799 (41)	£800–1000
St Vincent (348)	£550–650	London 13 March 1806 (27)	£1000–1200
Camperdown (298)	£550–600	Curacao 1 Jany 1807 (65)	£700–800
Nile (326)	£600–700	Stately 22 March 1808 (31)	£900–1000
12 Octr 1798 (78)	£600–700	Lissa (124)	£600–700
Egypt (618)	£320–350	Shannon with Chesapeake (42)	£3000–3500
Copenhagen (555)	£550–650	Gluckstadt 5 Jany 1814 (44)	£900–1000
Gut of Gibraltar (142)	£550–650	Gaieta 24 July 1815 (88)	£600–700
Trafalgar (1710)	£900–1000		
4 Novr 1805 (296)	£550–650	**Boat Service**	
St Domingo (396)	£350–400	16 July 1806 (51)	£850–950
Martinique (486)	£350–400	1 Novr 1809 (110)	£550–650
Basque Roads (529)	£450–500	28 June 1810 (25)	£800–900
Guadaloupe (483)	£350–400	29 Sepr 1812 (25)	£1000–1200
Java (665)	£350–400	8 Ap and May 1813 (57)	£1700–1900
St Sebastian (293)	£350–400	2 May 1813 (48)	£700–800
Algiers (1328)	£300–350	8 April 1814 (24)	£1800–2000
Navarino (1142)	£400–475	24 May 1814 (12)	£1000–1200
Syria (6978)	£200–220	14 Decr 1814 (205)	£800–1000

Miniature
Without clasp   £100–150, for each clasp add £50

95. ARMY GOLD CROSS

Date: 1813.
Campaigns: Peninsular War and War of 1812.
Branch of Service: British Army.
Ribbon: 38mm crimson edged with dark blue.
Metal: Gold. **Size:** 38mm.
Description: A cross pattée with a laurel border having a rose at the centre on each of the four flat ends. At the centre of the cross appears a British lion statant. The scrolled top of the cross is fitted with an elaborate ring decorated with laurel leaves looped through a plain swivel ring fitted to the suspender. The arms of the cross on both obverse and reverse bear the names of four battles in relief.
Clasps: Large borders of laurel leaves enclosing the name of a battle in raised relief within an elliptical frame, awarded for fifth and subsequent battles.
Comments: *Arguably the most prestigious award in the campaign series, the Army Gold Cross was approved by the Prince Regent in 1813. It was granted to generals and officers of field rank for service in four or more battles of the Peninsular War. Three crosses had six clasps, two had seven, while the Duke of Wellington himself had the unique cross with nine clasps, representing participation in thirteen battles.*

VALUE:

Gold cross without clasp (61)	From £10,000
Miniature	£350–450

96. MAIDA GOLD MEDAL

Date: 1806.
Campaign: Peninsular War, Battle of Maida 1806.
Branch of Service: British Army.
Ribbon: 38mm crimson edged with navy blue.
Metal: Gold. **Size:** 39mm.
Description: (Obverse) laureated profile of George III; (reverse) winged figure of Victory hovering with a laurel wreath over the head of Britannia, shield upraised, in the act of throwing a spear. The name and date of the battle appears on Britannia's left, with the *trinacria* or three-legged emblem on the right.
Clasps: None.
Comments: *This small gold medal was authorised in 1806 and awarded to the thirteen senior officers involved in the battle of Maida in Calabria when a small British force under General Sir John Stuart defeated a much larger French army with heavy loss. A small unknown number of gold and silver specimens are known to exist.*

VALUE: Rare

97. ARMY GOLD MEDAL

Date: 1810.
Campaigns: Peninsular War 1806-14 and War of 1812.
Branch of Service: British Army.
Ribbon: 38mm crimson edged with navy blue.
Metal: Gold.
Size: 54mm and 33mm.
Description: (Obverse) Britannia seated on a globe, holding a laurel wreath over the British lion and holding a palm branch in her left hand while resting on a shield embellished with the Union Jack. The name of the first action is generally engraved on the reverse.
Clasps: For second and third actions.
Comments: *The Maida medal (no. 96) established a precedent for the series of medals instituted in 1810. The name of the battle was inscribed on the reverse, usually engraved, though that for Barossa was die-struck. These medals were struck in two sizes, the larger being conferred on generals and the smaller on officers of field rank. Second or third battles were denoted by a clasp appropriately inscribed, while those who qualified for a fourth award exchanged their medal and bars for a gold cross. The award of these gold medals and crosses ceased in 1814 when the Companion of the Bath was instituted.*

VALUE:

Large medal	From £8000
Small medal	From £4000

98. MILITARY GENERAL SERVICE MEDAL

Date: 1847.

Campaigns: French Revolutionary and Napoleonic Wars 1793-1814.

Branch of Service: British Army.

Ribbon: 31mm crimson edged with dark blue.

Metal: Silver.

Size: 36mm.

Description: (Obverse) the Wyon profile of Queen Victoria; (reverse) a standing figure of the Queen bestowing victor's laurels on a kneeling Duke of Wellington. The simple inscription TO THE BRITISH ARMY appears round the circumference, while the dates 1793-1814 are placed in the exergue. Despite this, the earliest action for which a clasp was issued took place in 1801 (Abercromby's Egyptian campaign).

Clasps: Only 29 battle or campaign clasps were issued but multiple awards are much commoner than in the naval medal, the maximum being fifteen. While it is generally true to say that multi-clasp medals are worth more than single-clasp medals, there are many in the latter category (noted below) which command higher prices. The figures quoted below are based on the commonest regiments. Clasps awarded to specialists and small detached forces rate more highly than medals to the principal regiment in a battle or campaign. In particular, it should be noted that one naval officer, Lieut. Carroll, received the Military GSM and clasp for Maida, while a few other officers of the Royal Navy and Royal Marines received the medal with the clasps for Guadaloupe, Martinique or Java, and these, naturally, are now very much sought after. Paradoxically, the clasps for Sahagun and Benevente alone are very much scarcer than the clasp inscribed Sahagun and Benevente, awarded to surviving veterans who had participated in both battles. The clasps are listed below in chronological order.

Comments: *Like the Naval GSM, this medal was not sanctioned till 1847 and awarded the following year. Unlike the Naval medal, however, the Military GSM was confined to land actions up to the defeat of Napoleon in 1814 and the conclusion of the war with the United States.*

VALUE:

Egypt	£350–400	Chateauguay	£1400–1800
Maida	£320–380	Chrystler's Farm	£1500–1800
Roleia	£550–600	Vittoria	£250–300
Vimiera	£300–350	Pyrenees	£250–300
Sahagun	£500–600	St Sebastian	£300–350
Benevente	£4500–5500	Nivelle	£280–300
Sahagun and Benevente	£450–550	Nive	£280–300
Corunna	£300–350	Orthes	£280–300
Martinique	£350–400	Toulouse	£280–320
Talavera	£300–400	2 clasps	£320–360
Guadaloupe	£350–400	3 clasps	£350–380
Busaco	£320–350	4 clasps	£460–500
Barrosa	£320–350	5 clasps	£500–550
Fuentes D'Onor	£300–350	6 clasps	£650–700
Albuhera	£400–450	7 clasps	£750–850
Java	£350–380	8 clasps	£850–950
Ciudad Rodrigo	£300–350	9 clasps	£1000–1200
Badajoz	£350–400	10 clasps	£1200–1400
Salamanca	£300–350	11 clasps	£1600–1800
Fort Detroit	£1400–1800	12 or more clasps	From £2000

Miniature **without clasp**   £100–150, for each clasp add £50

99. WATERLOO MEDAL

Date: 1815.
Campaign: Waterloo 1815.
Branch of Service: British Army.
Ribbon: 38mm, crimson edged in dark blue.
Metal: Silver.
Size: 37mm.
Description: (Obverse) the profile of the Prince Regent; (reverse) the seated figure of Victory above a tablet simply inscribed WATERLOO with the date of the battle in the exergue.
Comments: *This was the first medal awarded and officially named to all ranks who took part in a particular campaign. It was also issued, however, to those who had taken part in one or more of the other battles of the campaign, at Ligny and Quatre Bras two days earlier. The ribbon was intended to be worn with an iron clip and split suspension ring but many recipients subsequently replaced these with a more practical silver mount which would not rust and spoil the uniform. Some 39,000 medals were issued. The value of a Waterloo medal depends to a large extent on the regiment of the recipient. Medals awarded to those formations which saw the heaviest action and bore the brunt of the losses are in the greatest demand, whereas medals named to soldiers in General Colville's reserve division which did not take part in the fighting, are the least highly rated.*

VALUE:

Heavy Cavalry	£600–700
Scots Greys	£1100–1400
Light Cavalry	£450–550
Royal Artillery	£400–500
Foot Guards	£600–700
1st, 27th, 28th, 30th, 42nd, 44th, 73rd, 79th, 92nd Foot	£650–1200
Other Foot regiments	£450–550
Colville's division (35th, 54th, 59th, 91st Foot)	£400–450
King's German Legion	£400–600
Miniature	£50–200

100. BRUNSWICK MEDAL FOR WATERLOO

Date: 1815.
Campaign: Battle of Waterloo 1815.
Branch of Service: Brunswick troops.
Ribbon: Yellow with light blue stripes towards the edges.
Metal: Bronze.
Description: (Obverse) Duke Friedrich Wilhelm of Brunswick who was killed in the battle; (reverse) a wreath of laurel and oak leaves enclosing the German text "Braunschweig Seinen Kriegern" (Brunswick to its warriors) and the names of Quatre Bras and Waterloo.
Comments: *The Prince Regent authorised this medal for issue to the contingent from the Duchy of Brunswick.*

VALUE: £180–200

101. HANOVERIAN MEDAL FOR WATERLOO

Date: 1815.
Campaign: Battle of Waterloo 1815.
Branch of Service: Hanoverian troops.
Ribbon: Crimson edged with light blue.
Metal: Silver.
Description: (Obverse) the Prince Regent, his name and title being rendered in German. (Reverse) a trophy of arms below the legend HANNOVERSCHER TAPFERKEIT (Hanoverian bravery), with the name and date of the battle wreathed in the centre.
Comments: *The Prince Regent authorised this medal on behalf of his father George III in his capacity as Elector of Hanover and this was conferred on survivors of the battle. Suspension was by iron clip and ring similar to the British Waterloo Medal.*

VALUE: £200–250

102. NASSAU MEDAL FOR WATERLOO

Date: 1815.
Campaign: Battle of Waterloo 1815.
Branch of Service: Nassau forces.
Ribbon: Dark blue edged in yellow.
Metal: Silver.
Size: 25mm.
Description: (Obverse) Duke Friedrich of Nassau; (reverse) the winged figure of Victory crowning a soldier with laurels, the date of the action being in the exergue.
Comments: *Friedrich Duke of Nassau distributed this medal on 23 December 1815 to all of his own troops who had been present at the battle.*

VALUE: £180–200

103. SAXE-GOTHA-ALTENBURG MEDAL

Date: 1815.
Campaign: Germany and Waterloo 1814-15.
Branch of Service: Saxe-Gotha-Altenburg Foreign Legion.
Ribbon: Green with black edges and gold stripes.
Metal: Gilt bronze or bronze.
Size: 42mm.
Description: (Obverse) a crown with the legend IM KAMPFE FUER DAS RECHT (in the struggle for the right); (reverse) an ornate rose motif with the name of the duchy and the dates of the campaign in roman numerals.
Comments: *Gilded medals were issued to officers, but other ranks received a bronze version.*

VALUE:
Gilt-bronze	£220–260
Bronze	£200–240

104. ARMY OF INDIA MEDAL

Date: 1851.
Campaigns: India 1803–26.
Branch of Service: British and HEIC troops.
Ribbon: 32mm pale blue.
Metal: Silver.
Size: 35mm.
Description: (Obverse) the Wyon profile of Queen Victoria; (reverse) the seated figure of Victory beside a palm tree, with a wreath in one hand and a laurel crown in the other. The medal is suspended by a rococo mount fitted to a plain suspender.
Clasps: The medal was not awarded without a campaign clasp and, unusually, in multi-clasp medals, the last clasp awarded was mounted closest to the medal itself, so that the battle roll has to be read downwards. There were two dies of the reverse, leading to the long- or short-hyphen varieties, both of comparable value. In all, some 4500 medals were awarded, but there is a very wide divergence between the commonest and rarest bars. Multi-clasp medals are rare, and medals awarded to Europeans are much scarcer than those to Indian troops.
Comments: *The last of the medals authorised in connection with the Napoleonic Wars, it was instituted and paid for by the Honourable East India Company in March 1851 for award to surviving veterans of the battles and campaigns in India and Burma between 1803 and 1826. Despite the dates 1799–1826 in the exergue, the medal was in fact awarded for service in one or other of four wars: the Second Mahratta War (1803–4), the Nepal War (1814–16), the Pindaree or Third Mahratta War (1817–18) and the Burmese War (1824–26), together with the siege of Bhurtpoor (1825–26). The medal is scarce, and examples with the clasps for the Second Mahratta War are much sought after, partly because few veterans were still alive 48 years after the event to claim their medals, and partly because of the war's association with Arthur Wellesley, the Duke of Wellington, who died in the very year in which the medal was awarded.*

Rev. die a, short hyphen

Rev. die b, long hyphen

VALUE:
Prices for medals bearing the following clasps are for European recipients. Medals to Indians are generally less expensive.

Allighur (66)	£2000–2500
Battle of Delhi (40)	£2500–2800
Assye (87)	£2000–2500
Asseerghur (48)	£2000–2500
Laswarree (100)	£1000–1200
Argaum (126)	£2000–2500
Gawilghur (110)	£2000–2500
Defence of Delhi (5)	Rare
Battle of Deig (47)	£2200–2500
Capture of Deig (103)	£1800–2200
Nepaul (505)	£550–700
Kirkee (5)	Rare
Poona (75)	£900–1100
Kirkee and Poona (88)	£950–1200
Seetabuldee (2)	Rare
Nagpore (155)	£800–900
Seetabuldee and Nagpore (21)	Rare
Maheidpoor (75)	£1000–1200
Corygaum (4)	Rare
Ava (2325)	£450–500
Bhurtpoor (1059)	£480–550
2 clasps (300)	Rare
3 clasps (150)	Rare
4 clasps (23)	Rare
5 or more clasps (10 x 5, 2 x 6, 1 x 7)	Rare
Miniature	
One clasp Ava	£100–150
Further clasps	£100–150 each

105. GHUZNEE MEDAL

Date: 1839.
Campaign: Ghuznee 1839.
Branch of Service: British and HEIC forces.
Ribbon: 35mm half crimson, half dark green.
Metal: Silver.
Size: 37mm.
Description: (Obverse) the impressive gateway of the fortress of Ghuznee; (reverse) a mural crown enclosed in a laurel wreath with the date of capture.
Comments: *This was the second medal awarded for a particular campaign (after Waterloo) and was granted to both British and Indian troops who took part in the assault on Ghuznee in July 1839 which brought the first Afghan War to a close, overthrew the pro-Russian Dost Mohamed and restored Shah Soojah who instituted the Order of the Dooranie Empire (awarded to British generals and field officers) in appreciation. The Ghuznee medal was issued unnamed by the Honourable East India Company, but many recipients subsequently had their names impressed or engraved in various styles. No clasps were issued officially, but unauthorised clasps are occasionally encountered.*

VALUE:

British recipient	£250–400
Indian recipient	£150–200
Unnamed as issued	£200–250
Miniature	£150–300

106. ST. JEAN D'ACRE MEDAL

Date: 1840.
Campaign: Syria 1840.
Branch of Service: Royal Navy, Royal Marines and British Army.
Ribbon: Red with white edges.
Metal: Gold, silver or copper (bronzed).
Size: 30mm.
Description: (Obverse) a fortress flying the Ottoman flag, with six five-pointed stars round the top. A commemorative inscription and date in Arabic appear at the foot; (reverse) the Toughra of the Sultan in a laurel wreath.
Comments: *Awarded by the Sultan of Turkey to British, Austrian and Turkish forces under Sir Charles Napier, taking part in the liberation of this important city on the Syrian coast after eight years of Egyptian occupation. The medal has a plain ring suspension. The clasp "Syria" to the Naval GSM was awarded in 1848 in respect to this operation, and this medal generally accompanies the St Jean d'Acre medal.*

VALUE:

		Miniature
Gold (captains and field officers)	£500–700	—
Silver (junior officers)	£100–120	£150–200
Copper (petty officers, NCOs and other ranks)	£50–65 —	

107. CANDAHAR, GHUZNEE, CABUL MEDAL

Date: 1842.
Campaign: Afghanistan 1841–42.
Branch of Service: British and HEIC troops.
Ribbon: 40mm watered silk of red, white, yellow, white and blue.
Metal: Silver.
Size: 35mm.
Description: Although the medals have a uniform obverse, a profile of the Queen captioned VICTORIA VINDEX, reverses are inscribed with the names of individual battles, or combinations thereof, within wreaths surmounted by a crown.
Comments: *The Honourable East India Company instituted this series of medals in 1842 for award to both HEIC and British troops who took part in the First Afghan War. The issue of this medal to units of the British Army, to Europeans serving in the Company's forces, and to Indian troops is further complicated by the fact that unnamed medals are generally common. In addition, the medal for Cabul is known in two versions, with the inscription CABUL or CABVL, the latter being a major rarity as only fifteen were issued. Beware of modern copies of the Candahar and Cabul medals.*

VALUE:	Imperial Regiments	Indian Units	Unnamed
Candahar	£400–500	£200–250	£220–250
Cabul	£300–350	£140–180	£150–200
Cabvl (15)	Rare	Rare	Rare
Ghuznee/Cabul	£400–600	£250–300	£200–250
Candahar/Ghuznee/ Cabul	£300–400	£200–250	£200–240
Miniature	from £200		

108. JELLALABAD MEDALS

Type 2 rev.

Type 1 obv.

Date: 1842.
Campaign: Afghanistan 1841-42.
Branch of Service: British and HEIC forces.
Ribbon: 44mm watered silk red, white, yellow, white and blue.
Metal: Silver.
Size: 39mm and 35mm.
Description: There are two different types of this medal, awarded by the HEIC to surviving defenders of the fortress of Jellalabad between 12 November 1841 and 7 April 1842. The first, struck in Calcutta, has a mural crown and JELLALABAD on the obverse, with the date of the relief of the garrison on the reverse; the second type shows the Wyon profile of Victoria (obverse) and the winged Victory with mountain scenery in the background and JELLALABAD VII APRIL round the top and the year in roman numerals in the exergue (reverse).
Comment: *The first type, struck in Calcutta, was considered to be unsuitable and holders were invited to exchange their medals for the second, more attractive, issue which was produced in London, although very few recipients took up the offer. The latter type was also awarded to the next of kin of soldiers killed in action.*

VALUE:	Imperial Regiments	Indian Units	Unnamed	*Miniature*
First type (Crown)	£450–550	£350–450	£380–450	£150–250
Second type (Victory)	£600–800	—	£450–550	£150–250

109. MEDAL FOR THE DEFENCE OF KELAT-I-GHILZIE

Date: 1842.
Campaign: Afghanistan 1842.
Branch of Service: European and native troops, HEIC.
Ribbon: 40mm watered silk red, white, yellow, white and blue.
Metal: Silver.
Size: 36mm.
Description: (Obverse) a shield bearing the name of the fort, surmounted by a mural crown and encircled by laurels; (reverse) a trophy of arms above a tablet inscribed INVICTA (unbeaten) and the date in roman numerals.
Comments: *Awarded to those who took part in the defence of the fort at Kelat-i-Ghilzie in May 1842, it is the rarest medal of the First Afghan War. No British imperial regiments took part, but 55 Europeans in the Company's service received the medal. It was also awarded to 877 native troops (including a contingent supplied by Shah Soojah) but few of their medals appear to have survived.*

VALUE:

European recipients	£4500–5500
Indian recipients	£1800–2300
Unnamed	£600–800
Miniature	£250–300

110. CHINA WAR MEDAL

Issued reverse

Date: 1842.
Campaign: China 1841-42.
Branch of Service: British and HEIC forces.
Ribbon: 39mm crimson with yellow edges.
Metal: Silver.
Size: 36mm.
Description: The medal has the usual Wyon obverse, but the reverse was to have shown a British lion with its forepaws on a dragon. This was deemed to be offensive to the Chinese and was replaced by an oval shield bearing the royal arms, a palm tree and a trophy of weapons with the Latin motto ARMIS EXPOSCERE PACEM (to pray for peace by force of arms) round the top and CHINA 1842 at the foot.
Comments: *Originally intended for issue to all ranks of the Honourable East India Company, it was subsequently awarded by the British government in 1843 to all who had taken part in the campaign in China popularly known as the First Opium War which ended with the seizure of Nanking.*

VALUE:

Royal Navy	£220–250
Indian and Bengal marine units	£250–350
British imperial regiments	£220–250
Indian Army	£160–180
Specimens of the original reverse	From £500
Miniature	£150–250

111. SCINDE MEDAL

Date: 1843.
Campaign: Scinde 1843.
Branch of Service: HEIC forces and 22nd Foot.
Ribbon: 44mm watered silk red, white, yellow, white and blue.
Metal: Silver.
Size: 36mm.
Description: The usual Wyon profile obverse was married to three different reverse types showing a crowned laurel wreath inscribed with the name of one or two campaigns and the date.
Comments: *Authorised in September 1843, this silver medal marked Sir Charles Napier's conquest of Scinde. The two major battles in the campaign, at Meeanee and Hyderabad, accomplished the complete rout of the forces of the Amirs of Scinde. The medals were originally issued with steel suspenders but the commanding officer of the 22nd Foot had the medals awarded to his men fitted with silver suspenders, at his own expense. Medals to the Indus Flotilla are particularly sought after by collectors.*

VALUE:

	22nd Foot	Indian units	HEIC ships
Meeanee	£600–800	£250–350	£1000–1100 (38)
Hyderabad	£500–600	£200–250	£1000–1100 (52)
Meeanee/Hyderabad	£400–500	£200–250	
Miniature	£150–250		

112. GWALIOR STAR

Date: 1843.
Campaign: Gwalior 1843.
Branch of Service: British and HEIC forces.
Ribbon: 44mm watered silk red, white, yellow, white and blue.
Metals: Bronze, with a silver centre.
Size: Max. width 45mm; max. height 52mm.
Description: Six-pointed bronze star with a silver centre star. The silver stars in the centre bear the name of one or other of the battles and the date 29 December 1843 on which both battles were fought. The plain reverse bears the name and regiment of the recipient.
Comments: *Bronze from guns captured at the battles of Maharajpoor and Punniar during the Gwalior campaign was used in the manufacture of these stars, thus anticipating the production of the Victoria Cross in the same manner. They were presented by the Indian government to all ranks who took part in these actions. When first issued, these stars were fitted with hooks to be worn like a breast decoration, but later ornate bar or ring suspensions were fitted to individual fancy and worn with the standard Indian ribbon of the period.*

VALUE:

		Miniature	
Maharajpoor	£250–300	£100–150	
Punniar	£280–340	£150–200	

Awards to Indian recipients are usually somewhat less.

113. SUTLEJ MEDAL

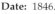

Date: 1846.
Campaign: Sutlej 1845-46.
Branch of Service: British and HEIC forces.
Ribbon: Dark blue with crimson edges.
Metal: Silver.
Size: 36mm.
Description: (Obverse) Wyon profile of Queen Victoria; (reverse) standing figure of Victory holding aloft a laurel crown, with a pile of captured weapons at her feet. The legend ARMY OF THE SUTLEJ appears round the top. The medal was fitted with an ornamental scroll suspender.
Clasps: Mounted above the suspender with roses between: Ferozeshuhur, Aliwal or Sobraon.
Comments: *The practice of issuing medals inscribed with different battles now gave way to the style of medals with specific battle or campaign clasps which set the precedent for the Naval and Military GSMs and later awards. As a compromise, however, the exergue of the reverse bears the name and date of the action for which the medal was first granted, and thus several different types are known.*

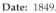

VALUE:	British regiments	Europeans in HEIC units	Indian units
Moodkee	£140–180	£120-140	£100–120
Moodkee 1 clasp	£180–220	£160–180	£140–160
Moodkee 2 clasps	£280–320	£200–240	£180–220
Moodkee 3 clasps	£400–450	£350–400	£240–280
Ferozeshuhur	£140–160	£150–200	£120–140
Ferozeshuhur 1 clasp	£220–250	£180–220	£150–180
Ferozeshuhur 2 clasps	£280–320	£300–350	£150–180
Aliwal	£160–180	£160–180	£120–140
Aliwal 1 clasp	£200–220	£180–200	£120–140
Sobraon	£180–200	£140–160	£80–120
Glazed gilt specimen	£250–300		
Miniature	£100–150, for each clasp add £50		

114. PUNJAB MEDAL

Date: 1849.
Campaign: Punjab 1848-49.
Branch of Service: British and HEIC forces.
Ribbon: Dark blue with yellow stripes towards the edges.
Metal: Silver.
Size: 36mm.
Description: (Obverse) Wyon profile of Queen Victoria; (reverse) Sir Walter Gilbert receiving the Sikh surrender. TO THE ARMY OF THE PUNJAB appears round the top and the year in roman numerals in the exergue. The medal has a scroll suspender.
Clasps: Mooltan, Chilianwala, Goojerat. Unusually the clasps read downwards from top to bottom
Comments: *This medal was granted to troops taking part in the campaigns which ended in the annexation of the Punjab. Unlike the Sutlej medal, however, this silver medal had a standard design. Large numbers of this medal were awarded to native troops, however many were melted down and therefore surprisingly few remain on the market in comparison with medals to European recipients.*

VALUE:	British units	Europeans in HEIC units	Indian units
No clasp	£100–140	£80–100	£60–80
Mooltan	£170–190	£140–160	£100–120
Chilianwala	£180–220	£140–160	£100–120
Goojerat	£170–190	£160–180	£140–160
Mooltan/Goojerat	£180–220	£180–200	£140–160
Chilianwala/Goojerat	£180–220	£180–200	£140–160
24th Foot casualty at Chilianwala	£320–360	—	—
Glazed gilt specimen	£250–300		
Miniature	£50–75, for each clasp add £25		

115. SOUTH AFRICA MEDAL

Date: 1854.
Campaigns: Southern Africa 1834–53.
Branch of Service: Royal Navy and Army.
Ribbon: Gold with broad and narrow deep blue stripes towards each end.
Metal: Silver.
Size: 36mm.
Description: (Obverse) Wyon profile of Queen Victoria; (reverse) a British lion drinking at a waterhole beside a protea shrub, the date 1853 being in the exergue.
Clasps: None.
Comments: *Authorised in November 1854, this medal was awarded in respect of three campaigns in southern Africa: 1834–35, 1846–47 and 1850–53, but as the medal was issued with a standard reverse and no campaign clasps it is impossible to tell when and where the recipient served without reference to the medal rolls. The majority of recipients were British troops but several hundred sailors of the Royal Navy also received the medal and a much smaller number of local forces. Of particular interest are medals awarded to men who survived the sinking of the troopship* Birkenhead *on its way to the Eastern Cape from Simons Town.*

VALUE:

	1834–35	1846–47	1850–53
British Army	£250–300	£220–270	£200–230
Royal Navy	£280–320	£250–290	£180–220
HMS *Birkenhead*			From £500
Local forces	£260–280	£230–250	£150–180
Miniature	£50–65	£50–65	£50–65

116. SIR HARRY SMITH'S MEDAL FOR GALLANTRY

Date: 1851.
Campaign: Eighth Kaffir War 1850-51.
Branch of Service: Cape Mounted Rifles.
Ribbon: Dark blue with crimson edges.
Metal: Silver.
Size: 34mm.
Description: (Obverse) British lion passant gardant with a laurel wreath over its head; date 1851 in the exergue. (Reverse) PRESENTED BY round top and FOR GALLANTRY IN THE FIELD round the foot. HIS EXCELLENCY SIR H. G. SMITH and the name of the recipient appear across the centre.
Comments: *Sir Harry Smith (1787–1860) served with distinction in the Kaffir War of 1834–35, gained his KCB in the Gwalior campaign and a baronetcy for his decisive victory at Aliwal in the Sikh War. In 1847 he returned to South Africa as governor of Cape Colony. Although short of troops he conducted the eighth Frontier War (1850–53) with great resourcefulness but was recalled to England in 1852 before the Xhosas had been subdued. Harrismith in the Orange Free State was named in his honour, while Ladysmith in Natal was named after his beautiful and spirited Spanish wife Juanita, the forces' sweetheart of her day. Sir Harry had this medal struck at his own expense and awarded to troopers of the Cape Mounted Rifles who took part in the epic ride through the enemy lines from Fort Cox to Kingwilliamstown in 1851. Only 31 medals were presented, of which 22 are believed to be still extant.*

VALUE:

Unnamed	£1200–1500
Named	£2000–3000

117. INDIA GENERAL SERVICE MEDAL

Date: 1854.

Campaigns: Indian 1854-95.

Branch of Service: British and Indian forces.

Ribbon: Three crimson and two dark blue bars of equal width.

Metal: Silver or bronze.

Size: 36mm.

Description: (Obverse) Wyon profile of Queen Victoria; (reverse) Victory crowning a semi-nude seated warrior.

Clasps: 24 (see below).

Comments: *This medal was the first of five general service medals issued to cover minor campaigns in India. It was instituted in 1854 and continued for forty-one years, retaining the original Wyon profile of Queen Victoria throughout the entire period. Although the medal itself is quite common, some of its clasps are very rare, notably* Kachin Hills 1892–93 *awarded to the Yorkshire Regiment and* Chin Hills 1892–93 *awarded to the Norfolk Regiment. The maximum number of clasps to one medal recorded is seven. At first the medal was awarded in silver to all ranks regardless of race or branch of the services, but from 1885 onwards it was issued in bronze to native support personnel such as bearers, sweepers and drivers.*

VALUE:

	British Army	Indian Army	Bronze
Pegu	£80–100	—	—
Persia	£80–100	£55–65	—
North West Frontier	£80–100	£50–60	—
Umbeyla	£80–100	£55–65	—
Bhootan	£80–100	£50–60	—
Looshai	—	£100–110	—
Perak	£80–100	£70–80	—
Jowaki 1877–78	£80–10	£60–70	—
Naga 1879–80	—	£130–150	—
Burma 1885–87	£60–80	£55–65	£50–60
Sikkim 1888	£120–140	£60–70	£80–100
Hazara 1888	£80–100	£80–90	£75–90
Burma 1887–89	£60–80	£40–50	£50–60
Burma 1887–9	£80–100	—	—
Chin Lushai 1889–90	£100–120	£40–50	£110–130
Lushai 1889-92	£280–320	£120–150	£170–190
Samana 1891	£80–100	£50–60	£60–70
Hazara 1891	£80–100	£40–50	£50–60
NE Frontier 1891	£90–110	£40–50	£80–90
Hunza 1891	—	£180–200	£350–380
Burma 1889–92	£70–90	£55–65	£50–60
Chin Hills 1892-93	£320–360	£110–130	£320–350
Kachin Hills 1892-93	£450–500	£180-200	£700–750
Waziristan 1894-95	£80–90	£40–50	£40–50

Miniature

£20–30, for each clasp add £10 (Hunza, Chin Hills and Kachin Hills clasps are rare)

118. BALTIC MEDAL

Date: 1856.
Campaign: Baltic Sea 1854–55.
Branch of Service: Royal Navy, Royal Marines and Royal Sappers and Miners.
Ribbon: Yellow with light blue edges.
Metal: Silver.
Size: 36mm.
Description: (Obverse) Wyon profile of Queen Victoria; (reverse) Britannia seated on a plinth decorated by a cannon, with a coastal scene in the background and BALTIC round the top.
Comments: *Authorised in 1856, this medal was granted to officers and men of the Royal Navy and Royal Marines for operations against Russia in the Baltic at the same time as the war in the Crimea. It was also awarded to about 100 members of the Royal Sappers and Miners engaged in the demolition of Russian fortifications of Bomarsund and Sveaborg. Medals were generally issued unnamed but often privately named afterwards, the exception being medals to the Sappers and Miners which were officially impressed.*

VALUE:

Unnamed	£60–70
Privately named	£70–90
Officially impressed to Sappers and Miners	£600–800
Miniature	£15–20

119. CRIMEA MEDAL

Date: 1854.
Campaign: Crimea 1854–56.
Branch of Service: British Army, Navy and Marines.
Ribbon: Pale blue with yellow edges.
Metal: Silver.
Size: 36mm.
Description: (Obverse) Wyon profile of Queen Victoria; (reverse) a Roman soldier, armed with circular shield and short sword, being crowned by a flying Victory.
Clasps: Unusually ornate, being shaped like oak leaves with acorn finials: Alma, Inkerman, Azoff, Balaklava, Sebastopol, but the maximum found on any medal is four. Unofficial clasps for Traktir, Mamelon Vert, Malakoff, Mer d'Azoff and Kinburn are sometimes found on medals awarded to French troops.
Comments: *Medals may be found unnamed, unofficially or regimentally named, or officially impressed. Medals awarded to participants in the most famous actions of the war—the Thin Red Line (93rd Foot) and the Charge of the Light and Heavy Brigades—rate a very high premium. The prices quoted are for medals officially impressed to the Army.*

VALUE :

No clasp	£80–120
Alma	£140–160
Inkerman	£150–170
Azoff	£110–130
Balaklava	£160–180
93rd Foot	£600–700
Heavy Bde	£600–700
Light Bde (Charger)	£3500–4000
Sebastopol	£80–120
2 clasps	£150–180
3 clasps	£200–250
4 clasps	£400–450
Miniature	£15–20, for each clasp add £10

120. TURKISH CRIMEA MEDAL

Date: 1855.
Campaign: Crimea 1855-56.
Branch of Service: British, French and Sardinian forces.
Ribbon: Crimson with green edges.
Metal: Silver.
Size: 36mm.
Description: (Obverse) a cannon, weapons and the four Allied flags with the name and date in the exergue; (reverse) the Toughra and Arabic date according to the Moslem calendar.
Clasps: None.
Comments: *Instituted by the Sultan of Turkey, this silver medal was conferred on troops of the three Allies who fought in the Crimea. The obverse types differed in the arrangement of the flags, corrsponding with the inscription in English, French or Italian in the exergue. Although the medals were intended to be issued to British, French and Sardinian troops respectively, they were issued haphazardly. They were unnamed, but many were privately engraved or impressed later. There is a dangerous copy emanating from the West Country of the UK.*

VALUE:		*Miniature*
CRIMEA (British Issue)	£50–60	£12–18
LA CRIMEE (French Issue)	£120–180	£12–18
LA CRIMEA (Sardinia Issue)	£45–55	£10–15

121. INDIAN MUTINY MEDAL

Date: 1858.
Campaign: Sepoy mutiny, India 1857-58.
Branch of Service: British Army, Navy and Indian forces.
Ribbon: White with two red stripes.
Metal: Silver.
Size: 36mm.
Description: (Obverse) Wyon profile of Queen Victoria; (reverse) the standing figure of Britannia bestowing victor's laurels, with the British lion alongside. INDIA appears round the top with the dates 1857-1858 in the exergue.
Clasps: Delhi, Defence of Lucknow, Relief of Lucknow, Lucknow, Central India. The maximum recorded for a single medal is four (Bengal Artillery) or three (imperial troops, 9th Lancers).
Comments: *This medal was awarded to troops who took part in operations to quell the Sepoy mutiny which had been the immediate cause of the uprising, although it also served to focus attention on the Honourable East India Company's conduct of affairs and led directly to the transfer of the administration of India to the Crown. Medals with the clasp for the defence of Lucknow awarded to the original defenders rate a considerable premium, as do medals awarded to members of the Naval Brigade which witnessed most of the fighting in the mopping-up operations.*

VALUE:

	British Navy	British Army	*Miniature*
No clasp	£350–450	£70–100	£12–15
Delhi	—	£140–180	£15–25
Defence of Lucknow			
original defender	—	£500–600	£35–45
first relief force	—	£300–350	
Relief of Lucknow	£500–600	£140–180	£15–25
Lucknow	£500–600	£120–150	£15–25
Central India	—	£120–150	£15–20, add
2 clasps	£600–700	£220–250	£10 for each
3 clasps (9th Lancers)	—	£450–500	additional clasp

*Medals to Indian recipients although scarcer on the market, generally bring a little less than their British counterparts. Four clasp medals to the Bengal Artillery bring from £800 if verified.

122. SECOND CHINA WAR MEDAL

Date: 1861.
Campaign: Second China War 1857-60.
Branch of Service: British Army and Navy.
Ribbon: 33mm crimson with yellow edges.
Metal: Silver.
Size: 36mm.
Description: As the First China War Medal (no. 110), but without the year 1842 at the foot.
Clasps: Fatshan 1857, Canton 1857, Taku Forts, Pekin 1860.
Comments: *This medal was awarded to British sevicemen who took part, alongside the French, in the campaign against China which had been provoked by hostile acts against European nationals. The Royal Navy, under Admiral Sir Michael Seymour, destroyed a Chinese flotilla at Fatshan Creek, preparing the way for the attack on Canton whose capture brought the first phase to an end in June 1858. Reinforcements were meanwhile diverted to help put down the Indian mutiny. Fighting broke out again and this time large numbers of troops were involved in the assault on the Taku forts and the sack of Pekin (Beijing). Examples of the China medal of 1842, with or without clasps for 1857-60, have been recorded to recipients who fought in the Second China War. Medals may be found unnamed or with names officially engraved (Indian Army) or impressed (British Army, India Marine). Although those to the Navy were all issued unnamed, they are occasionally encountered unofficially named. Awards to Army and Navy personnel are other factors governing values.*

VALUE:		Miniature
No clasp	£60–70	£18
China 1842	Rare	—
Fatshan 1857	£70–90	£45
Canton 1857	£130–160	£35
Taku Forts 1858	£70–90	£30
Taku Forts 1860	£120–140	£40
Pekin 1860	£120–140	£30
2 clasps	£200–240	£55
3 clasps	£180–220	£65

123. NEW ZEALAND MEDALS

Date: 1869.

Campaigns: First and Second Maori Wars 1845–47 and 1860–66.

Branch of Service: Army, Navy and local volunteers.

Ribbon: Blue with a central orange stripe.

Metal: Silver.

Size: 36mm.

Description: (Obverse) Veiled head of Queen Victoria. (Reverse) Date of service in a wreath, with NEW ZEALAND round the top and VIRTUTIS HONOR (honour of valour) round the foot. Suspender ornamented with New Zealand wattle.

Comments: *These medals were unusual in having the recipient's dates of service die-struck on the centre of the reverse, though medals were also issued without dates. As the medal was only awarded to surviving veterans, the numbers issued in respect of the earlier conflict are understandably small. Many of the dates are very scarce, especially those issued to naval personnel in the first war.*

VALUE:

First war

Undated	£160–180
1845–46	£275–300
1845–47	£300–330
1846–47	£320–350
1846	£550–600
1847	£450–500
1848	Rare

Second war

Undated	£150–165
1860	£550–600
1860-61	£200–240
1860-63	From £1500
1860-64	£210–250
1860-65	£200–240
1860-66	£210–250
1861	Rare
1861-63	Rare
1861-64	£220–275
1861-65	Rare
1861-66	£150–190
1862-66	Rare
1863	£450–500
1863-64	£200–240
1863-65	£190–220
1863-66	£190–220
1864	£210–250
1864-65	£190–210
1864-66	£150–175
1865	£330–360
1865-66	£180–200
1866	£180–200

Miniature	
Undated	£45
Dated	£60+

124. ABYSSINIAN WAR MEDAL

Date: 1869.
Campaign: Abyssinia (Ethiopia) 1867–68.
Branch of Service: Royal Navy, British and Indian Armies.
Ribbon: Red with broad white edges.
Metal: Silver.
Size: 33mm diameter.
Description: (Obverse) the veiled portrait of Victoria framed by a zigzag pattern with floral ornament alternating with the letters of the name ABYSSINIA. The recipient's name and unit were embossed in the centre of the reverse except most to Indian troops which were impressed. Suspension is by a ring via a large crown standing proud from the top of the medal.
Clasps: None.
Comments: *The imprisonment of British subjects by King Theodore of Abyssinia precipitated a punitive expedition under General Sir Robert Napier involving ships of the Royal Navy, a naval brigade and troops of the British and Indian armies. Because casualties were unusually light (only two killed and 27 wounded), medals from this campaign are not so highly rated as those from other nineteenth century wars.*

VALUE:

British troops	£140–180
Royal Navy	£140–160
RN Rocket Brigade	£250–300
Indian troops	£80–120
Miniature	£70

125. CANADA GENERAL SERVICE MEDAL

Date: 1899.
Campaign: Canada 1866–70.
Branch of Service: Royal Navy, British Army and Canadian units.
Ribbon: Red, white and red.
Metal: Silver.
Size: 36mm.
Description: (Obverse) crowned and veiled Old Head bust of Queen Victoria by Sir Thomas Brock (reflecting the very late issue of the medal). (Reverse) Canadian flag surrounded by maple leaves.
Clasps: Fenian Raid 1866, Fenian Raid 1870, Red River 1870.
Comments: *This medal was not authorised until January 1899, thirty years after the event, and was issued by the Canadian government to British and Canadian local forces who took part in operations to put down the Fenian raids of 1866 and 1870 and the Red River rebellion of the latter year. Of the 16,100 medals awarded, 15,000 went to local forces. Naval medals command a premium.*

VALUE:

	Canadian forces	British Army	Royal Navy	*Miniature*
Fenian Raid 1866	£130–150	£160–180	£180–220	£60
Fenian Raid 1870	£140–160	£180–200	—	£65
Red River 1870	£450–500	£550–650	—	£85
2 clasps	£200–220	—	—	£80
3 clasps	Rare	—	—	—

126. ASHANTEE MEDAL

Date: 1874.
Campaign: Gold Coast 1873–74.
Branch of Service: Royal Navy, Army and native troops.
Ribbon: Orange with black bars at the sides and two narrow black stripes towards the centre.
Metal: Silver.
Size: 36mm.
Description: The obverse and reverse are similar to the East and West Africa Medal of 1887–1900, differing solely in thickness and the method of naming. The veiled profile of Victoria graces the obverse while the reverse, designed by Sir Edwin Poynter, shows a skirmish in the jungle between British soldiers and Ashantee warriors.
Clasps: Coomassie.
Comments: *All ranks who took part in operations against King Kalkali of Ashantee, Gold Coast, were awarded this medal, approved in June 1874. The campaign lasted only four weeks but was fought with great ferocity and resulted in the award of four VCs. There was also a very high incidence of sickness and disease among the troops, notably the naval contingent. Unusually the medals are named in engraved capitals filled in with black.*

VALUE:

	Navy	Army	Natives	Miniature
No clasp	£100–110	£120–140	£70–90	£30
Coomassie	£180–220	£220–240	£100–130	£65

127. SOUTH AFRICA MEDAL

Date: 1879.
Campaign: South Africa 1877-79.
Branch of Service: Royal Navy, Army and colonial units.
Ribbon: Gold with thin dark blue stripes towards the edges and two thick dark blue stripes towards the centre.
Metal: Silver.
Size: 36mm.
Description: The same design as no. 115, except that the date 1853 in the exergue is replaced by a Zulu shield and four crossed assegais.
Clasps: 1877, 1877–8, 1877–9, 1877–8–9, 1878, 1878–9, 1879.
Comments: *The campaign began in 1877 with an attack on the Fingoes by the Galeka and Gaika tribes and culminated in the showdown between the Zulus and the British when Lord Chelmsford's column was annihilated at Isandhlwana. When the 3000 Zulus advanced on Rorke's Drift, however, they were checked with heavy losses by a tiny garrison of 139 men. During the defence no fewer than eleven VCs were won—the largest number for a single action. The campaign concluded with the defeat of Dinizulu and his warriors at Ulundi.*

VALUE:

	Navy	Army	Colonial	Miniature
No clasp	£100–140	£100–120	£80–100	£25
1877	—	Rare	£1100–1300	—
1877–8	£350–450	£200–250	£170–190	£40
1877–9	—	Unique	£4000–5000	—
1877–8–9	£400–500	£260–280	£170–190	£35
1878	—	£250–300	£180–200	£40
1878–9	£250–300	£250–280	£180–200	£35
1879	£160–180	£200–250	£150–180	£35
Isandhlwana casualty	£1650–2000			
Rorke's Drift participant	From £7500			

128. AFGHANISTAN MEDAL

Date: 1878.
Campaign: Afghanistan 1878–80.
Branch of Service: British and Indian Armies.
Ribbon: Dark green with broad crimson edges.
Metal: Silver or bronze.
Size: 36mm.
Description: (Obverse) veiled profile of Queen Victoria. (Reverse) a column on the march, with an elephant carrying cannon. The dates 1878–79–80 appear in the exergue.
Clasps: Ali Musjid, Peiwar Kotal, Charasia, Kabul, Ahmed Kel, Kandahar. Maximum number of clasps per medal is four.
Comments: *This medal was awarded to all who took part in the campaigns against Afghanistan known as the Second Afghan War. In 1877 the Amir refused to accept a British resident and the following year raised an army which began harrassing the Indian frontier. A treaty with Russia, however, granting it protective rights in Afghanistan, precipitated an armed response from Britain. In 1880 General Roberts led a column from Kabul to Kandahar to relieve General Burrows and the resulting battle led to the defeat of the Afghans and the conclusion of the war. Medals awarded to the 66th Foot (Berkshire regiment) and E Battery of B Brigade, Royal Artillery rate a high premium as these units sustained the heaviest casualties at the battle of Maiwand in July 1880.*

VALUE:	British units	Indian units	*Miniature*
No clasp bronze	—	£140–180	—
No clasp silver	£50–60	—	£20
Ali Musjid	£100–110	£40–60	£30
Periwar Kotal	£120–140	£40–60	£40
Charasia	£100–120	£40–60	£30
Kabul	£100–120	£40–60	£25
Ahmed Khel	£100–130	£40–60	£30
Kandahar	£100–120	£40–60	£30
2 clasps	£140–160	£60–80	£50
3 clasps	£200–250	£100–120	£65
4 clasps	£350–400	£140–180	£80
Maiwand casualties:			
66th Foot	£550–650	—	
E Bty, B Bde RA	£500–600	—	

129. KABUL TO KANDAHAR STAR

Date: 1880.
Campaign: Afghanistan 1878–80.
Branch of Service: British and Indian Armies.
Ribbon: Watered silk red, white, yellow, white and blue.
Metal: Bronze from captured guns.
Size: Height 60mm, width 45mm.
Description: (Obverse) a rayed five-pointed star surmounted by a crown with a ring for suspension. The centre is inscribed KABUL TO KANDAHAR with 1880 at the foot and the VRI monogram of the Queen Empress in the centre. Stars were either issued unnamed, or had the recipient's name impressed (to British) or engraved (to Indian troops) on the reverse.
Clasps: None.
Comments: *This star, struck by Jenkins of Birmingham, was awarded to those who took part in the epic 300-mile march from the Afghan capital to Kandahar, led by General Roberts to relieve the beleaguered forces of General Burrows.*

VALUE:	
Unnamed	£70–80
Impressed (British troops)	£120–130
Engraved (Indian troops)	£70–90
Miniature	£50

Maiwand (see no. 128)

130. CAPE OF GOOD HOPE GENERAL SERVICE MEDAL

Date: 1900.
Campaign: Uprisings in Transkei, Basutoland and Bechuanaland 1880-97.
Branch of Service: Local forces and volunteers.
Ribbon: Dark blue with a central yellow stripe.
Metal: Silver.
Size: 36mm.
Description: (Obverse) Jubilee bust of Queen Victoria by Sir Joseph Boehm; (reverse) arms of Cape Colony.
Clasps: Transkei, Basutoland, Bechuanaland.
Comments: *Instituted by the Cape government, this medal acknowledged service in putting down the Transkei (1880-1) and Bechuana (1896-7) rebellions and dealing with the unrest that erupted sporadically in Basutoland for much of this period. The medal was awarded, with one or more campaign clasps, to local forces and volunteer regiments. Ten medals were, however, officially awarded without a clasp.*

VALUE:

		Miniature
Transkei (1070)	£220–260	£50
Basutoland (2150)	£120–140	£50
Bechuanaland (2580)	£120–140	£45
2 clasps	£180–220	£65
3 clasps (23)	Rare	—
No clasp	Very rare	

131. EGYPT MEDAL

Dated rev.

Undated rev.

Date: 1882.
Campaign: Egypt 1882–89.
Branch of Service: Royal Navy and Army.
Ribbon: Three blue and two white stripes.
Metal: Silver.
Size: 36mm.
Description: (Obverse) the veiled profile of Queen Victoria; (reverse) the Sphinx.
Clasps: 13, listed below. Maximum number for one medal is 7, but only one such award was made. Common two-clasp combinations are denoted below by /.
Comments: *British involvement in Egypt deepened after the opening of the Suez Canal in 1869, many British officers being seconded to the Khedive's Army. When the Army mutinied in 1882 and triggered off a general anti-European uprising, an Anglo-French expedition was mounted. Subsequently the French withdrew before a landing was effected. Trouble erupted in the Sudan (under Anglo-Egyptian administration) in 1884 where General Gordon was besieged at Khartoum. Further campaigns aimed at the overthrow of the Mahdi and the reconquest of the Sudan. These prolonged operations created immense logistical problems. Nile transportation in particular was a matter resolved only when Canadian* voyageurs *were recruited to handle the river-boats. In addition, a contingent of troops from New South Wales "answered the Empire's call" and medals awarded to them for the Suakin campaign of 1885 are much sought after. Except where noted, the prices quoted below are for medals awarded to British Army personnel. Medals awarded to Indian or Egyptian troops are generally worth about 25 per cent less than comparable awards to British Army units.*

VALUE:		Miniature
No clasp (dated)	£35–45	£15
No clasp (undated)	£40–50	£20
Alexandria 11th July	£85–100	£22
Tel-el-Kebir	£100–120	£22
El-Teb	£100–120	£35
Tamaai	£130–150	£30
El-Teb/Tamaai	£120–130	£30
Suakin 1884	£75–90	£25
The Nile 1884-85	£80–95	£25
The Nile 1884-85/Abu Klea	£450–550	£30
The Nile 1884-85/Kirbekan	£130–150	£30
Suakin 1885	£85–100	£25
Suakin 1885/Tofrek	£120–150	£35
Gemaizah 1888	£100–120	£40
Toski 1889	£130–160	£50
2 clasps	£120–150	£40
3 clasps	£180–220	£50
4 clasps	£250–300	£60
5 clasps	£450–550	—
Canadian boatmen	£900–1000	
NSW units (Suakin 1885)	From £600	

132. KHEDIVE'S STAR

Date: 1882.
Campaign: Egypt 1892-91.
Branch of Service: Royal Navy and Army.
Ribbon: 37mm deep blue.
Metal: Bronze.
Size: Height 60mm; width 45mm.
Description: A five-pointed star with a circular centre showing the Sphinx and Pyramids surrounded by a band inscribed EGYPT followed by a year round the top, with 'Khedive of Egypt' and the year in the Moslem calendar in Arabic at the foot. (Reverse) the Khedive's monogram surmounted by a crown. The star is suspended by a ring from an ornamental clasp in the centre of which is a star and crescent.
Clasps: Tokar.
Comments: *This star, struck by Jenkins of Birmingham, was conferred by Khedive Tewfik of Egypt on those who qualified for the Egypt medal and it was invariably worn alongside, to the detriment of the silver medal which suffered abrasion from the points of the star. There was also an undated version found with or without a campaign clasp for Tokar, awarded in 1891. These stars were issued unnamed.*

VALUE:		*Miniature*
1882	£35–45	£10
1884	£45–50	£12
1884-86	£40–50	£12
Undated	£45–60	£12
Undated with Tokar bar	£120–140	£60

133. GENERAL GORDON'S STAR FOR THE SIEGE OF KHARTOUM

Date: 1884.
Campaign: Mahdist uprising, Sudan 1884.
Branch of Service: British and Sudanese forces.
Ribbon: Deep blue.
Metal: Silver or pewter.
Size: Height 80mm; maximum width 54mm.
Description: Star with three concentric circles and seven groups of rays on which are superimposed seven crescents and stars. Suspension by a ring from a Crescent and Star ornament.
Clasps: None.
Comments: *To boost the morale of the defenders Charles Gordon, commanding the garrison at Khartoum, had this star cast locally in a sand mould, using his own breast star of the Order of Mejidieh as the model. Exceptionally, recipients had to purchase their medals, the proceeds going to a fund to feed the poor.*

VALUE:	
Pewter	£300–350
Silver	£600–800
Silver gilt	£900–1200

134. NORTH WEST CANADA MEDAL

Date: 1885.
Campaign: Riel's rebellion 1885.
Branch of Service: Mainly local forces.
Ribbon: Blue-grey with red stripes towards the edges.
Metal: Silver.
Size: 36mm.
Description: (Obverse) bust of Queen Victoria; (reverse) the inscription NORTH WEST CANADA 1885 within a frame of maple leaves.
Clasps: Saskatchewan,
Comments: *Paradoxically, while the medal for the Fenian Raids of 1866–70 was not sanctioned till 1899, this medal for service in the North West was authorised immediately after the conclusion of operations against the Metis led by Louis Riel. It was issued unnamed, with or without the clasp for Saskatchewan where the bulk of the action took place. Of particular interest are medals to officers and men aboard the steamship Northcote involved in a boat action; exceptionally, their medals were impressed. Other medals may be encountered with unofficial naming. The medal was awarded to sixteen British staff officers but the majority of medals (5600 in all) went to local forces.*

VALUE:		Miniature
No clasp	£165–200	£35
Saskatchewan	£420–460	£65
Northcote recipient	£650–700	

135. ROYAL NIGER COMPANY'S MEDAL

Date: 1899.
Campaign: Nigeria 1886–97.
Branch of Service: Officers and men of the Company's forces.
Ribbon: Three equal stripes of yellow, black and white.
Metal: Silver or bronze.
Size: 39.5mm.
Description: (Obverse) the Boehm bust of Queen Victoria; (reverse) the Company's arms in a laurel wreath.
Clasps: Nigeria 1886-97 (silver), Nigeria (bronze).
Comments: *This medal was issued in silver to Europeans and bronze to natives for service in the vast territories administered by the Royal Niger chartered company. Silver medals were impressed in capitals, but those in bronze were more usually stamped with the recipient's service (constabulary) number. Specimens of both versions were later struck from the original dies but these lack name or number.*

VALUE:		Miniature
Silver named (85)	£1500–2000	
Original Silver specimen	£80–100	£130
Bronze named (250)	£450–500	
Original Bronze specimen	£60–80	—

136. IMPERIAL BRITISH EAST AFRICA COMPANY'S MEDAL

Date: 1890.
Campaign: East Africa (Kenya and Uganda) 1888–95.
Branch of Service: Company forces.
Ribbon: Plain blue.
Metal: Silver.
Size: 39mm.
Description: (Obverse) the Company badge, a crowned and radiant sun, with a Suaheli inscription in Arabic round the foot signifying "the reward of bravery"; (reverse) plain except for a wreath. Suspension is by a plain ring or an ornamental scroll.
Comments: *The rarest of the medals awarded by the chartered companies, this medal was originally intended solely as a gallantry award; but after the BEA Company was wound up in 1895 further issues were authorised by the Foreign Office for service in Witu (1890) and the Ugandan civil war (1890-91). Less than thirty medals are known.*

VALUE: From £600   *Miniature* £150

137. EAST AND WEST AFRICA MEDAL

Date: 1887.
Campaigns: East and West Africa 1887–1900.
Branch of Service: Royal Navy, Army and native forces.
Ribbon: Yellow with broad black bars at the edges and two thin black bars towards the centre (as for Ashantee Medal).
Metal: Silver or bronze.
Size: 36mm.
Description: As for the Ashantee Medal (q.v.), distinguished only by its clasps.
Clasps: 21 (see below). A 22nd operation (Mwele, 1895–96) was denoted by engraving on the rim of the medal.
Comments: *This medal was awarded for general service in a number of small campaigns and punitive expeditions. Though usually awarded in silver, it was sometimes struck in bronze for issue to native servants, bearers and drivers. British regiments as such were not involved in any of the actions, but individual officers and NCOs were seconded as staff officers and instructors and their medals bear the names of their regiments. Units of the Royal Navy were also involved in many of the coastal or river actions. Especially sought after are naval medals with the bar for Lake Nyassa 1893 in which the ships* Pioneer *and* Adventure *were hauled in sections overland through 200 miles of jungle.*

VALUE:

	Royal Navy	Europeans	Natives	*Miniature*
1887–8	£350–450	£130–140	£100–120	£40
Witu 1890	£120–140	£130–160	£80–100	£40
1891–2	£170–190	£140–160	£100–120	£40
1892	£130–150	£160–180	£100–120	£40
Witu August 1893	£150–180	—	£110–130	£60
Liwondi 1893	£1500–2000	—	—	—
Juba River 1893	£1500–2000	—	—	—
Lake Nyassa 1893	£1500–2000	—	—	—
1893–94	£150–200	£140–160	£90–110	£50
Gambia 1894	£120–140	—	£100–120	£45
Benin River 1894	£120–140	£120–140	£90–110	£40
Brass River 1895	£180–200	—	—	£45
M'wele 1895–6	£100–120	£100–120	£80–100	£100
1896–98	—	£300–350	£150–200	£30
Niger 1897	—	£250–300	£150–200	£30
Benin 1897	£100–120	£100–120	£150–200	£35
Dawkita 1897	—	Rare	Rare	—
1897–98	—	£130–150	£120–130	£40
1898	£600–800	£140–170	£120–140	£40
Sierra Leone 1898–99	£140–180	£130–160	£80–100	£30
1899	—	£220–250	£150–170	£35
1900	—	£200–220	£130–150	£35

138. BRITISH SOUTH AFRICA COMPANY'S MEDAL

1st type rev.

Mashonaland (2nd) obv.

Date: 1896.
Campaign: South Africa 1890-97.
Branch of Service: British Army and colonial units.
Ribbon: Seven equal stripes, four yellow and three dark blue.
Metal: Silver.
Size: 36mm.
Description: (Obverse) the Old Head bust of Queen Victoria; (reverse) a charging lion impaled by a spear, with a mimosa bush in the background and a litter of spears and a shield on the ground.
Clasps: Mashonaland 1890, Matabeleland 1893, Rhodesia 1896, Mashonaland 1897.
Comments: *Originally instituted in 1896 for award to troops taking part in the suppression of the Matabele rebellion, it was later extended to cover operations in Rhodesia (1896) and Mashonaland (1897). The medal, as originally issued, had the inscription MATABELELAND 1893 at the top of the reverse. The medal was re-issued with RHODESIA 1896 or MASHONALAND 1897 inscribed on the reverse, but holders of medals for their first campaign only added clasps for subsequent campaigns. Rather belatedly, it was decided in 1927 to issue medals retrospectively for the Mashonaland campaign of 1890; in this instance the name and date of the campaign were not inscribed on the reverse though the details appeared on the clasp. An unusually ornate suspender has roses, thistles, shamrocks and leeks entwined. Only one medal is known with all four clasps, while only fifteen medals had three clasps.*

VALUE:

	British regiments	Miniature
Mashonaland 1890	From £500	£30
Matabeleland 1893	£150–200	£30
with 1 clasp	£250–280	£50
with 2 clasps	From £450	£65
Rhodesia 1896	£130–160	£30
with 1 clasp	£230–260	£50
Mashonaland 1897	£150–200	£30

139. HUNZA NAGAR BADGE

Date: 1891.
Campaign: Hunza and Nagar 1891.
Branch of Service: Jammu and Kashmir forces.
Ribbon: Large (46mm x 32mm) with a broad red diagonal band and white centre stripe and green upper left and lower right corners.
Metal: Bronze.
Size: 55mm x 27mm.
Description: A uniface rectangular plaque featuring three soldiers advancing on the crenellated hill fort of Nilt, with mountains in the background. The inscription HUNZA NAGAR 1891 appears lower right. It was intended to be worn as a brooch at the neck but subsequently many were fitted with a suspender for wear with a red and green ribbon.
Clasps: None.

Comments: *Gurney of London manufactured this badge which was awarded by the Maharajah of Jammu and Kashmir to his own troops who served in the operation against the border states of Hunza and Nagar and qualified for the Indian general service medal with clasp for Hunza 1891. The punitive expedition was led by Colonel A. Durand in response to the defiant attitude of the Hunza and Nagar chiefs towards the British agency at Gilgit.*

VALUE: £450–500

140. CENTRAL AFRICA MEDAL

Date: 1895.
Campaigns: Central Africa 1891–98.
Branch of Service: Mainly local forces.
Ribbon: Three equal stripes of black, white and terracotta representing the Africans, Europeans and Indians.
Metal: Silver or bronze.
Size: 36mm.
Description: Obverse and reverse as the East and West Africa (Ashantee) medal, distinguished only by its ribbon.
Clasps: Originally issued without a clasp but one for Central Africa 1894–98 was subsequently authorised.
Comment: *Though generally issued in silver, a bronze version was awarded to native servants. The first issue of this medal had a simple ring suspension and no clasp. For the second issue a clasp, Central Africa 1894–98 was authorised and the medal was issued with a straight bar suspender, which is very rare.*

VALUE:

		Miniature
Without clasp (ring)	£250–300	£80
Clasp and ring suspension	£350–400	—
Clasp and bar suspension	£500–550	£40
Bronze	From £1000	—

141. HONG KONG PLAGUE MEDAL

Date: 1894.
Campaign: Hong Kong, May–September 1894.
Branch of Service: Royal Navy, Royal Engineers, KSLI and local personnel.
Ribbon: Red with yellow edges and two narrow yellow stripes in the centre.
Metal: Silver.
Size: 36mm.
Description: (Obverse) a Chinese lying on a trestle table being supported by a man warding off the winged figure of Death while a woman tends to the sick man. The year 1894 appears on a scroll in the exergue, while the name of the colony in Chinese pictograms is inscribed on the left of the field. (Reverse) inscribed PRESENTED BY THE HONG KONG COMMUNITY round the circumference, and FOR SERVICES RENDERED DURING THE PLAGUE OF 1894 in seven lines across the centre. It was fitted with a plain ring for suspension.
Clasps: None.
Comments: *The colonial authorities in Hong Kong awarded this medal to nurses, civil servants, police, British Army and Royal Navy personnel who rendered assistance when the crown colony was stricken by a severe epidemic of bubonic plague in May 1894. Despite stringent measures, over 2500 people died in the ensuing three months. About 400 medals were issued in silver and awarded to 300 men of the King's Shropshire Light Infantry, 50 petty officers and ratings of the Royal Navy and NCOs and other ranks of the Royal Engineers, as well as about the same number of police and junior officials, while 45 were struck in gold for award to officers, nursing sisters and senior officials.*

VALUE:

		Miniature
Gold (45)	From £3000	—
Silver (400)	£600–800	£50

142. INDIA MEDAL

Date: 1895.
Campaign: India 1895–1902.
Branch of Service: British and Indian forces.
Ribbon: Crimson with two dark green stripes.
Metal: Silver or bronze.
Size: 36mm.
Description: Issued with two different obverses, portraying Queen Victoria (1895–1901) and King Edward VII in field marshal's uniform (1901–02). (Reverse) British and Indian soldiers supporting a standard.
Clasps: Seven, mainly for actions on the North West Frontier (see below).
Comments: *This medal replaced the India GSM which had been awarded for various minor campaigns over a period of four decades from 1854. Combatant troops were given the medal in silver but native bearers and servants received a bronze version. Although the clasp Waziristan 1901–2 is rare to British recipients it was awarded to a number of regiments.*

VALUE:

	British regiments	Indian	Bronze	Miniature
Defence of Chitral 1895	—	£700–800	Rare	£60
Relief of Chitral 1895	£65–75	£35–45	£50–60	£20
Punjab Frontier 1897-98	£60–70	£35–45	£45–55	£15
pair with Malakand 1897	£80–90	£50–60	£60–70	£20–25
pair with Samana 1897	£80–90	£50–60	£70–80	£20–25
pair with Tirah 1897-98	£90–100	£40–50	£50–60	£20–25
Waziristan 1901-2	£200–250	£70–80	£60–70	£20–25
3 clasps	£100–135	£60–80	£80–100	£50–60
4 clasps	—	£80–100	—	£60–80

143. JUMMOO AND KASHMIR MEDAL

Date: 1895.
Campaign: Defence of Chitral 1895.
Branch of Service: Native levies.
Ribbon: White with red stripes at the edges and a broad central green stripe.
Metal: Bronze, silver.
Size: 35mm high; 38mm wide.
Description: This medal, by Gurney of London, has a unique kidney shape showing the arms of Jummoo (Jammu) and Kashmir on the obverse. (Reverse) a view of Chitral fort with troops in the foreground.
Clasps: Chitral 1895.
Comments: *Awarded by the Maharajah of Jummoo (Jammu) and Kashmir to the Indian troops who participated in the defence of Chitral (a dependency of Kashmir) during the siege of 4 March to 20 April by Chitralis and Afghans led by Umra Khan and Sher Afzul.*

VALUE:

Named	£350–400
Unnamed	£240–280
Silver	Rare

144. ASHANTI STAR

Date: 1896.

Campaign: Gold Coast 1896.

Branch of Service: British forces.

Ribbon: Yellow with two black stripes.

Metal: Bronze.

Size: 44mm.

Description: A saltire cross with a four-pointed star in the angles, surmounted by a circular belt inscribed ASHANTI 1896 around a British crown. The plain reverse is simply inscribed FROM THE QUEEN.

Clasps: None.

Comments: *Issued ed unnamed, but the colonel of the West Yorkshire Regiment had the medals of the second battalion engraved at his own expense. Some 2000 stars were awarded to officers and men serving in the expedition led by Major-General F.C. Scott against the tyrannical King Prempeh. It is believed that the star was designed by Princess Henry of Battenberg whose husband died of fever during the campaign.*

VALUE:

Unnamed	£110–120
Named to West Yorkshire Regiment	£220–240
Miniature	£35–40

INTERIOR OF CHITRAL FORT

(see nos. 142 & 143)

145. QUEEN'S SUDAN MEDAL

Date: 1899.
Campaign: Reconquest of the Sudan 1896–97.
Branch of Service: Royal Navy, Army and local forces.
Ribbon: Half-yellow and half-black representing the desert and the Sudanese nation, divided by a thin crimson stripe representing the British forces.
Metal: Silver or bronze.
Size: 36mm.
Description: (Obverse) the Jubilee bust of Queen Victoria. (Reverse) a seated figure of Victory holding palms and laurels with flags in the background, the word SUDAN appearing on a tablet at her feet.
Clasps: None.
Comments: *Unusually, no clasps were granted for individual actions which included the celebrated battle of Omdurman in which young Winston Churchill charged with the cavalry. Medals named to the 21st Lancers are especially desirable on that account.*

VALUE:

Bronze named	£120–180
Silver named	£110–130
21st Lancers (confirmed charger)	From £650
Miniature	£25–30

146. KHEDIVE'S SUDAN MEDAL

Date: 1897.
Campaign: Sudan 1896-1908.
Branch of Service: Royal Navy and British and Egyptian Armies.
Ribbon: 38mm yellow with a broad central deep blue stripe, symbolising the desert and the River Nile.
Metal: Silver or bronze.
Size: 39mm.
Description: (Obverse) an oval shield surrounded by flags and a trophy of arms; (reverse) an elaborate Arabic inscription. Bar suspender.
Clasps: Fifteen (see below) but medals with more than the two clasps 'The Atbara' and 'Khartoum' are unusual. Inscribed in English and Arabic.
Comments: *Instituted by the Khedive of Egypt in February 1897 and granted to those who served in the reconquest of Dongola province in the Sudan (1896-8) as well as in subsequent operations for the pacification of the southern provinces. It was awarded to officers and men of the British and Egyptian Armies and Royal Navy personnel who served on the Nile steamboats. In addition, the crews of the Royal Naval ships HMS* Melita *(139) and HMS* Scout *(149) were awarded silver medals with no clasps for Dongola 1896 (but were* not *awarded the Queen's Sudan Medal 1896–98).*

VALUE:

		Miniature				*Miniature*
No clasp silver	£60–70	£20	Jerok	£90–100	£45
No clasp silver (RN)	£90–120	—	Nyam-Nyam	£110–120	£40
No clasp bronze	£70–80	—	Talodi	£110–120	£45
Firket	£90–100	£30	Katfia	£110–120	£45
Hafir	£90–100	£30	Nyima	£100–110	£35
Abu Hamed	£90–100	£35			
Sudan 1897	£90–100	£35	2 clasps	£110–120	Add £10–15
The Atbara	£90–100	£25	3 clasps	£120–140	per clasp
Khartoum	£100–110	£25	4 clasps	£140–160	
Gedaref	£90–100	£40	5 clasps	£150–170	
Gedid	£90–100	£40	6 clasps	£160–180	
Sudan 1899	£90–100	£25	7 clasps	£180–200	
Bahr-el-Ghazal 1900–2	£120–150	£45	8 clasps	£200–240	

147. EAST AND CENTRAL AFRICA

Date: 1897.
Campaigns: East and Central Africa 1897–99.
Branch of Service: British, Indian and local forces.
Ribbon: Half yellow, half red.
Metal: Silver or bronze.
Size: 36mm.
Description: (Obverse) the Jubilee bust of Queen Victoria; (reverse) a standing figure of Britannia with the British lion alongside.
Clasps: Five (see below).
Comments: *Instituted for service in operations in Uganda and the southern Sudan, it was awarded in silver to combatants and in bronze to camp followers. Most of the medals were awarded to troops of the Uganda Rifles and various Indian regiments. The few British officers and NCOs were troop commanders and instructors seconded from their regiments and their medals are worth very much more than the prices quoted, which are for native awards.*

VALUE:

	Europeans	Natives	*Miniature*
No clasp silver	—	£180–200	£20
Lubwa's (with clasp Uganda 1897-98)	—	£250–280	£35
Uganda 1897-98	£350–400	£220–250	£35
1898 (silver)	—	£230–260	£35
1898 (bronze)	—	£350–400	—
Uganda 1899	—	£230–260	£35

147A. UGANDA STAR

Instituted: 1897–98.
Campaign: Mutiny of Sudanese troops in Uganda.
Branch of Service: African civilians and soldiers.
Ribbon: None.
Metal: Silver.
Description: An eight-pointed uniface star surmounted by a crown, with the dates 1897 and 1898 on a circular rim enclosing the Old Head or Veiled Bust of Queen Victoria. Brooch-mounted. Manufactured by Carrington of London and issued in a blue plush-lined case.
Comments: *This award, approved by the Foreign Office and sanctioned by Queen Victoria, acknowledged the loyalty of African tribal leaders but, in a few cases, was also awarded to Sudanese troops (one, in fact, a Tunisian) who fought gallantly in quelling the serious mutiny of Sudanese troops of the Uganda Rifles. It was for this action that British, Indian and Local forces were awarded the East and Central Africa Medal with the bar for Lubwa's (see above). Only 39 stars were awarded.*

VALUE:

Civilian award	Rare
Sudanese military award	Very rare

148. BRITISH NORTH BORNEO COMPANY'S MEDALS

1st type obv.

1st type rev.

Date: 1897.
Campaign: North Borneo 1897–1915.
Branch of Service: Company forces.
Ribbon: Originally 36mm gold watered silk, 32mm yellow with maroon edges and a central blue stripe (Punitive Expeditions and Rundum) or 32mm yellow with a central green stripe (Tambunan).
Metal: Silver or bronze.
Size: 39mm.
Description: (Obverse) the Company arms; (reverse) the British lion standing in front of a bush adorned by the Company flag, with a small wreath in the exergue.
Clasps: Four (see below).
Comments: *This series of medals was made by the British North Borneo Company for service in what is now Sabah. The medals, struck by Spink and Son of London, were issued in silver and bronze (except for Rundum) to British and Bornean officials, Sikh troops and a small number of servants. The first obverse showed the Company arms with supporters, crest and motto. This medal was issued unnamed and unnumbered. Specimens from the original dies are known with the S of Spink or Son erased and the word "Copy" on the rim. The medal was re-issued for a second expedition in 1898 and on this occasion it was named and numbered to the recipient. For a third expedition, in 1899–1900, the second obverse was used, showing the Company shield without supporters, motto or crest, but inscribed BRITISH NORTH BORNEO and with the date 1900 round the foot. This was used in conjunction with a new reverse showing the Company crest, two arms supporting a flag. This medal had a yellow ribbon with a central green stripe. In 1915 an expedition to raise the siege of Rundum was marked by the issue of a silver medal, similar to the 1897 medal but only struck in silver and fitted with a Rundum clasp.*

VALUE:

	Silver	Bronze	Miniature
Punitive Expedition (1897)	£60–80	£40–60	£40
Punitive Expeditions (1898)	£70–80	£40–60	£45
Tambunan	£70–80	£50–60	£45
Rundum	£80–100	—	£50
Originally named and numbered	Rare	£500–800	

2nd type obv.

2nd type rev.

149. SULTAN OF ZANZIBAR'S MEDAL

Date: 1896.
Campaign: East Africa 1896.
Branch of Service: Sultan's forces.
Ribbon: Plain bright scarlet.
Metal: Silver.
Size: 36mm.
Description: (Obverse) a facing bust of Sultan Hamid bin Thwain surrounded by a Suaheli inscription in Arabic; (reverse) same inscription set in four lines.
Clasps: Pumwani, Jongeni, Takaungu, Mwele (inscribed only in Arabic).
Comments: *Awarded to the Zanzibari contingent who served under Lieut. Lloyd-Matthews RN in East Africa alongside British and imperial forces.*

VALUE: £250–300   *Miniature*   £60

150. QUEEN'S SOUTH AFRICA MEDAL

Date: 1899.
Campaign: Anglo-Boer War 1899-1902.
Branch of Service: British and Imperial forces.
Ribbon: Red with two narrow blue stripes and a broad central orange stripe.
Metal: Silver or bronze.
Size: 36mm.
Description: (Obverse) the Jubilee bust of Queen Victoria; (reverse) Britannia holding the flag and a laurel crown towards a large group of soldiers, with warships offshore. The words SOUTH AFRICA are inscribed round the top.
Clasps: 26 authorised but the maximum recorded for a single medal is nine to the Army and eight to the Navy.
Comments: *Because of the large number of British and imperial forces which took part and the numerous campaign and battle clasps awarded, this is one of the most popular and closely studied of all medals, offering immense scope to the collector. A total of 178,000 medals were awarded. Numerous specialist units were involved for the first time, as well as locally raised units and contingents from India, Canada, Australia and New Zealand. Of particular interest are the medals awarded to war correspondents and nurses which set precedents for later wars. Although nurses received the medal they were not issued with clasps to which they were entitled. A small number of bronze medals without a clasp were issued to bearers and servants in Indian units. The original issue of the QSA depicts Britannia's outstretched hand pointing towards the R of AFRICA and bears the dates 1899–1900 on the reverse field. Less than 70 of these were issued to Lord Strathcona's Horse who had returned to Canada before the war ended, but as the war dragged on the date was removed before any other medals were issued, although some medals can be found with a "ghost" of this date still to be seen. On the third type reverse there is again no date but Britannia's hand points towards the F. The prices for clasps given below are for clasps issued in combination with others. Some clasps are much scarcer when issued singly than combined with other clasps and conversely some clasps are not recorded on their own. Verified ten-clasp medals to South African units are known.*

1st type rev.

continued overleaf

150. QUEEN'S SOUTH AFRICA MEDAL *continued*

VALUE:

	RN	British	SA/Indian	Aus/NZ	Canadian
No clasp bronze	—	—	£60–80	—	—
No clasp silver	£80–100	£30–40	£60–80	£75–85	£110–120
Cape Colony	£80–100	£35–45	£35–45	£45–50	£110–120
Rhodesia	—	£80–120	£90–100	£150–200	£260–280
Relief of Mafeking	—	—	£130–150	£150–160	£350–370
Defence of Kimberley	—	£80–120	£90–100	—	—
Talana	—	£125–135	£80–90	—	—
Elandslaagte	—	£110–130	—	—	—
Defence of Ladysmith	£160–180	£70–90	£70–80	—	—
Belmont	£90–110	£50–70	—	£180–200	—
Modder River	£95–120	£50–70	—	£180–200	—
Tugela Heights	—	£40–50	—	—	—
Natal	£120–140	£70–90	£60–70	—	£180–200
Relief of Kimberley	£250–400	£40–50	£40–50	£100–120	—
Paardeberg	£90–110	£40–50	£55–60	£90–100	£130–140
Orange Free State	£120–130	£30–40	£30–40	£50–60	£120–140
Relief of Ladysmith	£90–110	£45–55	£60–70	—	—
Driefontein	£90–110	£40–50	—	£40–50	£180–200
Wepener	—	£250–300	£160–190	—	—
Defence of Mafeking	—	—	£600–700	—	—
Transvaal	£80–100	£35–45	£35–45	£50–60	£180–200
Johannesburg	£100–120	£45–55	£50–60	£50–60	£120–130
Laing's Nek	£110–130	£60–75	—	—	—
Diamond Hill	£110–130	£45–55	£55–65	£60–70	£180–200
Wittebergen	—	£40–50	£90–100	£65–75	—
Belfast	£120–140	£60–70	£50–60	£60–70	£120–140
South Africa 1901	£60–70	£40–50	£40–50	£60–70	£140–150
South Africa 1902	£120–130	£40–50	£40–50	£60–70	£120–130
2 clasps	£110–140	£40–50	£40–50	£80–90	£120–130
3 clasps	£130–160	£50–60	£50–60	£90–110	£120–130
4 clasps	£150–200	£45–55	£50–60	£120–130	£140–150
5 clasps	£200–400	£50–60	£55–65	£150–180	£200–220
6 clasps	£300–500	£60–70	£90–100	£220–250	£250–300
7 clasps	£400–600	£150–200	£150–160	£350–450	—
8 clasps	£500–7500	£250–300	£350–400	—	—
Relief dates on reverse	—	—	—	—	£1900–2200
Nurses	—	£80–120	—	—	—
War Correspondents	—	£1000–1100	—	—	—

Miniature
From £5 with no clasp to £25 with 6 fixed clasps—"slip-on" style clasps approx. 20% less.

2nd type rev.   3rd type rev.

151. QUEEN'S MEDITERRANEAN MEDAL

Date: 1899.

Campaign: Mediterranean garrisons 1899-1902.

Branch of Service: British militia forces.

Ribbon: Red with two narrow dark blue stripes and a central broad orange stripe (as for Queen's South Africa Medal).

Metal: Silver.

Size: 36mm.

Description: Similar to the Queen's South Africa Medal but inscribed MEDITERRANEAN at the top of the reverse.

Clasps: None.

Comments: *Awarded to officers and men of the militia battalions which were sent to Malta and Gibraltar to take over garrison duty from the regular forces who were drafted to the Cape.*

VALUE:

Silver (5000)	£120–140	*Miniature*	£45–55

152. KING'S SOUTH AFRICA MEDAL

Date: 1902.

Campaign: South Africa 1901–02.

Branch of Service: British and imperial forces.

Ribbon: Three equal stripes of green, white and orange.

Metal: Silver.

Size: 36mm.

Description: (Obverse) bust of King Edward VII in field marshal's uniform; (reverse) as for Queen's medal.

Clasps: Two: South Africa 1901, South Africa 1902.

Comments: *This medal was never issued without the Queen's medal and was awarded to all personnel engaged in operations in South Africa in 1901–02 when fighting was actually confined to numerous skirmishes with isolated guerrilla bands. Very few medals were awarded to RN personnel as the naval brigades had been disbanded in 1901. Apart from about 600 nurses and a few odd men who received the medal without a clasp, this medal was awarded with campaign clasps—most men were entitled to both clasps, single clasp medals being very rare.*

VALUE:

No clasp (nurses)	£70–90
1901 / 1902 (RN)	£80–100
1901 / 1902 (Army)	£30–40
1901 / 1902 (Canada)	£50–60
1901 / 1902 (Aus, NZ)	£40–50
1901 alone	From £100
1902 alone	From £100
Miniature	£5–6

153. ST JOHN AMBULANCE BRIGADE MEDAL FOR SOUTH AFRICA

Date: 1902.
Campaign: South Africa 1899–1902.
Branch of Service: St John Ambulance Brigade.
Ribbon: Black with narrow white edges.
Metal: Bronze.
Size: 37mm.
Description: (Obverse) King Edward VII; (reverse) the arms of the Order with a legend in Latin, SOUTH AFRICA and the dates 1899 and 1902.
Clasps: None.
Comments: *Issued by the Order of St John of Jerusalem to the members of its ambulance brigade who served during the Boer War or who played an active part in the organisation, mobilisation and supply roles. Medals were engraved on the edge with the recipient's name and unit. It is most often associated with the two South Africa medals, but fourteen members who went on from South Africa to serve during the Boxer Rebellion were also awarded the China Medal.*

VALUE:

Bronze (1871)	£140–170	*Miniature*	£20–30

154. KIMBERLEY STAR

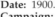

Date: 1900.
Campaign: Defence of Kimberley 1899–1902.
Branch of Service: British and local forces.
Ribbon: Half yellow, half black, separated by narrow stripes of red, white and blue.
Metal: Silver.
Size: Height 43mm; max. width 41mm.
Description: A six-pointed star with ball finials and a circular centre inscribed KIMBERLEY 1899–1900 with the civic arms in the middle. (Reverse) plain, but for the inscription MAYOR'S SIEGE MEDAL 1900. Suspended by a plain ring from a scrolled bar.
Clasps: None
Comments: *The Mayor and council of Kimberley awarded this and the following medal to the defenders of the mining town against the Boer forces. Two medals were struck in gold but about 5000 were produced in silver. Those with the "a" Birmingham hallmark for 1900 rate a premium over stars with later date letters.*

VALUE:

hallmark "a"	£110–125
later date letters	£90–110
Miniature	£60–80

155. KIMBERLEY MEDAL

Date: 1900.
Campaign: Defence of Kimberley 1899–1900.
Branch of Service: Local forces.
Ribbon: As above.
Metal: Silver
Size: 38mm.
Description: (Obverse) the figure of Victory above the Kimberley Town Hall, with the dates 1899–1900 in the exergue. (Reverse) two shields inscribed INVESTED 15 OCT. 1899 and RELIEVED 15 FEB. 1900. The imperial crown appears above and the royal cypher underneath, with the legend TO THE GALLANT DEFENDERS OF KIMBERLEY round the circumference.
Clasps: None.
Comments: *Although awarded for the same purpose as the above, this silver medal is a much scarcer award.*

VALUE:

Silver	£500–650

156. YORKSHIRE IMPERIAL YEOMANRY MEDAL

Date: 1900.
Campaign: South Africa 1900–02.
Branch of Service: Yorkshire Imperial Yeomanry.
Ribbon: Yellow.
Metal: Silver.
Size: 38mm.
Description: Three versions were produced. The first two had the numeral 3 below the Prince of Wales's feathers and may be found with the dates 1900–1901 or 1901–1902, while the third type has the figures 66, denoting the two battalions involved. The uniform reverse has the white rose of Yorkshire surmounted by an imperial crown and enclosed in a laurel wreath with the legend A TRIBUTE FROM YORKSHIRE.
Clasps: None.
Comments: *Many medals wre produced locally and awarded to officers and men of county regiments. The medals struck by Spink and Son for the Yorkshire Imperial Yeomanry, however, are generally more highly regarded as they were much more extensively issued, and therefore more commonly met with, than the others.*

VALUE:

3rd Battalion 1900–1901	£70–80
3rd Battalion 1901–1902	£80–100
66th Battalion 1900–1901	£120–150

157. MEDAL FOR THE DEFENCE OF OOKIEP

Date: 1902.
Campaign: Defence of Ookiep 1902.
Branch of Service: British and colonial forces.
Ribbon: Dark brown with a central green stripe.
Metal: Silver or bronze.
Size: 36mm.
Description: (Obverse) a miner and copper-waggon, with the Company name and date of foundation (1888) round the circumference; (reverse) a thirteen-line text. Fitted with a scroll suspender.
Clasps: None.
Comments: *This medal was awarded by the Cape Copper Company to those who defended the mining town of Ookiep in Namaqualand when it was besieged from 4 April to 4 May 1902 by a Boer commando led by Jan Christian Smuts, later Field Marshal, Prime Minister of South Africa and a member of the Imperial War Cabinet. The defence was conducted by Lieut. Colonel Sheldon, DSO and Major Dean, the Company's manager. The garrison consisted of 206 European miners, 660 Cape Coloureds, 44 men of the 5th Warwickshire militia and twelve men of the Cape Garrison Artillery.*

VALUE:

Silver (officers)	Rare
Bronze (other ranks)	£500–600

158. CHINA WAR MEDAL

Date: 1901.
Campaign: Boxer Rebellion 1900.
Branch of Service: British and imperial forces.
Ribbon: Crimson with yellow edges.
Metal: Silver or bronze.
Size: 36mm.
Description: (Obverse) bust of Queen Victoria; (reverse) trophy of arms , similar to the 1857-60 China Medal but inscribed CHINA 1900 at the foot.
Clasps: Taku Forts, Defence of Legations, Relief of Pekin.
Comments: *Instituted for service during the Boxer Rebellion and the subsequent punitive expeditions, this medal was similar to that of 1857-60 with the date in the exergue altered to 1900. There are three types of naming: in small, impressed capitals for European troops, in large impressed capitals for naval recipients, and in engraved cursive script for Indian forces. The medal was issued in silver to combatants and in bronze to native bearers, drivers and servants. The international community was besieged by the Boxers, members of a secret society, aided and abetted by the Dowager Empress. The relieving force, consisting of contingents from Britain, France, Italy, Russia, Germany and Japan, was under the command of the German field marshal, Count von Waldersee. The British Legation Guard, comprising 80 Royal Marines and a number of 'odd men', won the clasp for Defence of Legations, the most desirable of the campaign bars in this conflict.*

VALUE:

	Royal Navy	Army	Indian units	*Miniature*
Silver no clasp	£90–110	£100–120	£40–50	£10–15
Bronze no clasp	—	—	£70–80	—
Taku Forts	£300–320	—	—	£20–25
Defence of Legations	£3000–4000	—	—	£50–60
Relief of Pekin (silver)	£170–190	£180–200	£80–100	£20–25
Relief of Pekin (bronze)	—	—	£140–160	—
2 clasps	£400–450	—	—	£40–50
No-clasp medal to a nurse	£1000–1100			
To a War correspondent	£1000–1100			

159. TRANSPORT MEDAL

Date: 1903.
Campaigns: Boer War 1899-1902 and Boxer Rebellion 1900.
Branch of Service: Mercantile Marine.
Ribbon: Red with two blue stripes.
Metal: Silver.
Size: 36mm.
Description: (Obverse) bust of King Edward VII in the uniform of an Admiral of the Fleet; (reverse) HMS *Ophir* below a map of the world.
Clasps: S. Africa 1899-1902, China 1900.
Comments: *The last of the medals associated with the major conflicts at the turn of the century, it was instituted for award to the officers and men of the merchant vessels used to carry troops and supplies to the wars in South Africa and China.*

VALUE:

		Miniature
South Africa 1899–1902 (1219)	£260–280	£40–60
China 1900 (322)	£380–420	£50–70
Both clasps (178)	£450–550	£80–100

160. ASHANTI MEDAL

Date: 1901.
Campaign: Gold Coast 1900.
Branch of Service: British and local forces.
Ribbon: Black with two broad green stripes.
Metal: Silver or bronze.
Size: 36mm.
Description: (Obverse) bust of King Edward VII in field marshal's uniform. (Reverse) a lion on the edge of an escarpment looking towards the sunrise, with a native shield and spears in the foreground. The name ASHANTI appeared on a scroll at the foot.
Clasps: Kumassi.
Comments: *A high-handed action by the colonial governor provoked a native uprising and the siege of the garrison at Kumassi. The medal was awarded to the defenders as well as personnel of the two relieving columns. Very few Europeans were involved as most were in South Africa fighting the Boers. The medal was awarded in silver to combatants and bronze to native tansport personnel and servants.*

VALUE:

	Silver	Bronze	*Miniature*
No clasp	£150–170	£250–300	£20–25
Kumassi	£320–350	Rare	£40–50

161. AFRICA GENERAL SERVICE MEDAL

Date: 1902.
Campaigns: Minor campaigns in Africa 1902 to 1956.
Branch of Service: British and colonial forces.
Ribbon: Yellow with black edges and two thin central green stripes.
Metal: Silver or bronze.
Size: 36mm.
Description: (Obverse) effigies of Edward VII, George V and Elizabeth II; (reverse) similar to that of the East and Central Africa medal of 1897–99, with AFRICA in the exergue.
Clasps: 34 awarded in the reign of Edward VII, ten George V and only one Elizabeth II (see below).
Comments: *This medal replaced the East and West Africa Medal 1887–1900, to which 21 clasps had already been issued. In turn, it remained in use for 54 years, the longest-running British service medal. Medals to combatants were in silver, but a few bronze medals were issued during the 1903–04 operations in Northern Nigeria and the Somaliland campaigns of 1902 and 1908 to transport personnel and these are now much sought after, as are any medals with the effigy of George V on the obverse. With the exception of the 1902–04 Somali campaign and the campaign against the Mau Mau of Kenya (1952–56) European troops were not involved in any numbers, such personnel consisting mostly of detached officers and specialists.*

VALUE:	RN	British units	African/Indian regiments
N. Nigeria	—	—	£120–140
N. Nigeria 1902	—	—	£110–130
N. Nigeria 1903	—	—	£100–120
N. Nigeria 1903-04	—	—	£150–170
N. Nigeria 1903-04 (bronze)	—	—	£130–150
N. Nigeria 1904	—	—	£130–150
N. Nigeria 1906	—	—	£130–150
S. Nigeria	—	—	£180–200
S. Nigeria 1902	—	—	£130–150
S. Nigeria 1902-03	—	—	£130–150

continued overleaf

161. AFRICA GENERAL SERVICE MEDAL *continued*

S. Nigeria 1903	—	—	£120–140
S. Nigeria 1903-04	—	—	£150–170
S. Nigeria 1904	—	—	£120–140
S. Nigeria 1904-05	—	—	£150–170
S. Nigeria 1905	—	—	£250–300
S. Nigeria 1905-06	—	—	£140–160
Nigeria 1918	—	—	£110–130
East Africa 1902	—	—	£300–350
East Africa 1904	—	—	£170–190
East Africa 1905	—	—	£170–190
East Africa 1906	—	—	£170–190
East Africa 1913	—	—	£180–220
East Africa 1913-14	—	—	£170–190
East Africa 1914	—	—	£180–220
East Africa 1915	—	—	£200–250
East Africa 1918	—	—	£170–190
West Africa 1906	—	—	£170–190
West Africa 1908	—	—	£180–220
West Africa 1909-10	—	—	£180–200
Somaliland 1901	—	—	£250–300
Somaliland 1901 (bronze)	—	—	£200–250
Somaliland 1902-04	£75–85	£80–100	£50–60
Somaliland 1902-04 (bronze)	—	—	£220–250
Somaliland 1908-10	£80–90	—	£65–75
Somaliland 1908-10 (bronze)	—	—	£80–90
Somaliland 1920	£180–200	—	£80–90
as above but RAF	—	£250–280	—
Jidballi (with Somaliland 1902–04)	—	£150–180	£110–130
Uganda 1900	—	—	£170–190
B.C.A. 1899-1900	—	—	£120–150
Jubaland	£200–220	—	£90–100
Jubaland (bronze)	—	—	£250–300
Jubaland 1917-18	—	—	£160–180
Jubaland 1917-18 (bronze)	—	—	£125–150
Gambia	£240–260	—	£120–140
Aro 1901-1902	£200–250	—	£130–150
Lango 1901	—	—	£200–250
Kissi 1905	—	—	£350–400
Nandi 1905-06	—	—	£80–120
Shimber Berris 1914-15	—	—	£200–220
Nyasaland 1915	—	—	£120–150
Kenya	£75–85	£50–70	£40–50
Kenya (to RAF)	—	£55–60	—
2 clasps	£80–120	£100–150	£100–250
3 clasps	—	—	£200–400
4 clasps	—	—	£300–450
5 clasps	—	—	£350–500
6 clasps	—	—	£350–550

Miniature
Range from £10 to £60 depending upon clasp. "Slip-on" clasps are approx. 20% cheaper. Add £5 for each additional clasp.

162. TIBET MEDAL

Date: 1904.
Campaign: Tibet 1903–04.
Branch of Service: British and Indian regiments.
Ribbon: Green with two white stripes and a broad maroon central stripe.
Metal: Silver or bronze.
Size: 36mm.
Description: (Obverse) bust of King Edward VII; (reverse) the fortified hill city of Lhasa with TIBET 1903–04 at the foot.
Clasps: Gyantse.
Comments: *The trade mission led by Colonel Sir Francis Younghusband to Tibet was held up by hostile forces, against whom a punitive expedition was mounted in 1903. This medal was awarded mainly to Indian troops who took part in the expedition, camp followers being awarded the medal in bronze. A clasp was awarded to those who took part in the operations near Gyantse beteen 3 May and 6 July 1904.*

VALUE:

	British	Indian	Bronze	*Miniature*
Without clasp	£180–200	£100–120	£75–85	£20–25
Gyantse	£450–500	£170–200	£150–170	£50–60

163. NATAL REBELLION

Date: 1908.
Campaign: Natal 1906.
Branch of Service: Local forces.
Ribbon: Crimson with black edges.
Metal: Silver.
Size: 36mm.
Description: (Obverse) right-facing profile of King Edward VII. (Reverse) an erect female figure representing Natal with the sword of justice in her right hand and a palm branch in the left. She treads on a heap of Zulu weapons and is supported by Britannia who holds the orb of empire in her hand. In the background, the sun emerges from behind storm clouds.
Clasp: 1906.
Comments: *The Natal government instituted this medal for services in the operations following the Zulu rebellion. Local volunteer units bore the brunt of the action and it is interesting to note that one of the recipients was Sergeant-Major M. K. Gandhi who later led India to independence.*

VALUE:

		Miniature
without clasp (2000)	£90–110	£10–15
clasp 1906 (8000)	£120–140	£20–30
Natal Naval Corps (200)	£200–250	

163A. MESSINA EARTHQUAKE COMMEMORATIVE MEDAL

Date: 1908.
Campaign: Messina earthquake relief.
Branch of Service: Royal Navy.
Ribbon: Green with white edges and central white stripe.
Metal: Silver.
Size: 31.5mm.
Description: (Obverse) left-facing profile of King Victor Emanuel III; (reverse) A wreath of oak leaves within which are the words MEDAGLIA COMMEMORATIVA / TERREMOTO CALABRO SICULO 28 DICEMBRE 1908.
Clasp: —
Comments: *The King of Italy rewarded Royal Naval and other personnel who went to the aid of victims of the tragic earthquake that hit Messina in December 1908 with this silver medal. Officers and men serving on certain ships were eligible for the award as well as members of the Mercantile Marine and others who were engaged in relief operations. The Admiralty's published list of RN ships is as follows: HMS Duncan, HMS Euralyus, HMS Exmouth, HMS Lancaster, HMS Minerva and HMS Sutlej. However 52 medals were also awarded to personnel from HMS Boxer, which was omitted from the original list and a further 35 medals were awarded to the officers and men of HMS Philomel who had actually* 'been engaged in work which was directly attributable to the rescue operations'. *In addition to the commemorative medal a special Messina Earthquake Merit Medal was awarded in two sizes (40mm and 30mm) bronze, silver and gold to organisations, vessels and various key individuals who played a part in the rescue operations.*

VALUE:		Miniature
Royal Navy (c. 3500)	£50–60	—
Royal Marines (481)	£100–120	
Mercantile Marine (c. 400)	£100–120	
Other	Rare	

164. INDIA GENERAL SERVICE MEDAL

Date: 1908.
Campaigns: India 1908 to 1935.
Branch of Service: British and Indian forces.
Ribbon: Green with a broad blue central band.
Metal: Silver.
Size: 36mm.
Description: Three obverse types were used: Edward VII (1908–10), George V Kaisar-i-Hind (1910–30) and George V Indiae Imp (1930–35). (Reverse) the fortress at Jamrud in the Khyber Pass, with the name INDIA in a wreath at the foot.
Clasps: Fourteen, some in bronze (see below).
Comments: *This medal was awarded for a number of minor campaigns and operations in India before and after the First World War. The medals were struck at the Royal Mint in London and by the Indian government in Calcutta, the only difference being in the claw suspenders, the former being ornate and the latter plain. Medals with the bars* North West Frontier 1908 *and* Abor 1911–12 *were also issued in bronze to native bearers.*

VALUE:

	British Army	RAF	Indian regiments	Miniature
NW Frontier 1908	£55–65	—	£30–40	£20
bronze	—	—	£50–60	—
Abor 1911–12	—	—	£140–180	£20
bronze	—	—	£250–300	—
Afghanistan NWF 1919	£25–35	£100–120	£15–20	£10
*Mahsud 1919–20 & Waziristan 1919–21	£60–70	£120–150	£30–40	£10
Malabar 1921–22	£80–100	—	£25–35	£30
Waziristan 1921–24	£30–40	£70–90	£20–30	£12
Waziristan 1925	—	£500–550	—	£12
NW Frontier 1930–31	£30–40	£60–70	£15–20	£10
Burma 1930–32	£40–50	Rare	£25–30	£10
Mohmand 1933	£100–120	£180–200	£25–30	£10
NW Frontier 1935	£35–45	£60–70	£20–25	£10

Usually found in combination with Waziristan 1919-21, but 10 medals were awarded either with this clasp alone or with the Afganistan NWF clasp.

165. KHEDIVE'S SUDAN MEDAL

Date: 1911.

Campaign: Sudan 1910 to 1922

Branch of Service: British and Egyptian forces.

Ribbon: Black with thin red and green stripes on either side.

Metal: Silver or bronze.

Size: 36mm.

Description: (Obverse) an Arabic inscription signifying the name of Khedive Abbas Hilmi and the date 1328 in the Moslem calendar (1910 AD). He was deposed in December 1914 when Egypt was declared a British protectorate, and succeeded by his nephew who was proclaimed Sultan. Sultan Hussein Kamil changed the Arabic inscription and date to AH 1335 (1916–17) on later issues of the medal. (Reverse) a lion poised on a plinth with the sunrise in the background.

Clasps: 16, inscribed in English and Arabic.

Comments: *Introduced in June 1911 as a replacement for the previous Khedive's Sudan medal of 1896–1908, it was awarded for minor operations in the southern Sudan between 1910 and 1922. The silver medal was issued with clasps to combatants, and without a clasp to non-combatants, while the bronze version was granted to camp followers. The medal is usually found unnamed although a few British recipient's medals are found named in small impressed capitals or arabic script. The prices below are for unnamed examples.*

VALUE:

Silver without clasp type I	£100–120		
Silver without clasp type II	£130–150	Darfur 1916	£220–250
Bronze without clasp type I	£400–450	Fasher	£220–240
Bronze without clasp type II	£160–180	Lau Nuer	£240–260
Atwot	£220–240	Nyima 1917-18	£220–240
S. Kordofan 1910	£220–240	Atwot 1918	£220–240
Sudan 1912	£240–260	Garjak Nuer	£240–260
Zeraf 1913-14	£260–280	Aliab Dinka	£260–280
Mandal	£260–280	Nyala	£260–280
Miri	£260–280	Darfur 1921	£280–320
Mongalla 1915-16	£260–280	2 clasps	£280–300

Miniature
Silver — £20. Prices for clasps vary between £10 and £30.

166. 1914 STAR

Date: 1917.

Campaign: France and Belgium 1914.

Branch of Service: British forces.

Ribbon: Watered silk red, white and blue.

Metal: Bronze.

Size: Height 50mm; max. width 45mm.

Description: A crowned four-pointed star with crossed swords and a wreath of oak leaves, having the royal cypher at the foot and a central scroll inscribed AUG NOV 1914. Uniface, the naming being inscribed incuse on the plain reverse.

Clasps: 5th Aug. - 22nd Nov. 1914. The clasp was sewn on to the ribbon, the first of this type.

Comments: *Awarded to all those who had served in France and Belgium between 5 August and 22 November 1914. In 1919 King George V authorised a clasp bearing these dates for those who had actually been under fire during that period. The majority of the 400,000 recipients of the star were officers and men of the prewar British Army, the "Old Contemptibles" who landed in France soon after the outbreak of the First World War and who took part in the retreat from Mons, hence the popular nickname of Mons Star by which this medal is often known.*

VALUE:

		Miniature
1914 Star	£20–25	£2–3
With "Mons" clasp	£35–40	£3–4
To RN or RM	£40–60	

167. 1914-15 STAR

Date: 1917.
Campaign: First World War 1914–15.
Branch of Service: British and imperial forces.
Ribbon: Watered silk red, white and blue (as above).
Metal: Bronze.
Size: Height 50mm; max. width 45mm.
Description: As above, but AUG and NOV omitted and scroll across the centre inscribed 1914–15.
Clasps: None.
Comments: *Awarded to those who saw service in any theatre of war between 5 August 1914 and 31 December 1915, other than those who had already qualified for the 1914 Star. No fewer than 2,350,000 were awarded, making it the commonest British campaign medal up to that time.*

VALUE:

1914–15 Star	£7–10	*Miniature*	£2–3

168. BRITISH WAR MEDAL

Date: 1919.
Campaign: First World War, 1914–20.
Branch of Service: British and imperial forces.
Ribbon: Orange watered centre with stripes of white and black at each side and borders of royal blue.
Metal: Silver or bronze.
Size: 36mm.
Description: (Obverse) the uncrowned left-facing profile of King George V by Sir Bertram Mackennal. (Reverse) St George on horseback trampling underfoot the eagle shield of the Central Powers and a skull and cross-bones, the emblems of death. Above, the sun has risen in victory. The figure is mounted on horseback to symbolise man's mind controlling a force of greater strength than his own, and thus alludes to the scientific and mechanical appliances which helped to win the war.
Clasps: None.
Comments: *This medal was instituted to record the successful conclusion of the First World War, but it was later extended to cover the period 1919–20 and service in mine-clearing at sea as well as participation in operations in North and South Russia, the eastern Baltic, Siberia, the Black Sea and Caspian. Some 6,500,000 medals were awarded in silver, but about 110,000 in bronze were issued mainly to Chinese, Indian and Maltese personnel in labour battalions. It was originally intended to award campaign clasps, but 79 were recommended by the Army and 68 by the Navy, so the scheme was abandoned as impractical. The naval clasps were actually authorised (7 July 1920) and miniatures are known with them, though the actual clasps were never issued.*

VALUE:

		Miniature
Silver (6,500,000)	£6–10	£3–4
Bronze (110,000)	£40–50	£10–15

NB The 80th anniversary of the end of World War I sees the medals of that conflict enjoying increasing popularity which inevitably make the prices quite volatile. The prices quoted are for ordinary issues. Medals to casualties, special units, etc. continue to demand a premium.

169. MERCANTILE MARINE WAR MEDAL

Date: 1919.
Campaign: First World War 1914–18.
Branch of Service: Mercantile Marine.
Ribbon: Green and red with a central white stripe, symbolising port and starboard navigation lights.
Metal: Bronze.
Size: 36mm.
Description: (Obverse) Mackennal profile of King George V; (reverse) a steamship ploughing through an angry sea, with a sinking submarine and a sailing vessel in the background, the whole enclosed in a laurel wreath.
Clasps: None.
Comments: *Awarded by the Board of Trade to members of the Merchant Navy who had undertaken one or more voyages through a war or danger zone.*

VALUE:

Bronze (133,000)	£12–14	*Miniature*	£3–5

170. VICTORY MEDAL

Date: 1919.
Campaign: First World War 1914–19.
Branch of Service: British forces.
Ribbon: 38mm double rainbow (indigo at edges and red in centre).
Metal: Yellow bronze.
Size: 36mm.
Description: (Obverse) the standing figure of Victory holding a palm branch in her right hand and stretching out her left hand. (Reverse) a laurel wreath containing a four-line inscription THE GREAT WAR FOR CIVILISATION 1914–1919.
Clasps: None.
Comments: *Issued to all who had already got the 1914 or 1914–15 Stars and most of those who had the British War Medal, some six million are believed to have been produced. It is often known as the Allied War Medal because the same basic design and double rainbow ribbon were adopted by thirteen other Allied nations (though the USA alone issued it with campaign clasps). The Union of South Africa produced a version with a reverse text in English and Dutch (not Afrikaans as is often stated).*

VALUE:

British pattern	£3–5
South African pattern	£12–15
Miniature	
Normal	£1–2
"CIVILIZATION" variety	£3–4

171. TERRITORIAL FORCE WAR MEDAL

Date: 1919.
Campaign: First World War 1914–19.
Branch of Service: Territorial forces.
Ribbon: Watered gold silk with two dark green stripes towards the edges.
Metal: Bronze.
Size: 36mm.
Description: (Obverse) effigy of King George V; (reverse) a wreath enclosing the text FOR VOLUNTARY SERVICE OVERSEAS 1914–19.
Clasps: None.
Comments: *Granted to all members of the Territorial Force embodied before 30 September 1914, who had completed four years service by that date, and who had served outside the United Kingdom between 4 August 1914 and 11 November 1918. Those who had already qualified for the 1914 or 1914–15 Stars, however, were excluded. Only 34,000 medals were awarded, making it by far the scarcest of the First World War medals. The value of individual medals depends on the regiment or formation of the recipient.*

VALUE:

Infantry	£60–80
RA, RE or support units	£45–55
Yeomanry	£80–100
RFC or RAF	Rare
Nursing sisters	£80–120
Miniature	£5–6

172. MEMORIAL PLAQUE

Date: 1919.
Campaign: First World War.
Branch of Service: British forces.
Ribbon: None.
Metal: Bronze.
Size: 120mm.
Description: The plaque shows Britannia bestowing a laurel crown on a rectangular tablet bearing the full name of the dead in raised lettering. In front stands the British lion, with dolphins in the upper field, an oak branch lower right, and a lion cub clutching a fallen eagle in the exergue. The inscription round the circumference reads HE (or SHE) DIED FOR FREEDOM AND HONOVR. A parchment scroll was issued with each plaque giving the deceased's name and unit.
Comments: *Awarded to the next of kin of those who lost their lives on active service during the War.*

VALUE:

He died (1,355,000)	£15–18
She died (600)	£800–1200
Parchment scroll	£10–12

173. NAVAL GENERAL SERVICE MEDAL

Date: 1915.

Campaigns: Naval actions 1915 to 1962.

Branch of Service: Royal Navy.

Ribbon: White with broad crimson edges and two narrow crimson stripes towards the centre.

Metal: Silver.

Size: 36mm.

Description: (Obverse) effigy of the reigning monarch (see below). (Reverse) Britannia and two seahorses travelling through the sea.

Clasps: Seventeen (see below).

Comments: *Instituted for service in minor operations for which no separate medal might be issued, it remained in use for almost half a century. In that period five different obverses were employed: George V (1915-36), George VI Ind Imp (1936-49), George VI Fid Def (1949-52), Elizabeth II Br Omn (1952-53) and Elizabeth II Dei Gratia (1953-62). Medals issued with the first three clasps include the name of the recipient's ship but this lapsed in later awards. The Malaya clasp was issued with three types of medal: the George VI Fid Def and Eliuzabth II Dei Gratia being the most common, the Elizabeth II Br Omn type being awarded mainly to SAS for special duties. The clasp Bomb & Mine Clearance 1945–46 is very rare as it was apparently only awarded to the Royal Australian Navy.*

VALUE:		Miniature
Persian Gulf 1909-1914 (7,217)	£70–80	£10
Iraq 1919-20 (116)	£800–1000	£15
NW Persia 1920 (4)*	Rare	£15
NW Persia 1919-20 (4)*	Rare	£15
Palestine 1936-39 (13,600)	£60–70	£10
SE Asia 1945-46 (2,000)	£90–100	£10
Minesweeping 1945-51 (4,750)	£90–100	£10
Palestine 1945-48 (7,900)	£55–65	£10
Malaya (George VI, Elizabeth II		
2nd type) (7,800)	£55–65	£10
(Elizabeth II 1st type)	£120–130	£10
Yangtze 1949 (1,450)	£300–350	£10
to HMS *Amethyst*	£500–600	
Bomb and Mine Clearance		
1945-53 (117)	£450–475	£10
Bomb and Mine Clearance 1945–56	Very rare	—
Bomb and Mine Clearance		
Mediterranean (60)	£900–1000	£10
Cyprus (4,300)	£60–70	£10
Near East (17,800)	£50–60	£10
Arabian Peninsula (1,200)	£140–180	£10
Brunei (900)	£120–140	£10

   * The clasp NW Persia 1919–20 was withdrawn in favour of the clasp NW Persia 1920. Recipients were supposed to return their first clasp in exchange for the latter.

174. GENERAL SERVICE MEDAL ✱ ✓✓

Date: 1918.
Campaigns: Minor campaigns 1918 to 1962.
Branch of Service: Army and RAF.
Ribbon: Purple with a central green band.
Metal: Silver.
Size: 36mm
Description: (Obverse) five different effigies of the reigning monarch (see preceding entry). (Reverse) a standing figure of Victory in a Greek helmet and carrying a trident, bestowing palms on a winged sword.
Clasps: Sixteen (see below).
Comments: *Awarded to military and RAF personnel for numerous campaigns and operations that fell short of full-scale war. It did not cover areas already catered for in the Africa and India general service medals.*

VALUE:

	British units	RAF	Indian and local units	Miniature
S. Persia (Brit. officers)	£120–150	Rare	£30–40	£12
Kurdistan	£40–50	£80–100	£20–30	£12
Iraq	£35–45	£80–100	£20–25	£10
N.W. Persia	£40–50	£180–220	£25–35	£10
Southern Desert Iraq	—	£250–275	£80–100	£10
Northern Kurdistan	—	£650–850	£100–120	£10
Palestine	£30–40	£30–40	£20–30	£10
S.E. Asia 1945-46	£60–70	£50–60	£25–35	£10
Bomb and Mine Clearance 1945-49	£280–300	£280–300	—	£10
Bomb and Mine Clearance 1945-56	£400–500	£400–500	—	£10
Palestine 1945-48	£25–35	£20–30	£20–25	£10
Malaya (George VI)	£25–30	£25–30	£20–25	£10
Malaya (Elizabeth II)	£25–30	£25–30	£20–25	£10
✱ Cyprus	£25–30	£25–30	£20–25	£10
Near East	£40–50	£40–50	—	£10
Arabian Peninsular	£30–40	£30–40	£25–30	£10
Brunei	£120–150	£100–120	£60–80	£10

175. INDIA GENERAL SERVICE MEDAL

Date: 1937.
Campaign: India 1936–39.
Branch of Service: British and Indian Armies and RAF.
Ribbon: Grey flanked by narrow red stripes, with broad green stripes at the edges.
Metal: Silver.
Size: 36mm
Description: (Obverse) crowned effigy of King George VI; (reverse) a tiger with the word INDIA across the top.
Clasps: North-West Frontier 1936–37, North-West Frontier 1937–39.
Comments: *The fifth and last of the IGS series, it was introduced when the change of effigy from George V to George VI became necessary, anticipating a similarly long life. It was not awarded after the outbreak of the Second World War, while the partition and independence of the Indian sub-continent afterwards rendered it obsolete. The medal was struck at the Royal Mint, London for award to British Army troops and RAF personnel, but the Calcutta Mint struck the medals awarded to the Indian Army.*

VALUE	British Army	RAF	Indian Army	Miniature
North West Frontier				
1936-37	£40–50	£60–70	£20–25	£10
1937-39	£50–60	£60–80	£25–30	£10
2 clasps	£60–70	£100–120	£30–40	£12

176. NORTH BORNEO GENERAL SERVICE MEDAL

Date: 1937.
Campaign: British North Borneo 1937-41.
Branch of Service: British North Borneo Company Staff, Constabulary and Residents.
Ribbon: Half dark green, half yellow for general awards, with provision for a thin red central stripe in the case of awards for bravery.
Metal: Silver.
Size: 37mm.
Description: (Obverse) the seated figure of Britannia with shield and trident, and a laurel spray in the exergue; (reverse) the arms of the Company.
Clasps: None.
Comments: *Although it could be granted for meritorious service or individual acts of gallantry, as a rule it was granted for at least eighteen years service. The medal was no longer awarded after the Japanese occupation of North Borneo, January 19, 1942. 50 medals were manufactured in 1937. Between 1937 and 1941 a total of 44 were awarded, including one for bravery (1939). In 1947 one officially-named medal was issued to replace one lost during the Japanese occupation. Total issued was therefore 45, and all were officially named prior to issue.*

VALUE:
Silver   Rare

SECOND WORLD WAR STARS

Eight different campaign stars were issued for the Second World War. Apart from some Commonwealth issues, these were issued unnamed. It was decided that the maximum number of stars that could be earned by any one person was five, while those who qualified for more received a clasp to be sewn on the ribbon of the appropriate star. Only one clasp per ribbon was permitted. Thus the stars could bear the following clasps:

1 1939-45 (Battle of Britain)
2 Atlantic (Air Crew Europe or France and Germany)
3 Air Crew Europe (Atlantic or France and Germany)
4 Africa (North Africa 1942-43, 8th Army or 1st Army)
5 Pacific (Burma)
6 Burma (Pacific)
7 Italy
8 France and Germany (Atlantic)

The ribbons are believed to have been designed by King George VI personally and have symbolic significance in each case.

When ribbons alone are worn, the clasp is denoted by a silver rosette, the Battle of Britain being represented by a gilt rosette. As the clasps were sewn on to the ribbon and the stars issued unnamed, it is difficult to put valuations on examples with campaign clasps, however, the prices quoted are for medals with the *original* clasps. When purchasing expensive groups it is advisable that the medals be supported by documentary provenance or form part of a group in which at least one of the medals is named to the recipient.

Many of the medals and stars of the Second World War are still being produced, therefore there are a number of different die varieties available. There are also a number of dangerous forgeries in existence so care should be taken when purchasing expensive items.

177. 1939-45 STAR ✳ ✓

Date: 1945.
Campaign: Second World War 1939-45.
Branch of Service: British forces.
Ribbon: Equal stripes of dark blue, red and light blue symbolising the Royal Navy, Army and RAF respectively.
Metal: Bronze.
Size: Height 44mm; max. width 38mm.
Description: The six-pointed star has a circular centre with the GRI/VI monogram, surmounted by a crown and inscribed THE 1939-1945 STAR round the foot.
Clasps: Battle of Britain, sewn directly on to the ribbon.
Comments: *The first in a series of eight bronze stars issued for service in the Second World War, it was awarded to personnel who had completed six months' service in specified operational commands overseas, between September 3, 1939 and August 15, 1945, though in certain cases the minimum period was shortened. Any service curtailed by death, injury or capture also qualified, as did the award of a decoration or a mention in despatches. The clasp awarded to RAF aircrew for action during the Battle of Britain was denoted by a gilt rosette when the ribbon was worn alone.*

VALUE:		Miniature
1939-45 Star	£6–8	£3
With Battle of Britain clasp	£450–500	£10

178. ATLANTIC STAR

Campaign: Atlantic 1939-45.
Branch of Service: Mainly Royal Navy.
Ribbon: Watered silk blue, white and green representing the ocean.
Metal: Bronze.
Size: Height 44mm; max. width 38mm.
Description: As above, but inscribed THE ATLANTIC STAR.
Clasps: Air Crew Europe, France and Germany.
Comments: *This star was awarded in the Royal Navy for six months' service afloat between 3 September 1939 and 8 May 1945 in the Atlantic or home waters, and to personnel employed in the convoys to North Russia and the South Atlantic. Merchant Navy personnel also qualified, as did RAF and Army (air crews and maritime gunners) who served afloat. Entitlement to the France and Germany or Air Crew Europe stars was denoted by clasps to that effect, if the Atlantic Star was previously awarded.*

VALUE:		Miniature
Atlantic Star	£25–30	£3
Air Crew Europe clasp	£45–50	£10
France & Germany clasp	£25–30	£10

179. AIR CREW EUROPE STAR

Campaign: Air operations over Europe 1939-44.
Branch of Service: RAF aircrew.
Ribbon: Pale blue (the sky) with black edges (night flying) and a narrow yellow stripe on either side (enemy searchlights).
Metal: Bronze.
Size: Height 44mm; max. width 38mm.
Description: As above, but inscribed THE AIR CREW EUROPE STAR.
Clasps: Atlantic or France and Germany.
Comments: *Awarded for operational flying from UK bases over Europe, for a period of two months between 3 September 1939 and 4 June 1944. Entitlement to either the Atlantic Star or France and Germany Star was denoted by the appropriate bar. This star is by far the most coveted of all the Second World War stars. The officially named South African star is the rarest of all the Second Wold War medals.*

VALUE:		Miniature
Air Crew Europe Star	£100–120	£3
Atlantic Clasp	£150–155	£10
France & Germany Clasp	£100–110	£10

180. AFRICA STAR ❋ ✓

Campaign: Africa 1940-43.
Branch of Service: British and Commonwealth forces.
Ribbon: Pale buff symbolising the sand of the desert, with a broad red central stripe, a dark blue stripe on the left and a light blue stripe on the right symbolising the three services.
Metal: Bronze.
Size: Height 44mm; max. width 38mm.
Description: As above, but inscribed THE AFRICA STAR.
Clasps: North Africa 1942-43, 8th Army, 1st Army.
Comments: *Awarded for entry into an operational area in North Africa between 10 June 1940 (the date of Italy's declaration of war) and 12 May 1943 (the end of operations in North Africa), but service in Abyssinia (Ethiopia), Somaliland, Eritrea and Malta also qualified for the award. A silver numeral 1 or 8 worn on the ribbon denoted service with the First or Eighth Army between 23 October 1942 and 23 May 1943. A clasp inscribed North Africa 1942-43 was awarded to personnel of the Royal Navy Inshore Squadrons and Merchant Navy vessels which worked inshore between these dates. RAF personnel also qualified for this clasp, denoted by a silver rosette on the ribbon alone.*

VALUE:		Miniature
Africa Star	£10–15	£3
8th Army clasp	£15–20	£10
1st Army clasp	£15–20	£10
North Africa 1942-43 clasp	£15–20	£10

181. PACIFIC STAR

Campaign: Pacific area 1941-45.
Branch of Service: British and Commonwealth forces.
Ribbon: Dark green (the jungle) with a central yellow stripe (the beaches), narrow stripes of dark and light blue (Royal Navy and RAF) and wider stripes of red (Army) at the edges.
Metal: Bronze.
Size: Height 44mm; max. width 38mm.
Description: As above, but inscribed THE PACIFIC STAR.
Clasps: Burma.
Comments: *Awarded for operational service in the Pacific theatre of war from 8 December 1941 to 15 August 1945. Service with the Royal and Merchant navies in the Pacific Ocean, Indian Ocean and South China Sea and land service in these areas also qualified. Personnel qualifying for both Pacific and Burma Stars got the first star and a clasp in respect of the second.*

VALUE:		*Miniature*
Pacific Star	£25–35	£3
Burma clasp	£30–35	£10

182. BURMA STAR

Campaign: Burma 1941-45.
Branch of Service: British and Commonwealth forces.
Ribbon: Three equal bands of dark blue (British forces), red (Commonwealth forces) and dark blue. The dark blue bands each have at their centres a stripe of bright orange (the sun).
Metal: Bronze.
Size: Height 44mm; max. width 38mm.
Description: As above, but inscribed THE BURMA STAR.
Clasps: Pacific
Comments: *Qualifying service in the Burma campaign counted from 11 December 1941 and included service in Bengal or Assam from 1 May 1942 to 31 December 1943, and from 1 January 1944 onwards in these parts of Bengal or Assam east of the Brahmaputra. Naval service in the eastern Bay of Bengal, off the coasts of Sumatra, Sunda and Malacca also counted.*

VALUE:		*Miniature*
Burma Star	£20–25	£3
Pacific Clasp	£30–35	£10

183. ITALY STAR

Campaign: Italy 1943-45.
Branch of Service: British and Commonwealth forces.
Ribbon: Five equal stripes of red, white, green, white and red (the Italian national colours).
Metal: Bronze.
Size: Height 44mm; max. width 38mm.
Description: As above, but inscribed THE ITALY STAR.
Clasps: None.
Comments: *Awarded for operational service on land in Italy, Sicily, Greece, Yugoslavia, the Aegean area and Dodecanese islands, Corsica, Sardinia and Elba at any time between 11 June 1943 and 8 May 1945.*

VALUE:		*Miniature*
Italy Star	£8–10	£3

184. FRANCE AND GERMANY STAR * ✓

Date: 1945.
Campaign: France and Germany 1944-45.
Branch of Service: British and Commonwealth forces.
Ribbon: Five equal stripes of blue, white, red, white and blue (the national colours of the United Kingdom, France and the Netherlands).
Metal: Bronze.
Size: Height 44mm; max. width 38mm.
Description: As above, but inscribed THE FRANCE AND GERMANY STAR.
Clasps: Atlantic.
Comments: *Awarded for operational service in France, Belgium, the Netherlands or Germany from 6 June 1944 to 8 May 1945. Service in the North Sea, English Channel and Bay of Biscay in connection with the campaign in northern Europe also qualified. Prior eligibility for the Atlantic or Air Crew Europe Stars entitled personnel only to a bar for France and Germany. Conversely a first award of the France and Germany Star could earn an Atlantic bar.*

VALUE:		Miniature
Pacific Star	£15–20	£3
Atlantic Clasp	£70–80	£10

185. DEFENCE MEDAL * ✓

Date: 1945.
Campaign: Second World War 1939-45.
Branch of Service: British and Commonwealth forces.
Ribbon: Two broad bars of green (this green and pleasant land) superimposed by narrow stripes of black (the black-out), with a wide band of orange (fire-bombing) in the centre.
Metal: Cupro-nickel or silver.
Size: 36mm.
Description: (Obverse) the uncrowned effigy of King George VI; (reverse) two lions flanking an oak sapling crowned with the dates at the sides and wavy lines representing the sea below. The words THE DEFENCE MEDAL appear in the exergue.
Clasps: None.
Comments: *Awarded to service personnel for three years' service at home or six months' service overseas in territories subjected to air attack or otherwise closely threatened. Personnel of Anti-Aircraft Command, RAF ground crews, Dominion forces stationed in the UK, the Home Guard, Civil Defence, National Fire Service and many other civilian units qualified for the medal. The medal was generally issued unnamed in cupro-nickel, but a Canadian version was struck in silver.*

VALUE:		Miniature
Cupro-nickel	£10–12	£8
Silver	£14–18	£12

186. WAR MEDAL 1939–45 ✱ ✓

Date: 1945.
Campaign: Second World War 1939-45.
Branch of Service: British and Commonwealth forces.
Ribbon: Narrow red stripe in the centre, with a narrow white stripe on
   either side, broad red stripes at either edge and two intervening
   stripes of blue.
Metal: Cupro-nickel or silver.
Size: 36mm.
Description: (Obverse) effigy of King George VI; (reverse) a
   triumphant lion trampling on a dragon symbolising the Axis
   powers.
Clasps: None.
Comments: *All fulltime personnel of the armed forces wherever they were
   serving, so long as they had served for at least 28 days between 3 September
   1939 and 2 September 1945 were eligible for this medal. It was granted in
   addition to the campaign stars and the Defence Medal. A few categories of
   civilians, such as war correspondents and ferry pilots who had flown in
   operational theatres, also qualified. No clasps were issued with this medal
   but a bronze oak leaf denoted a mention in despatches. The medal was
   struck in cupro-nickel and issued unnamed, but those issued to Australian
   and South African personnel were officially named. The Canadian version
   of the medal was struck in silver.*

VALUE:		*Miniature*
Cupro-nickel	£7–10	£8
Named (Australian or South African)	£8–12	
Silver (Canadian)	£10–14	£12

187. INDIA SERVICE MEDAL

Date: 1945.
Campaign: India 1939-45.
Branch of Service: Indian forces.
Ribbon: Dark blue with two wide and one central thin pale blue
   stripes.
Metal: Cupro-nickel.
Size: 36mm.
Description: (Obverse) the effigy of the King Emperor; (reverse) a map
   of the Indian sub-continent with INDIA at the top and 1939-45
   round the foot.
Clasps: None.
Comments: *Awarded to officers and men of the Indian forces for three years'
   non-operational service in India. In effect, it took the place of the Defence
   Medal in respect of Indian forces.*

VALUE: £10–12   *Miniature*   £10–12

188. CANADIAN VOLUNTEER SERVICE MEDAL

Date: 1943.
Campaign: Second World War 1939-45.
Branch of Service: Canadian forces.
Ribbon: Narrow stripes of green and red flanking a broad central stripe of dark blue.
Metal: Silver.
Size: 36mm.
Description: (Obverse) seven men and women in the uniforms of the various services, marching in step; (reverse) the Canadian national arms.
Clasps: Maple leaf. A clasp inscribed DIEPPE and surmounted by the Combined Operations emblem, was instituted in 1994 for award to all servicemen who took part in the Dieppe raid of 1942.
Comments: *Awarded for eighteen months' voluntary service in the Canadian forces. The clasp denoted overseas service.*

VALUE:

		Miniature
Silver medal	£14–16	£8
With Maple leaf clasp	£18–22	£12

189. AFRICA SERVICE MEDAL

Date: 1943.
Campaign: Second World War 1939-45.
Branch of Service: South African forces.
Ribbon: A central orange stripe, with green and gold stripes on either side.
Metal: Silver.
Size: 36mm.
Description: (Obverse) depicts a map of the African Continent; (reverse) bears a leaping Springbok. Inscribed AFRICA SERVICE MEDAL on the left and AFRIKADIENS-MEDALJE on the right.
Clasps: None.
Comments: *Awarded to Union service personnel who served at home and abroad during the War for at least thirty days. Medals were fully named and gave the service serial number of the recipient, prefixed by the letters N (Native Military Corps), C (Cape Corps) or M (Indian and Malay Corps), no prefix indicated a white volunteer—a curious example of racism at work.*

VALUE:

Silver medal (190,000)	£8–12	Miniature	£10

190. AUSTRALIA SERVICE MEDAL

Date: 1949.
Campaign: Second World War 1939-45.
Branch of Service: Australian forces.
Ribbon: A broad central band of khaki bordered in red, with a dark blue and a light blue bar at either edge.
Metal: Cupro-nickel.
Size: 36mm.
Description: (Obverse) the effigy of King George VI; (reverse) the Australian arms supported by a kangaroo and an emu.
Clasps: None.
Comments: *Awarded to all Australian personnel who had seen eighteen months' overseas or three years' home service. The medals were named to the recipients and their service numbers were prefixed by the initial of their state: N (New South Wales), Q (Queensland), S (South Australia), T (Tasmania), V (Victoria) and W (Western Australia).*

VALUE:

Cupro-nickel medal (180,000)	£25–30	Miniature	£12

191. NEW ZEALAND WAR SERVICE MEDAL

Date: 1946.
Campaign: Second World War 1939-45.
Branch of Service: New Zealand forces.
Ribbon: Black with white edges.
Metal: Cupro-nickel.
Size: 36mm.
Description: (Obverse) effigy of King George VI; (reverse) the text
FOR SERVICE TO NEW ZEALAND 1939-45 with a fern leaf below.
Suspension was by a pair of fern leaves attached to a straight bar.
Clasps: None.
Comments: *Issued unnamed, to all members of the New Zealand forces who
completed one month full-time or six months part-time service between
September 1939 and September 1945.*

VALUE:

Cupro-nickel medal (240,000)   £18–20   *Miniature*   £7

192. SOUTH AFRICAN MEDAL FOR WAR SERVICE

Date: 1946.
Campaign: Second World War 1939-46.
Branch of Service: South African forces.
Ribbon: Three equal stripes of orange, white and blue, the South
African national colours.
Metal: Silver.
Size: 36mm.
Description: (Obverse) effigy of King George VI; (reverse) a wreath of
protea flowers enclosing the dates 1939 and 1945. Inscribed in
English and Afrikaans: SOUTH AFRICA FOR WAR SERVICES on
the left and SUID AFRIKA VIR OORLOGDIENSTE on the right.
Clasps: None.
Comments: *Men and women who served for at least two years in any official
voluntary organisation in South Africa or overseas qualified for this medal
so long as the service was both voluntary and unpaid. Those who already
had the South African War Service Medal were ineligible.*

VALUE:
Silver (17,500)   £25–35   *Miniature*   £14

193. SOUTHERN RHODESIA WAR SERVICE MEDAL

Date: 1946.
Campaign: Second World War 1939-45.
Branch of Service: Southern Rhodesian forces.
Ribbon: Dark green with black and red stripes at each edge.
Metal: Cupro-nickel.
Size: 36mm.
Description: (Obverse) King George VI; (reverse) the Rhodesian
national arms. FOR SERVICE IN SOUTHERN RHODESIA round
the top and the dates 1939-1945 at the foot.
Clasps: None.
Comments: *This very scarce medal was awarded only to those who served in
Southern Rhodesia during the period of the War but who were ineligible for
one of the campaign stars or war medals.*

VALUE:
Cupro-nickel (1700)   £160–175   *Miniature*   £14

194. NEWFOUNDLAND VOLUNTEER WAR SERVICE MEDAL

Date: 1981.
Campaign: Second World War 1939-45.
Branch of Service: Newfoundland forces.
Ribbon: Deep claret with edges of red, white and blue.
Metal: Bronze.
Size: 37mm
Description: (Obverse) the royal cypher of George VI surmounted by a crown topped by a caribou, the Newfoundland national emblem. (Reverse) Britannia on a scallop shell background guarded by two lions.
Clasps:
Comments: *While the Second World War was being fought, Newfoundland was still a separate British colony which did not enter the Canadian Confederation till 1947. Consequently Newfoundland servicemen did not qualify for the Canadian Volunteer Service medal, and this deficiency was not remedied until July 1981 when the Newfoundland provincial government instituted tis medal. Those who had served with the Canadian forces, on the other hand, and already held the Canadian medal, were not eligible for this award. The medal could be claimed by next-of-kin of those who died in or since the war.*

VALUE: £350–450   *Miniature*   £35

195. KOREA MEDAL

Date: July 1951.
Campaign: Korean War 1950-53.
Branch of Service: British and Commonwealth forces.
Ribbon: Yellow, with two blue stripes .
Metal: Cupro-nickel or silver.
Size: 36mm.
Description: (Obverse) Right-facing bust of Queen Elizabeth II by Mary Gillick; there are two obverse types, with or without BR: OMN. (Reverse) Hercules wrestling with the Hydra, KOREA in the exergue.
Clasps: None.
Comments: *Awarded to all British and Commonwealth forces who took part in the Korean War between July 1950 and July 27, 1953. British medals were issued in cupro-nickel impressed in small capitals, medals to Australian and New Zealand forces were impressed in large capitals and the Canadian version was struck in silver and has CANADA below the Queen's bust. Particularly prized are medals issued to the 'Glorious Gloucesters' who played a gallant part in the battle of the Imjin River.*

VALUE:		*Miniature*
British, first obverse	£50–70	£7
British, second obverse	£100–150	£7
To Gloucester Regiment	£250–300	
Australian or New Zealand naming	£70–90	
Canadian, silver (27,000)	£60–70	£9

196. SOUTH AFRICAN MEDAL FOR KOREA

Date: 1952.
Campaign: Korea 1950-53.
Branch of Service: South African forces.
Ribbon: Sky blue central band flanked by dark blue stripes and edges of orange.
Metal: Silver.
Size: 38mm.
Description: (Obverse) maps of South Africa and Korea with an arrow linking them and the words VRYWILLIGERS and VOLUNTEERS in the field. (Reverse) the then South African arms surmounted by the crowned EIIR.
Clasps: None.
Comments: *Awarded to the 800 personnel in the contingent sent to Korea by the Union of South Africa. Suspension is by a ring and claw.*

VALUE:

Silver (800)	£280–300	*Miniature*	£25

197. UNITED NATIONS KOREA MEDAL

Date: December 1950.
Campaign: Korea 1950-53.
Branch of Service: All UN forces.
Ribbon: Seventeen narrow stripes alternating pale blue and white.
Metal: Bronze.
Size: 35mm.
Description: (Obverse) the wreathed globe emblem of the UN; (reverse) inscribed FOR SERVICE IN DEFENCE OF THE PRINCIPLES OF THE CHARTER OF THE UNITED NATIONS.
Clasps: Korea.
Comments: *National variants were produced, but the British type was granted to all personnel of the British and Commonwealth forces who had served at least one full day in Korea or in support units in Japan. Moreover, as those who served in Korea after the armistice in July 1953 were also entitled to the UN medal it is sometimes found in groups without the corresponding British medal. The award was extended to cover the period up to July 27, 1954, the first anniversary of the Panmunjom Truce.*

VALUE:

	£22–25	*Miniature*	£8

198. GENERAL SERVICE MEDAL 1962

Date: 1964.
Campaign: Minor campaigns and operations since 1962.
Branch of Service: British forces.
Ribbon: Deep purple edged with green.
Metal: Silver.
Size: 36mm.
Description: (Obverse) a crowned bust of Queen Elizabeth II; (reverse) an oak wreath enclosing a crown and the words FOR CAMPAIGN SERVICE. It has a beaded and curved suspension above which are mounted campaign clasps.
Clasps: Twelve to date (see below); the maximum clasps awarded so far seems to be six.
Comments: *This medal was instituted for award to personnel of all services, and thus did away with the need for separate Army and Navy general service medals. Awards range from a mere 70 for South Vietnam to over 130,000 for service in Northern Ireland.*

VALUE:

		Miniature
Borneo	£30–40	£8–10
Radfan	£45–55	£8–10
South Arabia	£30–40	£8–10
Malay Peninsula	£30–40	£8–10
South Vietnam	Rare	£8–10
Northern Ireland	£30–40	£8–10
Dhofar	£120–140	£8–10
Lebanon	£450–500	£8–10
Mine Clearance	£650–800	£8–10
Gulf	£300–400	£8–10
Kuwait	£600–800	£8–10
N. Iraq & S. Turkey	£500–600	£8–10
2 clasps	£40–60	£12–16
3 clasps	£80–120	£14–18
4 clasps	From £140	£16–20

199. UNITED NATIONS EMERGENCY FORCE MEDAL

Date: 1957.
Campaign: Israel and Egypt 1956–57.
Branch of Service: All UN forces.
Ribbon: Sand-coloured with a central light blue stripe and narrow dark blue and green stripes towards each edge.
Metal: Bronze.
Size: 35mm.
Description: (Obverse) the UN wreathed globe emblem with UNEF at the top; (reverse) inscribed IN THE SERVICE OF PEACE. Ring suspension.
Clasps: None.
Comments: *Awarded to all personnel who served with the UN peace-keeping forces on the border between Israel and Egypt following the Six Day War of 1956. These medals were awarded to troops from Brazil, Canada, Colombia, Denmark, Finland, Indonesia, Norway, Sweden and Yugoslavia.*

VALUE:
Bronze	£20–25	Miniature	£7

200. VIETNAM MEDAL

Date: July 1968.
Campaign: Vietnam 1964-68.
Branch of Service: Australian and New Zealand forces.
Ribbon: A broad central band of bright yellow surmounted by three thin red stripes (the Vietnamese national colours) and bordered by broader red stripes, with dark and light blue stripes at the edges, representing the three services.
Metal: Silver.
Size: 36mm.
Description: (Obverse) the crowned bust of Queen Elizabeth II; (reverse) a nude male figure pushing apart two spheres representing different ideologies.
Clasps: None.
Comments: *Awarded to personnel who served in Vietnam a minimum of one day on land or 28 days at sea after 28 May 1964. The medal was impressed in large capitals (Australian) or small capitals (New Zealand).*

VALUE:

Australian recipient (18,000)	£140–160
New Zealand recipient (4000)	£140–160
Miniature	£10–12

201. SOUTH VIETNAM CAMPAIGN MEDAL

Date: 1964.
Campaign: Vietnam 1960-68.
Branch of Service: Allied forces in Vietnam.
Ribbon: White with two broad green stripes towards the centre and narrow green edges.
Metal: Bronze.
Size: Height 42mm; max. width 36mm.
Description: A six-pointed star, with gold rays in the angles. The gilt enamelled centre shows a map of Vietnam engulfed in flames; (reverse) a Vietnamese inscription in the centre.
Comments: *Awarded by the government of South Vietnam to Australian and New Zealand forces who served at least six months in Vietnam. The original issue, of Vietnamese manufacture, was relatively crude and issued unnamed. Subsequently medals were produced in Australia and these are not only of a better quality but bear the name of the recipient.*

VALUE:

Unnamed	£10–15
Named	£20–30
Miniature	£6–10

202. RHODESIA MEDAL

Date: 1980.
Campaign: Rhodesia 1979–80.
Branch of Service: British and Rhodesian forces.
Ribbon: Sky blue, with a narrow band of red, white and dark blue in the centre.
Metal: Rhodium-plated cupro-nickel.
Size: 36mm.
Description: (Obverse) the crowned bust of Queen Elizabeth II; (reverse) a sable antelope with the name of the medal and the year of issue.
Clasps: None.
Comments: *This medal was awarded to personnel serving in Rhodesia for fourteen days between 1 December 1979 and 20 March 1980, pending the elections and the emergence of the independent republic of Zimbabwe. Medals were issued unnamed or named in impressed capitals.*

VALUE:

Cupro-nickel (2500)	£300–350	*Miniature*	£9

203. SOUTH ATLANTIC MEDAL

Date: 1982.
Campaign: Falkland Islands and South Georgia 1982.
Branchof Service: British forces.
Ribbon: Watered silk blue, white, green, white and blue.
Metal: Cupro-nickel.
Size: 36mm.
Description: (Obverse) crowned profile of Queen Elizabeth II;
(reverse) laurel wreath below the arms of the Falkland Islands with
SOUTH ATLANTIC MEDAL inscribed round the top.
Clasps: None, but a rosette denoting service in the combat zone.
Comments: *Awarded to all personnel who took part in operations in the
South Atlantic for the liberation of South Georgia and the Falkland Islands
following the Argentinian invasion. To qualify, the recipient had to have at
least one full day's service in the Falklands or South Georgia, or 30 days in
the operational zone including Ascension Island. Those who qualified
under the first condition were additionally awarded a large rosette for wear
on the ribbon.*

VALUE:

Army (7000)	£180–200
Royal Navy (13,000)	£150–180
Royal Marines (3700)	£180–200
Royal Fleet Auxiliary (2000)	£120–150
RAF (2000)	£150–180
Merchant Navy and civilians (2000)	£110–120
Miniature	£6
with rosette	£9

203A. SOVIET 40th ANNIVERSARY MEDAL

Date: 1985.
Campaign: Second World War.
Branch of Service: British and Canadian forces who served
mainly in RN or MN ships on Arctic convoys.
Ribbon: One half red, the other orange with three black
stripes, edged with pale blue. Worn in the Russian
style.
Metal: Bronze.
Size: 32mm.
Description: (Obverse) Group of servicemen and women
in front of a five-pointed star flanked by oak leaves and
the dates 1945–1985 above; (reverse) 40th anniversary of
the Victory in the Great Patriotic War 1941–1945, in
Russian.
Clasps: None.
Comments: *In 1994 Her Majesty the Queen approved the
wearing of this medal awarded by the Soviet Government to
selected ex-Servicemen, bearing in mind the changed
circumstances in Russia since the award was first issued.*

VALUE:	British striking	£30
	Russian striking	£40

204. GULF MEDAL

Date: 1992.
Campaign: Kuwait and Saudi Arabia 1990-91.
Branch of Service: British forces.
Ribbon: Sand-coloured broad central band flanked by narrow stripes of dark blue, red and light blue (left) or light blue, red and dark blue (right) representing the sands of the desert and the three armed services.
Metal: Cupro-nickel.
Size: 36mm.
Description: (Obverse) crowned profile of Queen Elizbeth II; (reverse) an eagle and automatic rifle superimposed on an anchor, symbolising the three armed services. The dates of the Gulf War appear at the foot.
Clasps: 2 Aug 1990, 16 Jan–28 Feb 1991.
Comments: *Awarded to personnel who had thirty days continuous service in the Middle East (including Cyprus) between 2 August 1990 and 7 March 1991, or seven days between 16 January 1991 and 28 February 1991, or service with the Kuwait Liaison Team on 2 August 1990, the date of the Iraqi invasion. Two clasps were sanctioned and awarded to personnel who qualified for active service with the Liaison Team or in the operations to liberate Kuwait. A rosette is worn on the ribbon alone to denote the campaign clasps. Naming is in impressed capitals. More than 45,000 medals were awarded. See also the Kuwait and Iraq-Turkey clasps awarded to the Campaign Service Medal. About 1,500 civilian members of British Aerospace working at Dahran also received the medal with the clasp 16 Jan to 28 Feb 1991.*

VALUE:

No clasp	£80–100
16 Jan to 28 Feb 1991	Regiments: £150–200
	Corps and Artillery: £110–130
	Civilians: £100–130
2 Aug 1990	£1200–1600
Miniature	£10

205. SAUDI ARABIAN MEDAL FOR THE LIBERATION OF KUWAIT

Date: 1991.
Campaign: Gulf War 1991.
Branch of Service: British and Allied forces.
Ribbon: Green with edges of red, black and white (the Saudi national colours).
Metal: White metal.
Size: approx. 45mm across
Description: The white metal medal has a star of fifteen long and fifteen short round-tipped rays, surmounted by a bronze circle bearing a crowned and enwreathed globe on which appears a map of Arabia. Above the circle is a palm tree with crossed scimitars, the state emblem of Saudi Arabia. A scroll inscribed in Arabic and English LIBERATION OF KUWAIT appears round the foot of the circle.
Clasps: None.
Comments: *Awarded by the government of Saudi Arabia to all Allied personnel who took part in the campaign for the liberation of Kuwait, although only a few of the 45,000 British servicemen were subsequently given permission by the Foreign and Commonwealth Office to wear it. The contract for production was shared between Spink and a Swiss company, but subsequently a flatter version, more practicable for wear with other medals, was manufactured in the United States.*

VALUE: £15–20   *Miniature* £12

206. KUWAITI LIBERATION MEDALS

4th grade

Date: 1991.
Campaign: Liberation of Kuwait 1991.
Branch of Service: Allied forces.
Ribbon: Equal stripes of green, white and red (the Kuwaiti national colours).
Metal:
Size:
Description: The circular medals have different decorative treatments of the Kuwaiti state emblem on the obverse, enshrined in a five-petalled flower (Second Grade), a five-pointed star with radiate background (Third Grade) and a plain medallic treatment (Fourth Grade). All grades, however, have a straight bar suspender of different designs.
Clasps: None.
Comments: *This medal was issued in five grades and awarded according to the rank of the recipient. The Excellent Grade was only conferred on the most senior Allied commanders, the First Grade went to brigadiers and major-generals, the Second Grade to officers of field rank (colonels and majors), the Third Grade to junior officers (captains, lieutenants and equivalent ranks in the other services), and the Fourth Grade to all other ranks. HM Government has decreed that British personnel may accept their medals as a keepsake but permission to wear them in uniform has so far been refused. The Canadian Government has followed the same policy, but the personnel of other Allied nations are permitted to wear their medals.*

VALUE: 4th grade: £8–10

206A. NATO MEDAL

Instituted: December 20, 1994.
Campaigns: Any theatre or area of operations in the service of the North Atlantic Treaty Organization.
Branch of Service: NATO military and service personnel.
Ribbon: NATO blue with a narrow white stripe towards each edge.
Metal: Bronze
Size: 36mm
Description: (Obverse) the NATO star emblem set in a wreath of olive leaves; (reverse) the title NORTH ATLANTIC TREATY ORGANIZATION and the words IN SERVICE OF PEACE AND FREEDOM in English and French.
Clasp: Former Yugoslavia.
Comments: *The NATO medal was first instituted to reward personnel who took part in the Alliance operations in the former Yugoslavia. Any person serving under NATO command or operational control is eligible for the award. UK Service personnel cannot qualify for the NATO Medal and the UNPROFOR Medal (no. 207) in respect of the same period of service. The qualifying period for the medal is to be designated by the Secretary-General, however, for the operations in the former Yugoslavia the period has been set as 30 days continuous or accumulated service within the theatre of operations inside the former Yugoslavia and the Adriatic, or 90 days within the area of operations but outside the territory of the former Yugoslavia. The medal takes precedence equal to the General Service Medal in order of date of award.*

VALUE: —

207. UNITED NATIONS MEDAL

Date: 1951.
Campaigns: Various supervisory or observation roles since 1948.
Branch of Service: UN forces.
Ribbons: Various (see below).
Metal: Bronze.
Size: 35mm.
Description: (Obverse) the wreathed globe emblem surmounted by the letters UN; (reverse) plain.
Clasps: CONGO, UNGOMAP.
Comments: *Apart from the UN Korea and UNEF medals, there have been numerous awards to personnel who served in one or other of the UN peace-keeping actions around the world since the end of the Second World War. The all-purpose medal has been awarded with various distinctive ribbons for service in many of the world's trouble spots.*

UNTSO United Nations Truce Supervision Organization (Israel, Egypt, Syria since 1948).
Blue ribbon with two narrow white stripes towards the edges.
UNOGIL United Nations Observation Group in Lebanon (1958).
Same ribbon as UNTSO.
ONUC Organisation des Nations Unies au Congo (1960–64).
Originally the same ribbon as UNTSO with clasp CONGO, but a green ribbon, with white and blue edges was substituted in 1963.
UNTEA United Nations Temporary Executive Authority (Netherlands New Guinea, 1962).
Blue ribbon with a white central stripe bordered green.
UNMOGIP United Nations Military Observer Group in India and Pakistan since 1949.
Dark green ribbon shading to light green with white and blue edges.
UNIPOM United Nations India Pakistan Observation Mission (1965–66).
Ribbon as UNMOGIP.
UNYOM United Nations Yemen Observation Mission (1963–64).
Ribbon with brown centre, yellow stripes and light blue edges.
UNFICYP United Nations Force in Cyprus (1964–).
Pale blue ribbon with central white stripe bordered in dark blue.
UNEF 2 United Nations Emergency Force 2 patrolling Israeli-Egyptian cease-fire (1973–).
Pale blue ribbon with sand centre and two dark blue stripes.
UNDOF United Nations Disengagement Observer Force, Golan Heights (1974–).
Ribbon of red, white, black and pale blue.
UNIFIL United Nations Interim Force in Lebanon (1978–).
Pale blue ribbon with green centre bordered white and red.
UNGOMAP United Nations Good Offices in Afghanistan and Pakistan.
A bronze bar inscribed UNGOMAP was issued but as the mission was made up from observers from three other missions it can only be found on these ribbons: UNTSO, UNIFIL, UNDOF.
UNIIMOG United Nations Iran-Iraq Monitoring Observation Group.
Pale blue with red, white and green edges.
UNAVEM United Nations Angola Verification Mission.
Pale blue ribbon with yellow edges separated by narrow stripes of red, white and black.
ONUCA Observadores de las Naciones Unidas en Centro America (Nicaragua and Guatemala).
Pale blue ribbon with dark blue edges and nine thin central green or white stripes.
UNTAG United Nations Transitional Assistance Group (Namibia, 1990).
Sand ribbon with pale blue edges and thin central stripes of blue, green, red, sand and deep blue.
ONUSAL Observadores de las Naciones Unidas en El Salvador.
Pale blue ribbon with a white central stripe bordered dark blue.
UNIKOM United Nations Iraq Kuwait Observation Mission.
Sand ribbon with a narrow central stripe of pale blue.
MINURSO Mission des Nations Unies pour la Referendum dans le Sahara Occidental (UN Mission for the Referendum in Western Sahara).
Ribbon has a broad sandy centre flanked by stripes of UN blue.
UNAMIC United Nations Advanced Mission in Cambodia (Oct. 1991–March 1992)
Pale blue ribbon with central white stripe bordered with dark blue, yellow and red stripes.
UNTAC United Nations Transitional Authority in Cambodia (March 1992–Sept. 1993).
Green ribbon with central white stripe edged with red, pale blue and dark blue.
UNOSOM United Nations Operations in Somalia (1992–)
Pale yellow ribbon with central blue stripe edged with green.

UNMIH   United Nations Mission in Haiti
Pale blue ribbon with dark blue and red central stripes edged with white.
UNIMOZ   United Nations Operations in Mozambique (1992–)
Pale blue ribbon edged with white and green stripes.
UNPROFOR   United Nations Protection Force (1992–) operating in the former Yugoslavia, especially Bosnia.
Blue ribbon with central red stripe edged in white and green or brown edges.
UNOMIL   United Nations Observer Mission in Liberia (1993–)
Pale blue ribbon flanked with white stripes with dark blue or red edges.
UNOMUR   United Nations Observer Mission in Uganda/Rwanda (1993–)
Pale blue central stripe edged by white and flanked by equal stripes of black, orange and red.
UNOMIG   United Nations Observer Mission in Georgia (1993–)
Pale blue central stripe flanked by equal stripes of white, green and dark blue.
UNAMIR   United Nations Assistance Mission in Rwanda (1993–)
Pale blue central stripe edged with white and flanked by equal stripes of black, green and red.
UNHQ   General service at UN headquarters, New York.
Plain ribbon of pale blue, the UN colour.
UNPREDEP   United Nations Preventative Deployment in Yugoslavia.
Blue ribbon with central red stripe bearing four yellow lines and flanked by white edging.
UNMOP   United Nations Mission of Observers in Pravlaka.
Dark blue ribbon with central yellow stripe edged with white, and two pale blue stripes.
UNTAES   United Nations Transitional Authority in Eastern Slovenia.
Pale blue ribbon with yellow, red edged with white, and green stripes.
UNMOT   United Nations Peacekeeping Force in Tadjikistan.
Blue ribbon with central green stripe flanked by white stripes.
UNMIBH   United Nations Mission in Bosnia Herzegovina.
Blue ribbon with white central stripe, edged with one green and one red stripe.
UNMOGUA   United Nations Military Observers in Guatemala.
Purple with central blue stripe and two white stripes each with central green line.
UN SPECIAL SERVICE   Reward for special services.
Blue ribbon with white edges

VALUE:

Any current issue medal regardless of ribbon	£10–15
Original striking for Cyprus	£20–25
Miniature	£6–8

207A. NEW ZEALAND SERVICE MEDAL 1946–49

Instituted: 1995.
Branch of Service: Officers and men of J Force—New Zealand personnel who served in Japan as part of the British Commonwealth Occupation Force.
Ribbon: White with black edges and a red central stripe.
Metal: Rhodium plated steel.
Size: 38mm.
Description: (obverse) effigy of Queen Elizabeth; (reverse) royal arms of New Zealand. Swivel bar suspension.
Clasp: Malaya 1960–64.
Comments: *Awarded to about 7300 personnel despatched direct from New Zealand who had not had previous service in the Second World War, as well as about 5,000 troops stationed in Italy at the end of the war who were then sent to the Far East to take part in the police and peacekeeping operations in Japan from 1946 to 1949.*

VALUE: £100–150

LONG AND MERITORIOUS SERVICE MEDALS

A large, varied but until recently relatively neglected category comprises the medals awarded for long service and good conduct or meritorious service. Their common denominator is that the grant of such awards is made in respect of a minimum number of years of unblemished service—"undetected crime" is how it is often described in the armed forces. As their title implies, long service and good conduct medals combine the elements of lengthy service with no transgressions of the rules and regulations. Meritorious service, on the other hand, implies rather more. Apart from a brief period (1916-28) when awards were made for single acts of gallantry, MSMs have generally been granted to warrant officers and senior NCOs as a rather superior form of long service medal.

Long service and good conduct medals do not appear to excite the same interest among collectors as campaign medals. Perhaps this may be accounted for by their image of stolid devotion to duty rather than the romantic connotations of a medal with an unusual clasp awarded for service in some remote and all but forgotten outpost of the Empire. Nevertheless their importance should not be overlooked. Especially in regard to groups consisting primarily of the Second World War medals, they serve a useful purpose in establishing the provenance of the group, on account of the fact that they are invariably named to the recipient.

Service medals include not only such well known types as the Army LSGC (known affectionately as "the mark of the beast" on account of its high incidence on the chests of sergeant-majors), but also awards to the Territorial and Reserve forces, the auxiliary forces, the nursing services, and organisations such as the Royal Observer Corps and the Cadet Force, the Police, the Red Cross and St John's Ambulance Brigade. The Special Constabulary and Fire Brigades also have their own medals bestowed according to length of service and distinguished conduct. These medals may lack the glamour of naval and military awards but in recent years they have become increasingly fashionable with collectors and will certainly repay further study in their own right.

As many of these medals have been in use for eighty years or more with a standard reverse, variation usually lies in the obverse, changed for each successive sovereign. In addition, considerable variety has been imparted by the use of crowned or uncrowned profiles and busts, and changes in titles.

The following is a summary of the principal obverse types which may be encountered, referred to in the text by their type letters in brackets:

Queen Victoria (A) Young Head by William Wyon 1838-60
Queen Victoria (B) Veiled Head by Leonard C. Wyon 1860-87
Queen Victoria (C) Jubilee Head by Sir Joseph E. Boehm 1887-93
Queen Victoria (D) Old Head by Sir Thomas Brock 1893-1901
Edward VII (A) Bareheaded bust in Field Marshal's uniform
Edward VII (B) Bareheaded bust in Admiral's uniform
Edward VII (C) Coinage profile by George W. de Saulles
George V (A) Bareheaded bust in Field Marshal's uniform
George V (B) Bareheaded bust in Admiral's uniform
George V (C) Crowned bust in Coronation robes
George V (D) Crowned bust in Delhi Durbar robes
George V (E) Coinage profile by Bertram Mackennal 1931-36
George VI (A) Crowned bust in Coronation robes
George VI (B) Crowned profile IND: IMP 1937-48
George VI (C) Crowned profile FID: DEF 1949-52
George VI (D) Coinage profile IND: IMP 1937-48
George VI (E) Coinage profile FID: DEF 1949-52
Elizabeth II (A) Tudor crown 1953-80
Elizabeth II (B) Imperial crown 1980-
Elizabeth II (C) Coinage bust BR: OMN 1953-54
Elizabeth II (D) Coinage bust without BR: OMN 1955-

PRINCIPAL OBVERSE TYPES:

Queen Victoria (A) Young Head

Queen Victoria (B) Veiled Head

Queen Victoria (C) Jubilee Head

Queen Victoria (D) Old Head

Edward VII (A) Bareheaded bust in Field Marshal's uniform

Edward VII (B) Bareheaded bust in Admiral's uniform

George V (A) Bareheaded bust in Field Marshal's uniform

George V (B) Bareheaded bust in Admiral's uniform

George V (C) Crowned bust in Coronation robes

George V (E) Coinage profile by Bertram Mackennal

George VI (B) Crowned profile IND: IMP 1937-48

George VI (C) Crowned profile FID: DEF 1949-52

George VI (D) Coinage profile IND: IMP 1937-48

George VI (E) Coinage profile FID: DEF 1949-52

Elizabeth II (A) Tudor crown 1953-80

Elizabeth II (B) Imperial crown 1980-

Elizabeth II (C) Coinage bust BR: OMN 1953-54

Elizabeth II (D) Coinage bust without BR: OMN.

208. ROYAL NAVAL MERITORIOUS SERVICE MEDAL

Instituted: 14 January 1919, by Order in Council.
Branch of Service: Royal Navy.
Ribbon: Crimson edged in white, with a central white stripe.
Metal: Silver
Size: 36mm.
Description: (Obverse) effigy of the reigning monarch; (reverse) imperial crown surmounting a wreath containing the words FOR MERITORIOUS SERVICE. The medal was named in large seriffed capitals round the rim.
Comments: *Awarded without annuity or pension to petty officers and ratings of the Royal Navy. Originally it was awarded either for specific acts of gallantry not in the presence of the enemy or for arduous and specially meritorious service afloat or ashore in action with the enemy. Bars were granted for second awards. It was superseded in 1928 by the British Empire Medal for Gallantry or Meritorious Service, but re-instated on 1 December 1977. In this guise it has been awarded to senior petty officers of the Royal Navy, warrant officers and senior NCOs of the Royal Marines, and equivalent ranks in the WRNS and QARNNS, who have at least 27 years service and are already holders of the LSGC medal and three good conduct badges. The medal is not awarded automatically when these criteria are satisfied, as no more than 59 medals may be awarded annually. The revived medal is identical to the Army MSM and can only be distinguished by the naming giving rank and name of ship.*

VALUE:		Miniature
George V (B) (1020)	£180–220	£10–12
Elizabeth II (D)	£240–280	£10–12

210. ROYAL MARINES MERITORIOUS SERVICE MEDAL

Instituted: 15 January 1849, by Order in Council.
Branch of Service: Royal Marines.
Ribbon: Plain dark blue.
Metal: Silver.
Size: 36mm.
Description: (Obverse) effigy of the monarch; (reverse) a crowned laurel wreath enclosing the words FOR MERITORIOUS SERVICE.
Comments: *Annuities not exceeding £20 a year might be granted in addition to the medal for distinguished service. Sergeants with a minimum of 24 years service (the last fourteen as a sergeant), 'with an irreproachable and meritorious character' were considered eligible for the award which was extended to discharged sergeants in 1872 when the service qualification was reduced to 21 years. The award of the MSM for gallantry was discontinued in 1874 when the Conspicuous Gallantry Medal was reconstituted. Only six MSMs for gallantry were ever awarded. The medal was identical with the Army MSM, distinguished solely by its ribbon and the naming to the recipient. Under the royal warrants of 1916-19 Marine NCOs became eligible for immediate awards of the MSM for arduous or specially meritorious service. The medals in this case were worn with crimson ribbons with three white stripes and had the obverse showing the King in the uniform of an Admiral or a Field Marshal, depending on whether the award was for services afloat, or with the naval brigades on the Western Front. The use of this medal ceased in 1928 when the BEM for Gallantry was instituted. The Royal Marines MSM was revived in 1977 solely as a long service award and is the same as the naval MSM already noted, differing only in the details of the recipient.*

VALUE:	Rare	Miniature	£10–12

210. ARMY MERITORIOUS SERVICE MEDAL

Instituted: 19 December 1845.
Branch of Service: Army.
Ribbon: Plain crimson (till 1916), white edges added (1916-17), three white stripes (since August 1917).
Metal: Silver.
Size: 36mm.
Description: (Obverse) effigy of the monarch; (reverse) a crowned laurel wreath inscribed FOR MERITORIOUS SERVICE.
Comments: *A sum of £2000 a year was set aside for distribution to recipients in the form of annuities not exceeding £20, paid for life to NCOs of the rank of sergeant and above for distinguished or meritorious service. The number of medals awarded was thus limited by the amount of money available in the annuity fund, so that medals and annuities were only granted on the death of previous recipients or when the fund was increased. Until November 1902 holders were not allowed to wear the LSGC as well as the MSM, but thereafter both medals could be worn, the LSGC taking precedence. In 1979, however, the order of precedence was reversed. Until 1951 the MSM could only be awarded when an annuity became available, but since then it has often been awarded without the annuity, the latter becoming payable as funds permit. Since 1956 recipients must have at least 27 years service to become eligible. What was, in effect, a second type of MSM was introduced in October 1916 when immediate awards for exceptionally valuable and meritorious service were introduced. In January 1917 this was extended to include individual acts of gallantry not in the presence of the enemy. No annuities were paid with the immediate awards which terminated in 1928 with the institution of the Gallantry BEM. Bars for subsequent acts of gallantry or life-saving were introduced in 1916, seven being awarded up to 1928. The standard crown and wreath reverse was used but in addition to the wide range of obverse types swivelling suspension was used until 1926, and immediate and non-immediate awards may be distinguished by the presence or absence respectively of the recipient's regimental number. Recent awards of the Elizabethan second bust medals have reverted to swivelling suspension.*

VALUE:

		Miniature
Victoria (A) 1847 on edge (110)	£300–400	—
Victoria (A) 1848 below bust (10)	£1500–1600	—
Victoria (A) (990)	£175–200	£30
Edward VII (725)	£100–150	£25
George V (A) swivel (1050)	£50–75	£10–18
George V (A) non-swivel (400)	£75–100	£10–18
George V (A) Immediate awards 1916–28 (26,211+7 bars):		
For Gallantry (366+1 bar)	£160–180	—
Meritorious services (25,845+6 bars)	£60–80	—
George V (E) (550)	£120–150	£10–18
George VI (D) (1090)	£75–100	£10–18
George VI (E) (5600)	£50–75	£10–18
George VI (B) (55)	£750–800	£10–18
Elizabeth II (C) (125)	£160–180	£10–18
Elizabeth II (D) (2750)	£120–150	£10–18

211. ROYAL AIR FORCE MERITORIOUS SERVICE MEDAL

Instituted: June 1918
Branch of Service: Royal Air Force.
Ribbon: Half crimson, half light blue, with white stripes at the centre and edges.
Metal: Silver.
Size: 36mm.
Description: (Obverse) effigy of the monarch; (reverse) a crowned laurel wreath enclosing the words FOR MERITORIOUS SERVICE. Originally medals were named in large seriffed capitals and were issued in respect of the First World War and service in Russia (1918-20), but later medals were impressed in thin block capitals. The RAF version had a swivelling suspension, unlike its military counterpart.
Comments: *Awarded for valuable services in the field, as opposed to actual flying service. This medal was replaced by the BEM in 1928, but revived in December 1977 under the same conditions as the military MSM. No more than 70 medals are awarded annually. The current issue is similar to the naval and military MSMs, differing only in the naming which includes RAF after the service number.*

VALUE:		*Miniature*
George V (E) (854)	£200–250	£10–15
Elizabeth II (D)	£180–220	£10–15

212. COLONIAL MERITORIOUS SERVICE MEDALS

Instituted: 31 May 1895.
Branch of Service: Colonial forces.
Ribbon: According to issuing territory (see below).
Metal: Silver.
Size: 36mm.
Description: (Obverse) as British counterparts; (reverse) as British type, but with the name of the dominion or colony round the top.
Comments: *Awarded for service in the British dominions, colonies and protectorates.*

Canada: Ribbon as for British Army MSM. CANADA on reverse till 1936; imperial version used from then until 1958. No medals with the Victorian obverse were awarded, but specimens exist.
Cape of Good Hope: Crimson ribbon with central orange stripe. Only one or two Edward VII medals issued.
Natal: Crimson ribbon with a central yellow stripe. Exceptionally, it was awarded to volunteers in the Natal Militia. Fifteen Edward VII medals awarded.
Commonwealth of Australia: Crimson ribbon with two dark green central stripes. Issued between 1903 and 1975.
New South Wales: Crimson ribbon with a dark blue central stripe. Issued till 1903.
Queensland: Crimson ribbon with light blue central stripe. Issued till 1903.
South Australia: Plain crimson ribbon. Issued till 1903.
Tasmania: Crimson ribbon with a pink central stripe. Issued till 1903.
New Zealand: Crimson ribbon with a light green central stripe. Issued since 1898.

VALUE	Rare	*Miniature*	£20–30

213. INDIAN ARMY MERITORIOUS SERVICE MEDAL 1848

Instituted: 20 May 1848, by General Order of the Indian government.
Branch of Service: Forces of the Honourable East India Company and later the Indian armed services.
Ribbon: Plain crimson.
Metal: Silver.
Size: 36mm.
Description: (Obverse) the Wyon profile of Queen Victoria; (reverse) the arms and motto of the Honourable East India Company.
Comments: *Awarded with an annuity up to £20 to European sergeants, serving or discharged, for meritorious service. It was discontinued in 1873.*

VALUE:
      Victoria   £200–250

214. INDIAN ARMY MERITORIOUS SERVICE MEDAL 1888

Instituted: 1888.
Branch of Service: Indian Army.
Ribbon: Plain crimson (till 1917); three white stripes added (1917).
Metal: Silver.
Size: 36mm.
Description: (Obverse) the sovereign's effigy; (reverse) a central wreath enclosing the word INDIA surrounded by the legend FOR MERITORIOUS SERVICE with a continuous border of lotus flowers and leaves round the circumference.
Comments: *For award to Indian warrant officers and senior NCOs (havildars, dafadars and equivalent band ranks). Eighteen years of exceptionally meritorious service was the minimum requirement, subject to the availability of funds in the annuity. At first only one medal was set aside for each regiment and thereafter awards were only made on the death, promotion or reduction of existing recipients. On promotion the medal was retained but the annuity ceased. It became obsolete in 1947.*

VALUE:

		Miniature
Victoria (B)	£80–100	£45
Edward VII (A)	£40–50	£45
George V (D)	£30–40	£45
George V (C)	£30–50	£45
George VI (B)	£30–40	£25

215. AFRICAN POLICE MEDAL FOR MERITORIOUS SERVICE

Instituted: 14 July 1915.
Branch of Service Non-European NCOs and men of the colonial police forces in East and West Africa.
Ribbon: Sand-coloured with red edges.
Metal: Silver.
Size: 36mm
Description: (Obverse) effigy of the sovereign; (reverse) a crown surmounted by a lion passant gardant within a palm wreath and having the legend FOR MERITORIOUS SERVICE IN THE POLICE and AFRICA at the foot.
Comments: *Awarded for both individual acts of gallantry and distinguished, meritorious or long service. In respect of the lastnamed, a minimum of 15 years exemply service was required. It was superseded by the Colonial Police Medal in 1938.*

VALUE:

George V (A) IND: IMP 1915-31	£300–400
George V (A) INDIAE IMP 1931-7	£250–350
George VI (B) 1938	Rare

216. UNION OF SOUTH AFRICA MERITORIOUS SERVICE MEDAL

Instituted: 24 October 1914, by Government gazette.
Branch of Service: Service personnel of South Africa, Southern Rhodesia and Swaziland.
Ribbon: Crimson with blue edges and a central white, blue and white band.
Metal: Silver.
Size: 36mm.
Description: As British military MSM.
Comments: *A total of 46 gallantry and 300 meritorious service awards were made up to 1952 when the medal was discontinued. Of these only two were awarded to South Africans in the RNVR.*

VALUE: Rare

216A. ACCUMULATED CAMPAIGN SERVICE MEDAL

Instituted: January 1994.
Branch of Service: All branches of the armed services.
Ribbon: Purple and green with a gold stripe.
Metal: Silver.
Size: 36mm.
Description: (Obverse) crowned effigy of Queen Elizabeth; (reverse) the inscription FOR ACCUMULATED CAMPAIGN SERVICE set within a four-part ribbon surrounded by a branch of oak leaves with laurel and olive leaves woven through the motto ribbon.
Comments: *Awarded to holders of the General Service Medal 1962 on completion of 36 months* accumulated *campaign service since August 14, 1969. Further periods of 36 months accumulated campaign service will be denoted by a clasp, indicated as a silver rosette when the ribbon alone is worn.*

VALUE: £100–120

217. ROYAL HOUSEHOLD FAITHFUL SERVICE MEDALS

1st type obv.

1st type rev.

Instituted: 1872 by Queen Victoria.
Branch of Service: Royal Household.
Ribbon: Originally Royal Stuart tartan; later, a different ribbon for each monarch: dark blue and red diagonal stripes descending from left to right (George V), the same but descending from right to left (George VI) or dark blue with three red stripes (Elizabeth II).
Metal: Silver.
Size: 27mm (Victoria); 29mm (later awards).
Description: (Obverse) the sovereign's effigy; (reverse) the personal details of the recipient engraved on it. The Victorian medal has a very elaborate suspension ornamented with the crowned royal monogram, with a laurel bar brooch fitting at the top. This medal was not originally intended to be worn with a ribbon, although it had a strip of Royal Stuart tartan behind it. The same medal, but struck in 22 carat gold, was presented to John Brown, the Queen's personal servant. The concept was revived by George V, a silver medal of more conventional appearance being struck with the text FOR LONG AND FAITHFUL SERVICE on the reverse. Thirty, forty and fifty year service bars were also awarded.
Comments: *Intended as a reward to servants of the Royal Household for long and faithful service of at least 25 years. A further 10 years merited a bar. Different ribbons were used for each monarch, corresponding to the crowned cypher joining the medal to the suspension bar on either side of which the recipient's years of service were inscribed. Only two medals have been recorded with the profile of Edward VIII (1936).*

VALUE:

		Miniature
Victoria	From £500	£100–150
George V (E)	£200–250	£30–40
Edward VIII	Rare	—
George VI (D)	£240–280	£30–40
Elizabeth II (C)	£250–300	£30–40

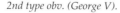

2nd type obv. (George V).

2nd type rev.

218. ROYAL NAVAL LONG SERVICE AND GOOD CONDUCT MEDAL

1st type obv.

1st type rev.

Instituted: 24 August 1831, by Order in Council.
Branch of Service: Royal Navy.
Ribbon: Plain dark blue (1831); dark blue with white edges (1848).
Metal: Silver.
Size: 34mm (1831); 36mm (1848).
Description: First type: (Obverse) an anchor surmounted by a crown and enclosed in an oak wreath; (reverse) the recipient's details. Plain ring for suspension.

Second type, adopted in 1848: (Obverse) the sovereign's effigy; (reverse) a three-masted man-of-war surrounded by a rope tied at the foot with a reef knot and having the legend FOR LONG SERVICE AND GOOD CONDUCT round the circumference. This medal originally had a wide suspender bar 38mm, but a narrow suspender was substituted in 1874. Normally the obverse was undated, but about 100 medals were issued in 1849-50 with the obverse of the Naval GSM, with the date 1848 below the Queen's bust. Between 1875 and 1877 a number of medals had the years of service added to the recipient's details, either engraved or impressed on the edge—these medals (about 60 known) are now sought after by collectors. Engraved naming was used from 1875 to 1877, but from then until 1901 impressed naming was adopted. Later medals used the various obverse effigies noted below.

Comments: *Originally awarded for 21 years exemplary conduct, but the period was reduced to 10 years in 1874, then later increased to 15 years. Bars for additional periods of 15 years were instituted by George V. In March 1981 commissioned officers of the naval services became eligible after 15 years service, provided at least 12 years were served in the ranks.*

VALUE:		Miniature
Anchor 1831-47 (644)	£350–450	—
Victoria (A) wide suspender (3572)	£160–200	—
1848 type (100)	Rare	—
Victoria (A) narrow suspender (4400)	£50–70	£30–40
Year on edge variety (c. 40)	£140–160	
impressed naming (18,200)	£45–55	
Year on edge variety (c. 20)	£180–200	
Edward VII (B)	£20–30	—
George V (B) 1910-30 swivel	£15–20	£5–10
non-swivelling bar	£20–25	£5–10
George V (E) 1931-36	£20–25	£5–10
George VI (D) 1937-48	£25–30	£5–10
George VI (E) 1949-52	£25–30	£5–10
Elizabeth II (C) 1953-54	£30–35	£5–10
Elizabeth II (D) 1954-	£30–35	£5–10

2nd type rev. wide suspender

2nd type rev. narrow suspender

2nd type obv. George V

219. ROYAL NAVAL RESERVE DECORATION

Instituted: 1908.
Branch of Service: Royal Naval Reserve.
Ribbon: Plain green ribbon, white edges being added from 1941 onwards.
Metal: Silver and silver-gilt.
Size: Height 54mm; max. width 33mm.
Description: A skeletal badge with the royal cypher in silver surrounded by an oval cable and reef knot in silver-gilt, surmounted by a crown and suspension ring.
Comments: *Granted for 15 years commissioned service (sub-lieutenant and above) in the Royal Naval Reserve, active service in wartime counting double. Bars are awarded for additional periods of 15 years. Recipients were entitled to the letters RD after their name, altered to VRD since 1966.*

VALUE:		*Miniature*
Edward VII	£90–100	£15
George V	£70–80	£10–12
George VI (GRI)	£70–80	£10–12
George VI (GVIR)	£70–80	£10–12
Elizabeth II	£110–130	£10–12

220. ROYAL NAVAL RESERVE LONG SERVICE AND GOOD CONDUCT MEDAL

Instituted: 1908.
Branch of Service: Royal Naval Reserve.
Ribbon: Plain green, white edges and a central white stripe being added in 1941. On the amalgamation of the RNR and RNVR in 1958 the ribbon was changed to five equal stripes of blue, white, green, white and blue.
Metal: Silver.
Size: 36mm.
Description: (Obverse) effigy of the monarch; (reverse) a battleship with the motto DIUTERNE FIDELIS (faithful for ever) at the foot.
Comments: *Awarded to petty officers and ratings of the RNR for 15 years service, war service counting double, with bars for additional 15 year periods.*

VALUE:		*Miniature*
Edward VII (B)	£20–25	£15–25
George V (B)	£15–20	£10–15
George V (E)	£20–25	£10–15
George VI (D)	£20–25	£10–15
George VI (E)	£20–25	£10–15
Elizabeth II (C)	£40–50	£10–15
Elizabeth II (D)	£30–40	£10–15

221. ROYAL NAVAL VOLUNTEER RESERVE DECORATION

Instituted: 1908.
Branch of Service: Royal Naval Volunteer Reserve.
Ribbon: 38mm originally plain dark green; dark blue with a central green stripe flanked by narrow red stripes (since 1919).
Metal: Silver and silver-gilt.
Size: Height 54mm; max. width 33mm.
Description: Similar to RNR decoration.
Comments: *Awarded to commissioned officers of the RNVR. The qualifying period was 20 years, service in the ranks counting half and war service counting double. In 1966 the decoration was replaced by the RD following the merger of the RNR and RNVR.*

VALUE:		Miniature
Edward VII	£100–120	£15–20
George V	£70–90	£10–12
George VI GRI	£70–80	£10–12
George VI GVIR	£70–90	£10–12
Elizabeth II	£110–130	£10–12

222. ROYAL NAVAL VOLUNTEER RESERVE LONG SERVICE AND GOOD CONDUCT MEDAL

Instituted: 1908.
Branch of Service: Royal Naval Volunteer Reserve.
Ribbon: Originally plain green, but subsequently a broad central green bar edged in red with blue stripes at the ends was adopted.
Metal: Silver.
Size: 36mm.
Description: Identical to the RNR medal, but distinguished by the ribbon and the naming which includes the letters RNVR, RCNVR (Canada), RSANVR (South Africa), etc.
Comments: *Awarded to petty officers and ratings for 12 years service with the necessary training, character assessed as 'very good' or better throughout the period. War service counted double. The award was extended to the Colonial Navies during the Second World War.*

VALUE:		Miniature
Edward VII (B)	Rare	£15–25
George V (B)	£30–40	£10–15
George V (E)	£40–50	£10–15
George VI (D)	£30–40	£10–15
George VI (E)	£30–40	£10–15
Elizabeth II (D)	£50–70	£10–15

223. ROYAL FLEET RESERVE LONG SERVICE AND GOOD CONDUCT MEDAL

Instituted: 1919.
Branch of Service: Royal Fleet Reserve.
Ribbon: Blue bordered with thin red stripes and white edges.
Metal: Silver.
Size: 36mm.
Description: Similar to the RNR LSGC but with ring suspension instead of a bar suspender.
Comments: *Awarded for 15 years service in the Fleet Reserve.*

VALUE:

		Miniature
George V (B)	£15–20	£12–15
George V (E)	£15–20	£8–10
George VI (D)	£20–25	£8–10
George VI (E)	£20–25	£8–10
Elizabeth II (C)	£40–50	£8–10
Elizabeth II (D)	£30–40	£8–10

224. ROYAL NAVAL AUXILIARY SICK BERTH RESERVE LONG SERVICE AND GOOD CONDUCT MEDAL

Instituted: 1919.
Branch of Service: Royal Naval Auxiliary Sick Berth Reserve.
Ribbon: Plaion g but later green with a white central stripe and white edges.
Metal: Silver.
Size: 36mm.
Description: Very similar to the RNR equivalent, but the letters RNASBR appear after the recipient's name.
Comments: *Arguably the longest title of any British medal, it continued until the RNASBR was disbanded in 1949. The Auxiliary Sick Berth Reserve was created in 1903, members being recruited from the St John Ambulance Brigade. About 780 medals were granted prior to the Second World War and a further 715 between 1939 and 1949.*

VALUE:

		Miniature
George V (B)	£70–90	£10–15
George V (E)	£80–100	£10–15
George VI (D)	£70–90	£10–15

225. ROYAL NAVAL WIRELESS AUXILIARY RESERVE LONG SERVICE AND GOOD CONDUCT MEDAL

Instituted: 1939.
Branch of Service: Royal Naval Wireless Auxiliary Reserve.
Ribbon: Broad green stripe with narrow red stripes on either side and blue edges.
Metal: Silver.
Size: 36mm.
Description: Similar to the RNR equivalent, but the letters RNWAR after the recipient's name. The last of the service medals with a battleship reverse.
Comments: *Issued till 1957 when the RNWAR was disbanded. It was awarded for 12 years service, only about 200 having been issued.*

VALUE:

		Miniature
George VI (D)	£140–160	£10–15
Elizabeth II (C)	£140–160	£10–15

226. ROYAL NAVAL AUXILIARY LONG SERVICE MEDAL

Instituted: July 1965.
Branch of Service: Royal Naval Auxiliary Service (RNXS), formerly the Royal Naval Minewatching Service.
Ribbon: Dark blue with a narrow green central stripe and broad white bars at the edges bisected by thin dark green stripes.
Metal: Cupro-nickel.
Size: 36mm.
Description: (Obverse) the Queen's effigy; (reverse) a fouled anchor in an oak wreath surmounted by a naval crown.
Comments: *Awarded for 12 years service.*

VALUE: Elizabeth II (D)   £120–160   *Miniature*   £8–10

227. ROCKET APPARATUS VOLUNTEER LONG SERVICE MEDAL

Instituted: 1911 by the Board of Trade.
Branch of Service: Rocket Life Saving Apparatus Volunteers,
Ribbon: Watered blue silk with broad scarlet edges.
Metal: Silver.
Size: 36mm.
Description: (Obverse) the effigy of the reigning monarch with the date 1911 below the truncation. (Reverse) exists in four types. The first refers to the Board of Trade but when that department handed over responsibility to the Ministry of Transport in 1942 the wording was amended to read ROCKET APPARATUS VOLUNTEER MEDAL round the circumference. In 1953 the inscription was changed to COAST LIFE SAVING CORPS and then in 1968 to COASTGUARD AUXILIARY SERVICE.
Comments: *Awarded for 20 years service with the Rocket Life Saving Apparatus Volunteers. The RLSAV became the Coast Life Saving Corps in 1953 and the Coastguard Auxiliary Service in 1968, these titles being reflected in the wording on the reverse.*

VALUE:

George V (E)	£30–40
George VI (D) BoT	£40–50
George VI (D) Rocket Apparatus	£40–50
Elizabeth II (E) Coast Life Saving	£60–80
Elizabeth II (E) Coastguard Auxiliary	£60–70

229. ARMY LONG SERVICE AND GOOD CONDUCT MEDAL

1st type obv. Trophy of Arms with badge of Hanover.

2nd type obv. with badge of Hanover omitted and swivel suspender.

Instituted: 1830.

Branch of Service: Army.

Ribbon: Plain crimson was used till 1917 when white stripes were added to the edges.

Metal: Silver.

Size: 36mm.

Description: Over the long period in which this medal has been in use it has undergone a number of changes. Until 1901 the obverse bore a trophy of arms with the royal arms in an oval shield in the centre while the reverse bore the inscription FOR LONG SERVICE AND GOOD CONDUCT. The first issue had the royal arms with the badge of Hanover on the obverse and small suspension ring with a plain crimson ribbon. A large ring was substituted in 1831. On the accession of Queen Victoria in 1837 the Hanoverian emblem was dropped from the arms. In 1855 a swivelling scroll suspension was substituted and in 1874 small lettering replaced the original large lettering on the reverse. From 1901, however, the effigy of the reigning sovereign was placed on the obverse although the reverse remained the same. In 1920 the swivelling scroll suspension gave way to a fixed suspender. In 1930 the title of the medal was changed to the Long Service and Good Conduct (Military) Medal; at the same time the design was modified. A fixed suspension bar was added, bearing the words REGULAR ARMY or the name of a dominion (India, Canada, Australia, New Zealand or South Africa). This replaced the Permanent Forces of the Empire LSGC Medal (see below).

Comments: *Originally awarded to soldiers of exemplary conduct for 21 years service in the infantry or 24 years in the cavalry, but in 1870 the qualifying period was reduced to 18 years. During the Second World War commissioned officers were permitted to acquire this medal so long as they had completed at least 12 of their 18 years service in the ranks. Canada discontinued the LSGC medal in 1950 when the Canadian Forces Decoration was instituted, while South Africa replaced it with the John Chard Medal later the same year. From 1930 onwards the lettering of the reverse inscription was in tall, thin letters. In 1940 bars for further periods of service were authorised. The LSGC is invariably named to the recipient. The William IV and early Victorian issues (to 1854) were impressed in the style of the Waterloo Medal and also bore the date of discharge and award. The 1855 issue was not dated, while lettering was impressed in the style of the Military General Service Medal. Later Victorian issues, however, were engraved in various styles, while medals from 1901 onwards are impressed in small capitals of various types. Medals to Europeans in the Indian Army are engraved in cursive script.*

1st type rev. large letters

2nd type rev. small letters with swivel suspender

3rd type obv. (George V).

229. ARMY LONG SERVICE & GOOD CONDUCT MEDAL *continued*

Modified design with fixed suspender obv. and (below) rev.

VALUE:		Miniature
William IV small ring 1830–31	£420–450	—
William IV large ring 1831–37	£380–420	—
Victoria without Hanoverian arms 1837–55	£100–120	—
Victoria swivelling scroll suspension 1855–74	£80–100	—
Victoria small reverse lettering 1874–1901	£50–65	£25–30
Edward VII (A) 1902–10	£30–40	£25–30
George V (A) 1911–20	£20–30	£6–10
George V (A) fixed suspender 1920–30	£20–30	£6–10
George V (C) 1930–36	£25–35	£6–10
Commonwealth bar	From £75	£10–20
George VI (D) 1937–48	£20–30	£6–10
Commonwealth bar	From £75	£10–20
George VI (E) 1949–52	£25–35	£6–10
Elizabeth II (C) 1953–54	£40–50	£6–10
Elizabeth II (D) 1954–	£40–50	£6–10
Commonwealth bar	From £100	£12–15

230. ULSTER DEFENCE REGIMENT MEDAL FOR LONG SERVICE AND GOOD CONDUCT

Instituted: 1982.
Branch of Service: Ulster Defence Regiment.
Ribbon: Similar to the Military LSGC medal but with a central black stripe in addition.
Metal: Silver.
Size: 36mm.
Description: (Obverse) the imperial crowned bust of Queen Elizabeth II; (reverse) similar to the Military LSGC medal. Fitted with a fixed suspension bar inscribed UDR.
Comments: *Granted to personnel for 15 years exemplary service after 1 April 1970, with bars for additional 15-year periods. It is also awarded to officers provided that at least 12 of their 15 years service was in the ranks.*

VALUE:
Elizabeth II (B)   £80–100   *Miniature*   £8–10

231. VOLUNTEER OFFICER'S DECORATION

Instituted: 25 July 1892.
Branch of Service: Volunteer Force.
Ribbon: Plain green.
Metal: Silver and silver-gilt.
Size: Height 42mm; max. width 35mm.
Description: An oval skeletal badge in silver and silver-gilt, with the royal cypher and crown in the centre, within a wreath of oak leaves. It is suspended by a plain ring with a laurel bar brooch fitted to the top of the ribbon. Although issued unnamed, many examples were subsequently engraved or impressed privately. Two versions of the Victorian decoration were produced, differing in the monogram—VR for United Kingdom recipients and VRI for recipients in the dominions and colonies.
Comments: *The basic qualification was 20 years commissioned service in the Volunteer Force, a precursor of the Territorial Army, non-commissioned service counting half. By Royal Warrant of 24 May 1894 the decoration was extended to comparable forces overseas, the qualifying period for service in India being reduced to 18 years. The colonial VD was superseded in 1899 by the Colonial Auxiliary Forces Officers Decoration and the Indian Volunteer Forces Officers Decoration. In the United Kingdom it was superseded by the Territorial Decoration, on the formation of the TF in 1908.*

VALUE:		*Miniature*
Victoria VR	£50–60	£10–20
Victoria VRI	£150–200	£25–35
Edward VII	£60–80	£15–25

232. VOLUNTEER FORCE LONG SERVICE AND GOOD CONDUCT MEDAL

Instituted: 1894.
Branch of Service: Volunteer Force.
Ribbon: Plain green, but members of the Honourable Artillery Company were granted a distinctive ribbon in 1906, half scarlet, half dark blue with yellow edges—King Edward's racing colours.
Metal: Silver.
Size: 36mm.
Description: (Obverse) effigy of the reigning monarch; (reverse) a laurel wreath on which is superimposed ribbons inscribed FOR LONG SERVICE IN THE VOLUNTEER FORCE.
Comments: *Awarded for 20 years service in the ranks, officers who failed to qualify for the VD being eligible on account of their previous non-commissioned service. It was extended to colonial forces in June 1896, the titles of the sovereign being appropriately expanded for this version, and superseded in Britain by the Territorial Force Efficiency Medal in 1908, although it continued to be awarded in India until 1930.*

VALUE:		*Miniature*
Victoria Regina (C) (UK)	£35–45	£20–25
Victoria Regina et Imperatrix (C) (overseas)	£55–85	£20–25
Edwardus Rex (A)	£30–45	£15–25
Edwardus Rex et Imperator (A) (colonial)	£35–45	£15–25
Edwardus Kaisar-i-Hind (A) (India)	£60–80	£15–25
George V (A) (India)	£25–35	£15–20

233. TERRITORIAL DECORATION

Instituted: 29 September 1908.
Branch of Service: Territorial Force, later Territorial Army.
Ribbon: 38mm plain dark green with a central yellow stripe.
Metal: Silver and silver-gilt.
Size: Height 46mm; max. width 35mm.
Description: A skeletal badge with the crowned monogram of the sovereign surrounded by an oval oak wreath, fitted with a ring for suspension.
Comments: *Awarded for 20 years commissioned service, service in the ranks counting half and war service double. It was superseded by the Efficiency Decoration in 1930.*

VALUE:			Miniature
Edward VII	£65–75	£15–20
George V	£65–75	£10–12

234. TERRITORIAL FORCE EFFICIENCY MEDAL

Instituted: 1908.
Branch of Service: Territorial Force.
Ribbon: 32mm plain dark green with a central yellow stripe.
Metal: Silver.
Size: Height 38mm; max. width 31mm.
Description: An oval medal fitted with claw and ring suspension. (Obverse) the sovereign's effigy; (reverse) inscribed with the name of the medal in four lines.
Comments: *Granted for a minimum of 12 years service in the Territorial Force. It was superseded in 1921 by the Territorial Efficiency Medal when the service was renamed.*

VALUE:		Miniature
Edward VII (A)	£50–60	£15–20
George V (A)	£25–35	£15–20

235. TERRITORIAL EFFICIENCY MEDAL

Instituted: 1921.
Branch of Service: Territorial Army.
Ribbon: 32mm plain dark green with yellow edges.
Metal: Silver.
Size: Height 38mm; max. width 31mm.
Description: As above, but with the name amended and inscribed in three lines.
Comments: *Introduced following the elevation of the Territorial Force to become the Territorial Army. It was superseded by the Efficiency Medal in 1930.*

VALUE:
| George V (A) | £20–30 | *Miniature* | £10–15

236. EFFICIENCY DECORATION

Instituted: 17 October 1930.

Branch of Service: Territorial Army (UK), the Indian Volunteer Forces and the Colonial Auxiliary Forces.

Ribbon: 38mm plain dark green with a central yellow stripe.

Metal: Silver and silver-gilt.

Size: Height 54mm; max. width 37mm.

Description: An oval skeletal badge in silver and silver-gilt with the crowned monogram in an oak wreath, the ring for suspension being fitted to the top of the crown. It differs also from the previous decorations in having a suspender bar denoting the area of service: Territorial (UK), India, Canada, Fiji or other overseas country being inscribed as appropriate, but the previous ribbon was retained.

Comments: *Recipients in Britain were allowed to continue using the letters TD after their names, but in the Commonwealth the letters ED were used instead. The 20-year qualification was reduced to 12 years in 1949, bars for each additional 6 years being added. In 1969 the British bar was changed to T & AVR, on the establishment of the Territorial and Army Volunteer Reserve, the ribbon being then altered to half green, half blue, with a central yellow stripe. In 1982 the title of Territorial Army was resumed, so the inscription on the bar reverted to TERRITORIAL but the blue, yellow and green ribbon was retained.*

VALUE:

	Territorial	T&AVR	Commonwealth
George V	£50–70	—	£70–80
George VI (GRI)	£50–60	—	£60–70
George VI (GVIR)	£60–70	—	—
Elizabeth II	£70–80	£100–120	—

Miniature £8–20

237. EFFICIENCY MEDAL

Instituted: 17 October 1930.

Branch of Service: Territorial Army (UK), Indian Volunteer Forces and Colonial Auxiliary Forces.

Ribbon: 32mm green with yellow edges. Members of the HAC wear the medal with the scarlet and blue ribbon edged in yellow.

Metal: Silver.

237. EFFICIENCY MEDAL *continued*

Size: Height 39mm; max. width 32mm.

Description: An oval silver medal. (Obverse) the monarch's effigy; (reverse) inscribed FOR EFFICIENT SERVICE. In place of the simple ring suspension, however, there was now a fixed suspender bar decorated with a pair of palm leaves surmounted by a scroll inscribed TERRITORIAL or MILITIA (for UK volunteer forces), while overseas forces had the name of the country.

Comments: *This medal consolidated the awards to other ranks throughout the volunteer forces of Britain and the Commonwealth. The basic qualification was 12 years service, but war service and peacetime service in West Africa counted double. The Militia bar was granted to certain categories of the Supplementary Reserve until the formation of the Army Emergency Reserve in 1951. In 1969 the bar inscribed T & AVR was introduced, along with a ribbon half blue, half green, with yellow edges. The bar TERRITORIAL was resumed in 1982 but the ribbon remained the same. For the distinctive medal awarded in the Union of South Africa see number 254. Instead of the second obverse of Queen Elizabeth II, Canada adopted a type showing the Queen wearing the Imperial Crown.*

VALUE:	Territorial	Militia	T&AVR	Commonwealth
George V (C)	£25–35	£40–50	—	£40–50*
George VI (A)	£15–20	£40–50	—	£80–90*
George VI (C)	£15–20	£40–50	—	£60–75*
Elizabeth II (A)	£40–50	—	—	*
Elizabeth II (B)	£40–50	—	£60–80	*

Miniature £6–20

*These prices are for the commoner Commonwealth types. However, some are extremely rare as can be seen in the table below where the issue numbers are indicated in brackets.

George V (C)	George VI (A)	George VI (C)	Elizabeth II (A)	Elizabeth II (B)
—	—	—	Antigua (3)	—
Australia	Australia	Australia	Australia	Australia
Barbados	Barbados	Barbados	Barbados	Barbados
Bermuda	Bermuda	Bermuda	Bermuda	Bermuda
British Guiana (15)	British Guiana	British Guiana	British Guiana	—
British Honduras (1)	British Honduras (23)	British Honduras (3)	British Honduras (13)	—
—	Burma (111)	—	—	—
Canada	Canada	Canada	Canada (Rare)	Canada (Rare)
Ceylon	Ceylon	Ceylon	Ceylon (69)	—
—	Dominica (130)	—	—	—
Falkland Islands (29)	Falkland Islands (29)	—	Falkland Islands	Falkland Islands
Fiji (29)	Fiji (35)	Fiji (9)	Fiji (7)	Fiji (33)
—	—	Gibraltar (15)	Gibraltar	Gibraltar
—	Gold Coast (275)	Gold Coast (35)	—	—
—	Grenada (1)	—	—	—
—	Guernsey (3)	Guernsey (4)	Guernsey (3)	Guernsey (35)
Hong Kong (21)	Hong Kong (50)	Hong Kong (224)	Hong Kong (145)	Hong Kong (268)
India	India	—	—	—
Jamaica	Jamaica	Jamaica	Jamaica	—

—	Jersey (40)	Jersey (7)	—	Jersey (1)
—	Kenya (1)	Kenya (159)	Kenya (36)	—
—	Leeward Islands (49)	Leeward Islands (14)	Leeward Islands (2)	—
—	Malaya	Malaya	Malaya (54)	—
—	Malta (320)	Malta (84)	Malta (7)	Malta (36)
—	—	—	Mauritius (71)	
—	—	—	—	Montserrat (6)
New Zealand (71)	New Zealand (34)	New Zealand	New Zealand	New Zealand
Nigeria (1)	—	Nigeria (7)	Nigeria (3)	—
—	—	—	Rhodesia/Nyasaland (7)	—
—	—	—	St Christopher Nevis (13)	—
—	St Lucia (2)	—	—	—
—	St Vincent (1)	—	—	—
S. Rhodesia (17)	S. Rhodesia (230)	S. Rhodesia (24)	S. Rhodesia (6)	—
—	Trinidad/Tobago (228)	Trinidad/Tobago (46)	Trinidad/Tobago (5)	—

238. ARMY EMERGENCY RESERVE DECORATION

Instituted: 17 November 1952.
Branch of Service Army Emergency Reserve.
Ribbon: 38mm dark blue with a central yellow stripe.
Metal: Silver and silver-gilt.
Size: Height 55mm; max. width 37mm.
Description: An oval skeletal badge, with the monarch's cypher surmounted by a crown in an oak wreath. Suspension is by a ring through the top of the crown and it is worn with a brooch bar inscribed ARMY EMERGENCY RESERVE.
Comments: *Awarded for 12 years commissioned service. Officers commissioned in the Army Supplementary Reserve or Army Emergency Reserve of Offices between 8 August 1942 and 15 May 1948 who transferred to the Regular Army Reserve of Officers after 10 years service were also eligible. War service counts double and previous service in the ranks counts half. The ERD was abolished in 1967 on the formation of the Territorial and Army Volunteer Reserve.*

VALUE:

Elizabeth II	£110–130	*Miniature*	£10–14

239. ARMY EMERGENCY RESERVE EFFICIENCY MEDAL

Instituted: 1 September 1953.
Branch of Service: Army Emergency Reserve.
Ribbon: 32mm dark blue with three central yellow stripes.
Metal: Silver.
Size: Height 39mm; max. width 31mm.
Description: This oval medal is similar to the Efficiency Medal previously noted, but has a scroll bar inscribed ARMY EMERGENCY RESERVE.
Comments: *Awarded for 12 years service in the ranks or for service in the Supplementary Reserve between 1924 and 1948 prior to transferring to the Army Emergency Reserve. War service counted double. It was abolished in 1967, following the formation of the Territorial and Army Volunteer Reserve.*

VALUE:

Elizabeth II	£140–160	*Miniature*	£10–12

240. IMPERIAL YEOMANRY LONG SERVICE AND GOOD CONDUCT MEDAL

Instituted: December 1904, by Army Order number 211.
Branch of Service: Imperial Yeomanry.
Ribbon: 32mm plain yellow.
Metal: Silver.
Size: Height 38mm; max. width 31mm.
Description: Upright oval. (Obverse) the sovereign's effigy; (reverse) inscribed IMPERIAL YEOMANRY round the top and the usual long service and good conduct inscription in four lines across the middle.
Comments: *Awarded to NCOs and troopers of the Imperial Yeomanry for 10 years exemplary service. It became obsolete in 1908 when the Territorial Force was created. Nevertheless 48 medals were awarded in 1909, one in 1910, one in 1914 and one in 1917. All medals were issued with the bust of King Edward VII on the obverse.*

VALUE:

Edward VII (A) (1674)   £170–190   *Miniature*   £25–30

241. MILITIA LONG SERVICE AND GOOD CONDUCT MEDAL

Instituted: December 1904, by Army Order number 211.
Branch of Service: Militia.
Ribbon: 32mm plain light blue.
Metal: Silver.
Size: Height 38mm; max. width 31mm.
Description: An upright oval medal. (Obverse) the effigy of the monarch; (reverse) similar to the preceding but inscribed MILITIA at the top of the reverse.
Comments: *Qualifying service was 18 years and 15 annual camps. It was superseded by the Efficiency Medal with the Militia bar in 1930.*

VALUE:

		Miniature
Edward VII (A) (1446)	£120–150	£20–30
George V (C) (141)	£140–160	£20–30

242. SPECIAL RESERVE LONG SERVICE AND GOOD CONDUCT MEDAL

Instituted: June 1908, by Army Order.
Branch of Service: Special Reserve.
Ribbon: Dark blue with a central light blue stripe.
Metal: Silver.
Size: Height 38mm; max. width 31mm.
Description: As the foregoing but inscribed SPECIAL RESERVE round the top of the reverse.
Comments: *Awarded to NCOs and men of the Special Reserve who completed 15 years service and attended 15 camps. A total of 1078 medals were awarded between 1908 and 1936, with solitary awards in 1947 and 1953.*

VALUE:

		Miniature
Edward VII (A)	£140–155	£20–30
George V (C)	£150–165	£20–30

243. INDIAN ARMY LONG SERVICE AND GOOD CONDUCT MEDAL (EUROPEAN)

Instituted: 20 May 1848, by General Order of the Indian government.
Branch of Service: Indian Army.
Ribbon: Plain crimson.
Metal: Silver.
Size: 36mm.
Description: (Obverse) a trophy of arms, not unlike its British counterpart, but a shield bearing the arms of the Honourable East India Company was placed in the centre. (Reverse) engraved with the recipient's name and service details. In 1859 some 100 medals were sent to India by mistake, with the Wyon profile of Queen Victoria on the obverse and a reverse inscribed FOR LONG SERVICE AND GOOD CONDUCT within an oak wreath with a crown at the top and a fouled anchor at the foot.
Comments: *Awarded to European NCOs and other ranks of the Indian Army on discharge after 21 years meritorious service. It was discontinued in 1873 after which the standard Army LSGC medal was granted.*

VALUE: *Miniature*
    HEIC arms   £275–350   —
    Victoria (A) (100)   £275–350   —

HEIC arms type.

Victoria type.

244. INDIAN ARMY LONG SERVICE AND GOOD CONDUCT MEDAL (INDIAN)

Instituted: 1888.
Branch of Service: Indian Army.
Ribbon: Originally plain crimson but white edges were added in 1917.
Metal: Silver.
Size: 36mm.
Description: (Obverse) the sovereign's effigy; (reverse) the word INDIA set within a palm wreath surrounded by a border of lotus flowers and leaves. The inscription FOR LONG SERVICE AND GOOD CONDUCT appears between the wreath and the lotus flowers.
Comments: *Awarded to native Indian NCOs and other ranks for 20 years meritorious service. The medal became obsolete in 1947 when India achieved independence.*

VALUE:		*Miniature*
Victoria (B) Kaisar-i-Hind	£70–90	£40–50
Edward VII (A) Kaisar-i-Hind	£40–50	£40–50
George V (D) Kaisar-i-Hind	£20–30	£25–30
George V (C) Rex Et Indiae Imp	£30–40	£25–30
George VI (B)	£20–30	£15-20

245. INDIAN VOLUNTEER FORCES OFFICERS' DECORATION

Instituted: May 1899, but not issued until 1903.
Branch of Service: Indian Volunteer Forces.
Ribbon: Plain green.
Metal: Silver and silver-gilt.
Size: Height 65mm; max. width 35mm.
Description: An oval skeletal badge with the royal monogram within an oval band inscribed INDIAN VOLUNTEER FORCE surmounted by a crown fitted with a suspension bar and an elaborate silver brooch.
Comments: *Awarded for 18 years commissioned service, with any service in the ranks counting half. It was superseded by the Efficiency Decoration with India bar in 1930.*

VALUE:		*Miniature*
Edward VII	£100–130	£20–25
George V	£130–150	£15–20

246. COLONIAL AUXILIARY FORCES OFFICERS' DECORATION

Instituted: 18 May 1899.
Branch of Service: Colonial Auxiliary Forces.
Ribbon: Plain green.
Metal: Silver and silver-gilt.
Size: Height 66mm; max. width 35mm.
Description: Similar to the previous decoration, with an oval band inscribed COLONIAL AUXILIARY FORCES.
Comments: *Awarded to officers of auxiliary forces everywhere except in India, service in West Africa counting double. Although issued unnamed, it was usually impressed or engraved privately. Examples to officers in the smaller colonies command a considerable premium. It became obsolete in 1930.*

VALUE:		*Miniature*
Victoria	£200–220	£20–30
Edward VII	£180–200	£15–25
George V	£120–140	£12–18

247. COLONIAL AUXILIARY FORCES LONG SERVICE MEDAL

Instituted: 18 May 1899.
Branch of Service: Colonial Auxiliary Forces.
Ribbon: Plain green.
Metal: Silver.
Size: 36mm.
Description: (Obverse) the effigy of the reigning monarch; (reverse) an elaborate rococo frame surmounted by a crown and enclosing the five-line text FOR LONG SERVICE IN THE COLONIAL AUXILIARY FORCES.
Comments: *Awarded for 20 years service in the ranks, West African service counting double. It was superseded in 1930 by the Efficiency Medal with the appropriate colonial or dominion bar.*

VALUE:		*Miniature*
Victoria (D)	£90–100	£25–35
Edward VII (A)	£80–90	£20–25
George V (A)	£70–80	£12–15

248. COLONIAL LONG SERVICE AND GOOD CONDUCT MEDALS

Instituted: May 1895.
Branch of Service: Indian and Colonial forces.
Ribbon: Crimson with a central stripe denoting the country of service (see below).
Metal: Silver.
Size: 36mm.
Description: Similar to its British counterpart except that the name of the country appeared on the reverse.
Comments: *Awarded to warrant officers, NCOs and other ranks for distinguished conduct in the field, meritorious service and long service and good conduct. Medals of the individual Australian colonies were superseded in 1902 by those inscribed COMMONWEALTH OF AUSTRALIA. The Colonial LSGC medal was replaced in 1909 by the Permanent Forces of the Empire Beyond the Seas LSGC award.*

VALUE: Rare

249. PERMANENT FORCES OF THE EMPIRE BEYOND THE SEAS LONG SERVICE AND GOOD CONDUCT MEDAL

Instituted: 1909.
Branch of Service: Colonial and Dominion forces.
Ribbon: Maroon bearing a broad white central stripe with a narrow black stripe at its centre.
Metal: Silver.
Size: 36mm.
Description: (Obverse) the effigy of the reigning sovereign; (reverse) the legend PERMANENT FORCES OF THE EMPIRE BEYOND THE SEAS round the circumference, with FOR LONG SERVICE AND GOOD CONDUCT in four lines across the centre.
Comments: *This award replaced the various colonial LSGC medals, being itself superseded in 1930 by the LSGC (Military) Medal with appropriate dominion or colonial bar. It was awarded for 18 years exemplary service.*

VALUE:		*Miniature*
Edward VII (A)	Rare	£50–60
George V (C)	£80–100	£40–50

250. ROYAL WEST AFRICA FRONTIER FORCE LONG SERVICE AND GOOD CONDUCT MEDAL

Instituted: September 1903.
Branch of Service: Royal West Africa Frontier Force.
Ribbon: Crimson with a relatively broad green central stripe.
Metal: Silver.
Size: 36mm.
Description: (Obverse) the effigy of the reigning monarch. Two reverse types were used, the word ROYAL being added to the regimental title in June 1928.
Comments: *Awarded to native NCOs and other ranks for 18 years exemplary service.*

VALUE:	Rare	*Miniature*	£25–30

251. KING'S AFRICAN RIFLES LONG SERVICE & GOOD CONDUCT MEDAL

Instituted: March 1907.
Branch of Service: King's African Rifles.
Ribbon: Crimson with a broad green central stripe.
Metal: Silver.
Size: 36mm.
Description: Very similar to the foregoing, apart from the regimental name round the top of the reverse.
Comments: *Awarded to native NCO's and other ranks for 18 years exemplary service.*

VALUE:	Rare	*Miniature*	£15–25

252. TRANS-JORDAN FRONTIER FORCE LONG SERVICE & GOOD CONDUCT MEDAL

Instituted: 20 May 1938.
Branch of Service: Trans-Jordan Frontier Force.
Ribbon: Crimson with a green central stripe.
Metal: Silver.
Size: 36mm.
Description: Similar to the previous medals, with the name of the Force round the circumference.
Comments: *This rare silver medal was awarded for 16 years service in the ranks of the Trans-Jordan Frontier Force. Service in the Palestine Gendarmerie or Arab Legion counted, so long as the recipient transferred to the Frontier Force without a break in service. Only 112 medals were awarded before it was abolished in 1948.*

VALUE: Rare

253. SOUTH AFRICA PERMANENT FORCE LONG SERVICE AND GOOD CONDUCT MEDAL

Instituted: 29 December 1939.
Branch of Service: South African forces.
Ribbon:
Metal: Silver.
Size: 36mm.
Description: (Obverse) Crowned effigy of King George VI; (reverse) FOR LONG SERVICE AND GOOD CONDUCT in four lines across the upper half and VIR LANGDURIGE DIENS EN GOEIE GEDRAG in four lines across the lower half. It also differs from its British counterpart in having a bilingual suspension bar.
Comments: *Awarded to NCOs and other ranks with a minimum of 18 years service.*

VALUE:		Miniature
George VI (B)	£120–140	£10–15
George VI (C)	£150–170	£10–15

254. EFFICIENCY MEDAL (SOUTH AFRICA)

Instituted: December 1939.
Branch of Service: Coast Garrison and Active Citizen Forces of South Africa.
Ribbon:
Metal: Silver.
Size: Height 38mm; max. width 30mm.
Description: An oval silver medal rather similar to the Efficiency Medal (number 235) but having a scroll bar inscribed UNION OF SOUTH AFRICA with its Afrikaans equivalent below. The reverse likewise bears a bilingual inscription.
Comments: *Awarded for 12 years non-commissioned service in the Coast Garrison and Active Citizen Forces. It was replaced in 1952 by the John Chard Medal.*

VALUE:	£55–65	Miniature	£10–20

254A. ROYAL HONG KONG REGIMENT DISBANDMENT MEDAL

Instituted: 1995.
Branch of Service: Royal Hong Kong Regiment (Volunteers).
Ribbon: Half red and half blue with a central yellow stripe.
Metal: Cupro-nickel.
Size: 38mm.
Description: (Obverse) Regimental badge with dates 1854 and 1995 either side and ROYAL HONG KONG REGIMENT THE VOLUNTEERS around. (Reverse) Coat of Arms of Hong Kong with DISBANDMENT MEDAL 3rdSEPTEMBER 1995 (date of disbandment) around.
Comment: *Available to those serving with the Regiment as the end of the Crown Colony became imminent. Recipients, however, had to purchase their medals.*

VALUE:	—	Miniature	—

255. CANADIAN FORCES DECORATION

Instituted: 15 December 1949.
Branch of Service: Canadian Forces.
Ribbon: 38mm red divided into four equal parts by three thin white stripes.
Metal: Silver-gilt (George VI) or gilded tombac brass (Elizabeth II).
Size: Height 35mm; max. width 37mm.
Description: A decagonal (ten-sided) medal. The George VI issue has a suspension bar inscribed CANADA and the recipient's details engraved on the reverse, whereas the Elizabethan issue has no bar, the recipient's details being impressed on the rim. The reverse has a naval crown at the top, three maple leaves across the middle and an eagle in flight across the foot. In the George VI version the royal cypher is superimposed on the maple leaves.
Comments: *Awarded to both officers and men of the Canadian regular and reserve forces for 12 years exemplary service, with a bar for each additional 10 years.*

VALUE:

		Miniature
George VI (E)	£50–60	£10–20
Elizabeth II (D)	£30–40	£10–20

256. VICTORIA VOLUNTEER LONG AND EFFICIENT SERVICE MEDAL

1st type obv.

Instituted: 26 January 1881 but not given royal sanction until 21 April 1882.
Branch of Service: Volunteer Forces, Victoria.
Ribbon: White, with broad crimson bars at the sides.
Metal: Silver.
Size: 39mm.
Description: (Obverse) the crowned badge of Victoria with LOCAL FORCES VICTORIA round the circumference; (reverse) inscribed FOR LONG AND EFFICIENT SERVICE. Two types of obverse exist, differing in the motto surrounding the colonial emblem. The first version has AUT PACE AUT BELLO (both in peace and war) while the second version is inscribed PRO DEO ET PATRIA (for God and country).
Comments: *Awarded to officers and men of the Volunteers in the colony of Victoria for 15 years service. Awards to officers ended in 1894 with the introduction of the Volunteer Officers Decoration. This medal was replaced by the Commonwealth of Australia LSGC medal in 1902.*

VALUE: Rare

2nd type obv.

257. NEW ZEALAND LONG AND EFFICIENT SERVICE MEDAL

Instituted: 1 January 1887.
Branch of Service: Volunteer and Permanent Militia Forces of New Zealand.
Ribbon: Originally plain crimson, but two white central stripes were added in 1917.
Metal: Silver.
Size: 36mm.
Description: (Obverse) an imperial crown on a cushion with crossed sword and sceptre and NZ below, within a wreath of oak-leaves (left) and wattle (right) and having four five-pointed stars, representing the constellation Southern Cross, spaced in the field; (reverse) inscribed FOR LONG AND EFFICIENT SERVICE. Plain ring suspension.
Comments: *Awarded for 16 years continuous or 20 years non-continuous service in the Volunteer and Permanent Militia Forces of New Zealand. It became obsolete in 1931 following the introduction of the LSGC (Military) medal with bar for New Zealand.*

VALUE: 1887-1931   £75–100   *Miniature*   £10–15

258. NEW ZEALAND VOLUNTEER SERVICE MEDAL

Instituted: 1902.
Branch of Service: Volunteer Forces, New Zealand.
Ribbon: Plain drab khaki.
Metal: Silver.
Size: 36mm
Description: (Obverse) a right-facing profile of King Edward VII with NEW ZEALAND VOLUNTEER round the top and 12 YEARS SERVICE MEDAL round the foot; (reverse) a kiwi surrounded by a wreath. Plain ring suspension.
Comments: *This rare silver medal (obsolete by 1912) was awarded for 12 years service. Two reverse dies were used. In type I (1902–04) the kiwi's beak almost touches the ground, whereas in Type II (1905–12) there is a space between the tip of the beak and the ground. Only about 100 of Type I were produced, but 636 of Type II.*

VALUE: **Type I**   £250–350   *Miniature*   —
           Type II   £180–220

259. NEW ZEALAND TERRITORIAL SERVICE MEDAL

Instituted: 1912.
Branch of Service: Territorial Force, New Zealand.
Ribbon: Originally as above, but replaced in 1917 by a ribbon of dark khaki edged with crimson.
Metal: Silver.
Size: 36mm.
Description: (Obverse) left-facing bust of King George V in field marshal's uniform; (reverse) similar to the above.
Comments: *It replaced the foregoing but became obsolete itself in 1931 when the Efficiency Medal with New Zealand bar was adopted.*

VALUE:
    George V   £75–100   *Miniature*   £10–15

261. ULSTER DEFENCE REGIMENT MEDAL

Instituted: 1982.
Branch of Service: Ulster Defence Regiment.
Ribbon: Dark green with a khaki central stripe edged in red.
Metal: Silver.
Size: 36mm.
Description: The medal is very similar to the foregoing but has a
   suspender of laurel leaves surmounted by a scroll bar bearing the
   regiment's initials.
Comments: *Awarded to part-time officers and men of the Ulster Defence
   Regiment with 12 years continuous service since 1 April 1970. A bar for
   each additional five-year period is awarded. Officers are permitted to add
   the letters UD after their names. This medal is to be superseded by the
   Northern Ireland Home Service Medal.*

VALUE:

Elizabeth II (B)	£150–200	*Miniature*	£6–8

262. CADET FORCES MEDAL

Instituted: February 1950.
Branch of Service: Cadet Forces.
Ribbon: A broad green central band bordered by thin red stripes
   flanked by a dark blue stripe (left) and light blue stripe (right, with
   yellow edges.
Metal: Cupro-nickel.
Size: 36mm.
Description: (Obverse) the effigy of the reigning monarch; (reverse) a
   hand holding aloft the torch of learning. Medals are named to
   recipients on the rim, in impressed capitals (Army and Navy) or
   engraved lettering (RAF).
Comments: *Awarded to commissioned officers and adult NCOs for 12 years
   service in the Cadet Forces. A bar is awarded for each additional 8 years.*

VALUE:

		Miniature
George VI (C)	£50–60	£8–12
Elizabeth II	£50–70	£8–12

263. ROYAL OBSERVER CORPS MEDAL

Instituted: 31 January 1950 but not awarded until 1953.
Branch of Service: Royal Observer Corps.
Ribbon: Pale blue with a broad central silver-grey stripe edged in dark
   blue.
Metal: Cupro-nickel.
Size: 36mm.
Description: (Obverse) effigy of the reigning monarch; (reverse) an
   artist's impression of a coast-watcher of Elizabethan times, holding a
   torch aloft alongside a signal fire, with other signal fires on hilltops
   in the background. The medal hangs from a suspender of two
   wings. An obverse die with the effigy of George VI was engraved,
   but no medals were struck from it.
Comments: *Awarded to officers and observers who have completed 12 years
   satisfactory service. A bar is awarded for each additional 12-year period.
   Home Office scientific officers and other non Royal Observer Corps
   members of the United Kingdom Warning and Monitoring Organisation
   were eligible for this medal until being stood down on September 30, 1991.
   This entailed serving for 15 years alongside ROC members who received
   their own medal for 12 years' service.*

VALUE:

		Miniature
Elizabeth II (C)	£60–70	£8–12
Elizabeth II (D)	£50–60	£8–12

264. CIVIL DEFENCE LONG SERVICE MEDAL

Instituted: March 1961.
Branch of Service: Civil Defence and other auxiliary forces.
Ribbon: Blue bearing three narrow stripes of yellow, red and green.
Metal: Cupro-nickel.
Size: 36mm.
Description: (Obverse) the effigy of the reigning monarch. (Reverse) two types. Both featured three shields flanked by sprigs of acorns and oak leaves. The upper shield in both cases is inscribed CD but the initials on the lower shields differ, according to the organisations in Britain and Northern Ireland respectively - AFS and NHSR (British) or AERS and HSR (Northern Ireland).
Comments: *Issued unnamed to those who had completed 15 years service in a wide range of Civil Defence organisations. It was extended to Civil Defence personnel in Gibraltar, Hong Kong and Malta in 1965. The medal became obsolescent in the UK after the Civil Defence Corps and Auxiliary Fire Service were disbanded in 1968, but members of the CD Corps in the Isle of Man and Channel Islands are still eligible.*

VALUE:			*Miniature*
British version		£15–20	£8–12
Northern Ireland version		£70–90	—

British rev.

Northern Ireland rev.

264A. AMBULANCE SERVICE (EMERGENCY DUTIES) LONG SERVICE AND GOOD CONDUCT MEDAL

Instituted: 5 July 1996.
Branch of Service: Ambulance services in England and Wales, Scotland, Northern Ireland, the Isle of Man and the Channel Islands.
Ribbon: Green with, on either side, a white stripe on which is superimposed a narrow green stripe.
Metal: Cupro-nickel.
Size: 36mm.
Description: (Obverse) crowned effigy of the reigning monarch, ELIZABETH II DEI GRATIA REGINA F.D.; (Reverse) FOR EXEMPLARY SERVICE round the top, with either the emblem of the Ambulance Services of Scotland or the remainder of the United Kingdom in the centre below. Fitted with a ring for suspension.
Comments: *Both full- and part-time members of Ambulance Services are eligible provided they are employed on emergency duties. Service prior to 1974 in ambulance services maintained by local authorities counts. For paramedics and technicians the qualifying service is 20 years. For ambulance officers and other management grades, at least seven of their 20 years' service must have been spent on emergency duties.*

VALUE:			*Miniature*	—
UK version	£20–30			
Scottish version	£30–40			

265. WOMEN'S VOLUNTARY SERVICE LONG SERVICE MEDAL

Instituted: 1961.
Branch of Service: Women's Royal Voluntary Service.
Ribbon: Dark green with twin white stripes towards the end and broad red edges.
Metal: Cupro-nickel.
Size: 36mm.
Description: (Obverse) three flowers, inscribed SERVICE BEYOND SELF round the circumference. Although the WVS acquired the Royal title in 1966 only one reverse has so far been used, with the interlocking initials WVS in an ivy wreath.
Comments: *Issued unnamed and awarded for 15 years service. Bars for additional 15 year periods are awarded. To date some 32,200 medals and 3000 bars have been awarded to women, but a small number of male recipients have been granted the medal for service in the headquarters administration.*

VALUE: WVS medal   £15–20   *Miniature*   £12–20

266. VOLUNTARY MEDICAL SERVICE MEDAL

Instituted: 1932.
Branch of Service: British Red Cross Society and the St Andrew's Ambulance Corps (Scotland).
Ribbon: Red with yellow and white stripes.
Metal: Originally struck in silver but since the 1960s it has been produced in cupro-nickel.
Size: 36mm.
Description: (Obverse) the veiled bust of a female holding an oil lamp, symbolic of Florence Nightingale; (reverse) the crosses of Geneva and St Andrew, with the inscription FOR LONG AND EFFICIENT SERVICE.
Comments: *Awarded for 15 years service, with a bar for each additional period of five years. The service bars are embellished with a Geneva cross or saltire (St Andrew) cross, whichever is the more appropriate.*

VALUE: Silver   £14–18   Cupro-nickel   £8–12   *Miniature*   £8–10

267. SERVICE MEDAL OF THE ORDER OF ST JOHN OF JERUSALEM

Instituted: 1898.

Branch of Service: Order of St John of Jerusalem.

Ribbon: Three black and two white stripes of equal width.

Metal: Silver (1898-1947), silvered base metal (1947-60), silvered cupro-nickel (1960-66) and rhodium-plated cupro-nickel (since 1966).

Size: 38mm.

Description: (Obverse) an unusual veiled bust of Queen Victoria with her name and abbreviated Latin titles round the circumference. A new obverse was adopted in 1960 with a slightly reduced effigy of Queen Victoria and less ornate lettering. (Reverse) the royal arms within a garter surrounded by four circles containing the imperial crown, the Prince of Wales's feathers and the badges of the Order. Between the circles are sprigs of St John's Wort. Round the circumference is the Latin inscription MAGNUS PRIORATUS ORDINIS HOSPITALIS SANCTI JOHANNIS JERUSALEM IN ANGLIA in Old English lettering.

Comments: *Originally awarded for 15 years service to the Order in the United Kingdom (12 in the Dominions and 10 in the Colonies) but the qualifying period has now been reduced to 12 years service, except that overseas service outside South Africa, New Zealand, Canada and Australia remains 10 years. A silver bar was introduced in 1911 for additional periods of five years. From then until 1924 the bar was inscribed 5 YEARS SERVICE but then a design showing a Maltese cross flanked by sprays of St John's Wort was substituted. Bars for 20 years service were subsequently instituted in silver-gilt. Suspension by a ring was changed in 1913 to a straight bar suspender. The medal is worn on the left breast.*

VALUE:		Miniature
Silver, ring suspension	£15–20	£15–20
Silver, straight bar suspension	£12–16	£12–15
Base metal, first obverse	£8–12	£6–10
Base metal, second obverse	£8–12	£6–10

268. ROYAL AIR FORCE LONG SERVICE AND GOOD CONDUCT MEDAL

Instituted: 1 July 1919.

Branch of Service: Royal Air Force.

Ribbon: Dark blue and maroon with white edges.

Metal: Silver.

Size: 36mm.

Description: (Obverse) the effigy of the reigning monarch; (reverse) the RAF eagle and crown insignia.

Comments: *Awarded to NCOs and other ranks of the RAF for 18 years exemplary service, reduced in 1977 to 15 years. Provision for bars for further periods of service was made from 1944 onwards. Before 1945 conduct below the required standard was permitted to count if the airman had displayed higher exemplary conduct against the enemy, gallantry or some special service in times of emergency. From 1944 prior service in the Navy and Army up to a maximum of four years could be counted. In 1947 officers became eligible for the medal provided they had had at least 12 years service in the ranks.*

VALUE:		Miniature
George V (E)	£60–70	£15–20
George VI (D)	£25–35	£10–15
George VI (E)	£30–40	£10–15
Elizabeth II (C)	£30–40	£10–15
Elizabeth II (D)	£30–40	£10–15

269. ROYAL AIR FORCE LEVIES LONG SERVICE AND GOOD CONDUCT MEDAL

Instituted: 1948.
Branch of Service: RAF Levies, Iraq.
Ribbon: As the preceding.
Metal: Silver.
Size: 36mm.
Description: Similar to the previous type but was fitted with a clasp inscribed ROYAL AIR FORCE LEVIES IRAQ.
Comments: *Awarded to the locally commissioned officers and men of the RAF Levies in Iraq, for 18 years service (the last 12 to be of an exemplary nature). The Iraq Levies were raised in 1919 and became the responsibility of the RAF in 1922, maintaining law and order by means of light aircraft and armoured cars. The force was disbanded in 1955 when the RAF withdrew from Iraq. Only about 300 medals were issued.*

VALUE:

George VI (E)	£800–1000
Elizabeth II (C)	£900–1100

270. AIR EFFICIENCY AWARD

Instituted: September 1942
Branch of Service: Royal Air Force.
Ribbon: Green with two light blue stripes towards the centre.
Metal: Silver.
Size: Height 38mm; max. width 32mm.
Description: An oval medal with a suspender in the form of an eagle with wings outspread. (Obverse) the effigy of the reigning monarch; (reverse) inscribed AIR EFFICIENCY AWARD in three lines.
Comments: *Granted for 10 years efficient service in the Auxiliary and Volunteer Air Forces of the United Kingdom and Commonwealth. A bar is awarded for a further ten-year period.*

VALUE:

George VI (D)	£60–70
George VI (E)	£70–80
Elizabeth II (C)	£80–90
Elizabeth II (D)	£70–80
Miniature (all)	£8–12

271. POLICE LONG SERVICE AND GOOD CONDUCT MEDAL

Instituted: 14 June 1951.
Branch of Service: Police Forces.
Ribbon: Dark blue with twin white stripes towards each end.
Metal: Cupro-nickel
Size: 36mm.
Description: (Obverse) the effigy of the reigning monarch; (reverse) a standing female allegorical figure of Justice, with scales in one hand and a wreath in the other.
Comments: *awarded for 22 years full-time service in any UK constabulary. By a Royal Warrant of 1 May 1956 it was extended to police forces in Australia, Papua New Guinea and Nauru. The Australian award was replaced in 1976 by the National Medal.*

VALUE:		Miniature
George VI (E)	£20–30	£5–8
Elizabeth II (D)	£40–50	£5–8
Elizabeth II (E)	£25–35	£5–8

272. SPECIAL CONSTABULARY LONG SERVICE MEDAL

Instituted: 30 August 1919.
Branch of Service: Special Constabulary.
Ribbon: A broad red stripe in the centre flanked by black and white stripes.
Metal: Bronze.
Size: 36mm.
Description: (Obverse) the effigy of the reigning monarch; (reverse) a partial laurel wreath with a six-line text inscribed FOR FAITHFUL SERVICE IN THE SPECIAL CONSTABULARY. A second reverse was introduced in 1970 for 15 years service in the Ulster Special Constabulary, the text being modified to permit the inclusion of the word ULSTER. A third type was introduced in 1982 for 15 years service in the RUC Reserve and is thus inscribed.
Comments: *Awarded to all ranks in the Special Constabulary for 9 years unpaid service, with more than 50 duties per annum. War service with at least 50 duties counted triple. A clasp inscribed THE GREAT WAR 1914-18 was awarded to those who qualified for the medal during that conflict. Clasps inscribed LONG SERVICE, with the date, were awarded for additional periods.*

VALUE:		Miniature
George V (C)	£25–35	£3–5
George V (E)	£6–8	£3–5
George VI (D)	£6–8	£3–5
George VI (E)	£50–75	£4–8
Elizabeth II (C)	£16–20	£4–8
Elizabeth II (D)	£16–20	£4–8
Elizabeth II (D) Ulster	£100–120	£8–12
Elizabeth II (D) RUC Reserve	£120–140	£8–12

273. ROYAL ULSTER CONSTABULARY SERVICE MEDAL

Instituted: 1982.
Branch of Service: RUC and its Reserve.
Ribbon: Green, with narrow central stripes of red, black and dark blue.
Metal: Cupro-nickel.
Size: 36mm.
Description: (Obverse) the effigy of Queen Elizabeth II; (reverse) the crowned harp insignia of the RUC with the words FOR SERVICE round the foot.
Comments: *Awarded for 18 months continuous service since 1 January 1971, but the award was made immediate on the recipient also being awarded a gallantry decoration or a Queen's commendation.*

VALUE:

Elizabeth II (D)	£80–100	*Miniature*	£25–30

273A. TAYSIDE POLICE MEDAL FOR MERITORIOUS CONDUCT

Instituted: 1996.
Branch of Service: Tayside Police.
Ribbon: Police blue, with two white stripes towards the centre, fitted with a brooch pin for suspension.
Metal: Silver.
Size: 36mm.
Description: (Obverse) a crowned thistle on a dark blue ground with the motto SEMPER VIGILO (always on guard) at the foot, in red, white, green and blue enamels; (reverse) details of the award.
Comments: *Awarded to police officers and members of the public for actions which fall short of national recognition but which are deemed to be above the standard required for a Chief Constable's commendation.*

VALUE: —

274. COLONIAL POLICE LONG SERVICE MEDAL

Instituted: 1934.
Branch of Service: Colonial police forces.
Ribbon: Green centre bordered with white and broad blue bars towards the edges.
Metal: Silver.
Size: 36mm.
Description: (Obverse) the effigy of the reigning monarch; (reverse) a police truncheon superimposed on a laurel wreath.
Comments: *Originally awarded to junior officers who had completed 18 years exemplary service but latterly awarded to officers of all ranks who have the required servic e qualification. A bar is awarded on completing 25 years service and a second bar after 30 years. These are represented on the ribbon bar in working dress by silver rosettes. The number (where applicable), rank and name as well as (for George VI and later issues) the relevant force in which the recipient is serving at the time of the award is engraved on the rim, often locally and therefore in a variety of styles.*

VALUE:

		Miniature
George V (C)	£80–100	£12–18
George VI (B)	£50–60	£10–15
George VI (C)	£50–60	£10–15
Elizabeth II (A)	£60–70	£10–15
Elizabeth II (B)	£60–70	£10–15

275. COLONIAL SPECIAL CONSTABULARY LONG SERVICE MEDAL

Instituted: 1957.
Branch of Service: Colonial Special Constabulary.
Ribbon: Two thin white stripes on a broad green centre, with broad blue edges.
Metal: Silver.
Size: 36mm.
Description: (Obverse) the effigy of the reigning monarch; (reverse) the crowned royal cypher above the words FOR FAITHFUL SERVICE in a laurel wreath.
Comments: *Awarded for nine years unpaid or 15 years paid service in a colonial special constabulary. A bar is awarded for further ten-year periods.*

VALUE:

Elizabeth II (B)	£180–220	*Miniature*	£15–20

276. ROYAL CANADIAN MOUNTED POLICE LONG SERVICE MEDAL

Instituted: 14 January 1933, by Order in Council.
Branch of Service: Royal Canadian Mounted Police.
Ribbon: Dark blue with two gold stripes towards the edges.
Metal: Silver.
Size: 36mm.
Description: (Obverse) the effigy of the reigning monarch; (reverse) the RCMP insignia with the legend FOR LONG SERVICE AND GOOD CONDUCT.
Comments: *Awarded to all ranks of the RCMP who had served 20 years. Bronze, silver or gold bars were awarded for 25, 30 or 35 years further service.*

VALUE:

		Miniature
George V (C)	£500–600	£15–25
George V (E)	£500–600	£15–25
George VI (B)	£450–500	£8–10
George VI (C)	£450–500	£5–10
Elizabeth II (A)	£250–300	£5–10

277. CEYLON POLICE LONG SERVICE AND GOOD CONDUCT MEDAL (I)

Instituted: 1925.
Branch of Service: Ceylon Police.
Ribbon: Very similar to that of the Special Constabulary Long Service Medal.
Metal: Silver.
Size: 36mm.
Description: (Obverse) coinage profile of King George V by Sir Bertram Mackennal; (reverse) an elephant surmounted by a crown. Ring suspension.
Comments: *Awarded for 15 years active service. It was superseded in 1934 by the Colonial Police Long Service Medal.*

VALUE:

George V (E)	£300–350	*Miniature*	—

278. CEYLON POLICE LONG SERVICE AND GOOD CONDUCT MEDAL (II)

Instituted: 1950.
Branch of Service: Ceylon Police.
Ribbon: Dark blue edged with khaki, white and pale blue.
Metal: Cupro-nickel.
Size: 36mm.
Description: (Obverse) the effigy of the reigning monarch; (reverse) similar to the foregoing, but without the crown above the elephant, to permit the longer inscription CEYLON POLICE SERVICE. Straight bar suspender.
Comments: *Awarded for 18 years exemplary service. Bars for 25 and 30 years service were also awarded. It became obsolete when Ceylon (now Sri Lanka) became a republic in 1972.*

VALUE:			Miniature
George VI (C)		£280–320	£15–20
Elizabeth II (A)		£250–300	£10–15

279. CYPRUS MILITARY POLICE LONG SERVICE AND GOOD CONDUCT MEDAL

Instituted: October 1929.
Branch of Service: Cyprus Military Police.
Ribbon: Yellow, dark green and yellow in equal bands.
Metal: Silver.
Size: 36mm.
Description: (Obverse) King George V; (reverse) the title of the police round the circumference and the words LONG AND GOOD SERVICE in four lines across the middle.
Comments: *Awarded to those who had three good conduct badges, plus six years exemplary service since the award of the third badge, no more than four entries in the defaulters' book and a minimum of 15 years service. Officers who had been promoted from the ranks were also eligible. No more than 7 officers and 54 other ranks were awarded this medal during its brief life before it was superseded in 1934 by the Colonial Police Long Service Medal.*

VALUE: George V   Rare

280. HONG KONG POLICE MEDAL FOR MERIT

Instituted: May 3, 1862.
Branch of Service: Hong Kong Police.
Ribbon: Various, according to class (see below).
Metal: Gold, silver or bronze.
Size: 36mm.
Description: (Obverse) the effigy of the reigning monarch; (reverse) inscribed in three lines HONG KONG POLICE FORCE FOR MERIT within a laurel wreath and beaded circle. Examples have been recorded with the effigy of Queen Victoria as on the Abyssinian and New Zealand Medals (123–124), and King George V types C and E.
Comment: *Exceptionally awarded in five different classes according to the length and type of service. The 1st Class medal was struck in gold and worn with a maroon (VC) ribbon, the 2nd Class in silver with a plain yellow ribbon, the 3rd Class in bronze with a central black stripe on the yellow ribbon, the 4th Class in bronze with two central black stripes in the yellow ribbon, and the 5th Class (confined to the Police Reserve) in bronze had a green ribbon with two black central stripes. The 4th Class was engraved on the reverse above the wreath. These medals were superseded in April 1937 by the Hong Kong Police Silver Medal, only four of which was awarded before it was replaced by the Colonial Police Medal for Meritorious Service 1938.*

VALUE:	1st class	2nd class	3rd class	4th class
Victoria	—	£450–500	£400–450	£250–300
Edward VII	Rare	£450–500	£350–450	£250–300
George V (B)	Rare	£400–450	£300–350	£225–275
George V (C)	Rare	£$00–450	£300–350	£225–275

280A. HONG KONG DISTRICT WATCH FORCE MERIT MEDAL

Instituted: 1868.
Branch of Service: District Watch Force.
Ribbon: Very dark green with a central deep red stripe.
Metal: Silver.
Size: 31mm with a prominent rim.
Description: (Obverse) four Chinese characters "Great Britain Hong Kong" above a watchman's lamp, superimposed on a cutlass and police baton, with the Chinese characters for "District Watch Force" and "Medal" at the sides; (reverse) DISTRICT WATCHMEN'S FORCE FOR MERIT within a laurel wreath.
Comment: *While the Hong Kong Police was principally a mixed force of Europeans and Indians, operated in the business and higher class residential areas, and was paid for out of the colony's revenues, the District Watch Force was a purely Chinese organisation, raised by prominent citizens of the colony to patrol and police the Chinese parts of the city. Its members had statutory powers, were uniformed and were trained and functioned in the style of the old parish constables, rather than in the gendarmerie style of the Hong Kong Police which was colonial in nature and imposed on society rather than integrated with it. The District Watch Force ceased to function at the time of the Japanese invasion in 1941 and was not revived on liberation.*

VALUE: £500

280B. ROYAL HONG KONG POLICE COMMEMORATION MEDAL

Instituted: 1996.
Branch of Service: Royal Hong Kong Police.
Ribbon: Black, magenta and old gold (colours of the turban worn by the original Punjabi constables).
Metal: Silver.
Size: 38mm.
Description: (Obverse) the RHKP crest; (reverse) crossed tipstaves inside a laurel wreath with the dates 1844 and 1997.
Comment: *The medal, approved by Commissioner Eddie Hui Kion, is available on purchase (HK$1,000, about £80) to those who served in the Hong Kong Police (1844–1969) and the Royal Hong Kong Police (1969–97). Made by Spink & Son and cased. Apparently only about 2,000 of the 40,000 eligible have purchased the medal owing to the cost. Purchasers' details are engraved in bold upright capitals in a variety of formats. The medal, worn on the right breast, has the same status as the Royal Hong Kong Regiment Disbandment Medal (254A).*

VALUE: £100   *Miniature*   £30

280C. ROYAL HONG KONG AUXILIARY POLICE COMMEMORATION MEDAL

Instituted: 1996.
Branch of Service: Royal Hong Kong Auxiliary Police.
Ribbon: Black, magenta and old gold (colours of the turban worn by the original Punjabi constables).
Metal: Silver.
Size: 38mm.
Description: Similar to the above, but inscribed ROYAL HONG KONG AUXILIARY POLICE FORCE.
Comment: *Similar to the above this medal is available for purchase. Some 5,000 auxiliary policemen and women being eligible for the award.*

VALUE: £120   *Miniature*   £30

281. HONG KONG ROYAL NAVAL DOCKYARD POLICE LONG SERVICE MEDAL

Instituted: 1920.
Branch of Service: Hong Kong Royal Naval Dockyard Police.
Ribbon: Yellow with two royal blue stripes towards the centre.
Metal: Gilt bronze or silver.
Size: 31mm.
Description: (Obverse) the effigy of the reigning monarch; (reverse) the title of the Police within a laurel wreath. Swivel ring suspension.
Comments: *Awarded for 15 years service. Although the Dockyard closed in 1961 men who transferred to other police divisions continued to be awarded the medal up to 1973. About 280 medals in all were issued.*

VALUE:		Miniature
George V (E)	£200–250	—
George VI (C)	£160–180	—
George VI (D)	£200–250	—
Elizabeth II (C)	£200–250	—

282. MALTA POLICE LONG SERVICE AND GOOD CONDUCT MEDAL

Instituted: 1921.
Branch of Service: Malta Police.
Ribbon: Dark blue with a narrow central silver stripe.
Metal: Silver.
Size: 36mm.
Description: (Obverse) the effigy of King George V; (reverse) an eight-pointed Maltese cross in a laurel wreath with the title of the service and FOR LONG SERVICE AND GOOD CONDUCT round the circumference.
Comments: *Awarded to sergeants and constables with 18 years exemplary service. Officers who had had 18 years in the ranks were also eligible for the award. It was superseded by the Colonial Police Long Service Medal in 1934. No more than 99 medals were awarded.*

VALUE:		Miniature
George V (E)	£300–350	£50–75
George V (C)	£350–400	£50–75

282B. MAURITIUS POLICE LONG SERVICE AND GOOD CONDUCT MEDAL

Instituted: 1921.
Branch of Service: Mauritius Police.
Ribbon: Two types: (a) 36mm half black, half white; (b) 33mm white with a broad royal blue central stripe.
Metal: Bronze.
Size: Oval, 40x33mm.
Description: (Obverse) crown surmounting crossed tipstaves with the legend POLICE DEPARTMENT round the top and MAURITIUS at the foot; (reverse) palm fronds enclosing a theee-line inscription FOR GOOD CONDUCT. Fitted with a ring for suspension. Medals with 33mm ribbon fitted at top with a pin brooch by Hunt & Roskill.
Comment: *It is believed that the different ribbons indicated different periods of service, but confirmation is sought. It is presumed that this medal was superseded by the Colonial Police Long Service Medal instituted in 1934.*

VALUE:	—	Miniature	—

283. NEW ZEALAND POLICE LONG SERVICE & GOOD CONDUCT MEDAL

Instituted: 1886.

Branch of Service: New Zealand Police.

Ribbon: Originally plain crimson but in 1917 it was changed to a pattern very similar to that of the Permanent Forces of the Empire Beyond the Seas LSGC medal.

Metal: Silver.

Size: 36mm.

Description: The original obverse was very similar to that of the NZ Long and Efficient Service Medal, with the crown, crossed sword and sceptre motif within a wreath of oak and fern leaves. Two types of suspension for this medal are known: the normal type has a bar suspender but a very rare variant has a ring suspender. By Royal Warrant of 8 September 1976 an obverse portraying Queen Elizabeth was introduced. The reverse was plain with the words FOR LONG SERVICE AND GOOD CONDUCT across the field.

Comments: *Awarded for 14 years service. Bars for further eight-year periods were added in 1959, reduced to seven years in 1963, the total length of service being indicated on the bar.*

VALUE:		*Miniature*
Regalia obverse, bar suspension	£100–120	£10–15
Regalia obverse, ring suspension	Rare	—
Elizabeth II	£90–110	£10–15

283A. SEYCHELLES POLICE LONG SERVICE AND GOOD CONDUCT MEDAL

Instituted: 1921.

Branch of Service: Seychelles Police.

Ribbon: Crimson.

Metal: Bronze.

Size: Oval, 40x33mm.

Description: (Obverse) crown surmounting crossed tipstaves with legend POLICE DEPARTMENT round the top and SEYCHELLES at the foot; (reverse) palm fronds enclosing a three-line inscription FOR GOOD CONDUCT. Fitted with a ring for suspension.

Comments: *Like the Mauritius Police Medal (282A) it is presumed that this medal became obsolete on the introduction of the Colonial Police Long Service Medal in 1934. Details of qualifying terms of service and other regulations are sought.*

VALUE: — *Miniature* —

284. SOUTH AFRICA POLICE GOOD SERVICE MEDAL

Instituted: 1923.

Branch of Service: South Africa Police.

Ribbon: Broad black centre, flanked by white stripes and green borders.

Metal: Silver.

Size: 36mm.

Description: (Obverse) South African coat of arms; (reverse) bilingual inscriptions separated by a horizontal line. Three versions of the medal have been recorded. In the first version inscriptions were in English and Dutch, the latter reading POLITIE DIENST with VOOR TROUWE DIENST (for faithful service) on the reverse. In the second, introduced in 1932, Afrikaans replaced Dutch and read POLISIE DIENS and VIR GETROUE DIENS respectively. In the third version, current from 1951 to 1963, the Afrikaans was modified to read POLISIEDIENS and VIR TROUE DIENS respectively.

Comments: *Awarded to other ranks for 18 years exemplary service or for service of a gallant or particularly distinguished character. In the latter instance a bar inscribed MERIT-VERDIENSTE was awarded. The medal was replaced by the South African Medal for Faithful Service.*

VALUE:

1st type	£20–30
2nd type	£15–25
3rd type	£15–25

285. SOUTH AFRICAN RAILWAYS AND HARBOUR POLICE LONG SERVICE AND GOOD CONDUCT MEDAL

Instituted: 1934.

Branch of Service: South African Railways and Harbour Police.

Ribbon: Similar to the Police Good Service Medal but with the colours reversed—a green central stripe flanked by white stripes and blue edges.

Metal: Silver.

Size: 36mm.

Description: (Obverse) the Union arms with S.A.R. & H. POLICE at the top and S.A.S.- EN HAWE POLISIE round the foot, but this was changed in 1953 to S.A.S. POLISIE at the top and S.A.R. POLICE at the foot. (Reverse) six line bilingual inscription.

Comments: *Awarded for 18 years unblemished service. Immediate awards for gallant or especially meritorious service earned a bar inscribed MERIT - VERDIENSTE (later with the words transposed). The medal was superseded in 1960 by the Railways Police Good Service Medal.*

VALUE:

1st type	£30–40
2nd type	£20–30

286. FIRE BRIGADE LONG SERVICE MEDAL

Instituted: 1 June 1954.
Branch of Service: Fire Services.
Ribbon: Red with narrow yellow stripes towards the end and yellow borders.
Metal: Cupro-nickel.
Size: 36mm.
Description: (Obverse) the Queen's effigy; (reverse) two firemen manning a hose. Ring suspension.
Comments: *Awarded to all ranks of local authority fire brigades, whether full- or part-time for 20 years exemplary service.*

VALUE:

Elizabeth II	£25–35	*Miniature*	£4–8

287. COLONIAL FIRE BRIGADE LONG SERVICE MEDAL

Instituted: 1934.
Branch of Service: Colonial Fire Services.
Ribbon: Blue with twin grey central stripes separated and bordered by thin white stripes.
Metal: Silver.
Size: 36mm.
Description: (Obverse) the effigy of the reigning monarch; (reverse) a fireman's helmet and axe. Ring suspension.
Comments: *Awarded to junior officers for 18 years full-time exemplary service. Bars are awarded for further periods of service.*

VALUE:

		Miniature
George V (E)	£300–350	£15–20
George VI (D)	£250–300	£10–15
George VI (E)	£250–300	£10–15
Elizabeth II (C)	£250–300	£10–15
Elizabeth II (D)	£250–300	£10–15

288. CEYLON FIRE BRIGADE LONG SERVICE AND GOOD CONDUCT MEDAL

Instituted: 1950.
Branch of Service: Ceylon Fire Service.
Ribbon: Similar to the Police Medal, but with a thin central white stripe through the dark blue band.
Metal: Silver.
Size: 36mm.
Description: As the Police Medal, but with a reverse inscribed CEYLON FIRE SERVICES.

VALUE:

		Miniature
George VI	£300–400	—
Elizabeth II	£300–400	—

289. COLONIAL PRISON SERVICE LONG SERVICE MEDAL

Instituted: October 1955.
Branch of Service: Colonial Prison Services.
Ribbon: Green with dark blue edges and a thin silver stripe in the centre.
Metal: Silver.
Size: 36mm.
Description: (Obverse) Queen Elizabeth II; (reverse) a phoenix rising from the flames and striving towards the sun.
Comments: *Awarded to ranks of Assistant Superintendent and below for 18 years exemplary service. Bars are awarded for further periods of 25 or 30 years service.*

VALUE:

Elizabeth II	£225–250	*Miniature*	£8–12

290. SOUTH AFRICAN PRISON SERVICE FAITHFUL SERVICE MEDAL

Instituted: September 1922.
Branch of Service: South African Prison Service.
Ribbon: ??
Metal: Silver.
Size: 36mm.
Description: (Obverse) arms of the Union of South Africa, with GEVANGENIS DIENST round the top and PRISONS SERVICE round the foot. (Reverse) inscribed FOR FAITHFUL SERVICE across the upper half and in Dutch VOOR TROUWE DIENST across the lower half.
Comments: *Awarded to prison officers with 18 years exemplary service. Immediate awards for gallantry or exceptionally meritorious service received the Merit bar. In 1959 this medal was superseded by a version inscribed in Afrikaans.*

VALUE: £30–40   *Miniature*   —

291. SOUTH AFRICA PRISONS DEPARTMENT FAITHFUL SERVICE MEDAL

Instituted: 1959.
Branch of Service: South African Prisons Department.
Ribbon: As above.
Metal: Silver.
Size: 36mm.
Description: (Obverse) arms of the Union of South Africa, with DEPARTEMENT VAN GEVANGENISS round the top and PRISONS DEPARTMENT round the foot. (Reverse) VIR TROUE DIENS across the upper half and FOR FAITHFUL SERVICE across the lower half.
Comments: *The conditions of the award were similar to the previous medal, the main difference being the change of title and the substitution of Afrikaans inscriptions for Dutch. This medal was superseded by the Prisons Department Faithful Service Medal of the Republic of South Africa, instituted in 1966.*

VALUE: £30–40   *Miniature*   —

CORONATION AND JUBILEE MEDALS

The first official royal medal was that cast by Henry Basse in 1547 for the accession of the young King Edward VI. It is known cast in gold or silver and is a curious example of bad design and poor workmanship for such an august occasion. No coronation medals were produced in honour of either Mary or Elizabeth I, but under James VI and I there was a small silver medal struck at the Royal Mint to mark the king's accession in 1603. These early medals celebrated the accession of the new sovereign, rather than the act of crowning itself.

To mark the coronation of James I, however, a small silver medalet was struck for distribution among the people who attended the ceremony, and this may be regarded as the forerunner of the modern series. This bore a Latin title signifying that James was Caesar Augustus of Britain and Heir to the Caesars. Thereafter medals in gold, silver or base metals were regularly struck in connection with the coronations of British monarchs. These were purely commemorative and not intended for wear, so they lack rings or bars for suspension.

By the early 19th century medals were being struck by many medallists for sale as souvenirs to the general public. At least fifteen different medals greeted the coronation of William IV in 1830 and more than twice that number appeared seven years later for the coronation of Queen Victoria. That paled into insignificance compared with the number produced for the coronation of Edward VII in 1902. On that occasion numerous civic authorities, organizations, industrial concerns and business firms issued medals in celebration—well over a hundred different medals and medalets were produced.

Sir George Frampton designed two silver medals, and one of these was mounted with a suspender and a blue ribbon with a thin white stripe and scarlet edges. This medal was distributed to notable personages attending the ceremony and established the precedent for subsequent coronation medals which came to be regarded as an award in recognition of services rendered in connection with the coronation, from the Earl Marshal of England to the private soldiers taking part in the ceremonial parades. In more recent times the coronation medal has even been given to people who were not present at the ceremony but who performed notable public service in the coronation year.

Many other royal events have been commemorated by medals over the centuries. Royal weddings and the birth of the heir to the throne were regularly celebrated in this manner. Important anniversaries in long reigns have been the subject of numerous commemorative medals. The Golden Jubilee of George III in 1809-10, for example, resulted in over 30 different medals. Five times that number greeted the Golden Jubilee of Queen Victoria in 1887, but among them was an official medal intended for wear by those on whom it was conferred.

Even this, however, was not the first of the royal medals intended to be worn. This honour goes to a very large medal celebrating the proclamation of Victoria as Empress of India in 1877. Although fitted with a suspender bar and worn from a ribbon round the neck, it was not permitted for officers and men to wear this medal while in uniform. Later medals, however, were permitted to be worn when in uniform, but after other orders, decorations and campaign medals.

292. EMPRESS OF INDIA MEDAL

Date: 1877.
Ribbon: 42mm crimson edged in gold.
Metal: Gold or silver.
Size: 58mm.
Description: (Obverse) a left-facing bust of Queen Victoria wearing a veil and a coronet, her name and the date of her elevation being inscribed round the circumference. (Reverse) a broad zigzag border enclosing the words EMPRESS OF INDIA and its equivalent in Punjabi and Hindi across the field.
Comments: *Issued to celebrate the proclamation of Victoria as Empress of India on 1 January 1877. It was awarded in gold to Indian princes and high-ranking British officials. Indian civilians and selected officers and men of the various British and Indian regiments serving in India at the time were awarded the silver medal. It was issued unnamed but many examples were subsequently engraved or impressed privately.*

VALUE:

		Miniature
Gold	£1,800–2,200	£250–350
Silver	£275–350	£100–150

292A. VISIT OF THE PRINCE OF WALES TO INDIA MEDAL

Date: 1875–76.
Ribbon:
Metal: Gold or silver.
Size: Oval 48mmx77mm.
Description:
Comments: *A large oval medal was struck to commemorate the state visit of HRH the Prince of wales (later King Edward VII) to India. It is believed that 14 were struck in gold and an unspecified number in silver. Further details are required.*

VALUE:

Gold	£7,000
Silver	£250

293. JUBILEE MEDAL

Date: 1887.
Ribbon: Broad central blue band with wide white stripes at the edges.
Metal: Gold, silver or bronze.
Size: 30mm.
Description: (Obverse) the bust of Queen Victoria by Sir Joseph Edgar Boehm; (reverse) an elaborate wreath in which are entwined the heraldic flowers of the United Kingdom. This encloses an eight-line inscription surmounted by a crown: IN COMMEMORATION OF THE 50th YEAR OF THE REIGN OF QUEEN VICTORIA 21 JUNE 1887.
Comments: *Struck to celebrate the 50th anniversary of Victoria's accession to the throne. The medal in gold was given to members of the Royal Family and their personal guests. The silver medal was given to members of the Royal Household, government ministers, senior officials, distinguished foreign visitors, naval and military officers involved in the Jubilee parade on 21 June 1887 and the captains of vessels taking part in the great Naval Review at Spithead. The bronze medal was given to selected NCOs and men who took part in the parade or the Spithead Review. All medals were issued unnamed with a ring for suspension. When the Diamond Jubilee was celebrated ten years later holders of the 1887 medal were given a clasp in the form of a cable entwined around the date 1897 and surmounted by an imperial crown. Twin loops at the ends enabled the clasp to be sewn on to the ribbon.*

VALUE:	without clasp	with clasp	Miniature
Gold	£1,100–1,300	Rare	—
Silver	£70–80	£110–120	£10–15 (add £5 for clasp)
Bronze	£60–70	£100–110	£10–15 (add £5 for clasp)

294. JUBILEE (POLICE) MEDAL

Date: 1887.
Ribbon: Plain dark blue.
Metal: Bronze.
Size: 36mm.
Description: (Obverse) the veiled profile of Queen Victoria; (reverse) a wreath surmounted by a crown and enclosing the inscription: JUBILEE OF HER MAJESTY QUEEN VICTORIA. The year appears at the foot and the name of the force round the top.
Comments: *Issued to all ranks of the Metropolitan and City of London Police involved in the parades and celebrations on 21 June 1887. Medals are believed to have been issued with the inscription POLICE AMBULANCE round the top but confirmation of this is required. Clasps for 1897 were likewise issued ten years later.*

VALUE:

	without clasp	with clasp	Miniature
Metropolitan Police	£18–20	£25–30	£8–12
City of London Police	£40–50	£30–40	£10–15 (add £5 for clasp)

295. JUBILEE MEDAL

Date: 1897.
Ribbon: Dark blue with two broad white bands and dark blue edges.
Metal: Gold, silver or bronze.
Size: 30mm.
Description: This medal is very similar to the 1887 issue, differing solely in the date and anniversary on the reverse.

VALUE:		*Miniature*
Gold (73)	£850–1000	—
Silver (3040)	£70–80	£8–12
Bronze (890)	£70–80	£8–12

296. JUBILEE MEDAL (MAYORS AND PROVOSTS)

Date: 1897.
Ribbon: White with two broad dark blue bands and white edges.
Metal: Gold or silver.
Size: Height 48mm; max. width 40mm.
Description: A diamond-shaped medal with ring suspension, reminiscent of the *Klippe* coinage of central Europe. Both sides had circular centres with trefoil ornaments occupying the angles. (Obverse) the Wyon profile of the young Victoria at the time of her accession; (reverse) Sir Thomas Brock's Old Head veiled bust of the Queen.
Comments: *The gold version was presented to Lord Mayors and Lord Provosts while the silver medal was granted to Mayors and Provosts. Small silver medals of more conventional circular format were produced with these motifs and sold as souvenirs of the occasion.*

VALUE:		*Miniature*
Gold (14)	Rare	£180–200
Silver (512)	£250–300	£80–120

297. JUBILEE (POLICE) MEDAL

Date: 1897.
Ribbon: Plain dark blue.
Metal: Bronze.
Size: 36mm.
Description: Very similar to the 1887 issue with the dates suitably amended and the name of the service round the top of the reverse.
Comments: *Separate issues were made in respect of the Police Ambulance service, St John Ambulance Brigade and the Metropolitan Fire Brigade. Holders of the previous medal merely received the 1897 clasp.*

VALUE:		*Miniature*
Metropolitan Police (7500)	£12–16	£10–15
City of London Police (535)	£40–50	£10–15
Police Ambulance (210)	£180–200	£25–30
St John Ambulance Brigade (910)	£60–70	£20–25
Metropolitan Fire Brigade (950)	£60–70	£30–35

298. CEYLON DIAMOND JUBILEE MEDAL

Date: 1897.
Ribbon: Plain red.
Metal: Gold.
Size: 35mm.
Description: (Obverse) the Boehm bust of Queen Victoria with the dates 1837-1897 at the foot. (Reverse) an elephant and a stupa (dome-shaped Buddhist shrine), with two lines of concentric inscriptions: TO COMMEMORATE SIXTY YEARS OF HER MAJESTY'S REIGN and, unusually, THE RT. HON. SIR J. WEST RIDGEWAY K.C.B., K.C.M.G., GOVERNOR. A crown above the rim was fixed to a ring for suspension.
Comments: *Awarded to local dignitaries and leading officials in the Ceylon government.*

VALUE:
    Gold   Rare   *Miniature*   —

299. HONG KONG DIAMOND JUBILEE MEDAL

Date: 1897.
Ribbon: Three equal bands of dark blue, maroon and dark blue.
Metal Silver, possibly also bronze.
Size: 36mm.
Description: (Obverse) the Boehm bust of Queen Victoria with the date 1897 at the foot; (reverse) a seascape with a British three-masted sailing ship and a Chinese junk in the background and two figures shaking hands in the foreground. The name of the colony appears at the top, while two concentric inscriptions read SIR WILLIAM ROBINSON G.C.M.G. GOVERNOR and TO COMMEMORATE SIXTY YEARS OF HER MAJESTY'S REIGN 1837-1897.
Comments: *Very little is known for certainty about this medal, on account of the fact that the colonial records were destroyed during the Japanese occupation.*

VALUE: —

299A. LAGOS DIAMOND JUBILEE MEDAL

Date: 1897.
Ribbon: Dark blue with two broad white stripes towards the edges.
Metal Silver.
Size: 34mm.
Description: (Obverse) the veiled crowned profile of Queen Victoria (similar to the Egypt Medal 1882, No. 131) inscribed VICTORIA QUEEN AND EMPRESS with a Tudor rose at the foot; (reverse) QUEEN'S DIAMOND JUBILEE LAGOS round the circumference, with JUNE 22ND 1897 in the centre.
Comments: *Issued to civil and military personnel associated with the Diamond Jubilee celebrations in the crown colony of Lagos (1886–1906 when it was incorporated in the colony and protectorate of Southern Nigeria).*

VALUE: Rare

300. VISIT TO IRELAND MEDAL

Date: 1900.
Ribbon: Plain dark blue.
Metal: Bronze.
Size: 36mm.
Description: (Obverse) a half-length version of the Boehm bust of Queen Victoria; (reverse) the female allegorical figure of Hibernia looking out over Kingstown (Dun Laoghaire) harbour in which the Royal Yacht can be seen (far left). Unusually, the medal was mounted with a suspension bar decorated with shamrocks.
Comments: *Commemorating Queen Victoria's visit to Ireland in 1900, this medal was awarded to officers of the Royal Irish Constabulary and Dublin Metropolitan Police who were involved in security and policing the various events connected with the visit. The medal was worn with the same ribbon as the Jubilee Police medals.*

VALUE:

Bronze (2285)	£60–70	*Miniature*	£25–35

301. CORONATION MEDAL

Date: 1902.
Ribbon: Dark blue with a central red stripe and white edges.
Metal: Silver or bronze.
Size: Height 42mm; max. width 30mm.
Description: (Obverse) the left-facing conjoined busts of King Edward VII and Queen Alexandra, both crowned and wearing coronation robes. (Reverse) the crowned royal cypher above the date of the actual ceremony. The medal has an elaborate raised rim decorated with a wreath culminating in a crown through which the ring for suspension was looped.
Comments: *This medal celebrated the coronation of King Edward VII on 9 August 1902. It was presented in silver to members of the Royal Family, foreign dignitaries, high officials of the government, senior officials and service officers involved in the celebrations. Selected NCOs and other ranks of the Army and Navy taking part in the parades were awarded the medal in bronze. Both versions were issued unnamed.*

VALUE:

		Miniature
Silver (3493)	£50–60	£5–10
Bronze (6054)	£35–40	£5–10

302. CORONATION MEDAL (MAYORS AND PROVOSTS)

Date: 1902.
Ribbon: Dark blue with a narrow white central stripe and crimson borders.
Metal: Silver.
Size: 32mm.
Description: (Obverse) conjoined right-facing busts of the King and Queen; (reverse) the crowned cypher and date. It differed from the ordinary medal by having flat, broad borders decorated with the heraldic flowers of the United Kingdom culminating at the top in a simple suspension ring.
Comment

VALUE:

Silver	£120–130	*Miniature*	£30–40

303. CORONATION (POLICE) MEDAL

Date: 1902.

Ribbon: Red, with a narrow dark blue central stripe.

Metal: Silver or bronze.

Size: 36mm.

Description: (Obverse) the conjoined busts of King Edward VII and Queen Alexandra; (reverse) a crown above a nosegay of heraldic flowers with the words CORONATION OF HIS MAJESTY KING EDWARD VII 1902 in the upper field. The name or initials of the service appeared round the top, LCC MFB signifying London County Council Metropolitan Fire Brigade.

Comments: *Issued to all ranks of the police and associated services involved in the coronation celebrations, and awarded in silver or bronze to officers and other ranks respectively.*

VALUE:

	Silver	Miniature	Bronze	Miniature
Metropolitan Police	£250–300 (51)	£15–20	£8–12 (16,700)	£12–15
City of London Police	£500–600 (5)	£15–20	£25–30 (1060)	£12–15
LCC MFB	£350–400 (9)	£30–35	£40–50 (1000)	£30–35
St John Ambulance Brigade	—	£15–20	£40–50 (912)	£15–20
Police Ambulance Service	—	£30–35	£180–120 (204)	£30–35

304. CEYLON CORONATION MEDAL

Date: 1902.

Ribbon: Plain blue.

Metal: Gold.

Size: 35mm.

Description: (Obverse) a crowned left-facing bust of King Edward VII; (reverse) the elephant and stupa motif previously used. The concentric inscription on the reverse now tactfully omitted any reference to the governor: IN COMMEMORATION OF THE CORONATION OF H.M. KING EDWARD VII 1902. The medal was fitted with a ring for suspension.

Comments: *Like its predecessor, this rare medal was struck for presentation to local dignitaries and government officials.*

VALUE:

Gold	Rare	Miniature	—

305. HONG KONG CORONATION MEDAL

Date: 1902.

Ribbon: None officially designated.

Metal: Bronze.

Size: 36mm.

Description: (Obverse) conjoined right-facing busts of King Edward VII and Queen Alexandra with their names round the circumference; (reverse) the maritime motif of the Diamond Jubilee medal with new inscriptions in two concentric curves: SIR HENRY A. BLAKE G.C.M.G. GOVERNOR (inner) and TO COMMEMORATE THE CORONATION OF THEIR MAJESTIES THE KING & QUEEN (outer). Fitted with a suspension ring.

Comments: *Issued to all British and Indian officers and other ranks serving in the colony as well as local police. Some 6,000 medals were produced by Edmonds & Son, London, and issued in cases.*

VALUE:

Bronze	£30–50	Miniature	—

305A. NATAL CORONATION MEDAL

Date: 1902.
Ribbon: Dark blue with a central claret stripe.
Metal: Silver.
Size: 30mm.
Description: (Obverse) a right-facing crowned bust of King Edward
  VII with the inscription TO COMMEMORATE THE
  CORONATION OF KING EDWARD VII: (reverse) Royal coat of
  arms above two running springbok, inscribed (round top)
  EDWARDUS DEI GRATIA BRITANNIAR REX F:D and (round
  bottom) COLONY OF NATAL 26 JUNE 1902. Ring suspension.

VALUE: Rare.

306. DELHI DURBAR MEDAL

Date: 1903.
Ribbon: Pale blue with three dark blue stripes.
Metal: Gold or silver.
Size: 38.5mm.
Description: (Obverse) a right-facing crowned
  bust of the King Emperor with DELHI
  DARBAR 1903 on the right side; (reverse) a
  three-line inscription in Farsi across the field,
  with an elaborate border of roses, thistles,
  shamrocks and Indian flowers. Ring
  suspension.
Comments: *Struck to celebrate the Durbar of the King
  Emperor at Delhi on 1 January 1903. It was
  awarded in gold to the rulers of the Indian princely
  states and in silver to lesser dignitaries, government
  officials, and officers and other ranks of the armed
  services actually involved in the celebrations.*

VALUE:		*Miniature*
Gold (140)	£800–1000	—
Silver (2570)	£80–100	£10–15

307. VISIT TO SCOTLAND MEDAL

Date: 1903.
Ribbon: Plain red.
Metal: Bronze.
Size: 36mm.
Description: Very similar to the Police Coronation medal but the year
  was changed to 1903 and the inscription SCOTTISH POLICE
  appeared round the top of the reverse.   The medal was named to
  the recipient on the rim. An ornate clasp decorated with a thistle
  was worn above the suspension bar.
Comments: *Struck to commemorate Their Majesties' post-coronation tour of
  Scotland in May 1903. It was awarded to the police and troops involved in
  parades and escort duties, as well as the ancillary services such as the Fire
  Brigade and the St Andrew's Ambulance Association.*

VALUE:

Bronze (2950)	£40–50	*Miniature*	£25–30

308. VISIT TO IRELAND MEDAL

Date: 1903.
Ribbon: Pale blue.
Metal: Bronze.
Size: 36mm.
Description: (Obverse) bust of King Edward VII; (reverse) as 1900 medal with the date altered at the foot. The suspension brooch is ornamented with shamrocks.
Comments: *Struck to mark the King's visit to Ireland in July 1903 and granted on the same terms as the medal of 1900.*

VALUE:

Bronze (7750)	£60–70	*Miniature*	£35–45

308A. VISIT OF THE PRINCE AND PRINCESS OF WALES TO INDIA

Date: 1905–06
Ribbon: Not known.
Metal: Silver.
Size: 35mm.
Description: (Obverse) The Prince of Wales's feathers within a garter and crown flanked by the initials G and M (George and Mary); (reverse) inscribed 'India 1905-6: T.R.H. George Prince of Wales and Victoria Mary Princess of Wales'.
Comments: *Struck for presentation to local dignitaries and government officials.*

VALUE: £40–60

309. CORONATION MEDAL

Date: 1911.
Ribbon: Dark blue with two thin red stripes in the centre.
Metal: Silver.
Size: 32mm.
Description: (Obverse) conjoined left-facing busts of King George V and Queen Mary in their coronation robes within a floral wreath; (reverse) the crowned royal cypher above the date of the coronation itself. Plain ring suspension.
Comments: *Medals were issued unnamed but may sometimes be found with unofficial engraving. Those who were also entitled to the Delhi Darbar Medal received a crowned clasp inscribed DELHI if they had previously been awarded the coronation medal. This was the first occasion that the medal might be awarded to those not actually present at the ceremony itself.*

VALUE:

Silver (16,000)	£20–25	*Miniature*	£4–8

310. CORONATION (POLICE) MEDAL

Date: 1911.
Ribbon: Red with three narrow blue stripes.
Metal: Silver.
Size: 32mm.
Description: (Obverse) a crowned left-facing bust of King George V; (reverse) an imperial crown with an ornate surround. The inscription CORONATION 1911 appears at the foot and the name of the service at the top. Ring suspension.
Comments: *By now the number of police and ancillary services had grown considerably, as witness the various reverse types which may be encountered in this medal.*

310. CORONATION (POLICE) MEDAL *continued*

VALUE:		Miniature
Metropolitan Police (19,783)	£10–15	£10–12
City of London Police (1400)	£40–50	£10–12
County and Borough Police (2565)	£55–65	£12–15
Police Ambulance Service*	£280–320	£30–35
London Fire Brigade (1374)	£40–50	£20–25
Royal Irish Constabulary (585)	£70–80	£20–25
Scottish Police (280)	£90–100	£20–25
St John Ambulance Brigade*	£40–50	£10–12
St Andrew's Ambulance Corps*	£120–150	£40–50
Royal Parks (119)	£240–280	£40–50

* *A total of 2623 medals was awarded to these three services, the Police Ambulance medal being the scarcest and St John Ambulance medal the commonest.*

311. VISIT TO IRELAND MEDAL

Date: 1911.
Ribbon: Dark green with thin red stripes towards either end.
Metal: Silver.
Size: 36mm.
Description: Very similar to the foregoing, distinguished only by the reverse which is inscribed CORONATION 1911 round the top, with the actual date of the visit round the foot.
Comments: *Granted to prominent civic dignitaries and members of the Irish police forces involved in the royal visit to Ireland which took place on 7-12 July 1911.*

VALUE:			
Silver (2500)	£45–50	*Miniature*	£25–30

312. DELHI DURBAR MEDAL

Date: 1911.
Ribbon: Dark blue with two narrow red stripes in the middle.
Metal: Gold or silver.
Size: 38.5mm.
Description: (Obverse) the conjoined crowned busts of King George V and Queen Mary in a floral wreath; (reverse) an elaborate Farsi text.
Comments: *This medal marked the Delhi Durbar held in the King Emperor's honour in December 1911. Most of the gold medals went to the Indian princely rulers and top government officials, while a good proportion of the 30,000 silver medals was awarded to officers and other ranks of the British and Indian Armies for exemplary service, without their necessarily being present at the Durbar itself.*

VALUE:		Miniature
Gold (200)	£800–850	—
Silver (30,000)	£25–30	£6–10

312A. VISIT OF KING GEORGE V AND QUEEN MARY TO INDIA

Date: 1911–12.
Ribbon: Not known.
Metal: Silver.
Size: Oval.
Description: A small oval medal. Further details required.

VALUE: £40–60

312B. VISIT OF THE PRINCE OF WALES TO INDIA

Date: 1921–22.
Ribbon: Not known.
Metal: Silver.
Size:
Description:
Comments: *Only 84 medals were awarded in connection with the visit of HRH the Prince of Wales (later King Edward VIII and Duke of Windsor) to India in the course of his world tour aboard HMS* Renown.

VALUE: £250

312C. WELCOME HOME MEDAL FOR THE PRINCE OF WALES

Date: 1922.
Ribbon: Not known.
Metal: Bronze.
Size: 35mm.
Description: Oval.
Comments: *Struck by F. Bowcher to mark the return of the Prince of Wales to England after his world tour.*

VALUE: £50–65

313. JUBILEE MEDAL

Date: 1935.
Ribbon: Red with two dark blue and one white stripes at the edges.
Metal: Silver.
Size: 32mm.
Description: (Obverse) left-facing conjoined half-length busts of King George V and Queen Mary in crowns and robes of state; (reverse) a crowned GRI monogram flanked by the dates of the accession and the jubilee.
Comments: *Issued to celebrate the Silver Jubilee of King George V and widely distributed to the great and good throughout the Empire.*

VALUE:
Silver (85,000)   £14–18   *Miniature*   £3–6

313A. ISLE OF MAN SILVER JUBILEE MEDAL

Date: 1935.
Ribbon: Black.
Metal: Silver.
Size:
Description: (Obverse) conjoined busts of King George V and Queen Mary in an inner circle surrounded by the legend 'KING GEORGE V & QUEEN MARY REIGNED 25 YEARS'; (reverse) Triskelion emblem with the legend IN COMMEMORATION OF THE SILVER JUBILEE 1935. Suspended from a brooch bar of seven overlapping panels. The centre panel has the royal cypher GvR while the outer panels have two leaves in each.
Comments: *Struck to celebrate the Silver Jubilee and presented to civic dignitaries and officials in the island.*

VALUE: £100–120

314. CORONATION MEDAL

Date: 1937.
Ribbon: Blue edged with one red and two white stripes.
Metal: Silver.
Size: 32mm.
Description: (Obverse) conjoined busts of King George VI and Queen Elizabeth in their robes of state without any inscription. The stark simplicity of this motif was matched by a reverse showing the crowned GRI over the inscription CROWNED 12 MAY 1937, with the names of the King and Queen in block capitals round the circumference.
Comments: *Issued to celebrate the coronation of King George VI on 12 May 1937.*

VALUE:
Silver (90,000)	£16–20	*Miniature* £3–6

315. CORONATION MEDAL

Date: 1953.
Ribbon: Dark red with two narrow blue stripes in the centre and narrow white edges.
Metal: Silver.
Size: 32mm.
Description: (Obverse) a right-facing bust of Queen Elizabeth II in a Tudor crown and robes of state, the field being otherwise plain. (Reverse) a similar crown over the royal monogram EIIR with the legend QUEEN ELIZABETH II CROWNED 2ND JUNE 1953 round the circumference. Ring suspension.
Comments: *This medal celebrated the coronation of Queen Elizabeth II on 2 June 1953. News that Edmund Hillary and Sherpa Tenzing had successfully attained the summit of Everest reached London on the morning of the Coronation. Subsequently the members of the Hunt Expedition were invited to Buckingham Palace on 16 July 1953 where, on Her Majesty's own initiative, they were presented with coronation medals engraved MOUNT EVEREST EXPEDITION on the rim, following the precedent of the Mwele medals of 1895-6.*

VALUE:
		Miniature
Silver (129,000)	£25–30	£5–10
Mount Everest Expedition (37)	£600	

316. JUBILEE MEDAL

Date: 1977.
Ribbon: White with thin red stripes at the edges, a broad blue stripe in the centre and a thin red stripe down the middle of it.
Metal: Silver.
Size: 32mm.
Description: (Obverse) Right-facing profile of Queen Elizabeth II wearing the imperial state crown—the first time this design was employed. (Reverse) a crown and wreath enclosing the words THE 25TH YEAR OF THE REIGN OF QUEEN ELIZABETH II 6 FEBRUARY 1977. A distinctive reverse was used in Canada, showing the dates of the reign flanking the royal monogram round the foot, CANADA round the top and a large stylised maple leaf in the centre.
Comments: *The 25th anniversary of the Queen's accession was marked by the release of this unnamed medal.*

VALUE:
		Miniature
General issue (30,000)	£130–150	£6–10
Canadian issue (30,000)	£70–90	£6–10

MEDALS FOR SAVING LIFE

Until the establishment of the government's own gallantry awards for the saving of life (the Sea Gallantry Medal (Foreign Services), instituted in 1841 and the Sea Gallantry Medal of 1854 and the Albert Medal of 1866), it was left entirely to private individuals and organizations to reward those who risked their own lives to save the lives of others. Although the medals granted from the late eighteenth century onwards are unofficial, they are of considerable human interest and are now very much sought after, preferably with the citations, diplomas, printed testimonials and other collateral material. The most commonly found of these medals are listed in broadly chronological order of their institution.

317. ROYAL HUMANE SOCIETY MEDALS

Date: 1774.

Ribbon: None (1774-1869); plain navy blue (1869); thin central yellow stripe and white edges added (silver medal, 1921).

Metal: Gold, silver or bronze.

Size: 51mm (1774-1869); 38mm (1869-).

Description: (Obverse) a cherub, nude but for a flowing cloak, blowing on a burnt-out torch explained by the Latin legend LATEAT SCINTILLVLA FORSAN (perhaps a tiny spark may be concealed). A three-line Latin text across the exergue reads SOC. LOND. IN RESUSCITAT INTERMORTUORUM INSTIT. with the date in roman numerals. (Reverse) an oak wreath containing the engraved details of the recipient and the date of the life-saving act. Round the circumference is a Latin motto HOC PRETIVM CIVE SERVATO TVLIT (He has obtained this reward for saving the life of a citizen). When the rescue attempt was unsuccessful, however, the medal was granted without this inscription. Later medals of similar design were struck also in bronze.

Comments: *The society was formed in 1774 for the specific purpose of diffusing knowledge about the techniques of resuscitation and saving life from drowning. From the society's inception large medals were struck in gold or silver. Monetary rewards, medals, clasps and testimonials were granted to those who saved life, or attempted to save life from drowning, but later the society's remit was broadened to include "all cases of exceptional bravery in rescuing or attempting to rescue persons from asphyxia in mines, wells, blasting furnaces or in sewers where foul air may endanger life".*

Although not intended for wear, the large medals were often pierced or fitted with a ring or bar for suspension from a ribbon. The details of the recipient and the act were engraved on the reverse.

In 1869 permission was given for the medals to be worn. As a result the diameter was reduced to 38mm and a scroll suspension was fitted for wear with a navy blue ribbon. At the same time the Latin text of the "unsuccessful" and "successful" medals was altered to read VIT. PERIC. EXPOS. D.D. SOC REG. HVM. (the Royal Humane Society presented this gift, his life having been exposed to danger) and VIT. OB. SERV. D.D. SOC, REG. HVM. (the Royal Humane Society presented this gift for saving life) respectively. Details of the recipient and the act were engraved on the rim. In 1921 the ribbon of the silver medal was changed to navy blue with a central yellow stripe and white edges, but the plain navy blue ribbon was retained for the bronze medal. Scrolled clasps with the initials R.H.S. were awarded for subsequent acts of lifesaving.

In 1873 the Stanhope Gold Medal, in memory of Captain C.S.S. Stanhope, RN, was instituted for award to the person performing the bravest act of life-saving during the year. The first Stanhope medals were similar to the society's small silver medal, differing only in the addition of a clasp inscribed STANHOPE MEDAL and the year, but since 1937 the Stanhope Medal has been identical to the other medals, differing solely in the metal. In 1921, however, the ribbon for the Stanhope Gold Medal was changed to one of navy blue with yellow and black edges.

VALUE:	Gold	Silver	Bronze
Large successful	—	£150–200	£70–80
Large unsuccessful	—	£250–300	£80–120
Small successful	—	£140–160	£40–60
Small unsuccessful	—	£150–180	£40–60
Stanhope Gold Medal	£1,500–2,000		
Miniature	£250–300	£10–15	£8–12

318. HUNDRED OF SALFORD HUMANE SOCIETY MEDALS

Date: 1824.
Ribbon: Plain dark blue.
Metal: Gold, silver or bronze.
Size: 32mm (circular type); height 49mm; max. width 41mm (cruciform type).
Description: Circular silver or bronze medals were awarded from 1824 onwards, with the recipient's name and details engraved on the reverse, and featuring a cherub kindling a spark similar to the Royal Humane Society's medal, on the obverse. Around the time of the society's centenary in 1889, however, a more elaborate type of medal was devised, with the circular medal superimposed on a cross of distinctive shape, so that the society's name could be inscribed on the arms. The recipient's details are again found on the reverse.
Comments: *This society was formed in 1789 to serve the needs of the Salford and Manchester area. After a few years it was dissolved, but was revived again in 1824. These awards ceased in 1922.*

VALUE:

	Gold	Silver	Bronze	*Miniature*
Circular medal	Rare	£110–130	£90–120	—
Cruciform medal	—	£60–80	—	—

319. ROYAL NATIONAL LIFEBOAT INSTITUTION MEDALS

Date: 1825.
Ribbon: Plain blue.
Metal: Gold, silver or bronze.
Size: 36mm.
Description: The first medals bore the effigy of George IV on the obverse and it was not until 1862 that this was replaced by a garlanded profile of Victoria by Leonard C. Wyon. Medals portraying Edward VII and George V were introduced in 1902 and 1911 respectively, but when permission to portray George VI was refused in 1937 the RNLI adopted a profile of its founder, Sir William Hillary, instead. All but the Edwardian medals have a reverse showing a drowning seaman being rescued by three men in a boat with the motto LET NOT THE DEEP SWALLOW ME UP. The Edwardian medals have the seated figure of Hope adjusting the lifejacket on a lifeboatman. The twin-dolphin suspension (first fitted in the 1850s) has a plain blue ribbon, and clasps inscribed SECOND SERVICE, THIRD SERVICE and so on are awarded for subsequent acts of gallantry.

Comments: *The RNLI was founded, as the Royal National Institution for the Preservation of Life from Shipwreck, on 4 March 1824 and began awarding medals the following year to "persons whose humane and intrepid exertions in saving life from shipwreck on our coasts are deemed sufficiently conspicuous to merit honourable distinction". Its title changed to the Royal National Lifeboat Institution in 1854.*

VALUE:	Gold	Silver	Bronze
George IV	£1,200–1,500	£200–250	—
Victoria	£1,200–1,500	£250–300	—
Edward VII	£1,500–1,800	£700–800	—
George V	£1,400–1,800	£400–500	£250–300
Hillary	£800–1,200	£400–500	£250–300

320. MEDALS OF THE SOCIETY OF THE PROTECTION OF LIFE FROM FIRE

Date: 1836.
Ribbon: Plain scarlet.
Metal: Silver or bronze.
Size: 52mm (I and II), 45mm (III), 42mm (IV &V) and 40mm (VI).
Description: The first medal (type I) had a radiate eye in garter on the obverse and a reverse giving the recipient's details in an oak-leaf wreath. They were fitted with a ring suspender. The Society was granted the Royal title in 1843 and a new medal (type II) was adopted the following year, with the word ROYAL added and the date at the foot of the obverse changed to 1844. In the early 1850s type III was introduced, with an obverse of a man carrying a woman away from a fire. This and type IV (1892) were struck in silver or bronze. As royal patronage ended with the death of Queen Victoria, a new medal (type V) was required in 1902 without the Royal title. Types IV and V show a man rescuing a woman and two children from a fire. The reverse of this medal has the words DUTY AND HONOR within a wreath, the recipient's details being placed on the rim. Type VI, awarded from 1984, is a bronze medal without suspension with the recipient's details engraved on the reverse.

VALUE:		Silver	Bronze
I	Eye and garter (1836)	£350–400	—
II	Eye and garter (1844)	£350–400	—
III	Man and woman (1850s)	£150–200	Rare
IV	Man, woman and children (1892)	£350–450	Rare
V	As type IV but "Royal" removed (1902)	£150–200	£100–150
VI	As type IV but details on rev.	—	Rare
Miniature (type IV)		£60–80	—

321. LLOYD'S MEDALS FOR SAVING LIFE AT SEA

Date: 1836.
Ribbon: Blue, striped white, red and white in the centre.
Metal: Gold, silver or bronze.
Size: 73mm or 36mm.
Description: Both large and small medals had similar motifs. (Obverse) the rescue of Ulysses by Leucothoe; (reverse) an ornate wreath.
Comments: *The first medals, introduced in 1836, had a diameter of 73mm and were not intended for wear, but in 1896 the diameter was reduced to 36mm and a ring fitted for suspension with a ribbon.*

VALUE:

		Miniature
Large silver	£400–500	—
Large bronze	£200–250	—
Small silver	£200–250	£60–80
Small bronze	£150–180	£40–50

322. LIVERPOOL SHIPWRECK AND HUMANE SOCIETY'S MARINE MEDALS

Date: 1839.
Ribbon: Plain dark blue.
Metal: Gold, silver or bronze.
Size: 54mm (type I), 45mm x 36mm (oval, type II) or 38mm (type III).
Description: (Obverse) a man on a spar of wreckage, taking an inert child from its drowning mother, with the stark legend LORD SAVE US, WE PERISH. This motif was retained for smaller, oval medals (type II) introduced around 1867 with the name of the Society round the edge, and a simple wreath reverse. The suspender was mounted with the Liver Bird emblem. A smaller circular version (type III) was adopted in 1874/75 and fitted with a scroll suspender. In this type the Liver Bird appeared in a wreath on the reverse. Bars engraved with the details were awarded for subsequent acts of life-saving. In addition to the general Marine medals there were distinctive awards in connection with specific marine rescues and funded separately. These had the type III obverse, but the reverse was inscribed CAMP & VILLAVERDE or BRAMLEY-MOORE. A glazed silver medal inscribed IN MEMORIAM was granted to the next of kin of those who lost their lives while attempting to save the lives of others.
Comments: *The Society was formed in 1839 to administer funds raised to help and reward those who distinguished themselves in saving life as a result of a hurricane which swept the Irish Sea in January of that year. The first medals were struck in 1844 and presented for rescues dating back to November 1839. They were large (54mm) in diameter, without suspension.*

VALUE:

	Gold	Silver	Bronze
Large (54mm) 1844	Rare	£250–300	—
Oval 1867	—	£400–450	—
Small (38mm) 1874/5	£800–1200	£60–150	£50–80
Camp & Villaverde	—	£400–600	£400–450
Bramley-Moore	—	£400–500	£350–400
In Memoriam	—	£350–400	—
Miniature (type III)	—	£90–100	—

323. SHIPWRECKED FISHERMEN AND MARINERS ROYAL BENEVOLENT SOCIETY MEDALS

Date: 1851.
Ribbon: Navy blue.
Metal: Gold or silver.
Size: 36mm.
Description: (Obverse) the Society's arms; (reverse) inscribed PRESENTED FOR HEROIC EXERTIONS IN SAVING LIFE FROM DROWNING with a quotation from Job 29: 13 at the foot. The circumference is inscribed ENGLAND EXPECTS EVERY MAN WILL DO HIS DUTY, a quotation from Lord Nelson's signal to the fleet at Trafalgar, 1805. The first medals had a straight suspender but by 1857 a double dolphin suspender had been adopted (five variations of this suspender can be identified). Details of the recipient's name and the date of the rescue are engraved on the edge.
Comments: *The Society was founded in 1839 to raise funds for shipwrecked fishermen and mariners and the families of those lost at sea.*

VALUE	Gold	Silver
Straight suspender	Rare	£150–200
Dolphin suspender	£800–1,200	£150–200
Miniature	—	£90–100

324. TAYLEUR FUND MEDAL

Date: 1854.
Ribbon: Dark blue.
Metal: Gold (2) or silver.
Size: 45mm.
Description: (Obverse) a sinking ship with the legend TAYLEUR FUND FOR THE SUCCOUR OF SHIPWRECKED STRANGERS; (reverse) details of the award engraved.
Comments: *In January 1854 the emigrant ship* Tayleur *foundered in Bantry Bay, Ireland. A fund was started for the relief of the survivors and the surplus used to issue silver life-saving medals. The first awards were made in 1861. Medals are known to have been awarded for eight separate rescues, the last in 1875. In December 1913 the residue of the Tayleur Fund was transferred to the RNLI and the issue of medals terminated.*

VALUE:	
Gold (2)	—
Silver (39)	£250–350

325. HARTLEY COLLIERY MEDAL

Date: 1862.
Ribbon: None.
Metal: Gold (1) or silver.
Size: 53mm
Description: (Obverse) an angel with mine rescuers and disaster victims. Details of the award were engraved on the reverse.
Comments: *Some 204 miners perished in the disaster which overtook the Hartley Colliery, Northumberland on 10 January 1862. This medal was awarded to those involved in the rescue operations.*

VALUE:	
Gold (1)	—
Silver (37)	£250–350

326. LIFE SAVING MEDAL OF THE ORDER OF ST JOHN

Date: 1874.
Ribbon: Black, embroidered with the eight-point cross in white (1874), black watered silk (1888), white inner and red outer stripes added, separated by a black line(1950) which was subsequently removed in 1954.
Metal: Gold, silver or bronze.
Size: 36mm.
Description: The first medals had a plain eight-pointed cross of the Order on the obverse with the legend AWARDED BY THE ORDER OF ST JOHN OF JERUSALEM IN ENGLAND. A second type of medal was adopted in 1888 and showed two tiny lions and two tiny unicorns in the interstices of the cross, the reverse shows sprigs of St John's wort and the legend FOR SERVICE IN THE CAUSE OF HUMANITY. Clasps for further awards were instituted in 1892.
Comments: *Instituted on 15 December 1874 and awarded for gallantry in saving life, these medals were originally granted in bronze or silver, but gold medals were also struck from 1907.*

VALUE:

	Gold	Silver	Bronze
1st type 1874	—	£500–600	£400–500
2nd type 1888	£1,000	£500–600	£400–500
Miniature	—	£40–50	£30–40

327. LIVERPOOL SHIPWRECK AND HUMANE SOCIETY'S FIRE MEDAL

Date: 1883.
Ribbon: Plain scarlet.
Metal: Gold, silver or bronze.
Size: 38mm.
Description: (Obverse) a fireman descending the stairs of a burning house carrying three children to their kneeling mother, her arms outstretched to receive them. (Reverse) the wreathed Liver Bird previously noted for the third type of Marine medal. The medal is fitted with a scroll suspender. Clasps engraved with the details are awarded for subsquent acts.
Comments: *The first recipient was William Oversly in November 1883, for rescuing a child from a burning house. The first woman recipient was Miss Julia Keogh (12 February 1895) who saved two children in a house fire.*

VALUE:

	Gold	Silver	Bronze
Fire medal	Rare	£250–300	£150–180
Miniature	—	£40–50	£40–50

328. LLOYD'S MEDALS FOR MERITORIOUS SERVICE

Date: 1893.
Ribbon: Red with blue stripes towards the edges (1893); blue with broad white stripes towards the edges (since 1900).
Metal: Silver or bronze.
Size: 36mm x 38mm (star), 39mm x 29mm (oval), 36mm (circular).
Description: The original medal was a nine-pointed rayed star in bronze with the arms of Lloyd's on the obverse, suspended by a ring from a red ribbon with blue stripes towards the edge. A silver oval medal was introduced in 1900 with Lloyd's arms on the obverse and details of the recipient engraved on the reverse. This medal was fitted with a twin dolphin suspender and a blue ribbon with broad white stripes towards the edge. A third type, introduced in 1913, was a circular medal, struck in silver or bronze, with Lloyd's shield on the obverse. The fourth type, still current, was introduced in 1936 and has the full arms, with crest, motto and supporters, on the obverse. The ribbon is suspended by a ring.
Comments: *These medals have been awarded to officers and men for extraordinary services in the preservation of vessels and cargoes from peril.*

VALUE:

	Silver	Bronze
Star 1893	—	£100–120
Oval 1900	£400–450	—
Circular 1913	£320–350	£280–320
Circular 1936	—	—
Miniature **(circular)**	£60–80	—

329. LIVERPOOL SHIPWRECK AND HUMANE SOCIETY'S GENERAL MEDAL

Date: 1894.
Ribbon: Five equal stripes, three red and two white.
Metal: Gold, silver or bronze.
Size: 38mm.
Description: (Obverse) a cross pattee with a wreathed crown at the centre and the legend FOR BRAVERY IN SAVING LIFE with the date 1894 at the foot; (reverse) the wreathed Liver Bird of the Marine medal, type III. Fitted with an ornate bar suspender. Bars for subsequent awards are granted.
Comments: *The first award was made on 9 June 1894 to Constables Twizell and Dean who were both injured whilst stopping runaway horses.*

VALUE:

	Gold	Silver	Bronze
General medal	Rare	£120–150	£60–100
Miniature	—	£80–100	—

330. DRUMMOND CASTLE MEDAL

Date: 1896.
Ribbon: Plain crimson.
Metal: Silver.
Size: 38mm.
Description: (Obverse) the veiled profile of Queen Victoria; (reverse) a wreath enclosing the name of the ship and the date of its sinking with the legend FROM QUEEN VICTORIA A TOKEN OF GRATITUDE. Fitted with a scrolled suspender.
Comments: *Presented on behalf of Queen Victoria by officials from the British Embassy in Paris to inhabitants of Brest, Ushant and Molene for their generosity and humanity in rescuing and succouring the survivors of the SS* Drummond Castle *which struck a reef off Ushant on 16 June 1896. Of the 143 passengers and 104 crew, all but three perished. 282 medals were struck and 271 of these were awarded to those who helped save the living and assisted in the recovery and burial of the victims.*

VALUE:

Silver (282)	£180–220	*Miniature*	—

331. CARNEGIE HERO FUND MEDAL

Date: 1908.
Ribbon: None.
Metal: Bronze.
Size: 90mm.
Description: (Obverse) an angel and a nude male figure surrounded by an inscription "HE SERVES GOD BEST WHO MOST NOBLY SERVES HUMANITY"; (reverse) two wreaths surrounding a central tablet inscribed "FOR HEROIC ENDEAVOUR TO SAVE HUMAN LIFE 19…" surrounding a further inscription "PRESENTED BY THE TRUSTEES OF THE CARNEGIE HERO FUND". Details of the recipient are engraved on the rim.
Comments: *The Carnegie Hero Fund Trust was established in Scotland by Andrew Carnegie in 1908. The first medallion was awarded posthumously on 26 November 1909 to Thomas Wright for a life saving act on 23 September 1908. To date 171 medllions have been awarded.*

VALUE:

Bronze	£250–350

332. C.Q.D. MEDAL

Date: 1909.
Ribbon: Plain dark blue.
Metal: Silver.
Size: 45mm.
Description: (Obverse) the SS Republic with the initials C.Q.D. at the top; (reverse) the words FOR GALLANTRY across the middle, with a very verbose inscription round the circumference and continued in eight lines across the field. Ring suspension.
Comments: *This medal takes its curious name from the CQD signal (Come Quick Danger) sent out by the Italian steamer* Florida *when it collided in thick fog with the White Star liner* Republic *on 21 January 1909. The liner* Baltic *responded to the call. The* Republic *was the more severely damaged vessel, but all of her passengers and crew were transferred, first to the* Florida *and then to the* Baltic, *before she sank. The saloon passengers of the* Baltic *and* Republic *subscribed to a fund to provide medals to the crews of all three ships in saving more than 1700 lives.*

VALUE:

Silver	£130–160

333. RSPCA LIFE-SAVING MEDAL

Date: 1909.
Ribbon: Blue with three white stripes in the centre, the central stripe being narrower than the others (silver); blue with a central white stripe flanked by narrow red and white stripes (bronze).
Metal: Silver or bronze.
Size: 36mm.
Description: (Obverse) a seated female figure surrounded by a cow, sheep, cat, dog, goat and horse; (reverse) plain, with an inscription. The recipient's name usually appears on the rim. Both medals have a brooch bar inscribed FOR HUMANITY.
Comments: *Instituted in 1909 by the Royal Society for the Prevention of Cruelty to Animals, this medal is awarded in silver or bronze for acts of gallantry in saving the lives of animals.*

VALUE:

		Miniature
Silver	£80–120	£15–20
Bronze	£50–60	£10–20

334. SCOUT ASSOCIATION GALLANTRY MEDALS

Date: 1909.
Ribbon: Red (bronze), blue (silver) or half red, half blue (gilt).
Metal: Bronze, silver and gilt.
Size: 33mm.
Description: A cross pattée with the Scout fleur-de-lis emblem at the centre with the motto "BE PREPARED" and the words "FOR GALLANTRY" or "FOR SAVING LIFE". The name and details of the recipient are engraved on the plain reverse. Suspension is by a straight bar. A plain bar can be awarded for additional acts of gallantry.
Comments: *The Scout movement began informally in 1907 and the Boy Scouts Association was founded a year later. Gallantry awards were instituted in 1908 and 1909. The bronze cross is the highest award of the Association for gallantry, granted for special heroism or action in the favce of extraordinary risk. The silver cross is awarded for gallantry in circumstances of consideravble risk. The gilt cross is awarded for gallantry in circumstances of moderate risk. A bar may be awarded to the holder of any gallantry award for further acts of galantry in circumstances of similar risk.*

VALUE:	Bronze	£350–450
	Silver	£250–300
	Gilt	£150–200

335. CARPATHIA AND TITANIC MEDAL

Date: 1912.

Ribbon: Dark blue.

Metal: Gold, silver or bronze.

Size: Height 40mm; max. width 35mm.

Description: The ornately shaped medal, in the best Art Nouveau style, has the suspension ring threaded through the head of Neptune whose long beard flows into two dolphins terminating in a fouled anchor and ship's spars. (Obverse) the Carpathia steaming between icebergs; (reverse) a twelve-line inscription, with the name of the manufacturer at the foot. It was worn from a straight bar suspender.

Comments: *This medal recalls one of the greatest tragedies at sea, when the White Star liner* Titanic *struck an iceberg on her maiden voyage and sank with the loss of 1490 lives. The 711 survivors were picked up by the* Carpathia *whose officers and men were subsequently awarded this medal in gold, silver or bronze according to the rank of the recipient.*

VALUE:

Gold (14)	Rare (an example sold at Sotheby's New York in July 1997 for $50,000)
Silver (110)	£400–600
Bronze (180)	£300–400

336. CORPORATION OF GLASGOW BRAVERY MEDAL

Date: 1924

Ribbon: Green with red edges.

Metal: Gold, silver or bronze.

Size: 38mm (type I) or 33mm (type II).

Description: Type I: (obverse) an angel blowing a trumpet and holding a laurel wreath in front of a circular scrolled cartouche inscribed FOR BRAVERY; (reverse) plain, engraved with the name and details of the recipient. Type II: (obverse) wreath enclosing the words "FOR BRAVERY"; (reverse) Arms of the Corporation of Glasgow and details of the recipient. Fitted with a ring suspension and an ornate thistle brooch inscribed GALLANTRY in a scroll.

Comments: *Following the reorganisation of local government in Scotland in 1975, the award ceased and was replaced by the Strathclyde Regional Council Medal for Bravery.*

VALUE:

	Type I	Type II
Gold	£200–250	£200–250
Silver	£100–150	£50–100
Bronze	£50–80	—

337. LLOYD'S MEDAL FOR SERVICES TO LLOYDS

Date: November 1913.

Ribbon: Blue with broad white stripes towards the edge.

Metal: Silver.

Size: 36mm.

Description: (Obverse) Neptune in a chariot drawn by four horses; (reverse) an oak-leaf wreath enclosing a scroll inscribed FOR SERVICES TO LLOYD'S. Fitted with ring suspension.

Comments: *Instituted by Lloyd's Committee, this medal was intended to reward services of a general nature.*

VALUE:

		Miniature
Gold (14)	£1500–2000	—
Silver (10)	£800–1000	£65–70

338. LLOYD'S MEDAL FOR BRAVERY AT SEA

Date: 1940.
Ribbon: White with broad blue stripes at the sides.
Metal: Silver.
Size: 36mm.
Description: (Obverse) a seated nude male figure holding a laurel wreath, extending his hand towards a ship on the horizon; (reverse) a trident surmounted by a scroll inscribed BRAVERY, enclosed in a wreath of oak leaves. It has a ring suspender.
Comments: *Instituted by Lloyd's Committee, it was awarded to officers and men of the Merchant Navy and fishing fleets for exceptional bravery at sea in time of war. A total of 523 medals was awarded up to December 1947 when it was discontinued.*

VALUE:

Silver	£500–700	*Miniature*	£65–75

339. LIVERPOOL SHIPWRECK AND HUMANE SOCIETY'S SWIMMING MEDAL

Date: 1885
Ribbon: Five equal bars, three blue and two white.
Metal: Silver or bronze.
Size: Height 44mm; max. width 30mm.
Description: This extremely ornate medal has a twin dolphin suspender and a free form. (Obverse) a wreath surmounted by crossed oars and a trident, with a lifebelt at the centre enclosing the Liver Bird emblem on a shield; (reverse) plain, engraved with the recipient's name and details.
Comments: *Not granted for life-saving as such, but for proficiency in swimming and life-saving techniques.*

VALUE:

Silver	£30–50
Bronze	£20–40

340. BINNEY MEMORIAL MEDAL

Date: 1947.
Ribbon: None.
Metal: Bronze.
Size: 48mm.
Description: (Obverse) a bust of Captain R.D. Binney, CBE, RN; (reverse) inscription FOR COURAGE IN SUPPORT OF LAW AND ORDER and AWARDED TO above the recipient's name on a raised tablet.
Comments: *Instituted in memory of Captain Binney who was killed on 8 December 1944 in the City of London while attempting to apprehend two armed robbers single-handedly. It is awarded annually to the British citizen who displays the greatest courage in support of law and order within the areas under the jurisdiction of the Metropolitan Police and the City of London Police. The medal is not intended for wear.*

VALUE:

Bronze	£400–600

MISCELLANEOUS MEDALS

Under this heading are grouped a very disparate range of medals whose only common denominator is that they do not fit conveniently into one or other of the preceding categories. They are not without considerable interest, the polar medals in particular having a very keen following and a buoyant market.

341. KING'S AND QUEEN'S MESSENGER BADGE

Instituted: 1485.
Ribbon: Plain blue.
Metal: Silver.
Size: 45mm x 35mm.
Description: An upright oval fitted with a plain suspension ring and having a greyhound suspended by a ring from the foot of the rim. (Obverse) the Garter inscribed HONI SOIT QUI MAL Y PENSE enclosing the crowned royal cypher. (Reverse) plain, engraved with dates of service. Occasionally found with additional dates and monarchs' details, indicating re-issue to other messengers.
Comments: *John Norman was the first gentleman messenger formally appointed by King Richard III. Henry VIII expanded the service into a corps of 40 King's Messengers under the control of the Lord Chamberlain. Nowadays the corps is controlled by the Foreign and Commonwealth Office. Originally the badge was worn at all times by messengers on duty; today it is only worn on formal occasions.*

VALUE: Rare

342. ARCTIC MEDAL

Instituted: 30 January 1857.
Ribbon: 38mm plain white.
Metal: Silver.
Size: Height 46mm; max. width 32mm.
Description: An octagonal medal with a beaded rim, surmounted by a nine-pointed star (representing the Pole Star) through which the suspension ring is fitted. (Obverse) an unusual profile of Queen Victoria, her hair in a loose chignon secured with a ribbon. (Reverse) a three-masted sailing vessel amid icebergs with a sledge party in the foreground and the dates 1818-1855 in the exergue. The medal was issued unnamed, but is often found privately engraved.
Comments: *Awarded retrospectively to all officers and men engaged in expeditions to the polar regions from 1818 to 1855, including those involved in the on-going search for the ill-fated Franklin Expedition of 1845-8. Thus the medal was granted to civilians, scientists, personnel of the French and US Navies and employees of the Hudson's Bay Company who took part in a number of abortive search parties for Sir John Franklin and his crew. Some 1106 medals, out of 1486 in all, were awarded to officers and ratings of the Royal Navy.*

VALUE:
   Silver £270–300   *Miniature* £150–200

343. ARCTIC MEDAL

Instituted: 28 November 1876.
Ribbon: 32mm plain white.
Metal: Silver.
Size: 36mm
Description: A circular medal with a raised beaded rim and a straight bar suspender. (Obverse) a veiled bust of Queen Victoria wearing a small crown, dated 1877 at the foot; (reverse) a three-masted ship icebound.

Comments: *Granted to officers and men of HM ships* Alert *and* Discovery *who served in the Arctic Expedition between 17 July 1875 and 2 November 1876. The medal was later extended to include the crew of the private yacht* Pandora *commanded by Allen Young which cruised in polar waters between 25 June and 19 October 1875 and from 3 June to 2 November 1876. Medals were impressed with the name and rank of the recipient. Only 170 medals were awarded.*

VALUE:
   Silver £900–1200 *Miniature* £200–250

344. POLAR MEDAL

Instituted: 1904.
Ribbon: 32mm plain white.
Metal: Silver or bronze.
Size: 33mm octagonal.
Description: (Obverse) the effigy of the reigning sovereign; (reverse) a view of the Royal Research Ship <u>Discovery</u> with a man-handling sledge party in the foreground.
Comments: *Originally issued in silver to officers and in bronze to petty officers and ratings, but the bronze medals were discontinued in 1939 and since then only silver medals have been awarded. Apart from the 1904 issue of bronze medals, all Polar Medals have been fitted with a clasp giving details of the service for which they were awarded. However, those receiving the bronze medal for the first time (21) in 1917 also had no clasp, the date being on the rim. Those already having a bronze medal (3) received a 1917 dated clasp. The 1904 bronze issue included four dated 1902–03, 23 dated 1902–04 and 33 1903–04. Only two women have received the Polar Medal: Lady Virginia Fiennes and the NZ scientist Mary Bradshaw. Medals are named to the recipient, engraved on the earlier and most recent issues and impressed in small capitals on the earlier Elizabethan issues. Clasps for subsequent expeditions are awarded. Altogether some 880 silver and 245 bronze medals for the Antarctic and 73 silver medals for the Arctic have been awarded to date. Of these almost 670 have been awarded in the present reign alone. 8 medals have been awarded for service in both the Arctic and Antarctic and 3 for Antarctic and Arctic (differentiating where first service took place). No bronze medals were issued for Arctic service.*

VALUE:	Silver	Miniature (no clasp)	Bronze	Miniature (no clasp)
Edward VII	from £1,250	£40–50	from £1,000	£20–30
George V (B)	from £1,000	£30–40	from £750	£20–30
George V (C)	—	£30–40	from £750	£20–30
George V (E)	from £1,000	£30–40	—	£20–30
George VI	from £800	£20–25	from £750	£15–20
Elizabeth II	from £800	£15–20	—	£15–20

345. KING EDWARD VII MEDAL FOR SCIENCE, ART AND MUSIC

Instituted: 1904
Ribbon: 35mm scarlet with a broad central band of dark blue and thin white stripes towards the edges.
Metal: Silver.
Size: 32mm.
Description: The raised rim consisted of a laurel wreath and has a ring for suspension. (Obverse) the conjoined busts of King Edward VII and Queen Alexandra; (reverse) the Three Graces engaged in various cultural pursuits.
Comments: *This short-lived medal was discontinued only two years later. It was awarded in recognition of distinguished services in the arts, sciences and music.*

VALUE:	
Silver	£700–800

346. ORDER OF THE LEAGUE OF MERCY

Date: 1900.
Ribbon: 38mm watered white silk with a central broad stripe of dark blue.
Metal: Silver.
Size: Height 51mm; max. width 39mm.
Description: An enamelled red cross surmounted by the Prince of Wales's plumes enfiladed by a coronet, with a central medallion depicting a group of figures representing Charity, set within a laurel wreath.
Comments: *Appointments to the Order are sanctioned and approved by the sovereign on the recommendation of the Grand President of the League of Mercy as a reward for distinguished personal service to the League in assisting the support of hospitals. Ladies and gentlemen who have rendered such aid for at least five years are eligible for the award. In 1917 King George V instituted a bar to be awarded to those who gave continuing service over a period of many years after receiving the Order itself. The Order was last awarded in 1946, the League itself ceasing to exist in 1947.*

VALUE:

Badge of the Order	£30–50	*Miniature*	£15–20

347. INDIAN TITLE BADGE

Instituted: 12 December 1911.
Ribbon: Light blue edged with dark blue (1st class); red edged with dark red (2nd class); or dark blue edged with light blue (3rd class).
Metal: Silver or silver-gilt.
Size: Height 58mm; max. width 45mm.
Description: A radiate star topped by an imperial crown with a curved laurel wreath below the crown and cutting across the top of a central medallion surrounded by a collar inscribed with the appropriate title. The medallion bears the left-facing crowned profile of King George V or the right-facing crowned bust of King George VI. (Reverse) plain, but engraved with the name of the recipient.
Comments: *Introduced by King George V on the occasion of the Delhi Durbar of 1911 and awarded in three classes to civilians and Viceroy's commissioned officers of the Indian Army for faithful service or acts of public welfare. Recipients proceeded from the lowest grade to higher grades, each accompanied by a distinctive title. Each grade was issued in Hindu and Muslim versions, differing in title: Diwan Bahadur (Muslim) or Sardar Bahadur (Hindu), Khan Bahadur (Muslim) or Rai or Rao Bahadur (Hindu) and Khan Sahib (Muslim) or Rai or Rao Sahib (Hindu), in descending order of grade. These title badges took precedence after all British and Indian orders and decorations, and before campaign medals.*

VALUE:

Diwan Bahadur	£60–70
Sardar Bahadur	£60–70
Khan Bahadur	£50–60
Rao Bahadur	£50–60
Khan Sahib	£40–50
Rao Sahib	£40–50
Miniature	£20–30

348. BADGES OF THE CERTIFICATE OF HONOUR

Instituted: 1920.
Ribbon: Plain yellow 38mm (neck) or 32mm (breast).
Metal: Bronze (African) or silver-gilt (non-African).
Size: 65mm x 48mm (neck); 45mm x 33mm (breast).
Description: Oval badges with a raised rim of laurel leaves terminating at the top in an imperial crown flanked by two lions. (Obverse) a crowned effigy of the reigning monarch; (reverse) the crowned cypher of the monarch or some emblem symbolic of the particular territory (Africa), or the colonial coat of arms (non-African colonies and protectorates), with the name of the territory inscribed round the top.
Comments: *Certificates of Honour were awarded to chiefs and other non-European dignitaries of the Empire for loyal and valuable service. Since 1954 recipients have been given the option of taking their award as a neck or breast badge. Both African and non-African types when worn as a breast badge take precedence over coronation and jubilee medals. These awards were quite distinct from the decorations known as the Native Chiefs Medals (see number 70).*

VALUE:

George V	—
George VI	—
Elizabeth II (neck)	—
Elizabeth II (breast)	—

349. NAVAL ENGINEER'S GOOD CONDUCT MEDAL

Instituted: 1842.
Ribbon: Originally plain dark blue but later broad blue with whiteedges.
Metal: Silver.
Size: 35mm.
Description: (Obverse) a two-masted paddle steamer with a trident in the exergue; (reverse) a circular cable cartouche enclosing a crowned fouled anchor and the legend FOR ABILITY AND GOOD CONDUCT. Between the cable and the rim the details of the recipient were engraved round the circumference. Considering the rarity of the award, it is even more remarkable that the medals have several unique features. Shaw's medal, for example, had oak leaves in the exergue, flanking the trident, but this feature was omitted from later medals. Medals have been recorded with a straight bar suspender, a steel clip and ring suspender or fixed ring suspension with one or two intermediate rings.
Comments: *This medal was abolished five years after it was instituted, only seven medals being awarded in that period: to William Shaw (1842), William Dunkin (1842), William Johnstone (1843), John Langley (1843), J.P. Rundle (1845), George Roberts (1845) and Samuel B. Meredith (1846). Restrikes were produced in 1875 and at a later date. The original medals have a grooved rim, the 1875 restrikes a diagonal grained rim and the later restrikes a plain, flat rim.*

VALUE:

Original	Rare
1875 restrike	£120–140
Later restrike	£80–100

350. INDIAN RECRUITING BADGE (GEORGE V)

Instituted: 1917.
Ribbon: Plain dark green.
Metal: Bronze.
Size: Height 45mm; max. width 48mm.
Description: A five-pointed star with ball finials, surmounted by a wreathed gilt medallion bearing a left-facing crowned bust of King George V, inscribed FOR RECRUITING WORK DURING THE WAR.
Comments: *Awarded to Indian officers and NCOs engaged in recruitment of troops. It could only be worn in uniform when attending durbars or state functions, but at any time in plain clothes.*

VALUE:

George V	£50–60	*Miniature*	£15–20

351. INDIAN RECRUITING BADGE (GEORGE VI)

Instituted: 1940.
Ribbon: Emerald green divided into three sections interspersed by narrow stripes of red (left) and yellow (right).
Metal: Silver and bronze.
Size: Height 42mm; max. width 39mm.
Description: A multi-rayed silver breast badge surmounted by an imperial crown with a suspension ring fitted through the top of the crown. In the centre is superimposed a bronze medallion bearing the left-facing crowned profile of King George VI, within a collar inscribed FOR RECRUITING.
Comments: *Awarded to selected civilian and military pensioners, full-time members of the Indian Recruiting Organisation, fathers and mothers having at least three children in the armed services, and wives having a husband and at least two children serving in the defence forces.*

VALUE:

George VI	£40–50	*Miniature*	£20–25

352. NAVAL GOOD SHOOTING MEDAL

Instituted: August 1902.
Ribbon: Dark blue with a red central stripe edged in white.
Metal: Silver.
Size: 36mm.
Description: (Obverse) the effigy of the reigning monarch; (reverse) a nude figure of Neptune holding five thunderbolts in each hand. In the background can be seen the bows of a trireme and the heads of three horses, with a trident in the field. The Latin motto AMAT VICTORIA CURAM (Victory loves care) appears round the circumference. Fitted with a straight suspension bar. The recipient's name, number, rank, ship and calibre of gun are impressed round the rim.
Comments: *Instituted to promote excellent gunnery performances in the annual Fleet Competitions, it was first awarded in 1903 but was discontinued in 1914. Subsequent success was marked by the issue of a clasp bearing the name of the ship and the date. A total of 974 medals and 62 bars was awarded. 53 men received one bar, three men got two bars and only one achieved three bars.*

VALUE:

		Miniature
Edward VII	£180–200	£50–60
George V	£200–220	£30–35

353. ARMY BEST SHOT MEDAL

Instituted: 30 April 1869.

Ribbon: Watered crimson with black, white and black stripes at the edges.

Metal: Bronze or silver.

Size: 36mm.

Description: (Obverse) the veiled diademmed profile of Queen Victoria; (reverse) Victory bestowing a laurel crown on a naked warrior armed with a quiver of arrows and a bow and holding a target, impaled with arrows, in his other hand. Fitted with a straight suspension bar.

Comments: *This medal, sometimes referred to as the Queen's Medal, was awarded annually to the champion in the Army marksmanship contests held at Bisley. It was originally struck in bronze, but was upgraded to silver in 1872. The award ceased in 1882, but was revived in 1923 and thereafter known as the King's Medal. The original reverse was retained, with the appropriate effigy of the reigning sovereign on the obverse. Since 1953 it has been known as the Queen's Medal again. In the post-1923 medals a bar bears the year of the award, with additional year clasps for subsequent awards. Until 1934 a single medal was awarded each year, but in 1935 two medals were granted, for the champion shots of the Regular and Territorial Armies respectively. Subsequently additional medals have been sanctioned for award to the military forces of India, Canada, Australia, New Zealand, Ceylon, Rhodesia, the British South Africa Police, the Union of South Africa, Pakistan, Jamaica and Ghana.*

VALUE:		Miniature
Victoria bronze	Rare	—
Victoria silver	Rare	—
George V	£700–800	£30–40
George VI	£700–800	£30–40
Elizabeth II	£700–800	£10–15

354. QUEEN'S MEDAL FOR CHAMPION SHOTS OF THE ROYAL NAVY AND ROYAL MARINES

Instituted: 12 June 1953.

Ribbon: Dark blue with a red central stripe bordered white.

Metal: Silver.

Size: 36mm.

Description: (Obverse) the effigy of Queen Elizabeth II; (reverse) Neptune (as on the Naval Good Shooting Medal).

Comments: *Instituted as the naval counterpart of the Army best shot medal.*

VALUE:			
Elizabeth II	£700–800	Miniature	£10–15

355. QUEEN'S MEDAL FOR CHAMPION SHOTS OF THE ROYAL AIR FORCE

Instituted: 12 June 1953.
Ribbon: Broad crimson centre flanked by dark blue stripes bisected by thin light blue stripes.
Metal: Silver.
Size: 36mm.
Description: (Obverse) the effigy of Queen Elizabeth II; (reverse) Hermes kneeling on a flying hawk and holding the caduceus in one hand and a javelin in the other. The recipient's details are engraved on the rim and the medal is fitted with a straight bar suspender.
Comments: *Competed for at the annual RAF Small Arms Meeting at Bisley.*

VALUE:

Elizabeth II	—	*Miniature*	£10–15

356. QUEEN'S MEDAL FOR CHAMPION SHOTS OF THE NEW ZEALAND NAVAL FORCES

Instituted: 9 July 1958.
Ribbon: Crimson centre bordered with white and broad dark blue stripes at the edges.
Metal: Silver.
Size: 36mm.
Description: (Obverse) the effigy of Queen Elizabeth II; (reverse) similar to that of the Naval Good Shooting Medal of 1903-14. Fitted with a clasp bearing the year of the award and a straight suspension bar.
Comments: *Awards were made retrospective to 1 January 1955. This medal is awarded for marksmanship in an annual contest of the New Zealand Naval Forces. Additional clasps are granted for further success.*

VALUE:

Elizabeth II	Rare	*Miniature*	—

357. UNION OF SOUTH AFRICA COMMEMORATION MEDAL

Instituted: 1910.
Ribbon: 38mm orange-yellow with a broad central dark blue stripe.
Metal: Silver.
Size: 36mm.
Description: (Obverse) the effigy of King George V; (reverse) a blacksmith beating on an anvil the links of a chain, symbolising the unification of the four countries (Cape Colony, Natal, Orange Free State and the Transvaal), with the date in the exergue.
Comments: *Awarded to those who played a prominent part in the ceremonies connected with the Union, as well as to certain officers and men of HMS Balmoral Castle, a Union Castle liner specially commissioned as a man-of-war to convey HRH the Duke of Connaught as the King's representative to South Africa for the celebrations.*

VALUE:

	Named	Unnamed	*Miniature*
George V	£250–300	£200–240	£10–15

358. LOYAL SERVICE DECORATION

Instituted: 1920.
Ribbon: A broad dark blue central stripe flanked on one side by a gold bar with a thin red stripe superimposed towards the edge, and on the other side by a yellow bar with a thin white stripe towards the edge. Transvaal recipients wore the ribbon with the red to the centre of the chest; Orange Free State recipients wore the ribbon with the white stripe to the centre of the chest.
Metal: Silver.
Size: 36mm.
Description: (Obverse) the arms of the Transvaal; (reverse) the arms of the Orange Free State. Fitted with a swivel suspender. Recipients wore the medal with the appropriate state arms showing.
Comments: *Awarded by the Union of South Africa to officers of the two former Boer republics for distinguished service during the Second Boer War of 1899-1902.*

VALUE:
  Silver (591)   £100–150

359. ANGLO-BOER WAR MEDAL

Instituted: 1920.
Ribbon: Broad green and yellow stripes with three narrow stripes of red, white and dark blue in the centre. Transvaal recipients wore the ribbon with the green to the centre of the chest, while Orange Free State recipients wore it with the yellow towards the centre.
Metal: Silver.
Size: 36mm.
Description: Both sides inscribed ANGLO-BOER OORLOG round the top, with the dates 1899-1902 round the foot. Medallions set in a border of a square and quatrefoil show the arms of the Orange Free State on one side and the Transvaal on the other. The medal was worn with the side showing the arms of the appropriate state uppermost. Fitted with a straight bar swivelling suspender.
Comments: *Awarded by the Union government to officers and men of the former Boer republics for loyal service in the war against the British.*

VALUE:
  Silver £60–70   *Miniature* £15–20

360. COMMONWEALTH INDEPENDENCE MEDALS

Since the partition of the Indian sub-continent in 1947 and the emergence of the Dominions of India and Pakistan, it has been customary for medals to be issued to mark the attainment of independence. As these medals are invariably awarded to British service personnel taking part in the independence ceremonies, they are appended here, in chronological order of institution, the date of the actual award, where later, being given in parentheses. These medals invariably have symbolic motifs with the date of independence inscribed. The distinctive ribbons are noted alongside. All are 32mm wide unless otherwise stated.

India 1947 (1948) three equal stripes of orange, white and green
Pakistan 1947 (1950) dark green with a central thin white stripe
Nigeria 1960 (1964) three equal stripes of green, white and green
Sierra Leone 1961 three equal stripes of green, white and blue
Jamaica 1962 black centre flanked by yellow stripes and green edges
Uganda 1962 (1963) six stripes of black, yellow, red, black, yellow and red
Malawi 1964 three equal stripes of black, red and green
Guyana 1966 36mm red centre flanked by yellow stripes and broad green edges. The green and yellow separated (left) by a thin black stripe and (right) by a thin pale blue stripe
Fiji 1970 Grey-blue with bars half red, half white, towards each end
Papua New Guinea 1975 Red bordered by thin stripes of yellow and white, with black edges
Solomon Islands 1978 five equal stripes of blue, yellow, white, yellow and green
Gilbert Islands (Kiribati) 1980 half red, half black, separated by a thin white stripe, and edged in yellow
Ellice Islands (Tuvalu) 1980 equal stripes of red, white and red edged yellow. the white stripe bisected by a thin black stripe
Zimbabwe 1980 Silver or bronze 38mm black centre flanked by red and yellow stripes with edges of green or blue
Vanuatu 1980 (1981) 25mm four equal stripes of red, black, yellow and dark brown
St Christopher, Nevis and Anguilla 1983 bars of green (left) and red (right) with a black central bar having two thin white stripes, flanked by yellow stripes

VALUE: From £20

361. MALTA GEORGE CROSS FIFTIETH ANNIVERSARY COMMEMORATIVE MEDAL

Instituted: 1992.
Ribbon: Watered dark blue with central stripes of white and red (the Maltese national colours).
Metal: Cupro-nickel.
Size: 36mm.
Description: (Obverse) the crowned arms of the island, which include the George Cross in the upper left corner, with the date 1992 at the foot. (Reverse) a replica of the George Cross with the eight-pointed Maltese Cross at the top and the date 1942 at the foot, with a legend BHALA SHIEDA TA'EROIZMU U DEDIKAZZJONI on one side and TO BEAR WITNESS TO HEROISM AND DEVOTION on the other. Suspension is by a fixed bar decorated with laurels, attached to a ring.
Comments: *Sanctioned by the government of Malta to celebrate the fiftieth anniversary of the award of the George Cross by King George VI to the island for its heroic resistance to prolonged Axis attack during the Second World War. The medal has been awarded to surviving veterans who served in Malta in the armed forces and auxiliary services between 10 June 1940 and 8 September 1943. Permission for British citizens to wear this medal was subsequently granted by the Queen.*

VALUE:
    Cupro-nickel   £80–100   *Miniature*   £8–10

362. SHANGHAI VOLUNTEER CORPS MEDAL

Date: 1854
Ribbon:
Metal: Silver.
Size: 38mm
Description:
Comment: *Awarded to the officers and men of the Shanghai Volunteers who took part in the battle of Soo Chow Creek (also known as the battle of Muddy Flats) which took place in April 28, 1854. Examples are of the greatest rarity and the last one to appear at auction was sold in 1991. Further details are sought.*

VALUE: £800

363. SHANGHAI JUBILEE MEDAL

Instituted: 1893.
Ribbon: Watered silk half bright red, half white.
Metal: Silver or bronze.

Size: 36mm

Description: (Obverse) triple-shield arms of the municipality surrounded by a band with thistles, shamrocks and roses round the foot and NOVEMBER 17 1843 round the top. (Reverse) a scrolled shield with the words SHANGHAI JUBILEE and NOVEMBER 17 1843 and inscribed diagonally across the centre with the recipient's name in block capitals. The shield is flanked by Chinese dragons and above is a steamship and the sun setting on the horizon. The rim is engraved 'Presented by the Shanghai Municipality'. Issued with a small suspension ring, but often replaced by a straight bar.

Comments: *The British settlement in Shanghai was founded in 1843 and formed the nucleus of the International Settlement established in 1854 under the control of an autonomous Municipal Council. In effect the International Settlement functioned as an autonomous City State administered by a Municipal Committee formed from those nations comprising the Settlement. This was abolished when Shanghai was overrun by Imperial Japanese troops in 1941.*

VALUE:

Silver (625)	£250–300
Bronze (100)	£250–300

364. SHANGHAI FIRE BRIGADE LONG SERVICE MEDAL

Instituted: Before 1904.
Ribbon: Black with broad crimson borders.
Metal: Silver.
Size: 31mm.
Description: (Obverse) an armorial device featuring a Chinese dragon standing on a symbolic high-rise building on which is displayed a flame on a pole crossed by a hook and ladder, with MIH-HO-LOONG SHANGHAI round the top and the motto "Say the word and down comes your house" round the foot; (reverse) blank. It seems strange that no Chinese characters appear on the medal. Ring and double claw suspension, with a broad silver brooch bar at the top of the ribbon.
Comment: *Awarded for a minimum of twelve years regular service with the Municipal Fire Brigade. The award was presumably in abeyance following the Japanese invasion in 1937 and the wholesale destruction of the international commercial metropolis.*

VALUE: £300

365. SHANGHAI VOLUNTEER FIRE BRIGADE LONG SERVICE MEDAL

Instituted: 1904.
Ribbon: Red with white edges.
Metal: Gold, silver or bronze.
Size: 36mm.
Description: (Obverse) the arms and motto of the Municipality surrounded by a collar inscribed SHANGHAI VOLUNTEER FIRE BRIGADE ESTABLISHED 1866. (Reverse) a pair of crossed axes surmounted by a fireman's helmet under which is a horizontal tablet on which are engraved the recipient's dates of service. Round the circumference is inscribed FOR LONG SERVICE (top) and WE FIGHT THE FLAMES (foot) with quatrefoil ornaments separating the two inscriptions. Fitted with a swivelling scroll suspender.
Comments: *The medal in silver was awarded to members of the Volunteer Fire Brigade for five years service, for eight years service a clasp was added to the ribbon and for 12 years service the medal was awarded in gold. Bronze medals exist but are believed to have been specimens only.*

VALUE: £450–500.

366. SHANGHAI VOLUNTEER CORPS LONG SERVICE MEDAL

Instituted: 1921.
Ribbon: Equal bands of red, white and blue, the red bisected by a thin green stripe, the white by black and the blue by yellow.
Metal: Silver.
Size: 36mm.
Description: (Obverse) an eight-pointed radiate star bearing a scroll at the top inscribed 4th APRIL 1854. The arms of the Municipality superimposed on the star and surrounded by a collar inscribed SHANGHAI VOLUNTEER CORPS. Round the foot of the medal is a band inscribed FOR LONG SERVICE. (Reverse) plain, engraved with the name of the recipient and his period of service.
Comments: *The Volunteer Corps was raised in 1853 to protect the British and other foreign settlements. The date on the scroll alludes to the Corps' first engagement, the Battle of Muddy Flat. The Corps was cosmopolitan in structure, although the British element predominated. It was disbanded in September 1942, nine months after the Japanese overran the International Settlement. Awarded for 12 years good service, the last medal was awarded in 1941.*

VALUE
Silver   £250–300   *Miniature —*

367. SHANGHAI MUNICIPAL POLICE DISTINGUISHED CONDUCT MEDAL

Instituted: 1924.
Ribbon: Red with a central blue stripe (1st class); red with a blue stripe at each edge (2nd class).
Metal: Silver or bronze.
Size: 36mm.
Description: (Obverse) arms of the Municipality and the inscription SHANGHAI MUNICIPAL POLICE; (reverse) the words FOR DISTINGUISHED CONDUCT. The recipient's name and rank was engraved round the rim.
Comments: *Awarded to officers and men of the Municipal Police in two classes, distinguished solely by their ribbons and the metal used (silver or bronze). A sliding clasp was fitted to the ribbon to denote a second award; this featured the Municipal crest and was engraved on the reverse with the details of the award. Only six awards were ever made, including two to Europeans.*

VALUE:
Silver   £800–900
Bronze   £650–750

368. SHANGHAI MUNICIPAL POLICE LONG SERVICE MEDAL

Instituted: 1925.

Ribbon: Brown with a central yellow band edged in white.

Metal: Silver.

Size: 36mm.

Description: (Obverse) arms of the Municipality within a collar inscribed SHANGHAI MUNICIPAL POLICE; (reverse) plain apart from the inscription FOR LONG SERVICE in two lines across the centre. The recipient's name and rank were engraved round the rim in upper and lower case lettering. Awards to Indians were named in cursive script with the Hindi equivalent alongside. Fitted with a swivelling scroll suspender.

Comments: *Awarded for 12 years good service in the Shanghai Municipal Police, an international force composed largely of Sikhs, Chinese and White Russians as well as British ex-soldiers and policemen. Dated clasps for further five year periods of service were awarded. The medal was abolished in 1942.*

VALUE:

		Miniature
Silver	£280–300	£45–50
With clasp	£350–400	£50–60

369. SHANGHAI MUNICIPAL POLICE (SPECIAL) LONG SERVICE MEDAL

Instituted: 1929.

Ribbon: Dark brown with three white bars, each bisected by a thin yellow stripe.

Metal: Silver.

Size: 36mm.

Description: (Obverse) the arms of the Municipality with the motto OMNIA JUNCTA IN UNO (all joined in one) round the circumference. (Reverse) inscribed SHANGHAI MUNICIPAL POLICE (SPECIALS) FOR LONG SERVICE in six lines. A unique award to A.L. Anderson (1930) was inscribed on the reverse FOR DISTINGUISHED AND VALUABLE SERVICES.

Comments: *Awarded for 12 years active and efficient service in the Special Constabulary. Some 52 medals and 8 clasps for additional service are recorded in the* Shanghai Gazette, *but the actual number awarded was probably greater. The medal was discontinued in 1942.*

VALUE:

With clasp	Very rare
Without clasp	£450–500

370. SHANGHAI MUNICIPAL COUNCIL EMERGENCY MEDAL

Instituted: 1937.

Ribbon: 38mm bright red, having a broad white central stripe bordered black and yellow edges separated from the red by thin black stripes.

Metal: Bronze.

Size: 40mm.

Description: An eight-pointed star with ring suspension. (Obverse) a central medallion superimposed on the radiate star with the triple-shield arms of the Municipality surrounded by a collar inscribed SHANGHAI MUNICIPAL COUNCIL. (Reverse) a laurel wreath enclosing the words FOR SERVICES RENDERED - AUGUST 12 TO NOVEMBER 12 1937.

Comments: *Awarded to members of the Police, Volunteer Corps, Fire Brigade and civilians for services during the emergency of August-November 1937 when fighting between the Chinese and Japanese in and around Shanghai threatened to encroach on the International Settlement. Issued unnamed, but accompanied by a certificate bearing the name and unit of the recipient. Examples have been seen with the recipient's name engraved on the reverse.*

VALUE:

Bronze star	£80–100	*Miniature*	£40–50

ABBREVIATIONS AND INITIALS

O Observer

The medal collector is constantly coming across initials and abbreviations on medals and in documents—many of which are commonplace and easily decipherable. However, there are many more which can cause problems when trying to identify a medal recipient. The following list represents only a small selection of the inexhaustible number of abbreviations encountered, but hopefully it will be of some assistance to the collector. The *"Token Book of Militarisms"* contains literally hundreds more if you cannot find the abbreviation you are looking for (see page 000).

1 E Ang   1st East Anglian Regiment
1 R Dgns   1st Royal Dragoons
1 QDG   1st Queen's Dragoon Guards
11H   11th Royal Hussars
12L   12th Royal Lancers
13/18H   13th/18th Royal Hussars
14/20H   14th/20th Royal Hussars
15/19H   15th/19th Royal Hussars
3 E Ang   3rd East Anglian Regiment
4 QOH   4th Queen's Own Hussars
4H   4th Royal Hussars
5 DGds   5th Royal Inniskilling Dragoon Guards
7QOH   7th Queen's Own Hussars
7GR   7th Gurkha Rifles
A/   Acting
A Avn   Army Aviation
Abn Inf   Airborne Infantry
A/CWEM   Acting Chief Weapons Engineering Mechanic
A/LMEM   Acting Leading Marine Engineering Mechanic
A/LRO(G)   Acting Leading Radio Operator (General)
A/PO   Acting Petty Officer, Acting Pilot Officer
A&SH   The Argyll and Sutherland Highlanders
AAC   Army Air Corps
AAU   Air Ambulance Unit
AB   Able Seaman; Airborne
ABDS   Army Bomb Disposal Squad
AC1   Aircraftman 1st Class
ACC   Army Catering Corps, Armoured Car Company
ACF   Army Cadet Force
ADALS   Assistant Director, Army Legal Service
AE   Army Education Officer, Air Efficiency Award
AER   Army Emergency Reserve
AFC   Air Force Cross
AFM   Air Force Medal
AGS   Africa General Service Medal
AIY   Ayrshire Imperial Yeomanry
ALO   Air Liaison Officer
ALS   Army Legal Services

AM   Albert Medal
AM1   Air Mechanic 1st Class
AMA   Acting Master at Arms
AMS   Assistant Military Secretary; Army Medical Staff
AOC   Army Ordnance Corps
APC   Army Pay Corps
APL   Aden Protectorate Levies
APTC   Army Physical Training Corps
AQ   Assistant Quartermaster; Administrative Quartermaster
Armd   Armoured
ASC   Army Service Corps; Air Service Command
ATO   Ammunition Technical Officer
B&H   The Bedfordshire & Hertfordshire Regiment
B&R   Blues & Royals
BAAT   British Army Advisory Team
BATT   British Army Training Team
BAO   British Army of Occupation
Bdr   Bombadier
BDU   Bomb Disposal Unit
BEM   British Empire Medal
BF   British Forces
BGS   Brigadier, General Staff
BIY   Bedford Imperial Yeomanry
BM   Brigade Major
BORD.R   Border Regiment
BR   British
Brig   Brigadier
Br Coy   Bearer Company
BSA Police   British South Africa Police
Buffs   The Buffs (Royal East Kent Regiment)
BW   Black Watch (Royal Highland Regiment)
BWM   British War Medal
C&TC   Commissariat and Transport Corps
C/Sgt   Colour Sergeant
C&S   Command & Staff
CAC   Canadian Armoured Corps
CADAC   Canadian Army Dental Corps
CAEA   Chief Air Engineering Artificer
CAHTC   Cape Auxiliary Horse Transport Corps
CAMN HIGH   Cameron Highlanders
Capt   Captain

CAR   Central African Rifles
CASC   Canadian Army Service Corps
CATO   Commander Ammunition Technical Officers
CB   Commander of the Order of the Bath
CBE   Commander of the Order of the British Empire
CBF   Commander British Forces
CC   Cadet Corps; Coastal Command; Combat Command
CCAEA   Charge Chief Air Engineering Artificer
CCCC   Cape Colony Cyclist Corps
CCF   Combined Cadet Force
CCMEA   Charge Chief Marine Engineering Artificer
CCS   Casualty Clearing Station
CD   Clearance Diver
C de G   Croix de Guerre
Cdr   Commander
CE   Canadian Engineers
CEO   Chief Executive Officer; Chief Education Officer
CG   Coast Guard; Commanding General
CGM   Conspicuous Gallantry Medal
Cheshire   The Cheshire Regiment
CI   Crown of India, Imperial Order; Counter-Intelligence
CIV   City Imperial Volunteers
CIE   Companion of the Order of the Indian Empre
CLY   County of London Yeomanry
CMEM   Chief Marine Engineering Mechanic
CMFR   Commonwealth Monitoring Force Rhodesia
CMG   Companion of the Order of St Michael and St George
CMM   Commander of the Order of Military Merit
CMO   Chief Medical Officer
CMMP   Corps of Military Mounted Police
CMP   Corps of Military Police
CMSC   Cape Medical Staff Corps
CMR   Cape Mounted Riflemen
CO   Commanding Officer
Col   Colonel
Coldm Gds   Coldstream Guards
Comd   Commander
COS   Chief of Staff
CP   Cape Police
Cpl   Corporal
CPO   Chief Petty Officer
CPOAEA   Chief Petty Officer Air Engineering Artificer
CPOWEA   Chief Petty Officer Weapons Engineering Artificer
CSI   Companion of the Order of the Star of India
CSM   Company Sergeant Major; Campaign Service Medal
CT, C/T, Ch Tech   Chief Technician
CVO   Commander of the Royal Victorian Order
D   Diver
D Comd   Deputy Commander
D&D   The Devon and Dorset Regiment
DAD   Deputy Assistant Director
DADOS   Deputy Assistant Director of Ordnance Services
DADVRS   Deputy Assistant Director Veterinary & Remount Section
DAMA   Department of the Army Material Annex
DANS   Director of Army Nursing Services
DAPM   Deputy Assistant Provost Marshall
DAT   Director of Army Training

DBE   Dame Commander, Order of the British Empire
DCLI   The Duke of Cornwall's Light Infantry
DCM   Distinguished Conduct Medal
DCMG   Dame Commander of the Order of St Michael and St George
DCO   Duke of Cambridge's Own; Duke of Connaught's Own
DCOS   Deputy Chief of Staff
DCVO   Dame Commander of the Royal Victorian Order
DDSD   Deputy Director Staff Duties
DEO   Duke of Edinburgh's Own
DERR   The Duke of Edinburgh's Royal Regiment (Berkshire & Wiltshire)
Det   Detached; Detachment
Devon   The Devonshire Regiment
DFC   Distinguished Flying Cross
DFM   Distinguished Flying Medal
DG   Dragoon Guards
DI   Defence Intelligence
DLI   The Durham Light Infantry
DMT   District Mounted Troops
Dorset   The Dorset Regiment
DOS   Director of Ordnance Services
DS   Defence Secretary; Deputy Secretary; Defensive Section
DSC   Distinguished Service Cross
DSM   Distinguished Service Medal
DSO   Distinguished Service Order
DWR   The Duke of Wellington's Regiment
EAR   East African Rifles
ED   Efficiency Decoration
EF   Expeditionary Force
EGM   Empire Gallantry Medal
EM   Edward Medal; Efficiency Medal
EOD   Explosive Ordnance Disposal
ERD   Emergency Reserve Decoration
ERE   Extra Regimentally Employed
FA   Field Ambulance
FANYC   First Aid Nursing Yeomanry Corps
FBRA   Field Battery Royal Artillery
FC   Fighter Command
Fd   Field
FELF   Far East Land Forces
FF   Field Force
FFL   French Foreign Legion
FFR   Frontier Force Rifles
FL, F/L, Flt Lt   Flight Lieutenant
FM   Field Marshal
FMR   Frontier Mounted Rifles
FO, F/O, Fg Off   Flying Officer
FS   Fighter Squadron; Field Security
FS, F/S, F/Sgt   Flight Sergeant
Fus   Fusilier
G Howards   Green Howards (Alexandra, Princess of Wales's Own Yorkshire Regiment)
G Or   General Operational Requirements
GBE   Grand Cross, Order of the British Empire
GC   George Cross, Group Captain
GCB   Knight Grand Cross Order of the Bath
GCH   Knight Grand Cross Hanoverian Order
GCIE   Knight Grand Commander Order of the Indian Empire
GCLH   Grand Cross Legion of Honour
GCM   Good Conduct Medal

GCMG Knight Grand Cross Order of St Michael and St George
GCSI Knight Grand Commander Order of the Star of India
GCVO Knight Grand Cross Royal Victorian Order
Gdsmn Guardsman
GLI Guernsey Light Infantry
Glosters The Gloucestershire Regiment (28th/61st Foot)
GM George Medal
Gnr Gunner
GOC General Officer Commanding
Gordons The Gordon Highlanders (75th/92nd Regiment)
GPR Glider Pilot Regiment
GR Gurkha Rifles
GS General Service
GSC General Service Corps
GSM General Service Medal
GSO General Staff Officer
HA Horse Artillery
HAC Honourable Artillery Company
HBM Her Britannic Majesty
HCR Household Cavalry Regiment
HG Home Guard; Horse Guards
HLI The Highland Light Infantry
HQ Headquarters
IAOC Indian Army Ordnance Corps
IASC Indian Army Service Corps
IC In Charge
IDSM Indian Distinguished Service Medal
IE Order of the Indian Empire
IG Irish Guards
Int Intelligence
Int Corps Intelligence Corps
Int & Sy Coy Intelligence and Security Company
IO Intelligence Officer
IOM Indian Order of Merit
IRC Infantry Reserve Corps
ISM Imperial Service Medal
ISO Imperial Service Order
IY Imperial Yeomanry
JSSC Joint Services Staff College
KAR King's African Rifles
KB Knight Bachelor
KBE Knight of the Order of the British Empire
KC Knight Commander
KCB Knight Commander Order of the Bath
KCH Knight Commander of the Royal Hanoverian Guelphic Order
KCIE Knight Commander Order of the Indian Empire
KCIO King's Commissioned Indian Officer
KCMG Knight Commander Order of St Michael and St George
KCSI Knight Commander Order of the Star of India
KCVO Knight Commander Royal Victorian Order
KDG King's Dragoon Guards
KG Knight of the Order of the Garter
KGCB Knight Grand Cross Order of the Bath
KGL King's German Legion
Kings The King's Regiment (Liverpool)
KLH Knight of the Legion of Honour
KM King's Medal
KOM Knight of the Order of Malta
KORB The King's Own Royal Border Regiment

KOSB The King's Own Scottish Borderers
KOYLI The King's Own Yorkshire Light Infantry
KPM King's Police Medal
KRRC The King's Royal Rifle Corps
KSG Knight of the Order of St George
KSLI The King's Shropshire Light Infantry
KT Knight of the Order of the Thistle
L/Cpl Lance Corporal
L/Sgt Lance Sergeant
LAC Leading Aircraftman
Lanc Fusiliers The Lancashire Fusiliers
Lanc R The Queen's Lancashire Regiment
LC Labour Corps
Leic The Royal Leicestershire Regiment
LG Life Guards; London Gazette
LI Light Infantry
Linc The Royal Lincolnshire Regiment
LM Legion of Merit
LMA Leading Medical Assistant
LS Leading Seaman
Lt Lieutenant
Lt-Cdr Lieutenant Commander
Lt-Col Lieutenant-Colonel
MA Military Attache
Maint Maintenance
Maj Major
Maj-Gen Major-General
Mal.LBC Maltese Labour Corps
MBE Member of the Order of the British Empire
MC Military Cross
MEM Marine Engineering Mechanic
MFA Mercantile Fleet Auxiliary
MFS Medical Field Service
MGC Machine Gun Corps
MH Medal of Honour
MI Mounted Infantry
MID Mentioned in Despatches
MKW Military Knights of Windsor
MM Military Medal; Medal of Merit
MMGS Motor Machine Gun Service
Mne Marine
MMR Mercantile Marine Service
MR Middlesex Regiment
MRCVS Member Royal College of Veterinary Surgeons
MSC Medical Staff Corps
MSM Meritorious Service Medal
MTO Motor Transport Office
MVO Member of the Royal Victorian Order
NACS Naval Air Commando Squadron
NAS Naval Air Squadron
NCO Non-Commissioned Officer
NFA Natal Field Artillery
NGS Naval General Service (Medal)
NZEF New Zealand Expeditionary Force
OBE Officer of the Order of the British Empire
OBLI Ox and Bucks Light Infantry
OC Officer Commanding
OCS Officer Cadet School
OEO Ordnance Executive Officer
OHBMS On Her Britannic Majesty's Service
OM Order of Merit
OR Operational Requirements; Other Ranks; Organised Reserve
Ord Ordnance
OS Ordinary Seaman; Ordnance Survey

PAOCVA   Prince Albert's Own Cape Volunteer Rifles
PAVG   Prince Albert's Volunteer Guard
Para   The Parachute Regiment
PO   Petty Officer
PO/AC   Petty Officer Aircrewman
POMA   Petty Officer Medical Assistant
POMEM   Petty Officer Marine Engineering Mechanic
PR   Public Relations
PSO   Personnel Selection Officer
Pte   Private
PVCP   Permanent Vehicle Check Point
PWO   The Prince of Wales's Own Regiment of Yorkshire
Q Ops   Quartermaster General Branch Operations
QARANC   Queen Alexandra's Royal Army Nursing Corps
QCBC   Queen's Commendation for Brave Conduct
QFSM   Queen's Fire Service Medal
QDG   The Queen's Dragoon Guards
QGM   Queen's Gallantry Medal
QLR   The Queen's Lancashire Regiment
QM   Quartermaster
QMAAC   Queen Mary's Auxiliary Ambulance Corps
QPM   Queen's Police Medal
QRIH   Queen's Royal Irish Hussars
QSA   Queen's South Africa (Medal)
Queens   The Queen's Regiment—Queen's Division
R Anglian   Royal Anglian Regiment
R Fus   Royal Fusiliers (City of London Regiment)
R Innis   Royal Inniskilling
R Signals   Royal Corps of Signals
RA   Regiment of Artillery
RAC   Royal Armoured Corps
RAChD   Royal Army Chaplains Department
RAEC   Royal Army Educational Corps
RAFVR   Royal Airforce Volunteer Reserve
RAMC   Royal Army Medical Corps
RAOC   Royal Army Ordnance Corps
RAPC   Royal Army Pay Corps
RARO   Regular Army Reserve of Officers
RASC   Royal Army Service Corps
RAVC   Royal Army Veterinary Corps
RB   The Rifle Brigade
RTC   Royal Corps of Transport
RE   Corps of Royal Engineers
RECC   Reconnaissance Corps
REME   Corps of Royal Electrical and Mechanical Engineers
RF   Royal Fusiliers
RFA   Royal Field Artillery
Rfmn   Rifleman
RGJ   Royal Greenjackets
RHA   Royal Horse Artillery
RHF   The Royal Highland Fusiliers
RHG   Royal Horse Guards
RI   Royal Irish Rangers (27th (Inniskilling), 83rd and 87th)
RI Regt   Royal Irish Regiment
RIC   Royal Irish Corps
RIF   The Royal Irish Fusiliers
RM   Royal Marines
RMC   Royal Military College/Royal Military Academy

RMLI   Royal Marine Light Infantry
RMP   Corps of Royal Military Police
RNF   The Royal Northumberland Fusiliers
RNR   Royal Naval Reserve
RNVR   Royal Naval Volunteer Reserve
RO   Radio Operator
RPC   Royal Pioneer Corps
RRC   Royal Red Cross (Medal)
RRF   Royal Regiment of Fusiliers
RRW   Royal Regiment of Wales
RS   The Royal Scots (The Royal Regiment)
RSDG   Royal Scots Dragoon Guards
RSF   Royal Scots Fusiliers
R Sig   Royal Signals
RSM   Regimental Sergeant Major
RSO   Regimental Supply Officer
RTR   Royal Tank Regiment, Royal Armoured Corps
RUR   The Royal Ulster Rifles
RVM   Royal Victorian Medal
RVO   Royal Victorian Order
RWF   The Royal Welsh Fusiliers
RWK   The Queen's Own Royal West Kent Regiment
RW Kent R   Royal West Kent Regiment
S/L, S/Ldr, Sqn Ldr   Squadron Leader
S/Sgt   Staff Sergeant
SAC   Senior Aircraftman
SAS   Special Air Service Regiment
SC   Staff College; Staff Captain; Second in Command; Signal Corps
SF   Special Forces
SG   Scots Guards
SGM   Sea Gallantry Medal
Sgmn   Signalman
Sgt   Sergeant
SI   Star of India (Order)
SJAB   St John Ambulance Brigade
SMIO   Special Military Intelligence Officer
SMIU   Special Military Intelligence Unit
Smn   Seaman
SO1   Staff Officer, Grade 1
Som LI   Somerset Light Infantry
SWB   The South Wales Borderers
TA   Territorial Army
T&AVR   Territorial and Army Volunteer Reserve
TD   Territorial Decoration
TEM   Territorial Efficiency Medal
TF   Territorial Force
TG   Town Guard
Trg Gp   Training Group
UKLF   United Kingdom Land Forces
UNM   United Nations Medal
UNSM   United Nations Service Medal
V&A   Victoria and Albert (Order)
VC   Victoria Cross
WAAF   Women's Auxiliary Air Force
WAFF   West Afican Frontier Force
W/C, W/Cdr, Wg Cdr   Wing Commander
W&S   Worcestershire & Sherwood Foresters
WEA   Weapons Engineering Artificer
WG   Welsh Guards
Wilts   Wiltshire Regiment
WO   Warrant Officer
WOI   Warrant Officer Class I
WOII   Warrant Officer Class II
WRAC   Women's Royal Army Corps
WRAF   Women's Royal Air Force

RESEARCHING YOUR MEDALS

The fact that many British medals are named enables the serious collector to engage in researching both the life and service history of the recipient as well as being able to learn about the history of the regiment/ship/unit or whatever with which he served. There is no easy or definitive guide to the range of research materials that are available, nor to the range of information likely to be found. The sort of information available varies greatly depending on whether the recipient was an officer or other rank, the service and unit with which he served, and the period during which he served. The experience and perseverence of the researcher can also affect the outcome.

When researching a medal and its recipient, experienced collectors regularly refer to a mixture of manuscript and printed sources:

Manuscript Sources

The Public Record Office (PRO, Ruskin Avenue, Kew, Middx) and the India Office Library and Records (IOR, Blackfriars Bridge Road, London SE1) are the two major depositories of official records of interest to the medal collector. Generally speaking the collector of medals to the British Armed Services will find the PRO records essential to their enquiries, whilst anyone interest in the Indian Army and Navy (formerly the armed services of the Honourable East India Company), also the participation of British Forces in Indian campaigns, will find the IOR to be an essential source of information. County Record Offices, National Libraries and Museums, and also Regimental Museums can also have important holdings of manuscript records.

A first visit to the PRO and the IOR can be daunting. The range of records held by both Record Offices is also awe-inspiring once research has gone beyond consulting medal rolls and service papers.

Whilst there is no substitute for *experience* in learning successfully to branch out from the main stream of records, it is essential to be well prepared. It is important to have some idea of where to start looking and to realise the scope and limitations of the documents—it should be noted that the PRO is subject to the standard 30 year closure rule for records, with many personal records being closed for longer periods. A great deal of time can be spent in simply locating the relevant references. To help you be more informed and to help eliminate time-wasting there are a number of important guides available that will aid in the location of the most relevant documents:

Cox, J. and Padfield, T., *Tracing your Ancestors in the Public Record Office* (1983).

Farrington, A., *Guide to the Records of the India Office Military Department* (1981).
Hamilton-Edwards, Gerald, *In Search of Army Ancestry* (1977).
Holding, N., *The Location of British Army Records: A National Directory of World War I Sources* (1984).
Holding, N., *World War I Army Ancestry* (1982).
Rodger, N.A.M., *Naval Records for Genealogists* (1988).

In addition it is worth noting that
1. The Public Record Office produces a range of leaflets which provide useful information about particular classes of records—records relating to military, naval and air services are particularly well-covered. The leaflets are free to visitors to the PRO.
2. The Mormons have published a wide range of guides to genealogical research which cover subjects of interest to medal/military researchers.
3. The National Army Museum occasionally holds a study day on the subject of military research.
4. New information is becoming available all the time and in new forms: for example, the PRO has been producing a video on genealogical research.

Medal Entitlement/Verification

Most collectors start their research by checking with the campaign medal roll (if available) that the recipient is indeed entitled to the medal and any clasps. It is a logical point at which to begin. This is often regarded as a simple, routine procedure, but for the unwary there are pitfalls and complications. The following points should always be borne in mind:

1. Printed medal rolls will always contain errors in transcription, thus any discrepancies between a medal and the roll should, whenever possible, be checked back with the original manuscript roll. The more complex the original roll, the more transcription errors are likely to occur (for example, the claimaints'

lists for the Naval General Service Medal 1793-1840 and even the Military General Service Medal 1793-1814 are good examples of rolls where difficulties are likely to arise).

2. Some rolls have not survived—for example that for the Gwalior Campaign 1843. In such instances prize or bhatta rolls may exist at either the Public Record Office or the India Office. The inclusion of a recipient's name will at least indicate that he was most likely "entitled" to a medal and/or clasp (prize rolls indicate the share of money—realised from the loot captured in an action and then sold—allocated to each participant; bhatta is an extra allowance of pay made for field service).

3. Some medal rolls are incomplete, as with some of the regimental rolls for the Crimea Medal 1854–56.

4. With some campaign medal rolls, supplementary lists and late claimants' documentation have not survived.

5. Some medal rolls are difficult to search and therefore one has to take time in understanding the background to the documents one is looking at—the various lists of recipients for the Military General Service Medal 1794–1840 is a case in point.

It is important to note that the establishment of a recipient's entitlement is not the same thing as verifying a medal. Verification also requires the numismatic knowledge to know that the medal and clasps appear genuine. Where entitlement cannot be confirmed from the medal rolls, some collectors may be happy to rely on their numismatic knowledge to assure themselves that a medal is "genuine".

Published Sources

The published literature on medals is far-reaching and diverse, ranging from simply-produced booklets to detailed studies published in several volumes. A full bibliography of medallic and related works would in itself fill several volumes, particularly if fully cross-referenced.

The references which follow seek to provide a useful list of publications which either relate to orders, decorations and medals in general or to specific items in particular; the list includes medal rolls and casualty lists. No attempt has been made to include journal articles, as this would be an immense task; however a list of useful periodicals, some of which publish regular indexes, appears at the end.

Suggestions for other works that might be considered for inclusion in the next Yearbook are welcomed.

Most collectors seek to build up a solid library which reflects their main interests, but inevitably there are always books that have to be consulted elsewhere. Major libraries and national museums, such as the British Museum Library, the National Army Museum, the Imperial War Museum, the Hendon Royal Air Force Museum, the Greenwich Maritime Museum, and the Portsmouth Naval Musuem have extensive holdings of relevant material which can be consulted on the premises. City and County Reference Libraries are important for collectors who rarely visit London. Some Regimental Museums have libraries attached. Most libraries of any size will have a subject index to their collection of books (and sometimes manuscripts and photographs).

ORDERS, DECORATIONS AND MEDALS

GENERAL WORKS
(listed in alphabetical order by author)

Alexander, E.G.M., Barron, G.K.B. and Bateman, A.J., *South African Orders, Decorations and Medals* (1986).

Blatherwick, Surg. Cmdr. F.J., *Canadian Orders, Decorations and Medals* (1983).

Brine, F., *British Decorations from 1348 to the Present Time, Together with Those Given by Allies* (1880).

Burke, J.B., *The Book of Orders of Knighthood and Decorations of Honour of All Nations* (1858).

Downey, M., *The Standard Catalogue of Orders, Decorations and Medals Awarded to Australians* (1971).

Central Office of Information, *Honours and Titles*. Part of the Aspects of Britain series.

Eaton, Col.Hon.H.F., (later Lord Cheylesmore)., *Naval and Military Medals* (1897).

Elvin, C.N., *A Handbook of the Orders of Chivalry, War Medals and Crosses with Their Clasps and Ribbons and Other Decorations* (1892).

Gibson, J.H., *British War Medals and Other Decorations, Military and Naval* (1866).

Gibson, J.H., *British Military and Naval Medals and Decorations* (1880).

Gordon, Major L.L., *British Orders and Awards* (1959).

Hall, D.C., (in association with Wingate, C.) *British Orders, Decorations and Medals* (1973).

Hastings Irwin, D., *War Medals and Decorations* (1910).

Hieronymussen, Paul, *Orders, Medals and Decorations of Britain and Europe* (1967).

Hayward, J. B. & Son (pub.) *Honours and Awards of the Army, Navy and Air Force 1914-20* (1979).

Irwin, Ross W. , *War Medals and Decorations of Canada* (1969).

Jocelyn, A., *Awards of Honour* (1956).

Johnson, S.C., *Medals of our Fighting Men* (1916).

Johnson, S.C., *The Medal Collector* (1921).

Johnson, S.C., *Everybodys Medals: Including Medals, Decorations, Honours and Orders* (1914).

Joslin, E., C., *The Observers Book of British Awards and Medals* (1974).

Letcher, Owen., *Medals and Decorations of the British Commonwealth of Nations - Medaljes en Dekorasies van de Britse Gemenebes van Nasies* (1941).

Litherland, A.R. and Simpkin, B.T., *Spink's Standard Catalogue of British Orders, Decorations and Medals* (1990).

Mayo, J.H., *Medals and Decorations of the British Army and Navy* (1897).

Mericka, V., *Book of Orders and Decorations* (1975).

Monick, S., *South African Military Awards 1912-1987* (1988).

Monick, S., *Awards of the South African Uniformed Public Services 1922-1987* (1988).

Narbeth, Colin, *Collecting Military Medals* (1971).

Nicolas, N.H., *History of the Orders of Knighthood of the British Empire; of the Order of the Guelphs of Hanover, and of the Medals, Clasps and Crosses, Conferred for Naval and Military Services* (1842).

Pamm, Anthony M., *Honours and Rewards of the British Empire and Commonwealth*, 2 vols. (1996).

Payne, A.A., *A Handbook of British and Foreign Orders, War Medals and Decorations awarded to the Army and Navy* (1911).

Purves, A.A., *Collecting Medals and Decorations* (1968).

Purves, A.A., *The Medals, Decorations and Orders of the Great War 1914-18* (1975).

Purves, A.A., *The Medals, Decorations and Orders of World War II 1939-45* (1986).

Purves, Alec A., *Orders, Decorations and Medals, a Select Bibliography* (1958).

Seedie's Roll of Naval Honours & Awards 1939-1959.

Seedie's List of Submarine Awards for World War II.

Seedie's List of Fleet Air Arm Awards 1939–1969.

Seedie's List of Coastal Forces Awards for World War II.

Seedie's List of Awards to the Merchant Navy for World War II (1997).

Steward, W.A., *War Medals and Their History* (1915).

Steward, W.A., *The ABC of War Medals and Decorations* (1918).

Tancred, G., *Historical Record of Medals and Honorary Distinctions* (1891).

Taprell-Dorling, Captain H. (ed. Alec A. Purves), *Ribbons and Medals* (1983).

ORDERS
(listed by the Order of Precedence)

GENERAL

CB Printers Group (Pubr)., *Orders of Chivalry and Gallantry Awards* (1963)

De la Bere, Sir I. *The Queen's Orders of Chivalry* (1961).

Harbord, R.E., *Supplement to the Royal Family Orders, Badges of Office, Royal Household Medals and Souvenirs* (1954)

Hunter, John., *A Concise Description of the Insignia of the Orders of British Knighthood*

James, G.P.L., *The Royal Family Orders, Badges of Office, Royal Household Medals and Souvenirs* (1951)

Neville, D.G. *A History of the Early Orders of Knighthood and Chivalry.*

Patterson, Stephen, *Royal Insignia* (1996).

Risk, J.C., *British Orders and Decorations* (1973).

ORDER OF THE GARTER

Anstis, J., *The Register of the Most Noble Order of the Garter* (1724).

Ashmole, E., *The Institution, Laws and Ceremonies of the Most Noble Order of the Garter* (1672).

Ashmole, E., *History of the Most Noble Order of the Garter* (1715).

Beltz, G.F., *Memorials of the Most Noble Order of the Garter* (1839).

Buswell, J., *An Historical Account of the Knights of the Most Noble Order of the Garter* (1757).

Dawson, T., *Memoirs of St George The English Patron: And of the Most Noble Order of the Garter* (1714).

Fellowes, Rev. E.H., *The Knights of the Garter 1348-1939* (1939).

Harrison, A.P., *Order of the Garter: Armorial Registry of the Sovereign and the Knights of the Most Noble Order of the Garter - Their Names, Titles, Election, Installment and Demise* (1845).

Heylyn, P., *The History of that Most Famous Saint and Soldier of Christ Jesus: St George of Cappadocia...The Institution of the Most Noble Order of St George, named The Garter. A Catalogue of all the Knights Thereof Until this Present* (1631).

Hope, W.H. St J., *The Stall Plates of the Knights of the Order of the Garter 1348-1485* (1901).

Leake, S.M., *The Statutes of the Most Noble Order of The Garter* (1766).

ORDER OF THE THISTLE

Innes of Learney, Sir T., *The Foundation of the Most Ancient and Most Noble Order of the Thistle* (1959).

Lyon King of Arms, Lord, and Warrack, J., *The Knights of the Most Ancient and Most Noble Order of the Thistle* (1911).

ORDER OF ST PATRICK

Galloway, Peter, *The Order of St Patrick* (1983).

Grierson, G.A. and Grierson, J.F., *Statutes and Ordinances of the Most Illustrious Order of St. Patrick* (1831).

ORDER OF THE BATH

Anstis, J., *Observations Introductory to an Historical Essay Upon the Knighthood of the Bath* (1725).

Perkins, Canon J., *The Most Honourable Order of the Bath* (1913).

Risk, J.C., *The History of the Order of the Bath and its Insignia* (1982).

ORDER OF ST MICHAEL AND ST GEORGE

Abela, A.E., *The Order of St Michael and St George in Malta* (1988).

ROYAL VICTORIAN ORDER

Malloch, R.J., *The Royal Victorian Chain and Other Honors of the Sovereign,* (The Orders and Medals Society of America 1990).

Royal Victorian Order: Statutes and Lists of Members (1930).

ORDER OF THE BRITISH EMPIRE

Burke, *Handbook to the Order of the British Empire* (1921).

Galloway, Peter, *The Order of the British Empire* (1996).

Thorpe, A. Winton (ed.), *Burke's Handbook to the Most Excellent Order of the British Empire* (1921).

ORDER OF ST JOHN OF JERUSALEM

Bedford, W.K.R., and Holbeche, R., *The Order of the Hospital of St John of Jerusalem* (1902).

Fincham, H.W., *The Order of the Hospital of St John of Jerusalem and its Grand Priory of England* (1915).

The Grand Priory in the British Realm of the Venerable Order of the Hospital of St John of Jerusalem, *Roll of the Order 1931; Centenary Issue* (1936).

King, Col. E.J., *The Knights of St John in England* (1924).

King, Col. E.J., *The Knights of St John in the British Empire, Being the Official History of the British Order of the Hospital of St John of Jerusalem* (1934).

Luke, Sir H., *An Examination of Certain Claims to be an Order of St John* (1965).

Puddy, E., *A Short History of the Order of the Hospital of St John of Jerusalem in Norfolk* (1961).

Renwick, E.D., *A Short History of the Order of St John* (1959).

Tozer, C.W., *The Insignia and Medals of the Grand Priory of the Most Venerable Order of the Hospital of St John of Jerusalem* (1975).

DECORATIONS
(listed in alphabetical order by name of medal)

GENERAL
Abbott, P.E. and Tamplin, J.M.A., *British Gallantry Awards* (1981).

Abela, A.E., *Maltas George Cross and War Gallantry Awards*.

Bles, G (pub.) *Naval Honours and Awards 1939-1940* (1942).

Brown, G.A., *Commando Gallantry Awards of World War II*.

Campbell, G.L., *Royal Flying Corps (Military Wing)—Honours, Awards and Casualties 1914-17* (1917).

Chatterton-Dickson, W.W.F., *Seedie's List of Coastal Forces Awards for World War II*.

Chatterton-Dickson, W.W.F., *Seedies List of Fleet Air Arm Awards 1939-1969*.

Chatterton-Dickson, W.W.F., *Seedie's Roll of Naval Honours & Awards 1939-59* (1990).

Clarke, John D., *Gallantry Medals and Awards of the World* (1993).

Greenhill (pub.) *South African Honours and Awards 1899-1902*.

Hayward J. B. & Son (pub.) *Honours & Awards to the Indian Army 1914-21* (1992).

Hayward J. B. & Son (pub.) *Honours & Awards of the Old Contemptibles* (1992).

Hypher, P.P., *Deeds of Valour Performed by Indian Officers and Soldiers During the Period from 1860 to 1925* (1927).

Jacob, J.R., *Court Jewellers of the World* (1978).

McInness, I. and Webb, J.V., *Contemptible Little Flying Corps* (1991).

Midland (pub.) *Tank Corps Honours & Awards 1916-1919* (1982).

O'Shea, P., *An Unknown Few: The Story of Those Holders of the George Cross, the Empire Gallantry Medal, and the Albert Medals Associated with New Zealand*.

Pamm, Anthony N., *Honours and Rewards in the British Empire* (1995) (2 vols.).

Royal Flying Corps: Casualties and Honours During the War of 1914-17 (1987).

Sainsbury, Major J.D., *For Gallantry in the Performance of Military Duty* (1980).

Stanistreet, A. *'Gainst All Disaster: Above and Beyond the Call of Duty* (1986).

Wilson, Sir A., and McEwen, Capt. J.H.F., *Gallantry* (1939).

ALBERT MEDAL
Henderson, D.V., *For Heroic Endeavour* (1988).

CHIEFS' MEDALS
Jamieson, A.M., *Indian Chief Medals and Medals to African and Other Chiefs* (1936).

CONSPICUOUS GALLANTRY MEDAL
Cooper, A.W., *In Action With The Enemy: The Holders of the Conspicuous Gallantry Medal (Flying)*.

Brown, G. and Penhall, R., *Conspicuous Gallantry Medal* (1977).

DISTINGUISHED CONDUCT MEDAL
Abbott, P.E., *The Distinguished Conduct Medal 1855-1909* (1987).

Ashton, M., *The Canadian Medal Rolls—Distingushed Conduct and Military Medal (1939-45 & 1950-53)*.

Mackinlay, Gordon, *True Courage: The Distinguished Conduct Medal to Australians 1939-1972* (1993).

McDermott, P., *For Distinguished Conduct in the Field: The Register of the DCM 1920-22* (1994).

Polaschek, A.J., *The Complete New Zealand Distinguished Conduct Medal* (1978).

Walker, R.W., *The Distinguished Conduct Medal 1914-20* (1981).

DISTINGUISHED FLYING CROSS
Carter, Nick and Carol, *Register of the Distinguished Flying Cross, 1918–1995*, 3 vols. (1996).

DISTINGUISHED FLYING MEDAL
Ashton, M., *The Canadian Medal Rolls—Distinguished Flying Medal (1939-1945)*.

Tavender, Ian, *The Distinguished Flying Medal: A Record of Courage* (1990).

DISTINGUISHED SERVICE CROSS
Fevyer, W. H., *Distinguished Service Cross 1901-1938* (1990).

Witte, R. C., *Fringes of the Fleet and the Distinguished Service Cross* (1997).

DISTINGUISHED SERVICE MEDAL
Fevyer, W.H., *The Distinguished Service Medal, 1914–1920* (1982).

Fevyer, W.H., *The Distinguished Service Medal, 1939–1946* (1981).

DISTINGUISHED SERVICE ORDER
Creagh, General Sir O'Moore and Humphris, H.M., *The D.S.O.: A Complete Record of Recipients* (1978).

EDWARD MEDAL
Henderson, D.V., *For Heroic Endeavour* (1988).

EMPIRE GALLANTRY MEDAL
Henderson, D.V., *For Heroic Endeavour* (1988).

GEORGE CROSS
Bisset, Lieut. Colonel Ian. *The George Cross (1961)*.

Dowling, Dr C., *The Victoria Cross and George Cross* (1970).

Hare-Scott, K., *For Gallantry—The George Cross* (1951).

Smyth, Sir J., *The Story of the George Cross* (1968).

This England (pub.), *The Register of the George Cross* (1990).

GEORGE MEDAL
Fevyer, W.H., *The George Medal*.

Henderson, D.V., *Dragons Can Be Defeated* (1984).

Henderson, D.V., *Fashioned into a Bow* (1995).

INDIAN ORDER OF MERIT
Hypher, P.P., *Deeds of Valour of the Indian Soldier Which Won the Indian Order of Merit During the Period From 1837 to 1859* (1925).

MERITORIOUS SERVICE MEDAL
McInnes, Ian, *The Annuity Meritorious Service Medal* (1996).

MILITARY MEDAL

Abbink, H. and C., *The Military Medal: Canadian Recipients 1916-1922.*

Ashton, M., *The Canadian Medal Rolls—Distingushed Conduct and Military Medal (1939-45 & 1950-53).*

Bate, Chris and Smith, Martin, *For Bravery in the Field: Recipients of the Military Medal 1919-1939, 1939-1945* (1991).

VICTORIA CROSS

Biggs, M., *The Story of Gurkha VCs.*

Clayton, Ann, *Chavasse, Double VC* (1992).

Clayton Ann, *Martin-Leake, Double VC* (1995).

Creagh, General Sir O'Moore and Humphris, H.M., *The Victoria Cross 1856-1920* (1993).

Crook, M.J., *The Evolution of the Victoria Cross* (1975).

Dowling, Dr C., *The Victoria Cross and George Cross* (1970).

Gerard, M., *The Victoria Cross* (1892).

Hare-Scott, K., *For Valour—The Victoria Cross* (1949).

Haydon, A.L., *The Book of the Victoria Cross* (1906).

Lee, P.H., *The Victoria Cross* (1912).

Lennox, Lord W., *The Victoria Cross: The Rewarded and Their Services* (1857).

Leyland, R., *For Valour: The Story of the Victoria Cross.*

Little, M.G., *The Royal Marines Victoria Crosses.*

Muddock, J.E., *For Valor—the Victoria Cross 1856-1895* (1895).

Mundell, F., *Stories of the Victoria Cross* (1890).

O'Byrne, R.W., *The Victoria Cross* (1865).

Pallinger, D. and Staunton, A., *Victoria Cross Locator* (1991).

Parry, D.H., *Britain's Roll of Glory, or the Victoria Cross, Its Heroes and Their Valour* (1895)

Parry, D.H., *The Victoria Cross, Its Heroes and Their Valour* (1913).

RAMC Historical Museum, *The Medical Victoria Crosses.*

Smyth, Brig. Sir John, *The Story of the Victoria Cross* (1964).

Snelling, Stephen, *VCs of the First World War: Gallipoli* (1995).

Stewart, Lt.Col.Rupert., *The Victoria Cross: The Empire's Roll of Valour* (1916).

This England (pub.), *Register of the Victoria Cross* (1988).

Toomey, T.E., *The Victoria Cross and How Won 1854-1889* (1889).

Toomey, T.E., *Heroes of the Victoria Cross* (1895).

Turner, J.F., *VCs of the Air* (1961).

Turner, J.F., *VCs of the Army 1939-51* (1962).

Turner, J.F., *VCs of the Royal Navy* (1956).

Wilkins, P.A., *The History of the Victoria Cross* (1904).

ANIMAL AWARDS

Le Chene, Evelyn, *Silent Heroes: The Bravery and Devotion of Animals in War* (1994).

CAMPAIGN MEDALS

(listed in chronological order by date of campaign medal)
GENERAL

Carter, T. and Long, W.H., *War Medals of the British Army 1650-1891* (1972).

Douglas-Morris, Captain K.J., *Naval Medals 1793-1856* (1987).

Douglas-Morris, Capt K.J. *Naval Medals Vol. II 1856-1880.*

Johnson, Derek E., *War Medals* (1971).

Joslin, E.C., Litherland, A.R. and Simpkin, B.T., *British Battles and Medals* (1988).

Kerr, Major W.J.W., *Notes on War Medals 1794-1840* (1948).

Laffin, J., *British Campaign Medals.*

Long, W.H., *Medals of the British Navy* (1895).

Poulsom, Major N.W.A., *Catalogue of Campaign and Independence Medals Issued During the Twentieth Century to the British Army* (1969).

Power, J.R., *Identification Data on British War Medals and Their Interpretation* (1962).

Power, J.R., *Addenda and Corrigenda to Identification Data on British War Medals and their Interpretation* (1963).

Purves, A.A., *Some Notes on War Medals for the Collector* (1958).

Steward, W., Augustus, *War Medals and their History* (1915).

Vernon S.B., *Collector's Guide to Orders, Medals and Decorations* (With Valuations) (1990).

Williams, R.D. *Medals to Australians: with Valuations.*

MILITARY GENERAL SERVICE MEDAL 1793-1814

Foster, Col. Kingsley O.N., *The Military General Service Medal Roll 1793-1814* (1947).

Mullen, A.L.T., *The Military General Service Medal 1793-1814.*

Newnham, A.J., *The Peninsula Medal Roll 1793-1814* (privately produced).

Vigors, Lieutenant Colonel D.D. and Macfarlane, Lieutenant Colonel A.M., *The Three Great Retrospective Medals 1793-1840 Awarded to Artillerymen* (1986).

Wilson, B., *Canadian Recipients of the MGS, Egypt (1882-9) and NW Canada Medals.*

NAVAL GENERAL SERVICE MEDAL 1793-1840

Douglas-Morris, Captain K.J., *The Naval General Service Medal Roll, 1793-1840* (1982).

Hailes, Colonel D.A., *Naval General Service Medal Roll 1793-1840* (privately produced).

MacKenzie, Col R.H., *The Trafalgar Roll: The Ships and the Officers* (1989).

Message, C.W., *Alphabetical Naval General Service Medal Roll 1793-1840* (1995).

Newnham A.J., *Naval General Service Medal Roll 1793-1840* (privately produced).

O'Byrne, William, *Naval Biographical Dictionary* (2 vols, 1849).

Roberts, *The Trafalgar Roll* (1995).

Vigors, Lieutenant Colonel D.D. and Macfarlane, Lieutenant Colonel A.M., *The Three Great Retrospective Medals 1793-1840 Awarded to Artillerymen* (1986).

ARMY OF INDIA MEDAL 1799-1826

Gould, R.W. and Douglas-Morris, Captain K.J., *The Army of India Medal Roll 1799-1826* (1974).

Vigors, Lieutenant Colonel D.D. and Macfarlane, Lieutenant Colonel A.M., *The Three Great Retrospective Medals 1793-1840 Awarded to Artillerymen* (1986).

WATERLOO MEDAL

Dalton, C., *The Waterloo Roll Call* (1904).

INDIAN CAMPAIGN MEDALS

Biddulph, Major H., *Early Indian Campaigns and the Decorations Awarded for Them* (1913).

Cook, H. C. B., *The Sikh Wars 1845–6, 1848–9* (1975).

Stone, A.G., *The First Afghan War 1839-1842 and Its Medals* (1967).

Stiles, Richard G. M., *The Story of the India General Service Medal 1908–35* (1996).

SOUTH AFRICA MEDAL 1835-53

Everson, Gordon R., *The South Africa 1853 Medal Roll* (1978).

Sole, T.E., *The Military Casualties of south Africa: Vol 1 1834-1878.*

NEW ZEALAND MEDAL 1845-66

Cowan, J., *The New Zealand Wars* (2 volumes) (1969).

Gudgeon, T.W., *Heroes of New Zealand and Maori History of the War* (1887).

Longley, H.G., *The New Zealand Wars 1845-1866* (1967).

INDIA GENERAL SERVICE MEDAL 1854-95

Parritt, Colonel B.A.H., *Red With Two Blue Stripes* (1974).

CRIMEA MEDAL 1854-56

Cook, F. and Cook, A., *Casualty Roll for the Crimea 1854-55* (1976).

Lummis, Canon W.M., *Honour the Light Brigade* (1973).

Research Publications and Productions (pub.), *Returns Relating to Officers of the Army in the Crimea* (1989).

INDIA MUTINY MEDAL 1857-59

Tavender, I.T., *Casualty Roll for the India Mutiny 1857-59* (1983).

CANADA GENERAL SERVICE MEDAL 1866-70

Neale, G. N. and Irwin, R. W., *The Medal Roll of the Red River Campaign in 1870 in Canada* (1982).

ABYSSINIAN WAR MEDAL 1867–68

Bates, Darrell, *The Abyssinian Difficulty* (1979).

SOUTH AFRICA MEDAL 1877-79

Forsyth, D.R., *South African War Medal 1877-8-9: The Medal Roll.*

Holme, N., *The Silver Wreath. The 24th Regiment at Isandhlwana and Rorke's Drift 1879* (1979).

Knight, Ian, *Brave Men's Blood* (1990).

Mackinnon, J.P. and Shadbolt, S.H., *The South Africa Campaign of 1879* (1882).

Sole, T.E. *The Military Casualties of South Africa: Vol 1 1834-1878.*

Tavender, I.T., *Casualty Roll for the Zulu and Basuto Wars, South Africa 1877-79* (1985).

Whybra, J., *The Roll Call for Isandhlwana and Rorke's Drift* (1990).

AFGHANISTAN MEDAL 1878-80

Farrington, A., *The Second Afghan War 1878-80 Casualty Roll* (1986).

Robson, Brian, *The Road to Kabul: The Second Afghan War 1878–1881* (1986).

Shadbolt, S.H., *The Afghanistan Campaigns of 1878-80* (1882).

CAPE OF GOOD HOPE GENERAL SERVICE MEDAL 1880-97

Forsyth, D.R., *Cape of Good Hope General Service Medal: The Medal Roll.*

EGYPT MEDAL 1882-89

Maurice, Colonel J.F., *The Campaign of 1882 in Egypt.*

Webb, J.V., *Abu Klea Medal Roll.*

KHARTOUM STAR 1884

Fearon, D., *General Gordon's Khartoum Star* (1967).

NORTH WEST CANADA MEDAL 1885

Pacific Publishing Co (pub.), *North-West Canada Medal Roll (The Riel Rebellion 1885)* (1974).

BRITISH SOUTH AFRICA COMPANY MEDAL 1890-97

Forsyth, D.R., *British South Africa Co. Medal 1890-1897.*

Owen, C.R., *British South African Company Medal Roll 1890-1897.*

Roberts (pub.), *The British South Africa Company Medal Rolls 1890-1897* (1993).

INDIA MEDAL 1895–1902

Farrington, A., *India General Service Casualty Roll* (1987).

Barthorp, Michael, *The Frontier Ablaze: The North-West Frontier Rising 1897–98* (1996).

ASHANTI STAR 1896

McInnes, Ian and Fraser, Mark, *The Ashanti Campaign 1896.*

QUEEN'S & KING'S SOUTH AFRICA MEDAL 1899-1902

British Naval Brigades in the South Africa War 1899-1902 (Reprint).

Dooner, M.G., *The Last Post: A Roll of All Officers Who Gave Their Lives in the South African War 1899-1902* (1980).

Fevyer, W.H. and Wilson, J.W., *The Queen's South Africa Medal to the Royal Navy and Royal Marines* (1983).

Gray, S., *The South African War 1899-1902 - Service Records of British and Colonial Women.*

Hayward, J. B. & Son (pub.), *List of Casualties of the South Africa Frontier Force* (Reprint 1972).

Hayward, J. B. & Son (pub.), *South African War Casualty Roll: Natal Field Force* (1980).

Lusted, C.A (pub.), *The Queens South Africa Medal 1898-1902* (1974).

Mitchell, Dr F.K., *Roll Of The Bar, Defence of Mafeking, on the Queen's Medal for South Africa, 1899-1902* (1963).

Stirling, J., *British Regiments in South Africa 1899-1902* (reprint) (1994).

Stirling, J., *The Colonials in South Africa* (1990).

CAPE COPPER COMPANY'S MEDAL 1902

Forsyth, D.R., *Medal Roll of the Cape Copper Company's Medal.*

CHINA MEDAL 1900

Fevyer, W.H. and Wilson, J.W., *The China War Medal 1900 to the Royal Navy and Royal Marines* (1985).

Narbeth, C., *Taku Forts* (1980).

OOKIEP DEFENCE MEDAL

Kieran, Brian L., *O'okiep* (1996).

AFRICA GENERAL SERVICE MEDAL 1902

Fevyer, W.H. and Wilson, J.W. *African General Service Medal to the RN and RM.*

Magor, R.B., *African General Service Medals.*

TIBET MEDAL 1903–04
Fleming, Peter, *Bayonets to Lhasa* (revised 1985).
Roberts (pub.), *The Tibet Campaign 1904 and the Royal Fusiliers*.

NATAL REBELLION MEDAL 1906
Forsyth, D.R., *Natal Native Rebellion 1906: The Medal Roll*.
Roberts Medals Publications Ltd (pub.), *The Natal Zulu Rebellion 1906*.

INDIA GENERAL SERVICE MEDAL 1908–35
Styles, Richard G. M., *The Story of the India General Service Medal 1908–35* (1992).
Naval & Military Press (pub.), *India General Service Medal 1908–1935 to the Royal Air Force* (1994).

FIRST WORLD WAR MEDALS 1914-19
Adler, Revd. M (ed.), *British Jewry Book of Honour* (1922).
Bell, E.W., *Soldiers Killed on the First Day of the Somme* (1977).
Christie, N.M. *Officers of the Canadian Expeditionary Force who Died Overseas 1914-1919*.
Fevyer, W. H. and Wilson, J. W., *The 1914 Star to the Royal Navy and the Royal Marines* (1995).
Hayward, J. B. & Son (pub.), *Officers Died in the Great War* (1988).
Hayward, J. B. & Son (pub.), *Soldiers Died in the Great War* (80 parts).
Hobson, C., *Airmen Died in the Great War 1914-18: The Roll of Honour of the British and Commonwealth Air Services of the First World War* (1995)
Imperial War Museum (pub.), *Drake, Royal Naval Division Roll of Honour*.
Imperial War Museum (pub.), *Hawke, Royal Naval Division Roll of Honour*.
Imperial War Museum (pub.), *Hood, Royal Naval Division Roll of Honour*.
Imperial War Museum (pub.), *Howe, Royal Naval division Roll of Honour*.
Imperial War Museum (pub.), *Nelson, Royal Naval division Roll of Honour*.
Jarvis, S.D. and Jarvis, D.B., *The Cross of Sacrifice* (1990-1994) (several volumes).
Laslo, A.J., *The Interallied Victory Medals of WWI* (1986).
Mitchell, F.K., *Medals of the Great War Awarded to South Africans* (1983).
New Zealand Expeditionary Force Roll of Honour (Reprint).
Parks, Major Edwin, *The Royal Guernsey Militia* (1993).
Ruvigny, Marquis de., *The Roll of Honour 1916-1919*.
Walker, R., *To What End Did They Die?—Officers Died At Gallipoli*.
Williams, R.D., *Guide to Collecting and Researching Campaign Medals of the Great War* (1993).
Williamson, H.J., *The Roll of Honour, Royal Flying Corps and Royal Air Force for the Great War 1914-18* (1992).

SECOND WORLD WAR MEDALS
Hayward, J. B. & Son (pub.), *Prisoners of War (British, Empire and Commonwealth Forces)* (3 volumes, reprint).
Purves, A. A., *The Medals, Decorations & Orders of World War II* (1986).

NAVAL GENERAL SERVICE MEDAL 1915
Fevyer, W.H. and Wilson, J.W., *NGS Medal 1915-1962 to the Royal Navy and Royal Marines for the Bars Persian Gulf 1909-1914, Iraq 1919-1920, NW Persia 1920* (1995).

KOREA MEDALS 1950-53
Dyke, P., *Korea 1950-53: Mentions-in-Despatches* (1989).
Gaston, P., *Korea 1950-1953, Prisoners of War, The British Army*.
Harding, Colonel E.D., *The Imjin Roll* (1976).
Ingraham, Kevin R., *The Honors, Medals and Awards of the Korean War 1950-1953* (1993).

MERITORIOUS SERVICE MEDALS
McInnes, Ian, *The Meritorious Service Medal to Aerial Forces* (1984).
McInnes, Ian, *The Meritorious Service Medal to Naval Forces* (1983).
McInnes, Ian, *Meritorious Service Medal to Naval Forces* (1983).
McInnes, Ian, *Meritorious Service Medal. The Immediate Awards 1916-1928* (1992).
McInnes, Ian, *The Annuity Meritorious Service Medal* (1994).

LONG SERVICE & GOOD CONDUCT MEDALS
(listed alphabetically by author)
Douglas-Morris, Captain K.J., *The Naval Long Service Medals* (1991).
Lees, J.R., *Recipients of the Long Service & Good Conduct Medal 1833-1916 to the Somerset Light Infantry (Prince Alberts)*.
Pallas, S.M., *Canadian Recipients of the Colonial Auxiliary Forces Officers Decoration and the Colonial Auxiliary Forces Long Service Medal*.
Tamplin, J.M.A., *The Army Emergency Reserve Decoration and the Efficiency Medal (Army Emergency Reserve)* (1989).
Tamplin, J.M.A., *The Colonial Auxiliary Forces Long Service Medal* (1984.)
Tamplin, J.M.A., *The Colonial Auxiliary Forces Officers' Decoration: the Indian Volunteer Forces Officers' Decoration* (1981).
Tamplin, J.M.A., *The Efficiency Decoration Instituted 1930* (1987).
Tamplin, J.M.A., *The Imperial Yeomanry Long Service and Good Conduct Medal* (1978).
Tamplin, J.M.A., *The Militia Long Service and Good Conduct Medal* (1979).
Tamplin, J.M.A., *The Special Reserve Long Service and Good Conduct Medal* (1979).
Tamplin, J.M.A., *The Territorial Decoration 1908-1930* (1983).
Tamplin, J.M.A., *The Territorial Force Efficiency Medal 1908-1921 and the Territorial Efficiency Medal 1922-1930* (1980).
Tamplin, J.M.A., *The Volunteer Long Service Medal* (1980).
Tamplin, J.M.A., *The Volunteer Officers' Decoration* (1980).
Scarlett, R. J., *Under Hazardous Circumstances* (1992).
Williams, R.D., *The Victoria Volunteer Long and Efficient Service Medal & the Volunteer Officers' Decoration* (1976).

LIFESAVING MEDALS
Brown, G., *Lloyds War Medal for Bravery at Sea* (1992)
Cumming, Sir J., *Literature of the Life-Boat 1785-1947* (1947)
Dibdin, C., *History of the Institution's Gold and Silver Medals* (1909)
Gawler, J., *Lloyds Medals 1836-1989*.

Jeffery, S., *The Liverpool Shipwreck and Humane Society 1839-1939* (1939)

Lamb, Sir J.C., *The Life Boat and Its Work* (1911)

Mundell, F., *Stories of the Royal Humane Society* (1895)

Young, L., *Acts of Gallantry: Being a Detailed Account of Each Deed of Bravery in Saving Life from Drowning in All Parts of the World for which the Gold and Silver Medals and Clasps of the Royal Humane Society Have Been Awarded from 1830-1871.*

OTHER MEDALS

Balmer, Major J L *TD, British and Irish Regimental and Volunteer Medals 1745-1895.*

Cole, H.N., *Coronation and Royal Commemorative Medals 1887-1977* (1977).

Condon, Major J.P.B., MBE, *The Kings and Queens Medals for Shooting (Regular Army).*

Duckers, P., *The Delhi Durbar Medal 1911 to The British Army* (1995).

Hibbard, M.G., *Boer War Tribute Medals* (1982).

James G.P.L., *The Royal Family Orders, Badges of Office, Royal Household Medals and Souvenirs* (1951).

Poulsom, Major N.W., *The White Ribbon: a Medallic Record of British Polar Expeditions* (1968).

Poulsom, Major N.W.A., *Catalogue of Campaign and Independence Medals Issued During the Twentieth Century to the British Army* (1969).

Scarlett, R.J., *The Naval Good Shooting Medal 1903-1914* (1990).

Wilson, J.W. and Perkins, R., *Angels in Blue Jackets: The Navy at Messina, 1908.*

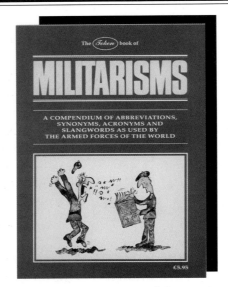

SYDNEY B. VERNON

PO BOX 890280YB
TEMECULA CA 92590–0280, USA
Tel: 909 698 1646   Fax: 909 698 7091
e-mail: svernon@inland.net
website: http://home.earthlink.net/~svernon/

PUBLICATIONS

1. THE MEDAL COLLECTORS' COMPANION—Collecting and Identify Orders, Medals and Decorations.

At last a work dealing with information on how to collect and identify Orders, Medals and Decorations which covers countries using the Roman, Cyrillic and Greek alphabets, especially Europe and the United States. Items are identified by inscriptions, dates, monarchs' ciphers, ribbons and ribbon devices. Profusely illustrated, with over 200 pages, it has a comprehensive glossary and bibliography. It is softbound with a sturdy binding. A fitting companion for your VERNON'S COLLECTORS' GUIDE TO ORDERS MEDALS AND DECORATIONS (3rd edn.) ISBN 0–96235–75–2–9 Price: $22.95 (post /handling, N. America $3.00, elsewhere $8.00

2. VERNON'S COLLECTORS' GUIDE TO ORDERS, MEDALS AND DECORATIONS (with valuations) III edition 1995.

Softbound 512 pages, covers Europe, USA, Japan Boxer Rebellion, and many other areas. Over 11,000 items valued, with 122 pages of photographs. Price $28.95 (post/handling $3.00 N. America, elsewhere $8.00. The definitive work on the subject.
CALIFORNIAN RESIDENTS ADD CORRECT LOCAL SALES TAX.
VISA/MASTERCARD—WRITTEN AUTHORISATION REQUIRED.

3. SALES CATALOGUE

Issued 6 times yearly. I have been offering a comprehensive selection of Orders, Medals and Decorations from around the world since 1967. Between 400–600 items are offered from the rare to the common. All items are guaranteed to be to your satisfaction. VISA/MASTERCARD for book & medal sales; written authorization required. Subscription for 10 issues is $8.00 for N. America, $20.00 elsewhere.

SOCIETIES FOR MEDAL COLLECTORS

Listed here are some of the many societies around the world that cater for the medal collector. The addresses given are mostly the private addresses of the membership secretaries to whom all correspondence should be sent. *We would appreciate information from other Societies who would like their details included in the next YEARBOOK.*

Association de Collectionneurs de Decorations et Médailles (MEDEC) (Paasbloemstraat 81, 2060 Merksem, Belgium).

Birmingham Medal Society (229 Rednal Road, King's Norton, Birmingham B38 8EA).

Bund Deutscher Ordenssammler e.v. (Postfach 1260, Eisenbergstr 10, D-6497 Steinau a.d. Str., Germany).

Crown Imperial (history, traditions, regalia, insignia) (37 Wolsey Close, Southall, Middlesex UB2 4NQ).

Indian Military Historical Society (37 Wolsey Close, Southall, Middlesex UB2 4NQ).

Life Saving Awards Research Society ("Little Sadlers", 10 Upper Edgeborough Road, Guildford, Surrey GU1 2BG).

Medal Society of Ireland (1 The Hill, Stillorgan, Co. Dublin, Ireland).

Mid-Western Orders & Medals Society (MIDOMS) (5847 Gilbert Avenue, La Grange, IL 60525, USA).

Military Collector's Club of Canada (MCCofC) (15 Abel Place, St Albert, Alta T8N 2Z5).

Military Medal Society of South Africa (1 Jacqueline Avenue, Northcliff 2195, South Africa).

Naval Historical Collectors and Research Association (17 Woodhill Avenue, Portishead, Bristol BS20 9EX).

Orders & Medals Society of America (OMSA) (PO Box 484, Glassboro, NJ 08028, USA).

Orders & Medals Research Society (OMRS) (21 Colonels Lane, Chertsey, Surrey KT16 8RH).

Orders & Medals Research Society, Australia Branch (Sydney) (10/8 Pacific Parade, Dee Why 2099, NSW, Australia).

ditto, Canada Branch (Ottawa) (17 Ella Street, Ottawa, Ontario, Canada K1S 2S3).

ditto, Canada Branch (Toronto) (346 Manor Road East, Toronto, Ontario, Canada M4S 1S2).

ditto, Hong Kong Branch (Flat 23, 11/F Mt Nicholson Gap, 103 Mt Nicholson Road, Hong Kong).

ditto, Northern Branch (Manchester) (7 St Michael's Avenue, Great Lever, Bolton, Lancs BL3 2LP).

ditto, Scottish Branch (21 Hartington Place, Edinburgh EH10 4LF).

ditto, Sussex Branch (9 Mereryfield Drive, Horsham, West Sussex RH12 2AA).

ditto, Cotswold Branch (Cheltenham) (12 The Verneys, Cheltenham, Glos GL53 7DB).

ditto, Northumbrian Branch (41 Ashdown Avenue, Durham DH1 1DB).

ditto, Medal Ribbon Branch (7 Durham Way, Rayleigh, Essex SS6 9RY).

ditto, Miniatures Branch (31 Gatcombe, Great Holm, Milton Keynes, Bucks MK8 9EA).

Ordenshistorik Selskab (Falkoneralle 79, DK 2000 Frederiksberg, Denmark).

Société Suisse de Phaleristique (Box 1, CH-1137 Yens, Switzerland).

Victorian Military Society (20 Priory Road, Newbury, Berks RG14 7QN).

MUSEUMS AND COLLECTIONS

The majority of the museums listed below are the regimental museums of the British Army, Militia, Yeomanry and Territorials, but we have included other museums pertaining to the Royal Navy, the Royal Marines and the Royal Air Force where medals form a significant part of the collections. So, too, the museums of the police forces, fire brigades, Red Cross, Royal National Lifeboat Institution and similar bodies have been included where relevant. Readers should also bear in mind that many general museums in our towns and cities boast fine collections of military medals pertaining to their local regiments. We have included those of which we are aware. The date of foundation is shown in brackets after the name.

Some service museums have been undergoing refits, relocations and amalgamations. We would welcome further information from readers about these changes and about other general museums in their areas with a good coverage of medals to local regiments.

Space prevents us from going into details regarding the scope of individual museum holdings. We give the postal address, telephone number, and the name of the curator wherever possible, also the hours of opening and admission charges (where applicable) at the time of going to press. Where two charges are listed, the first denotes the full adult price and the second the concessionary charge (OAPs, students and children). Where three charges are given the first is the full adult price, the second the OAP concession and the third the children's charge. It is always sensible, particularly before travelling long distances to visit a museum or collection, to telephone and check that the published details are still correct.

Some museums may have libraries holding archival material; this should be checked out and the conditions for use ascertained as such holdings will not have the resources to answer detailed research enquiries.

Where museums are devoted to one particular regimental/service/unit or whatever, they are listed by title in alphabetical order. This may not always accord with the exact official name of the museum which is given on the address line. The well-known national museums are listed alphabetically by name. More general museums which include medal collections are listed by the name of the town. If you cannot see the name of the museum you require at first glance, it may be worth searching through the full list, as some museums escape neat classification and would require extensive cross-referencing to do them full justice.

Aberdeen Maritime Museum (1984)
Provost Ross's House, Shiprow, Aberdeen. 01224 5857888. Monday - Saturday, 10am - 5pm. Admission free.

Airborne Forces Museum (1969)
Browning Barracks, Aldershot, Hants GU11 2BU. 01252 349619. £1.25 / 60p. Tuesday-Sunday, 10am - 4.30pm. Major D.M. Cuthbertson-Smith.

Aldershot Challenge (1989)
Wavell House, Cavans Road, Aldershot, Hants GU11 2LQ. 01252 21048. Only by appointment at present.

Aldershot Military Museum (1984)
Queen's Avenue, Aldershot, Hants GU11 2LG. 01252 314598. £1.50 / £1 / 50p. March-October, 10am - 5pm; November-February 10am - 4.30pm daily. Closed Christmas and New Year. Ian Maine.

Argyll and Sutherland Highlanders Regimental Museum (1945)
Stirling Castle. 01786 475165. Free. Easter-September, Monday-Saturday, 10am - 5.30pm; Sunday, 11am - 5pm. October-Easter, Monday-Saturday, 10am - 4.30pm; Sunday, 11am - 4pm.

Army Physical Training Corps Museum (1949)
Army School of Physical Training, Queen's Avenue, Aldershot, Hants GU11 2LB. 01252 347131. Free. Monday-Friday, 8.30am - 12.30pm; 2pm - 4pm. Weekends by appointment. Closed in August, and two weeks each at Easter and Christmas. A.A. Forbes and J. Pearson.

Army Transport Museum (1983)
Flemingate, Beverley, Humberside HU17 0NG. 01482 860445. £2.50 / £1.50. Daily, 10am - 5pm. Closed 24-26 December. David Dawson.

Arundel Toy and Military Museum (1978)
Dolls House, 23 High Street, Arundel, West Sussex.
01903 507446/882908. £1.25 / 90p. June-August,
10.30am - 5pm daily. Otherwise open on Bank
Holidays and weekends in winter.

**Aylmer Military Collection and Isle of Wight Home
Guard Museum (1984)**
Nunwell House, Brading, Isle of Wight PO36 0JQ.
01983 407240. £2.30/£1.80 / 60p (children
accompanied by adults). July-September, Sunday-
Thursday, 10am - 5pm. Otherwise by appointment.
J.A. Aylmer.

Ayrshire Yeomanry Museum
Rozelle House, Monument Road, Alloway by Ayr
KA7 4NQ. 01292 264091. Monday - Saturday 10am -
5pm, Sundays, April - October, 2 - 5pm.

Bangor, Museum of Welsh Antiquities (1898)
Ffordd Gwynedd, Bangor, Gwynedd, LL57 1DT.
01248 353368. 50p. Tuesday-Friday, 12.30pm -
4.30pm; Saturday, 10.30am - 4.30pm. Includes medals
and militaria of the Welsh regiments. Patricia
Benneyworth.

Bath Police Museum (1985)
Manvers Street, Bath, Avon BA1 1JN. 01225 444343.
Free, by appointment only. Sergeant Mike Stanton.

Bedale, Badges and Battledress Museum(1990)
The Green, Crakehall, Bedale, North Yorkshire, DL8
1PH. 01677 424444. £1 / 80p / 50p. Easter-
September, Tuesday-Friday, 11am - 5pm; Saturday
and Sunday, 1pm - 5pm. Barrie Morris.

**Bedfordshire and Hertfordshire Regimental
Museum**
Luton Museum, Wardown Park, Luton, Beds LU2
7HA. Monday - Friday, 10am - 5pm, Sunday, 1pm -
5pm.

Black Watch Museum (1924)
Balhousie Castle, Perth PH1 5HR. 01738 21281 ext
8530. Free. Easter-September, Monday-Friday, 10am -
4.30pm; Sundays and Bank Holidays, 2pm - 4.30pm.
Major A.R. McKinnell, MBE.

**Border Regiment and King's Own Royal Border
Regiment Museum (1973)**
Queen Mary's Tower, The Castle, Carlisle, Cumbria
CA3 8UR. 01228 32774. £2 / £1.50 / £1. April-
September, Monday-Saturday, 10am - 4pm; Sunday,
10am - 6pm. October-March, 10am - 4pm daily.
Stuart Eastwood.

British Red Cross Museum and Archives (1984)
Barnett Hill, Wonersh, Guildford, Surrey GU5 0RF.
01483 898595. Free, by appointment. Monday-Friday,
9.30am - 4.30pm. Margaret Poulter.

**Burnley, Towneley Hall Art Gallery and Museum
(1902)**
Burnley, Lancs BB11 3RQ. 01282 424213. Free.
Monday-Friday, 10am - 5pm; Sunday, 12pm - 5pm.
Small collection including two VCs, other unique
items seen by appointment. Susan Bourne.

Caenarfon Air Museum
Caernarfon Airport, Dinas Dinlle, Caernarfon,
Gwynedd LL54 5TP. £2.50/£1.50. March - November
9.30am - 5.30pm.

**Cambridge, Scott Polar Research Institute Museum
(1920)**
Lensfield Road, Cambridge CB2 1ER. 01223 336540.
Free. Monday-Saturday, 2.30pm - 4pm. Robert
Headland.

**Cameronians (Scottish Rifles) Regimental Museum
(1928)**
Mote Hill, off Muir Street, Hamilton, Lanarkshire
ML3 6BY. 01698 428688. Free. Monday-Wednesday,
Friday-Saturday, 10am - 1pm; 2pm - 5pm. John
McGourty.

Chester, Cheshire Military Museum (1972)
The Castle, Chester CH1 2DN. 01244 327617. 50p /
25p. Daily, 9am - 5pm. Lieut. Colonel R.C. Peel.

City of London Police Museum (1964)
37 Wood Street, London EC2P 2NQ. 0171 601 2705.
Free, by appointment only. Roger Appleby.

Colchester, Military Miniatures Museum (1978)
13 Cheveling Road, Old Heath, Colchester, Essex CO2
8DL. 01206 794473. Free, by appointment only.
Daily, 9am - 5pm. Anthony Debski.

Coldstream Museum
13 Market Square, Coldstream. 01361 82600. Easter -
end October, Monday - Saturday 10am - 5pm, Sunday
2 - 5pm.

Colne, British in India Museum (1972)
Newtown Street, Colne, Lancs BB8 0JJ. 01282 613129/
870215. £1.20 / 50p. Monday-Saturday, 10am - 4pm.
Closed December, January and Bank Holidays.
Devonshire Regiment Museum
Wyvern Barracks, Barrack Road, Exeter, Devon EX2
6AE. Monday-Friday, 10am-4.30pm. Closed Bank
Holidays. Lieutenant Colonel D.R. Roberts.

Dingwall Museum (1975)
Town Hall, High Street, Dingwall, Ross-shire IV15
9RY. 01349 65366. 50p / 25p. May-September,
Monday-Saturday, 10am - 5pm. Otherwise by
appointment only. Includes medals and militaria of
the Seaforth Highlanders, Duke of Ross-shire's Buffs.
Dr Anthony Woodham.

Diss, 100th Bomb Group Memorial Museum (1978)
Common Road, Dickleburgh, near Diss, Norfolk.
0379 740708. Medals and memorabilia of the Eighth
Air Force and 100th Bomb Group. Free. May-
September, Saturday, Sunday and Wednesday, 10am-
5pm. October-April, weekends only, 10am - 4.30pm.
S.P. Hurry.

Dorchester, Dorset Military Museum (1927)
The Keep, Bridport Road, Dorchester, Dorset DT1
1RN. 01305 264066. £1 / 50p. Monday-Saturday,
9.30am - 5pm. Major J. Carroll.

**Duke of Cornwall's Light Infantry Regimental
Museum (1925)**
The Keep, Bodmin, Cornwall PL31 1EG. 01208 72810.
£1/50p. Monday-Friday, 8am-5pm. Major W.H.
White.

Duke of Wellington's Regiment Museum(1960)
Bankfield Museum, Boothtown Road, Halifax HX3
6HQ. 01422 352334 / 354823. Free. Tuesday-
Saturday, 10am - 5pm; Sunday, 2.30pm - 5pm.

Durham Light Infantry Museum (1969)
Aykley Heads, Durham DH1 5TU. 0191 384 2214.
Free. Tuesday-Saturday, 10am - 5pm; Sunday, 2pm -
5pm. Stephen D. Shannon.

East Lancashire Regimental Museum (1934)
Blackburn Museum and Art Gallery, Museum Street,
Blackburn, Lancs BB1 7AJ. 01254 667130. Free.
Tuesday-Saturday, 10am - 5pm.

Essex Regimental Museum (1973)
Oaklands Park, Moulsham Street, Chelmsford, Essex
CM2 9AQ. 01245 260614. Free. Monday-Saturday,
10am - 5pm; Saturday, 2pm - 5pm. Ian Hook.

Feltham, Army Museums Ogilby Trust (1954)
Falklands House, Elwood Avenue, Feltham,
Middlesex TW13 7AA. 0181 844 1613. Free, Daily,
9am - 4pm. Colonel P.S. Walton.

Fleet Air Arm Museum (1962)
RNAS Yeovilton, Somerset BA22 8HT. 01935 840565.
£4.80 / £3.50 / £2.70. Daily, 10am - 5.30pm. Closed
4.30pm, November-February. Graham Mottram.

Glasgow Art Gallery and Museum (1854)
Kelvingrove, Glasgow G3 8AG. 0141 359 3929. Free.
Monday-Saturday, 10am - 5pm; Sunday, 11am - 5pm.
Includes medals of the Glasgow Yeomanry, Highland
Light Infantry and regiments associated with the city.

Gloucestershire Regiments Museum (1989)
Gloucester Docks, Gloucester GL1 2HE. 01452
522682. £2.50 / £1.50 / £1.25. Tuesday-Sunday and
Bank Holidays, 10am - 5pm. Christine Beresford.

Gordon Highlanders' Regimental Museum (1961)
Regimental Headquarters, Viewfield Road, Aberdeen,
AB1 7XH. 01224 318174. April-October, 2 days a
week, 10am - 4pm, two weekends a month, 10am -
4pm. October-March by appointment only. Major
David White.

Green Howards Regimental Museum
Trinity Church Square, Richmond, Yorkshire DL10
4QN. 01748 822133. £1/75p/50p. April - October,
Weekdays 9.15am - 4.30pm, Sundays 2 - 4.30pm.
Restricted hours the rest of the year

Guards Museum (1988)
Wellington Barracks, London SW1E 6HQ. 0171 414
3271. £2 / £1. Monday-Thursday, weekends, 10am -
4pm. Captain David Horn.

Gurkha Museum (1974)
Peninsular Barracks, Romsey Road, Winchester,
Hants SO23 8TS. 01962 842832. £1.50 / 75p.
Tuesday-Saturday, 10am - 5pm. Brigadier C. Bullock.

Hawkinge, Kent, Battle of Britain Museum (1969)
Hawkinge, Kent CT18 7AG. 0130 389 3140. £2.50 /
£2 £1.50. Easter-end of May, October, 11am - 4pm.
July-September, 10am - 5pm. Mike Llewellyn.

Hertford Regiment Museum
8 Bull Plain, Hertford SG14 1DJ. Tuesday-Saturday,
10am - 5pm.

Hertfordshire Yeomanry Museum
Paynes Park, Hitchin, Herts SG5 1EQ. 01462 434476.
Free. Monday-Saturday, 10am - 5pm; Sunday, 2pm -
4pm. Closed Bank holidays.

Hornsea Folk Museum (19780
Burn's Farm, 11 Newbegin, Hornsea, East Yorkshire
HU18 1BP. 01964 533443. £1.50/£1. Easter w/e, 1 May
- 30 September, Monday to Saturday, 11am - 5pm and
Sunday 2 - 5pm. A section featuring East Yorkshire
Regt, East Riding Yeomanry, Royal Artillery, 158
Squadron and The Home Front. Dr J. E. S. Walker.

Honourable Artillery Company Museum
Armoury House, City Road, London EC1 2BQ.
Apply in writing for a visit.

Imperial War Museum (1917)
Lambeth Road, London SE1 6HZ. 0171 416 5000.
£3.70 / £2.70 / £1.85. Daily, 10am - 6pm.

Imperial War Museum (1976)
Duxford Airfield, Duxford, Cambridge CB2 4QR.
01223 835000. £5.50 / £3.80 / £2.75. March-October,
10am - 6pm daily; October-March, 10am - 4pm daily.

Inns of Court and City Yeomanry Museum (1947)
10 Stone Buildings, Lincoln's Inn, London WC2A
3TG. 0171 405 8112. Free. Monday-Friday, 10am -
4pm. Major R.J.B. Gentry.

Intelligence Corps Museum
Templar Barracks, Ashford, Kent, TN23 3HH. 01233
657208. Free. Tuesdays and Thursdays, 9.30am -
12.30pm; 2pm - 4.30pm. Dick Shaw.

Kent and Sharpshooters Yeomanry Museum
Hever Castle, Tonbridge, Kent TN8 7NG. April -
October 12 - 6pm

**King's Own Royal Regiment (Lancaster) Museum
(1929)**
City Museum, Market Square, Lancaster LA1 1HT.
01524 64637. Free. Monday-Saturday, 10am - 5pm.

**King's Own Scottish Borderers Regimental
Museum (1954)**
Berwick Barracks, The Parade, Berwick-upon-Tweed
TD15 1DE. 01289 307426. £1.80 / 40p. Monday-
Friday, 9.30am - 4.30pm; Saturday, 9.30am - 12pm.
Lieut. Colonel C.G.O. Hogg.

**King's Own Yorkshire Light Infantry Regimental
Museum (1932)**
Museum and Art Gallery, Chequer Road, Doncaster,
South Yorkshire DN1 2AE. 01302 734293. Monday-
Saturday, 10am - 5pm; Sunday, 2pm - 5pm. Major
C.M.J. Deedes.

King's Regiment (Liverpool) Museum
William Brown Street, Liverpool L3 8EN. 0151
2070001. Daily, 10am-5pm, Sunday 2pm-5pm. G.S.
Boxer.

**15th/19th King's Royal Hussars (Light Dragoons)/
Northumberland Hussars**
Tyne & Wear Museums, Newcastle Discovery,
Blandford Square, Newcastle-upon-Tyne NE1 4JA.
0191 232 6789. Monday-Friday, 9am - 4pm.

Lamanva Military Vehicles
Lamanva, Nr Mabe, Falmouth, Cornwall TR10 9BJ
01326 72446. £2,75/£1.50. Easter - October 10am -
5pm, Rest of year 10am-4pm

Lancashire Fusiliers Regimental Museum (1933)
Wellington Barracks, Bury, Lanc BL8 2PL. 0161 764
2208. 50p / 25p. Monday-Saturday (closed
Wednesday), 9.30am - 4.30pm.

17th/21st Lancers Regimental Museum (1964)
Belvoir Castle, Grantham, Lincs NG 31 6BR. 01476
870161. £3.20 / £2.20. April-October, Tuesday-
Thursday, Saturday and Sunday, 11am - 5pm. Bank
Holiday Mondays, 11am - 5pm. Major W.M. Walton.

Light Infantry Museum (1990)
Peninsular Barracks, Romsey Road, Winchester.
01962 828530. £1.50 / 75p. Tuesday-Saturday, 10am -
5pm; Sunday, 12pm - 4pm. Patrick Kirby.

Liverpool Scottish Regimental Museum
Forbes House, Score Lane, Childwell, Liverpool L16
6AN. 0151 6474342. By appointment. D. Reeves.

London Fire Brigade Museum (1967)
94A Southwark Bridge Road, London SE1 0EG. 0171
587 4273. Free. Monday-Friday, 9am - 4.30pm. John
Rodwell.

London Scottish Regimental Museum (1935)
Regimental Headquarters, 95 Horseferry Road,
London SW1P 2DX. 0171 630 1639. Free, by
appointment only.

Manchesters Museum (1987)
Town Hall, Ashton-under-Lyne, Lancs. 0161 342 3078
or 0161 343 1978. Free. Monday-Saturday, 10am -
4pm. Dr Alan Wilson.

Metropolitan Police Historical Museum (1969)
New Scotland Yard, London SW1H 0BG. 0181 305
2824. By appointment only. Richard Sharp.

**Monmouth, The Castle and Regimental Museum
(1989)**
The Castle, Monmouth, Gwent NP5 3BS. 01600
772175 / 712935. Free. Summer daily, 2pm - 5pm;
winter weekends 2pm - 5pm. Other times by
appointment. Dr Eric Old.

National Army Museum (1960)
Royal Hospital Road, Chelsea, London SW3 4HT.
0171 730 0717. Free. Daily, 10am - 5.30pm. Ian G.
Robertson.

National Maritime Museum (1934)
Romney Road, Greenwich, London SE10 9NF. 0181
858 4422. £7.45 / £5.45. Summer, Monday-Saturday,
10am - 6pm; Sunday, 12pm - 5pm. Winter, Monday-
Saturday, 10am - 5pm; Sunday, 2pm - 5pm. Richard
Ormond.

National Museum of Ireland (1877)
Kildare Street, Dublin 2, Republic of Ireland. 01
618811. Free. Tuesday-Saturday, 10am - 5pm;
Sunday, 2pm - 5pm. Includes medals of the former
Irish regiments.

Newark Air Museum (1968)
Winthrop Airfield, Newark-on-Trent NG24 2NY.
01636 707170. £2.50 / £1.50. April-October, Monday-
Friday, 10am - 5pm; weekends, 10am - 6pm.
November-March, daily 101am - 4pm. Mike Smith.

Northamptonshire Regimental Museum
Abington Park Museum, Abington, Northampton.
01604 35412. Colonel J.P. Wetherall.

Order of St. John of Jerusalem Museum
St. John's Gate, St. John's Lane, Clerkenwell, London
EC1M 4DA. 0171 253 6644. Tuesday-Friday 10am -
5pm, Saturday 10am - 4pm. Pamela Willis.

Oxfordshire & Buckinghamshire Light Infantry
TA Centre, Slade Park, Headington. Oxford OX3 7JL.
01865 716060. Free. Monday-Friday 10am - 4pm.

Polish Institute and Sikorski Museum
20 Princes Gate, London SW7 1QA. 0171 589 9249.
Monday - Friday 2pm -4pm.

Preston, County and Regimental Museum (1987)
Stanley Street, Preston, Lancs PR1 4YP. 01772 264075.
£1 / children free. Monday-Saturday (closed
Thursday), 10am - 5pm. Stephen Bull.

**Prince of Wales's Own 9th /12th Lancers Regimental
Museum (1972)**
City Museum and Art Gallery, The Strand, Derby
DE1 1BS. 01332 255581. Free. Monday, 11am - 5pm;
Tuesday-Saturday, 10am - 5pm; Sunday and Bank
Holidays, 2pm - 5pm. Nick Forder.

**Prince of Wales Regiment of Yorkshire and
Regimental Museum of the 4th/7th Royal Dragoon
Guards (1925)**
3A Tower Street York YO1 1SB. 01904 642 038. 50p /
25p. Monday-Friday, 9.30am - 4.30pm; Saturday,
10am - 4.30pm. Brigadier J.M. Cubiss.

Princess of Wales's Regimental Museum (1987)
Inner Bailey, Dover Castle, Kent CT16 1HU. 01304
240121. £5 / £3.70 / £2.50. Summer, 10am - 6pm
daily; winter, 10am - 4pm. Lieut. Colonel L.M.
Wilson, MBE.

Princess Patricia's Canadian Light Infantry Museum
Hatch Court, Hatch Beauchamp, Taunton, Somerset
TA3 6AA. 01823 480120. £2.80 / £1. June-September,
Tuesday and Bank Holiday Mondays, 2.30pm - 5pm.
Otherwise by appointment. Dr and Mrs Odgers.

**Queen Alexandra's Royal Army Nursing Corps
Museum (1953)**
Regimental Headquarters, Royal Pavilion,
Farnborough Road, Aldershot, Hants GU11 1PZ.
01252 349301 / 349315. Free. Monday-Friday, 9.30 - 12
noon; otherwise by appointment. Major McCombe.

Queen's Dragoon Guards Regimental Museum
Cardiff Castle, Cardiff, South Glamorgan CF1 2RB.
01222 222253. £3 / £2 / £1.50. March, April and
October, 10am - 5pm daily. May-September, 10am -
6pm. November-February, 10am-4.30pm. Gareth Gill.

Queen's Lancashire Regiment (1929)
Fulwood Barracks, Preston, Lancs PR2 4AA. 01772
716 543 ext 2362. Free. Tuesdays and Thursdays only,
9am - 12pm; 2pm - 4pm. Major A.J. Maher, MBE.

Queen's Own Highlanders Regimental Museum
Fort George, Ardersier, Inverness-shire. 01463
224380. Free. April-September, Monday-Friday,
10am - 6pm; Sunday, 2pm - 6pm. October-March,
Monday-Friday, 10am - 4pm.

**Queen's Own Royal West Kent Regimental
Museum (1966)**
St Faith's Street, Maidstone, Kent ME14 1LH. 01622
754497. Free. Monday-Saturday, 10.30am - 5.30pm;
Sunday, 2pm - 5pm. Colonel H.B.H. Waring, OBE.

Queen's Royal Surrey Regimental Museum (1979)
Clandon Park, Guildford, Surrey GU4 7RQ. 01483
223419. April-October, closed Thursday and Friday,
1.30pm - 5.30pm. Penny James.

Royal Air Force Museum (1963)
Grahame Park Way, Hendon, London NW9 5LL.
0181 205 2266. £4.50 / £2.25. Daily, 10am - 6pm. Dr
M.A. Fopp. Medal queries: A. Cormack.

Royal Air Force Regiment Museum (1965)
Royal Air Force Regiment Depot, Royal Air Force
Honington, Bury St Edmunds, Suffolk IP31 1EE.
01359 269561. Initially by appointment. Ask for
Museum Director/staff.

**Royal Air Force Museum Reserve
Collection (1965)**
RAF Cardington, Beds MK42 0TH. 01234 742711.
Free, by appointment only. Bruce James.

Royal Armouries Museum (1996)
Waterfront, Leeds City Centre. 0113-245 6465.
£6.95+concessions. Daily (except Christmas Eve,
Christmas Day and New Year's Day). 10am - 5pm
(winter), 10am - 6pm (summer).

**Royal Army Chaplains' Department Museum
(1968)**
Bagshot Park, Bagshot, Surrey GU19 5PL. 01276
471717, ext. 2845. Free. Monday-Friday, 10am - 4pm,
by appointment. Closed in August. Major Margaret
Anne Easey.

Royal Army Dental Corps Museum (1958)
Headquarters RADC, Evelyn Woods Road,
Aldershot, Hants GU11 2LS. 01252 347782. Free.
Monday-Friday, 10am - 12pm; 2pm - 4pm. Closed on
bank holidays. Major Vincent Ward.

Royal Army Educational Corps Museum (1967)
Wilton Park, Beaconsfield, Bucks HP9 2RP. 01494
683290. Free, by appointment only. Simon Anglim.

Royal Army Medical Corps Museum (1952)
Keogh Barracks, Ash Vale, Aldershot, GU12 5RQ.
01252 340212. Free. Monday-Friday, 8.30am - 4pm;
weekends and evenings by appointment. Lieut.
Colonel Roy Eyeions, OBE.

**Royal Army Ordnance Corps (Logistics) Museum
(1993)**
Blackdown Barracks, Deepcut, near Camberley
Surrey GU16 6RW. 01252 340634. Free. Monday-
Friday, 8.30am - 12.30pm; 1.30pm - 4.30pm. Lieut.
Colonel W.P. Masterson.

Royal Artillery Regimental Museum (1946)
Old Royal Military Academy, Woolwich, London
SE18 4DN. 0181 781 5628. Free. Monday-Friday,
12.30pm - 4.30pm. Brigadier Ken Timbers.

Royal Corps of Signals Outstation Museum (1987)
Helles Barracks, Catterick Garrison, North Yorkshire
DL9 4HH. 01748 873778. Free. Monday-Thursday,
10am - 4pm; Friday, 10am - 3pm. Lieut. Colonel F.M.
Orr, OBE.

Royal Corps of Transport Museum (1945)
Regimental Headquarters, Royal Corps of Transport,
Buller Barracks, Aldershot, Hants GU11 2BX. 01252
348834. Free. Monday-Friday, 9am - 12pm; 2pm -
4pm. Weekends by appointment. Closed on Bank
Holidays. Lieut. Colonel M.H.G. Young.

Royal Devon Yeomanry (1845)
Museum of North Devon, The Square, Barnstaple,
Devon EX32 8LN. 01271 46747. £1 / 50p .Tuesday-
Saturday, 10am - 4.30pm. Jerry Lee.

**Royal East Kent Regiment, Third Foot (The Buffs)
Museum (1961)**
Royal Museum and Art Gallery, High Street,
Canterbury, Kent CT1 2JE. 01277 452747. Free.
Monday-Saturday, 10am - 5pm. Kenneth Reedie.

**Royal Electrical and Mechanical Engineers Museum
(1958)**
Isaac Newton Road, Arborfield Garrison, Reading,
Berks, RG2 9LN. 01734 763567. Free. Monday-
Friday, 9am - 12.30pm; 2pm - 4pm. Weekends by
appointment. Closed on Bank Holidays. Lieut.
Colonel Larry LeVar.

Royal Engineers Museum
Brompton Barracks, Chatham, Kent ME4 4UG. 01634
406397. £1/50p. Tuesday-Friday, 11.30am - 5pm,
Spring/Summer Bank Holidays 10am - 5pm.
Colonel G.W.A. Napier.

Royal Fusiliers Museum (1962)
HM Tower of London, EC3N 4AB. 0171 488 5612.
25p. Daily, 9.30am-4.30pm. Major B.C. Bowes-Crick.

**Royal Gloucester, Berkshire, Wiltshire (Salisbury)
Regimental Museum (1982)**
The Wardrobe, 58 The Close, Salisbury, Wilts SP1
2EX. 01722 414 536. £1.80 / £1.50p. Major J.H.
Peters, MBE.

Royal Hospital Chelsea
Hospital Road, Chelsea, London SW3 4SL. 0171 730
0161. Free. Daily, 10am - 12pm; 2pm - 4pm. Major
R.A.G. Courage, CVO, MBE.

Royal Green Jackets Museum
Peninsular Barracks, Romsey Road, Winchester.
01962 863846. £2 / £1. Monday-Saturday, 10am -
5pm; Sunday, 12pm - 4pm.

Royal Hampshire Regimental Museum (1933)
Serle's House, Southgate Street, Winchester, Hants
SO23 9EG. 01962 863658. Free. All year Monday-
Friday 10am - 12.30pm, 2pm - 4pm. Weekends/Bank
Holidays April to October only, midday - 4pm. Lt-
Col. H.D.H. Keatinge.

**Royal Highland Fusiliers Regimental Museum
(1960)**
518 Sauchiehall Street, Glasgow G2 3LW. 0141 332
0961. Free. Monday-Thursday, 9am - 4.30pm; Friday,
9am - 4pm. W. Shaw, MBE.

Royal Hussars Museum (1980)
Home Headquarters (South): Peninsular Barracks,
Romsey Road, Winchester. 01962 828539. £1.50 / 75p.
Tuesday - Friday, 10am - 4pm; weekends and Bank
Holidays, 12pm - 4pm. Major P.J.C. Beresford,
Regimental Secretary. Home Headquarters (North):
Fulwood Barracks, Preston, Lancs PR2 8AA.

**13th/18th Royal Hussars (Queen Mary's Own)
Regiment (1957)**
Cannon Hall Museum, Cawthorne, Barnsley, South
Yorkshire S75 4AT. 01226 790270. Free. Tuesday-
Saturday and Bank Holiday Mondays, 10.30am -
5pm; Saturday and Sunday, 2.30pm - 5pm. Brian
Murray.

**Royal Inniskilling Fusiliers Regimental Musuem
(1938)**
The Castle, Enniskillen, Co. Fermanagh, Northern

Ireland BT74 7BB. 01365 323142. £1 / 75p. Summer, Monday-Friday, 9.30am - 5pm; weekends, 2pm - 5pm. Winter, Monday-Friday, 930am - 12.30pm; 2pm - 5pm. Major George Stephens, MBE.

Royal Irish Fusiliers
Sovereign's House, The Mall, Armagh BT61 9AJ. 01861 522911. Weekdays 10am - 4.30pm. Major M. Wright.

Royal Irish Regiment Museum (1993)
Regimental Headquarters, Royal Irish Rangers, St Patrick's Barracks, Ballymena, BFPO 808, Northern Ireland. 01266 661388. Free. Monday-Friday, 10am - 4.30pm. Lieut. Carol Liles.

Royal Leicestershire Regiment Museum (1969)
The Magazine, Oxford Street, Leicester. 0116 2473220. Free. Monday-Thursday, Saturday, 10am - 5.30pm; Sunday, 2pm - 5.30pm. Y.C. Courtney.

Royal Lincolnshire Regimental Museum (1985)
Burton Road, Lincoln LN1 3LY. 01522 528468. £1 / 50p. May-September, daily, 10am - 5.30pm. October-April, Monday-Saturday, 10am - 5,30pm; Sunday, 2pm - 5.30pm.

Royal Marines Museum (1956)
Southsea, Hants PO4 9PX. 01705 819385. £2.50 / £1.50 / £1.25. Whitsun-September, 9.30am - 5pm. Winter, 9.30am - 4.30pm. Col. K.N. Wilkins, OBE.

Royal Military Police Museum (1979)
Rousillon Barracks, Broyle Road, Chichester, West Sussex PO19 4BN. 01243 786311 ext 4225. Free. April-September, Tuesday-Friday, 10.30am-12.30pm; 1.30pm-4.30pm; Sat-Sunday, 2pm-6pm. October-March, Tuesday-Friday, 10.30am-12.30pm; 1.30pm-4.30pm. Closed January. Lt-Col. Maurice Squier.

Royal National Lifeboat Institution Museum(1937)
Grand Parade, Eastbourne, East Sussex BN21 4BY. 01323 730717. Free. April-December, 9.30am - 5pm daily. January-March, Monday-Friday, 9.30am - 5pm. J.M. Shearer.

Royal National Lifeboat Institution Museum (1969)
Pen-y-Cae, Barmouth, Gwynedd. Free. Easter-October, 10.30am - 6.30pm, daily.

Royal Naval Museum (1911)
HM Naval Base, Portsmouth PO1 3LR. 01705 733060. £2 / £1.75. Daily, 10.30am - 5pm. H. Campbell Murray.

Royal Norfolk Regimental Museum (1945)
Shirehall, Market Avenue, Norwich NR1 3JQ. 01603 223649. 80p / 40p. Monday-Saturday, 10am - 5pm; Sunday, 2pm - 5pm. Kate Thaxton.

Royal Northumberland Fusiliers Regimental Museum (1970)
The Abbot's Tower, Alnwick Castle, Alnwick, NE66 1NG. 01665 602152 / 510211. Easter-October, 11am - 5pm daily. Captain Peter H.D. Marr.

Royal Scots Regimental Museum (1951)
The Castle, Edinburgh EH1 2YT. 0131 310 5016. Free. March-September, Monday-Saturday, 9.30am - 4.30pm; Sunday, 11am - 4.30pm. October-April, Monday-Friday, 9.30am - 4pm. Major Dick Mason.

Royal Signals Museum (1967)
Blandford Camp, Blandford, Dorset DT11 8RH. 01258 482248. Free. Monday-Friday, 10am - 5pm; Saturday, Sunday (June-September only) 10am-4pm.

Royal Sussex Regimental Museum (1930)
Redoubt Fortress, Royal Parade, Eastbourne, East Sussex BN21 4BP. 01323 410300. £1.50 / £1. April-October. Other times by appointment. B.R. Burns.

Royal Tank Regiment Museum (1923)
Bovington Camp, near Wareham, Dorset BH20 6JG. 01929 403463 / 403329 / 463953. £4 / £2. Daily, 10am-5pm. Closed at Christmas. Colonel J. Woodward.

Royal Ulster Constabulary Museum (1983)
Brooklyn, Knock Road, Belfast BT5 6LE. 01232 650222. Free. Monday-Friday, 9am - 5pm. Robin Sinclair.

Royal Ulster Rifles Museum (1935)
Regimental Headquarters, The Royal Irish Rangers, 5 Waring Street, Belfast BT1 2EW. 01232 232086. Free. Monday-Friday, 10am -12pm; 2pm - 4pm. Major M.B. Murphy.

Royal Warwickshire Regimental Museum (1928)
St John's House, Warwick CV34 4NF. 01926 491653. Free. Tuesday-Saturday, 10am - 12.30pm; 1.30pm - 5.30pm; Sunday, 2.30pm-5pm. Brigadier J.K. Chater.

Royal Welch Fusiliers Museum (1955)
Queen's Tower, Caernarfon Castle, Gwynedd LL55 2AY. 01286 673362. £3 / £2. March-October, 9.30am - 6.30pm daily; winter 9.30am - 4pm; Sunday, 2pm - 4pm. Captain Bryan H. Finchett-Maddock.

St Helier, Elizabeth Castle and Militia Museum
St Helier, Jersey, Channel Islands. 01534 23971. £2 / £1. April-October, daily, 10am - 5pm.

Sandhurst Royal Military Academy (1960)
Royal Military Academy Sandhurst, Camberley GU15 4PQ. 01276 63344 ext 2457. Free, by appointment only.

School of Infantry and Small Arms School Corps Weapons Museum (1953)
School of Infantry, Warminster, BA12 0DJ. 01985 842487. Free. Daily, 9am - 4,30pm. Lieut. Colonel Tug Wilson, MBE.

Scottish Horse Museum
The Cross, Dunkeld, Perthshire. 50p Easter - September 10am - 5pm

Scottish National War Memorial
The Castle, Edinburgh. 0131 220 4733. Free. Same hours as above. Thomas Barker.

Scottish United Services Museum (1930)
The Castle, Edinburgh. 0131 225 7534. Free. Same hours as above. Stephen Wood.

Sherwood Foresters Regimental Museum (1923)
The Castle, Nottingham. 0115 9483504. Free. Daily, 10am - 5.30pm. Major R.A. Creamer.

Shropshire Regimental Museum (1985)
Copthorne Barracks, Shrewsbury, Salop. 01743 262402. By appointment only. Geoffrey Archer Parfitt.

South Lancashire Regiment (Prince of Wales's Volunteers) and the Lancashire Regiment Museum (1934)
Fulwood Barracks, Preston, Lancs PR2 8AA. 01772 716543. Free. Tuesday-Thursday, 9am-4.30pm. Otherwise by appointment. Major Glover.

South Nottinghamshire Hussars Museum (1974)
TA Centre, Hucknall Lane, Bulwell, Nottingham NG6 8AB. 0115 9272251. Free, by appointment only.

South Wales Borderers and Monmouthshire Regimental Museum (1934)
The Barracks, Brecon, Powys LD3 7EB. 01874 623111 ext 2310. £1. October-March, Monday-Friday, 9am - 1pm; 2pm - 5pm. April-September, daily except Sunday, same hours. Major Bob Smith.

South Wales Police Museum (1950)
Police Headquarters, Cowbridge Road, Bridgend, Mid Glamorgan CF31 3SU. 01656 655555 ext 427. Free. Monday-Thursday, 10am - 1pm; 2pm - 4.30pm; Friday, 10am - 1pm; 2pm - 4pm. Jeremy Glenn.

Staff College Museum (1958)
Staff College, Camberley, Surrey GU15 4NP. 01276 412662 / 412647 / 412650. Free, by appointment only. Colonel Philip S. Newton, MBE.

Staffordshire Regimental Museum (1962)
Whittington Barracks, Lichfield, Staffs WS14 9PY. 0121 311 3240 / 3229. Free. Monday-Friday, 9am - 4.30pm. Major R.D.W. McLean.

Suffolk Regimental Museum (1967)
The Keep, Gibraltar Barracks, Bury St Edmunds, Suffolk IP33 1HF. 01284 752394. Free. Weekdays, 10am - 12pm; 2pm - 4pm. Major A.G.B. Cobbold.

Tangmere, Military Aviation Museum (1992)
Tangmere, near Chichester, West Sussex PO20 6ES. 01243 775223. £3 / 50p. February-November, daily, 11am - 5.30pm. Andy Saunders.

Taunton, Somerset Military Museum (1974)
County Museum, The Castle, Taunton, Somerset TA1 1AA. 01823 255504. £1.20 / 80p / 30p. Monday-Saturday, 10am - 5pm. Brigadier A.I.H. Fyfe.

Welch Regiment Museum (1927)
The Black and Barbican Towers, Cardiff Castle, Cardiff, South Glamorgan CF1 2RB. 01222 229367. £2/ £1. Lieut. Bryn Owen, RN.

Wellington Museum
Apsley House, 149 Piccadilly, Hyde Park Corder, London W1V 9FA. 0171 499 5676. £2/£1. Tuesday - Sunday 11am - 5pm. J. Voak.

West Midlands Police Museum (1991)
Sparkhill Police Station, 641 Stratford Road, Birmingham B11 6EA. Free, by apppointment only.

Woodbridge, 390th Bomb Group Memorial Air Museum (1981)
Parham Airfield, Parham, Woodbridge, Suffolk. 01359 51209. Free. Sundays and Bank Holidays, 11am - 6pm.

Worcestershire Regimental Museum (1973)
City Museum and Art Gallery, Foregate Street, Worcester. Free. Monday-Wednesday, Friday, 9.30am - 6pm; Saturday, 9.30am - 5pm. Brian Owen

York, Divisional Kohima Museum (1991)
Imphal Barracks, Fulford Road, York YO1 4AY. 01904 662381. Free, by appointment only.

York, Yorkshire Air Museum and Allied Air Forces Memorial (1984)
Halifax Way, Elvington, York YO4 5AU. 01904 605595. £2.50 / £1.50. Monday-Friday, 10.30am - 4pm; weekends, 10.30am - 5pm. Peter Douthwaithe.

York and Lancaster Regimental Museum (1947)
Brian O'Malley Central Library and Art Gallery, Walker Place, Rotherham, Yorkshire S65 1JH. 01709 382 121 ext 3625. Free. Tuesday-Saturday, 10am–5pm. Don Scott.

PROFESSIONAL DIRECTORY

On the following pages are the names and addresses of auctioneers, dealers, booksellers and fair organisers, all of whom will be of assistance to the medal collector. Most are full time and many have retail shops and the collector is usually welcome during normal business hours. Some have extensive stocks of medals whilst others include medals in a more diverse inventory. A number of dealers are part time or work from small premises or from home and appointments are necessary as many keep their stock in the bank for security. Telephone numbers have been included where known and it is always sensible to make contact before travelling any distance.

AUCTIONEERS

The following hold regular medal auctions or feature medals in general numismatic or militaria sales.

Bonham's
Montpelier Street, Knightsbridge, London SW7 1HH. 0171 584 9161 (fax 0171 589 4072). Auctioneers and valuers. 3–4 general numismatic sales (including medals) a year.

Bosley's
42 West Street, Marlow, Bucks SL7 2NB. 01628 488 188. Specialist military auctioneers with occasional interesting groups of medals.

Croydon Coin Auctions
272 Melfort Road, Thornton Heath, Surrey CR7 7RR. Tel/fax 0181 684 6515 or 6565 4583. Regular coin sales which often feature interesting medals.

Dix Noonan Webb
1 Old Bond Street, London W1X 3TD. 0171 499 5022 (fax 0171 499 5023). Auctioneers and valuers. Regular auctions of medals.

Floyd, Johnson & Paine
6427 W. Irving Park Road, Suite 160, Chicago, Illinois 60634, USA. (312) 777 0499 (fax 312 777 4017). Auctions of medals and militaria.

Glendining's
101 New Bond Street, London W1Y 9LG. 0171 493 2445 (fax 0171 491 9181). Auctioneers and valuers. Approximately four sales per year.

Jeffrey Hoare Auctions Inc.
345 Talbot Street, London, Ontario, Canada N6A 2R5. (519) 663 1087 (fax 519 473 1541). Regular sales devoted to Canadian, British and world medals, badges and militaria.

Imperial Auctions
11 Avenue Parade, Accrington, BB6 6PN. tel/fax: 01254 393323. Regular sales of medals, badges and coins.

Sotheby's
Summers Place, Billingshurst, West Sussex RH14 9AD. 01403 783933. Auctioneers and valuers. Regular sales of medals and militaria.

Spink & Son Ltd (Christie's International)
5-7 King Street, St James's, London SW1Y 6QS. 0171 930 7888 (fax 0171 839 4853). Auctioneers, valuers and dealers. Regular sales of medals and militaria.

Wallis & Wallis
West Street Auction Galleries, Lewes, Sussex BN7 2NJ. 01273 480208 (fax 01273 476562). Auctioneers and valuers of militaria, arms, armour and military medals. Monthly general sales and half-yearly connoisseurs' sales.

DEALERS

Ackley Unlimited
PO Box 82144, Portland, Oregon, USA 97282-0144. (503) 659 4681. Orders, medals and decorations. Free quarterly lists on request.

Armoury of St. James's
17 Piccadilly Arcade, Piccadilly, London SW1Y 6NH. 0171 493 5082 (fax 0171 499 4422). Orders, decorations, medals, militaria.

Michael Autengruber
Schillstrasse 7B, D-63067 Offenbach, Germany. (69) 88 69 25 evenings. Orders, medals, literature. Catalogues $US3 (Europe), $US6 (elsewhere).

A. H. Baldwin & Sons Ltd
11 Adelphi Terrace, London WC2N 6BJ. 0171 839 1310. Orders, medals and decorations.

Bonus Eventus
Aartshertoginnestratt 27, 8400 Oostende, Belgium. (059) 801696. Medals and miniature medals. Free medal lists (specify full-size or miniatures).

Bostock Militaria
"Pinewood", 15 Waller Close, Leek Wootton, near Warwick CV35 7QG. 01926 56381. British orders, medals and decorations. Sae for free current lists. Callers welcome by appointment.

Andrew Bottomley
The Coach House, Huddersfield Road, Thongsbridge, Holmfirth, West Yorkshire HD7 2TT. Arms and armour, some medals. Catalogue £5.

Paul Boulden
Parade Antiques Market, 17 The Parade, The Barbican, Plymouth, Devon. 01752 221443. Fax: 01589 632686. Medals and militaria. 6 lists p.a. (£3, £6 overseas)

Philip Burman
Blackborough End, Middleton, King's Lynn, Norfolk PE32 1SE. 01553 840350. Large and varied stock of orders, medals and decorations. Send large sae for lists, issued 6 times a year.

John Burridge
91 Shenton Road, Swanbourne, Western Australia 6010. British and Commonwealth medals and decorations.

Mark Carter
PO Box 470, Slough SL3 6RR. 01753 534777. British and foreign orders, medals, decorations and miniatures. Fairs organiser. Lists £5 (UK and BFPO), £7.50 (overseas airmail).

Castle Medals
PO Box 11, Brecon, Powys LD3 7WG. 01874 665617. Order, medals and decorations. Wants lists welcomed.

Central Antique Arms & Militaria
Smith Street Antiques Centre, Warwick CV34 4JA. 0926 400554. British orders, decorations, medals and militaria. Lists 50p.

Coldstream Military Antiques
55a High Street, Marlow, Bucks. Tel/fax 01628 822503. Medals, badges, insignia.

Collector's Lair
#205 - 15132 Stony Plain Road, Edmonton, Alberta, Canada T5P 3X8. (403) 486 2907. Medals, badges and uniforms.

Norman W. Collett
PO Box 235, London SE23 1NS. 0181 291 1435 (fax 0181 291 3300). British medals and decorations, and military books. Regular catalogues issued. Send 50p in stamps for the current 48 page medal list or 32 page book list.

Command Post of Militaria
578 Yates Street, Victoria, British Columbia, Canada V8W 1K8. (604) 383 4421. Medals, badges and uniforms.

Conglomerate Coins & Medals
206 Adelaide Street, Brisbane, Queensland 4000, Australia. (07) 2211217 (fax 07 2299128). Medals and medallions.

Peter R. Cotrel
7 Stanton Road, Bournemouth, Dorset BH10 5DS. Mail order only—callers by appointment. 01202 516801. British, American and general foreign medals and decorations. Medal albums and accessories. Lists (sae for a sample).

C.J. & A.J. Dixon Ltd
23 Prospect Street, Bridlington, East Yorkshire YO15 2AE. 01262 676877 (fax 01262 606600). 4 large lists a year £6 (UK), £9 (overseas).

D.M.D. Services
6 Beehive Way, Reigate, Surrey RH2 8DY. 01737 240080. Victorian campaign medals and decorations.

Downie's Militaria
7th Floor, 343 Little Collins Street, Melbourne, Vic 3000, Australia. (03) 670 0500 (fax 03 670 0311). Emphasis on Australian and UK medals.

Frank Draskovic
PO Box 803, Monterey Park, CA 91754, USA. Worldwide orders and medals, especially European and Far Eastern.

M.J. Dyas Coins and Medals
30 Shaftmoor Lane, Acocks Green, Birmingham B27 7RS. 0121 707 2808. All medals—memorial plaques a speciality. Lists £1 (UK), £2 (overseas).

Edinburgh Coin Shop (Hiram T. D. Brown)
2 Polwarth Crescent, Edinburgh EH11 1HW. 0131 229 2915 / 3007. British medals and decorations. 4 lists and 10 auctions a year.

Gateway Militaria
Box 24049, 13 - 1853 Grant Avenue, Winnipeg, Manitoba, Canada R3N 1ZO. (204) 489 3884 (fax 204 489 9118). Medals and badges.

Glance Back
17 Upper Church Street, Chepstow, Gwent NP6 5EX. 01291 626562. Large stock of Medals, badges and military books.

Gordons Medals & Military Collectables
Stand G16–17, Grays Antique Centre, South Molton Lane, London W1Y 2LP. 0171 495 0900 (fax 0171 495 0115). Monday-Friday, 10.30am–6pm. Campaign medals, militaria, German and Third Reich documents and awards. Bimonthly catalogues £8 (UK), £16 (overseas airmail).

Louis E. Grimshaw
612 Fay Street, R.R. #1 Kingston, Ontario, Canada K7L 4VI. (613) 549 2500. Military antiques and collectables, including medals. Catalogues of arms, medals and militaria . Single copies $C5 (Canada), $US4 (USA), $US6 (elsewhere).

Great War Medals
22 Selborne Road, Southgate, London N14 7DH. Mainly WW1 medals and books. 36 page catalogue of medals and decorations, £7.50 (UK), £11 (overseas).

W.D. Grissom
PO Box 12001, Suite 216, Chula Vista, California, USA 91912. American medals. Free lists.

H & B Medals Ltd
38 Chetwood Drive, Widnes, Cheshire WA8 9BL. 051 424 0630 / 0151 228 6421. Callers by appointment only. British orders, decorations and medals. 4–6 lists a year, £3 (UK), £6 (overseas).

Tom Halpin
268 Gilmore Street, Mineola, NY 11501, USA. 516-248-4673. Fax: 516 248 6082. Worldwide awards with other military (all services) items. Large newspaper-style list.

A. D. Hamilton & Co.
7 St Vincent Place, Glasgow G1 2DW. 0141 221 5423 (fax 0141 248 6019). British and foreign medals, groups and collections, badges and militaria. Monday-Saturday, 9am - 5.30pm.

Harpers Military Medals Ltd
PO Box 9273, London E14 3YF. 0171 515 5661 (fax: 0171 515 5662). Mainly British orders, medals and decorations. 4 lists per year, £8 (UK), £12 (overseas). Also special auction agent service available.

Raymond D. Holdich
Trafalgar Square Collectors' Centre, 7 Whitcomb Street, London WC2. 0171 930 1979. Monday–Friday, 11am–5.30pm. Saturday by appointment only. British gallantry awards and campaign medals, cap badges, world medals and decorations.

Invicta International
740 Gladstone Avenue, Ottawa, Ontario, Canada K1R 6X5. (613) 232 2263. Worldwide medals, badges, insignia, wings, books and prints.

Steve Johnson
USA: PO Box 4076, Aurora, Illinois 60507, USA. (630) 851-0744 (fax (630) 851-0866). UK: Woodbridge, Derwent Avenue, Rowlands Gill, Tyne & Wear NE39 1BZ. All world orders, medals, decorations and militaria.

Paul Laycock
6 Poplar Terrace, Moldgreen, Huddersfield, W. Yorks HD5 8AB. British medals and decorations. Regular lists.

Liverpool Medal Company Ltd
42 Bury Business Centre, Kay Street, Bury, Lancs BL9 6BU. 0161 763 4610/4612 (fax 0161 763 4963). British and world medals and decorations. Regular lists.

March Medals
113 Gravelley Hill North, Erdington, Birmingham B23 6BJ. 0121 384 4901. Orders of chivalry, decorations, campaign medals, military antiques, books, ribbons and accessories. Regular lists. Monday-Friday, 10am–5pm; Saturday, 10am - 2pm.

Medals of Service
926 Old Northern Road, Glenorie NSW 2157, Australia. 61 02 9652 2022 (fax 61 02 9652 2950). Specialising in replica medals.

Merseyside Collectors Centre
Unit C110-111, Market Hall, Grange Precinct, Birkenhead, Merseyside L41 2YH. Tel/fax: 0151 666 1431. Medals and militaria.

Militaria House
238 Davenport Road, PO Box 99, Toronto, Ontario Canada M5R 1J6. Mail bid auctions of decorations, medals, insignia and militaria. 4 catalogues per year $25 (US and Canada), $30 (overseas).

The Military Shop
1350 Stratford Road, Hall Green, Birmingham B28 9EH. Medals and decorations, groups and medal literature. Lists available.

Miniature Medals
The Post Office, Moreton Morrell, Warwickshire CV35 9AL. Tel/fax 01926 651500. Miniature medal specialist. Lists.

Peter Morris
1 Station Concourse, Bromley North Railway Station, Kent. Postal: PO Box 223, Bromley, Kent BR1 4EQ. 0181 313 3410 (shop hours), 0181 466 1762 (other times). Monday-Friday, 10am–6pm; Saturday, 9am–2pm. Other times by appointment. Free quarterly lists of medals and decorations on request.

Neate Militaria & Antiques
PO Box 3794, Preston St Mary, Sudbury CO10 9PX. 01787 248168 (fax 01787 248363). Monday-Friday, 9am-6pm. Lists available, £6 (UK, EC), £10 (overseas).

Detlev Niemann
Ballindamm 9, V Floor, 20095 Hamburg 1, Germany. 0049 40 3252 5354 (fax 0049 40 3252 5454). Specialist in German orders, decorations, militaria, etc. Catalogue subscription £20 for 4 issues.

Pieces of History
PO Box 4470, Cave Creek, AZ 85331, USA. (602) 488 1377 (fax 602 488 1316). Worldwide medals badges, patches, accessories etc. Lists available.

Pobjoy Mint
Mint House, 92 Oldfields Road, Sutton, Surrey. 0181 641 0370 (fax 0181 644 1028). Manufacturers of orders, medals, decorations, commemorative medals, etc.

Q & C Militaria
22 Suffolk Road, Cheltenham, Gloucestershire GL50 2AQ. Tel/fax 01242 519815. British and Commonwealth orders, medals, decorations and miltaria.

R & M International
PO Box 6278, Bellevue, Washington DC, USA 98008-0278. Well illustrated 64 page lists of medals and decorations of the world, $US2.50.

Barbara Radman
Denver House, 17 Witney Street, Burford, Oxfordshire OX18 4RU. 01993 822040. Fax: 01993 822769. British and Foreign orders, medals and decorations.

Roberts
PO Box 1, Brimpton, Reading, RG7 4RJ. 01734 713543. Fax 01734 811176. Campaign medals. Medal and book lists £9 (UK), £15 (overseas).

Romsey Medals
5 Bell Street, Romsey, Hampshire SO51 8GY. 01794 512069 (fax 01794 830332). Orders, medals and decorations.

George M. Shank
1574 Arnold Ct., Huntingdon, W. Va. 25705, USA. 304-736-8730. Worldwide orders, medals and decorations. Large lists.

Southern Medals
16 Broom Grove, Knebworth, Herts SG3 6BQ. 32 page lists of British and Commonwealth medals and decorations. £6 (UK), £9 (overseas).

Spink & Son Ltd (Christie's International)
5-7 King Street, St James's, London SW1Y 6QS. 0171 930 7888 (fax 0171 839 4853). Dealers, auctioneers and valuers. The Medal Gallery, Monday-Friday, 9am–5.30pm (Tuesday to 7.30pm). Publishers of *Spink Medal Quarterly*, £8 (UK), £15 or $US25 (overseas).

Sunset Militaria
Dinedor Cross, Herefordshire HR2 6PF. 01432 870420. Quarterly lists of medals, badges, militaria and literature, sae for sample.

Suttle Medals and Militaria
50 Lackey Street, Summer Hill, NSW 2130, Australia. Tel/fax 61 02 9798 6113. Medals, militaria, books, uniforms, etc.

Jeremy Tenniswood
28 Gordon Road, Aldershot, Hants GU11 1ND. 01252 319791 (fax 01252 342339). Orders, medals decorations and militaria and related books.

Toad Hall Medals
Court Road, Newton Ferrers, near Plymouth, South Devon PL8 1DH. 01752 872672 (fax 01752 872723). Lists available.

Toye, Kenning & Spencer Ltd
Regalia House, Newtown Road, Bedworth, Warwickshire CV12 8QR. 01203 315 634 (fax 01203 643 018). Manufacturers of miniature medals, medal ribbons, badges, etc.

Eugene G. Ursual
PO Box 8096, Ottawa, Ontario, Canada K1G 3H6. (613) 521 9691 (fax 613 523 3347). Medals, orders, decorations, miniatures and militaria. 10 lists a year $12 (Canada), $15 (USA), $20 (overseas).

Vernon
Box 1560MN, Wildomar, California, USA 92595. Worldwide orders, medals and decorations. Lists 10 times a year, $3 (USA), $20 (oversea airmail).

Welsh Medals & Militaria
1A Pontcanna Street, Cardiff CF1 9HQ. 01222 374202. Medals, coins and militaria.

Fred S. Walland
17 Gyllyngdune Gardens, Seven Kings, Essex IG3 9HH. 0181 590 4389. Orders, medals and decorations. Lists £7.50 (UK and BFPO), £15 (overseas).

Yeovil Collectors Centre
16 Hendford, Yeovil, Somerset BA20 1TE. 01935 433739. Medals, badges, etc. Occasional lists.

BOOKSELLERS/DEALERS

In addition to the names listed below, it should be noted that a number of the medal dealers listed above regularly or occasionally include books on their medal lists.

Aviation Bookshop
656 Holloway Road, London N19 3PD. 0171 272 3630. Aviation history—books, magazines, posters and videos.

Michael Bartlett
Hillside, Lancarfen, Nr Barry, Glamorgan CF6 9AD. 01446 781442. British military history, particularly the First World War. Regular lists available.

Bufo Books
32 Tadfield Road, Romsey, Hants SO51 8AJ. 01794 517149. Mainly 20th century military history, especially the Second World War.

Bunker to Bunker Books
PO Box 342, 1631 St Mary's Road, Winnipeg, Canada MB R2N 3X9. General but with a focus on Canadian-related material.

Andrew Burroughs
24 St. Martins, Stamford, Lincolnshire PE9 2LJ. 01780 51363. Military history. Lists available.

Buttercross Books
2 The Paddock, Bingham, Nottingham NG13 8HQ. Tel/fax 0115 9 837147. Napoleonic era and First World War. Lists available.

Caliver Books
816/818 London Road, Leigh-on-Sea, Essex SS9 3NH. Tel/fax 01702 73986. Military history up to 1900. Shop and mail order. Lists available.

Chelifer Books
Todd Close, Curthwaite, Wigton, Cumbria CA7 8BE. General military history, including unit histories. Lists available.

The Collector
36 The Colonnade, Piece Hall, Halifax, West Yorks HX1 1RS. Military, naval and aviation history, all periods.

Q.M. Dabney & Company
PO Box 42026-MH, Washington, DC 20015, USA. Military books of all periods. Lists $US1 each.

Peter de Lotz
20 Downside Crescent, Hampstead, London NW3 2AP. 0171 794 5709. (fax 0171 284 3058). Military, naval and aviation history, with emphasis on regimental and divisional histories.

Tom Donovan Military Books
52 Willow Road, Hampstead, London NW3 1TP. 0171 431 2474 (fax 0171 431 8314). Printed works, documentation and manuscript material relating to the British Military Services. Regular lists.

Francis Edwards
13 Great Newport Street, Charing Cross Road, London WC2H 4JA. 0171 379 7669 (fax 0171 836 5977). All aspects of military history. Lists available.

Chris Evans Books
Unit 6, Jervoise Drive, Birmingham B31 2XU. Tel/fax 0121 477 6700. General military history. Lists available.

Falconwood Transport and Military Bookshop.
5 Falconwood Parade, The Green, Welling, Kent DA16 2PL. 0181 303 8291. Military, naval and aviation history.

Kenneth Fergusson
The Book Room, The Post Office, Twyning, Tewkesbury, Glos GL20 6DF. 01684 295855. Military and aviation history.

Ken Ford Military Books
93 Nutshalling Avenue, Rownhams, Southampton SO1 8AY. 01703 739437. British colonial wars. Lists available.

John Gaunt
21 Harvey Road, Bedford MK41 9LF. 01234 217686. Numismatic books including medal reference works.

GM Services
98 Junction Road, Andover, Hampshire SP10 3JA. Tel/fax 01264 362048. Postal auctions of military books.

Tony Gilbert Antique Books
101 Whipps Cross Road, Leytonstone, London E11 1NW. 0181 530 7472. Military, naval and aviation history.

Martin Gladman
235 Nether Street, Finchley, London N3 1NT. 0181 343 3023. Military, naval and aviation history.

G. L. Green.
18 Aldenham Avenue, Radlett, Herts WD7 8HX. 01923 857077. Naval and maritime history.

George Harris
Heathview, Habberley Road, Bewdley, Worcs DY12 1JH. 01299 402413. Napoleonic, Victorian campaigns and the First World War.

David Hayles Military Books
35 St. Marks Road, Maidenhead, Berks SL6 6DJ. 01628 39535. Regular lists.

Hersant's Military Books
17 The Drive, High Barnet, Herts EN5 4JG. Tel/fax 0181 440 6816. General military history. Lists available by period.

Michael Hicks Beach
99 York Mansions, London SW11 4BN. 0171 622 2270. British and Imperial military history.

Jerboa-Redcap Books
PO Box 1058, Highstown, N.J. 08520, USA. (609) 443 3817. British military books (all services), including collectables. Catalogues $US2.

Keegan's Bookshop
Merchant's Place, Reading RG1 1DT. Phone/fax 01734 587253. Secondhand booksellers with good stock of military titles. Shop in town centre. Parking nearby.

Roger Knowles
26 Church Road, Norton Canes, Cannock, Staffs WS11 3PD. 01543 279313. Military history

John Lewcock
6 Chewells Lane, Haddenham, Ely, Cambs CB6 3SS. 01353 741152. Naval history.

Liverpool Medal Company Ltd
42 Bury Business Centre, Kay Street, Bury, Lancs BL9 6BU. 0161 763 4610/4612 (fax 0161 763 4963). Medal dealers, but publish an occasional separate book catalogue four times a year.

Ian Lynn
258 Upper Fant Road, Maidstone Kent ME16 8BX. 01622 728525. Military history.

Marcet Books
4a Nelson Road, Greenwich, London SE10 9JB. 0181 853 5408. Naval history.

G. & D. I. Marrin & Sons
149 Sandgate Road, Folkestone, Kent CT20 2DA. 01303 253016 (fax 01303 850956) Specialises in material relating to the First World War.

McLaren Books
91 West Clyde Street, Helensburgh, Dunbartonshire G84 8BB. 01436 676453. Naval history.

Military Bookman
29 East 93rd Street, New York, NY 10128, USA. (212) 348 1280. Large stock of military history relating to all services worldwide and all periods.

Military Bookworm
PO Box 235, London SE23 1NS. 0181 291 1435. Decorations & medals, regimental & divisional histories, and campaign histories. Subscription to lists £9 (approx 9 per year)

Military History Bookshop
2 Broadway, London N11 3DU. Tel/fax 0181 368 8568. Lists, subscription £2.50 (4 issues).

Military Parade Bookshop
The Parade, Marlborough, Wilts SN8 1NE. 01672 515470 (fax 01980 630 150). Wide ranging new and secondhand books. Lists available.

Motor Books
St Martins Court, London WC2N 4AL. 0171 836 5376 (fax 0171 497 2539). Comprehensive stock of military books in print.

Military & Naval History
54 Regis Road, Tettenhall, Wolverhampton WV6 8RW. 01902 756402. British Military history. Lists available.

Palladour Books
Cartref, Aberporth, Nr Cardigan, Dyfed SA43 2EN. 01239 811658. Mainly WW1 and 2.

Anthony J. Simmonds
23 Nelson Road, Greenwich, London SE10 9JB. 0181 853 1727. Naval and maritime history. Occasional catalogues.

Andrew Skinner
42 Earlspark Avenue, Newlands, Glasgow G43 2HW. 0141 632 4903 (fax 0141 632 8453). General military history stock with special emphasis on Scotland. Monthly lists.

Frank Smith Maritime Aviation Books
98/100 Heaton Road, Newcastle upon Tyne. 91 265 6333. Naval, maritime and aviation history.

Spink & Son Ltd (Christie's International)
5-7 King Street, St James's, London SW1Y 6QS. 0171 930 7888 (fax 0171 839 4853). Specialist Book Department also the Medal Department lists some books in the *Spink Medal Quarterly*, £8 (UK), £15 or $US25 (overseas).

Squirrel Publishing
6 & 7 Castle Gates, Shrewsbury SY1 2AE. 01743 272140 (fax 01743 366041). Numismatic books with good stock of medal reference works.

Stephen Tilston
37 Bennett Park, Blackheath, London SE3 9RA. Tel/fax 0181 318 9181. General stock, but specialising in the First World War. Lists available

THCL Books
185 Lammack Road, Blackburn, Lancs BB1 8LH. Military book specialist aand publishers of collectors' cards of medal heroes. Lists available.

Ken Trotman Ltd
Unit 11, 135 Ditton Walk, Cambridge CB5 8QD. 01223 211030 (fax 01223 212317). Large, wide-ranging stock. Lists available: 3 per year.

Brian Turner Military Books
1132 London Road, Leigh-on-Sea, Essex SS9 2AJ. Tel/fax 01702 78771. Printed works and documentation relating to military, naval and

aviation history, specialising in the First World War, India and Africa.

Robin Turner
30 Great Norwood Street, Cheltenham, Glos GL50 2BH. 01242 234303. Military, specialising in the Napoleonic period.

Mark Weber
35 Elvaston Place, London SW7 5NW. 0171 225 2506 (fax 0171 581 8233). Specialises in official war histories and books by and about Sir Winston Churchill.

Terence Wise
Pantiles, Garth Lane, Knighton, Powys LD7 1HH. Military history especially regimental and divisional histories. Lists available.

Woodford Books
The Lodge, Well Street, Docking, King's Lynn, Norfolk PE31 8LQ. 01485 518700. Medal and military books, photograph albums, letters, ephemera. Lists available.

Woolcott Books
Kingston House, Higher Kingston, Nr Dorchester, Dorset DT2 8QE. 0135 267773 (fax 01305 848218). Military and colonial history, specialising in India, Africa and 19th century campaigns.

World War Books
Oaklands, Camden Park, Tunbridge Wells, Kent TN2 5AE. 01892 538465. Military, naval and aviation books and documents, particularly First World War, regimental histories, maps, diaries and photographs. Lists available.

World War II Books
PO Box 55, Woking, Surrey GU22 8HP. 01483 722880 (fax 0483 721548). Second World War military history. 12 lists per year.

R.J. Wyatt.
33 Sturges Road, Wokingham, Berks RG11 2HG. 01734 780325. All aspects of British military history, with an emphasis on the First and Second World Wars, Volunteers, and the Territorial Army.

FAIRS

Many fairs are held regularly and organised by professionals, in addition a number of societies organise fairs for the public (Victorian Military Society, Aldershot Militaria Society, etc.). The dates are usually well advertised in MEDAL NEWS and other publications, however, times and venues are liable to change so it is advisable in every instance to telephone the organisers beforehand. Listed below are the major fair organisers and the events known to us.

Aldershot Militaria and Medal Fair
Princes Hall, Barrack Road, Aldershot, Surrey.
Mark Carter, 01753 534777.

Arms, Shooters, Militaria and Medal Fair
The Premier, Compton and Manx Suites, The National Motorcycle Museum, Birmingham. Up to 150 tables. Central Arms Fairs, 11 Berwick Close, Warwick CV34 5UF. 01926 400554/497340.

Bedford Arms Fair
The Corn Exchange, Bedford. Arms & Armour UK, 58 Harpur Street, Bedford MK40 2QT. 01234 344831.

Birmingham, Midlands Militaria Fair
St John's Hotel, Warwick Road, Solihull, Birmingham. Watergate Antiques, 56 Watergate Street, Chester. 0244 344516.

Britannia Medal Fair
Victory Services Club, 63-79 Seymour Street, Marble Arch, London W2. Six p.a. Britannia Enterprises, 28 Raglan Place, Burnopfield, Gateshead NE16 6NN. 01267 71869.

Bromley Medal and Militaria Fair
Civic Centre, Bromley, Kent. Ray Brough. 0181 766 0329.

Cheshunt Militaria Fair
Wolsey Hall, Windmill Lane, Cheshunt, Herts. Ron Sparks. 01703 453 418.

Chessington Militaria Fair
Community Sports College, Garrison Lane, Chessington, Surrey. Ron Sparks. 01703 453 418.

Collectors' Market
London Bridge Main Line Station, London SE1. Every Saturday. Over 60 stands comprising medals, badges and militaria. 0181 398 8065.

Crowthorne Militaria Fair
Wellington College Sports Club, Duke's Ride, Crowthorne. Ron Sparks. 01703 453 418.

Didcot Militaria Fair
Civic Hall, Britwell Road, Didcot, Berks. Ron Sparks. 01703 453 418.

Dorking Militaria Fair
Dorking Halls, Reigate Road, Dorking, Surrey. Ron Sparks. 01705 839400/831804.

Dunstable Arms & Armour Fair
The Queensway Hall, Dunstable. Arms & Armour UK, 58 Harpur Street, Bedford MK40 2QT. 01234 344831.

Farnham Militaria Fair
The Maltings, Bridge Squre, Farnham, Surrey. Ron Sparks. 01703 453 418.

Farnham Annual Militaria Fair
The Maltings, Bridge Street, Farnham, Surrey. Aldershot Militaria Society. 01705 839400 / 831804.

Gloucester Militaria and Medal Fair
Gloucester Leisure Centre, Bruton Way, Inner Ring Road, Gloucester. Mark Carter. 01753 534777.

London Arms Fairs
The Paragon Hotel, Lillie Road, London SW6. 4 shows p.a. Douglas Fryer. 01273 475 959.

London Military Market—Islington
Angel Arcade, Camden Passage, Islington, London N1. Every Saturday, 8am–2pm. Over 35 stands. 0162882 2503 or 01455 556971.

London—Militaria and Medals—Paxton Mews
Paxton Mews Warehouse, Paxton Mews, 65/67 Westow Street, Crystal Palace, London SE19 Every Saturday, 8am–3pm. Over 70 stands. 0181 653 7700 or 0181 768 1672.

Maidenhead Medal and Militaria Fair
The Magnet Leisure Centre, Maidenhead, Kent. Ray Brough. 0181 766 0329.

Midhurst Militaria Fair
The Grange, Bepton Road, off the A286, Midhurst, Surrey. Ron Sparks. 01705 839400/831804.

Sandhurst Militaria and Medal Fair
Memorial Park, Sandhurst, Berks. Sovereign Arms Fairs. 01438 811657 or 01923 448903.

Surbiton Militaria Fair
Assembly Rooms, Maple Road, Surbiton Road, near Kingston-on-Thames. Ron Sparks. 01705 839400/831804.

Tunbridge Wells
The Camden Centre, Market Square, Camden Road, Tunbridge Wells, Kent. Ray Brough. 0181 766 0329.

Victorian Military Fair
Victorian Military Society, 49 Belsize Park, London NW3 4EE. 0171 722 5542.

Wakefield Medal and Militaria Fair
H & B Medals, 38 Chetwood Drive, Widnes, Cheshire WA8 9BL. 0151 424 0630/0151 228 6421.

Watford Arms, Militaria and Medal Fair
Bushey Hall School, London Road, Bushey, near Watford, Herts. Sovereign Fairs. 01438 811657 or 01923 448903.

West Country Militaria and Medal Fair
Yate Leisure Centre, Kennedy Way, Yate, near Chipping Sodbury, Bristol. Mark Carter. 01753 534777.

MEDAL RIBBONS

In this section we feature the majority of the ribbons for the medals included in the main section of the book. Where the same ribbon is used for more than one medal, only one is illustrated here.

24. Victoria Cross

24. Victoria Cross, Navy to 1918

24A. Conspicuous Gallantry Cross

25. New Zealand Cross

26. George Cross

27. Distinguished Service Order

28/29. Imperial Service Order/Medal

31. Royal Red Cross

32. Distinguished Service Cross

33. Military Cross

34. Distinguished Flying Cross 1919

35. Air Force Cross 1919

39. Albert Medal (2nd Class, Sea)

39. Albert Medal (2nd Class, Land)

40. SA Queen's Medal for Bravery

41/42. Distinguished Conduct Medal

43. DCM (KAR and WAFF)

44. Conspicuous Gallantry, Navy

44. Conspicuous Gallantry, RAF

45. George Medal

46/49. King's Police Medal 1916

46. King's Police Medal (Gallantry)

50/51. Edward Medal

52. Indian Distinguished Service Medal

54. Distinguished Service Medal

55. Military Medal

56. Distinguished Flying Medal

57. Air Force Medal

58. Constabulary Medal Ireland 1872

59. Indian Police Medal (Meritorious Service)

60. Burma Police Meritorious Service Medal

61. Colonial Police Medal (Gallantry)
62. Colonial Fire Brigade Medal (Gallantry)

61. Colonial Police Medal (Meritorious Service)
62. Colonial Fire Brigade (Meritorious Service)

63. Queen's Gallantry Medal

64. Allied Subjects Medal

65. King's Medal for Courage
in the Cause of Freedom

66. King's Medal for Service in the
Cause of Freedom

67/68. Sea Gallantry Medal

79. Seringapatam

93. Naval Gold Medal

94. Naval General Service Medal

95. Army Gold Cross/96. Maida Gold Medal
97. Army Gold Medal

98. Military General Service Medal

99. Waterloo Medal

102. Nassau Medal for Waterloo

104. Army of India

105. Ghuznee Medal

106. St Jean D'Acre Medal

107. Candahar, Ghuznee, Cabul Medal
108. Jellalabad, 109. Kelat-I-Ghilzi

110. China War Medal

111. Scinde Medal/112. Gwalior Star

113. Sutlej Medal

114. Punjab Medal

115/127. South Africa Medal

117. India General Service 1854–95

118. Baltic Medal

119. Crimea

120. Turkish Crimea

121. Indian Mutiny

122. Second China War

123. New Zealand Medals

124. Abyssinia 1867–68

125. Canada General Service

126. Ashantee/137. E&W Africa

128. Afghanistan 1878–80

129. Kabul to Kandahar Star

130. Cape of Good Hope GSM

131. Egypt Medal

132. Khedive's Star
133. Gordon's Khartoum Star

134. North West Canada

135. Royal Niger Company's Medal

138. BSA Co's Medal

140. Central Africa

141. Hong Kong Plague

142. India Medal 1895–1902

143. Jummoo and Kashmir

144. Ashanti Star

145. Queen's Sudan

146. Khedive's Sudan Medal

147. East and Central Africa

148. BNB Co's Medal (2)

148. BNB Co's Medal (3)

150. Queen's South Africa/151. Queen's Mediterranean

152. King's South Africa

153. St John's Ambulance Brigade Medal for South Africa

154/155. Kimberley Star and Medal

156. Yorkshire Imperial Yeomanry

157. Medal for the Defence of Ookiep

158. China War Medal

159. Transport Medal

160. Ashanti Medal

161. Africa General Service 1902–56

162. Tibet Medal

163. Natal Medal

164. India General Service 1908–35

165. Khedives Sudan

166/167. 1914/1914–15 Star

168. British War Medal

169. Mercantile Marine

170. Victory Medal

171. Territorial Force War Medal

173. Naval General Service 1915–62

174. General Service 1918–62

175. India General Service 1936–39

177. 1939–45 Star

178. Atlantic Star

179. Air Crew Europe Star

180. Africa Star

181. Pacific Star

182. Burma Star

183. Italy Star

184. France and Germany Star

185. Defence Medal

186. War Medal 1939–45

187. India Service Medal

188. Canadian Volunteer Service

189. Africa Service Medal

190 Australia Service Medal

191. New Zealand War Service

192. South Africa Service

193. Southern Rhodesia War Service

195. Korea Medal

196. South African Medal for Korea

197. United Nations Korea Medal

198. General Service Medal 1962

199. UN Emergency Force

200. Vietnam Medal

201. South Vietnam Campaign Medal

202. Rhodesia Medal

203. South Atlantic Medal

203A. Soviet 40th Anniversary Medal

204. Gulf Medal

205. Saudi Medal for Liberation of Kuwait

206. Kuwait Liberation Medals

206A. NATO

207. UNTSO, UNOGIL

207. ONUC

207. UNTEA

207. UNMOGIP, UNIPOM

207. UNYOM

207. UNFICYP

207. UNEF 2

207. UNDOF

207. UNIFIL

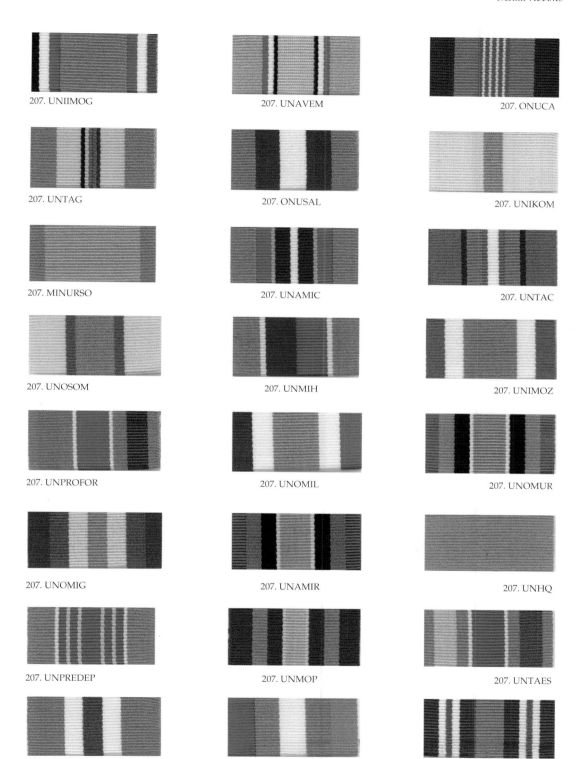

207. UNIIMOG

207. UNAVEM

207. ONUCA

207. UNTAG

207. ONUSAL

207. UNIKOM

207. MINURSO

207. UNAMIC

207. UNTAC

207. UNOSOM

207. UNMIH

207. UNIMOZ

207. UNPROFOR

207. UNOMIL

207. UNOMUR

207. UNOMIG

207. UNAMIR

207. UNHQ

207. UNPREDEP

207. UNMOP

207. UNTAES

207. UNMOT

207. UNMIBH

207. UNMOGUA

207. UN Special Service

208/210/214. Meritorious Service

211. RAF Meritorious Service

216A. Accumulated Campaign Service

217. Royal Household FS GVIR

217. Royal Household FS EIIR

218. RN LS & GC (i)

218. RN LS & GC (ii)

219. RNR Decoration

220. RNR LS & GC (i)

220. RNR LS & GC (ii)

221. RNVR Decoration 1919

222. RNVR LS& GC

223. RFR LS & GC

226. RNA LS

227. Rocket Apparatus Vol LS

229. Army LS & GC

231. Volunteer Decoration
232. Volunteer Force LS & GC

232. Volunteer Force LS & GC (HAC)

233. Territorial Decoration
236. Efficiency Decoration (i)

234. Territorial Force Efficiency

235. Territorial Efficiency
237. Efficiency Medal

236. Efficiency Decoration (ii)

237. Efficiency Medal 1969

237. Efficiency Medal HAC

238. AER Decoration

239. AER Efficiency Medal

240. Imperial Yeomanry LS & GC

241. Militia LS & GC

242. Special Reserve LS & GC

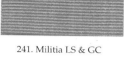
243. Indian Army LS & GC (European)

244. Indian Army LS & GC 1917

245. Indian VF Officers Decoration

246/247. Colonial AF Decoration/LS Medal

249. Permanent Forces LS & GC

255. Canadian Forces Decoration

260. UDR LS & GC

261. Ulster Defence Regiment Medal

262. Cadet Forces Medal

263. Royal Observer Corps Medal

264. Civil Defence LS

265. WVS LS

266. Voluntary Medical Service

267. Service Medal of the Order of St John

268/269. RAF LS & GC

270. Air Efficiency Award

271. Police LS & GC

272. Special Constabulary LS

273. RUC Service Medal

274. Colonial Police LS

275. Colonial Special Constabulary LS

278. Ceylon Police LS & GC (II)

280B. Royal Hong Kong Police Commemoration Medal

286. Fire Brigade LS

287. Colonial Fire Brigade LS

289. Colonial Prison Service

292. Empress of India Medal

293/295. Jubilee (VR) 1887/1897

294/297. Jubilee (Police) 1887/1897

296. Jubilee 1897 (Mayors & Provosts)

300. Visit to Ireland 1900

301. Coronation 1902

302. Coronation 1902 (Mayors & Provosts)

303. Coronation 1902 (Police)

306. Delhi Durbar 1903

307. Visit to Scotland 1903

308. Visit to Ireland 1903

309. Coronation 1911
312. Delhi Durbar 1911

310. Coronation 1911 (Police)

311. Visit to Ireland 1911

313. Jubilee 1935

314. Coronation 1937

315. Coronation 1953

316. Jubilee 1977

317. Royal Humane Society

317. Stanhope Gold Medal

320. Society of the Protection of Life from Fire
327. Liverpool Shipwreck & Humane Society (Fire)

329. Liverpool Shipwreck & Humane
Society (General)

337. Lloyd's Medal for Services to Lloyds

338. Lloyd's Medal for Bravery at Sea

342./343. Arctic Medal

344. Polar Medal

346. League of Mercy

352. Naval Good Shooting

353. Army Best Shot

354. Queen's Medal for Champion Shot
(RN/RM)

355. Queen's Medal for Champion Shot
(RAF)

359. Anglo-Boer War Medal

360. Nigeria Independence Medal

360. Pakistan Independence Medal

360. Zimbabwe Independence Medal

361. Malta GC Anniversary

370. Shanghai Municipality Council
Emergency Medal

INDEX TO MEDAL NEWS

In this issue of the MEDAL YEARBOOK we include the complete **Cumulative Subject Index** to the parent magazine MEDAL NEWS, commencing with the March 1989 issue, when it became a separate publication.

MEDAL NEWS was born in 1981 from the amalgamation of *Medals International* and *Coins & Medals*, into the popular title *Coin & Medal News*. However, the success of this magazine and the continuing growth of both the coin and the medal collecting hobbies prompted the separation of the two sections in March 1989. Since then both *Coin News* and MEDAL NEWS have grown from strength to strength and today are the hobby's leading publications, not only in the UK but MEDAL NEWS is the *only* independent magazine in the world devoted to the collecting and study of medals. A small number of some back issues of MEDAL NEWS are available at £5 each—please enquire whether we have the issue you require.

NOTES

References are indicated **year, month: page,** for example 9004.18 means April 1990 issue, page 18; 9306.24 means June/July 1993 issue, page 24.

Each year runs from February to December. For example the year 1990 includes the December 1990/January 1991 issue.

Names of ships are indicated in italics.

Names of people have been included where they appear to be the major subject of an article or where more than trivial information is included.

Abbreviations used:
(cr)   Indicates the inclusion of a full or partial casualty list.
(mr)   Indicates the inclusion of a medal roll.
(nr)   Indicates nominal roll.
(i)   Indicates that the reference gives information rather than the object itself. For example it tells you where to find a medal roll rather than reproducing the roll itself.
(p)   Indicates that the reference is to a picture of a person or object where little or no other information is given.
(mp)   Same as (p) except that the picture is of medals.
(br)   Indicates Book Review.

A

East Surrey Regt
  badges
    Territorial Battn 9108.25-26
    tropical helmet 9405.22-23
    Wandsworth Battalion WWI 9012.22
East Yorkshire Regt
  badges 9512.22-23
    Cyclist Battn 9104.22
    Musician 9403.24
economy badges 9112.24-25
Edgar, William H.V., Lt Cdr RAN: Zeebrugge (1918) 9104.19-20
Edinburgh: Queen's Visit (1881) 9412.16-17
Edlund, Flt Lt, DFC/AFM group (mp) 9509.05
Edmunds, Robert S., Cpl RAFVR: British Empire Medal (1947) 9505.15
Edwardes, John, Lt Col: OBE (Vitez) 9602.17
Edward Medal: register (i) 9212.04
Edwards, Jimmy RAF (p) 8904.25
Efficiency Medal (T): Militia bar 8904.27-28
Egerton, Charles C., Maj Gen Sir: Somaliland (1903-04) 9006.14-15
Egypt (1917): Anzac forces (VC mr) 8905.24-25
Egypt (1956): award of GSM 9508.10-11
Egypt Campaign (1801): badges 9002.24-25
Egyptian Expeditionary Force (1917) 8905.25
Egypt Medal (1882-89): naming 9004.18
8th Army: clasp to Africa Star; entitlement 9504.10
Eimer, C. 'Medallic Portraits of the Duke of Wellington' (br) 9412.20
Eisenhower, Dwight D., Gen: award of Africa Star 9609.13, 9611.26
Elandslaagte (1899) (mr Manchersters) 9510.14-18
Ellsworth, Lincoln, Antarctic rescue 8904.13
Elphinstone, Howard, Gen Sir (p) 9011.11
El Teb (1884): DCMs 8906.19
emblems on medal ribbons see ribbon emblems
Emergency Service Medal (1939-46) (Ireland) 9204.20-21
Empire Gallantry Medal
  Quetta Earthquake (mr) 9305.11-13
  register (i) 9212.04
Empire Hamble: damaged (1942) 9504.12-13
enemy aliens in Britain WWII 9009.14-17
Enquiry List No. 14 (British Red Cross & St John's) 8908.06-07
Erica: WWII 8908.25
Essex & Kent Scottish: badge 9106.27
Essex & Suffolk Cyclist Battn: badge 9104.22-23
Essex Regt: Musician badge 9403.24-25
Essex Scottish: badge 9106.26
ethics code (OMSA) 9003.27
European Bengal Fusiliers 9005.28
European History centre of the Second World War 9603.06
Evans, David Hywel, Sub/Lt RNVR: Glatton (1918) 8909.16-17
Evans, E.R.G.R, Lt RN: 2nd Antarctic Expedition 9402.18-19
Evans, Samuel, 26th Regt (1839-1851) 9605.24
Everard, Mathias, Maj Gen (1790-1857) 9303.28

F

Faithful Service, Cross for (Germany) 8909.13
Falkland Islands Dependencies Survey 9003.12-14
Falklands campaign: gallantry award stats 9105.16-17
Fane's Horse: badge 9409.23
'Farmer' Circuit (French Resistance) 9612.15-16
Feddon, Edward A., Able Seamn [I]Bellona[i] WWII 9412.13-15

Federal Defence Forces, Decoration of Honour for the (Germany) 8903.09
Federation of Firemen of France badge: to Norfolk, James, Sgt 9602.26
Fenian raids (1866): newspaper cutting 9210.26
Fenton, William, Sgt: El Teb (1884) 8906.19
Ferguson, Francis 20/Hussars: Sudan (1885) 9308.17-18
Fernie, Thomas S., LAC RAF: BEM (Military) Padang (1945) 9605.13
Ferret Force: Malaya 9512.26
Fidelity 9112.27
Field Ambulance, 157(lowland) RAMC: piper's badge 9003.25
Fielding, Xan 'One Man in His Time' (br) 9102.20
Fife & Forfar Yeomanry: badge 9209.25
50 Years of Marriage Medal (Poland) 9011.23
Finch, A., Sjt (mp) 9412.06
Finnecy, Peter: Arctic Medal (1818-55) 9312.19-20
Finnish Women's Auxiliary Defence Service Medals (i) 9502.06
Finsbury Rifles badge 9110.27
Fire Brigades Cross of Honour (Germany) 8903.09
Fire Queen 8908.23
First Aid Nursing Yeomanry: badge 9212.24-25
Fitzsimmons, H., Pte: Quetta Earthquake 9305.12
fleur-de-lys badges 9009.22-23
72/ Foot see Seaforth Highlanders, 1st
93/ Foot see Highlanders
01/ Foot: Balaklava (Crimea) 8908.15-18
04/ Foot: Balaklava (Crimea) 8908.15-18
07/ Foot: Balaklava (Crimea) 8908.15-18
19/ Foot
  Balaklava (Crimea) 8908.15-18
  Crimea Medal (mr) 8908.16-17
  Hazara (1868) 9310.12-14
  names not on recruit roll (1854) (nr) 9611.17
20/ Foot
  Musician badges 9403.24
  tropical helmet badge 9404.2
23/ Foot: Balaklava (Crimea) 8908.15-18
25/ Foot: Port Natal 8912.16
27/ Foot
  Port Natal (1842) (cr) 9004.26-27
  Port Natal 8912.15-17
28/ Foot: Balaklava (Crimea) 8908.15-18
29/ Foot
  pouch & valise badge 9411.23
  tropical helmet badge 9404.23
30/ Foot: Balaklava (Crimea) 8908.15-18
33/ Foot: Balaklava (Crimea) 8908.15-18
36/ Foot: Musician badges 9403.24
38/ Foot: Balaklava (Crimea) 8908.15-18
41/ Foot: Balaklava (Crimea) 8908.15-18
44/ Foot: Balaklava (Crimea) 8908.15-18
47/ Foot: Balaklava (Crimea) 8908.15-18
50/ Foot: Balaklava (Crimea) 8908.15-18
53/ Foot 8910.20-21
55/ Foot
  Balaklava (Crimea) 8908.15-18
  Dewangiri 8910.15-19
57/ Foot: tropical helmet badge 9404.23
58/ Foot: tropical helmet badge 9404.23
60/ Foot
  history 9503.13-14
  nationalities of soldiers 9503.13-14
62/ Foot 9503.13
63/ Foot: badge 9009.22-23
66/ Foot: Bobbie (Regt mascot0 9503.20
72/ Foot: Afghanistan (1878-80) (mr) (i) 8903.13

(nr) (i) 9403.26
origins as 60/ Foot 9503.13-14
Sambre-Oise (1918) 8909.10-11
Somaliland (1903-04) (mr) 9006.14-17
Spion Kop (1900) (cr) 9408.14-17
Wagon Hill (1900) (cr) 9306.14-18
King's Shropshire Light Infantry 8910.20-21
King's South Africa Medal
naming 9004.18
Rifle Brigade (mr) 8904.15-18
Kinne, Derek G, 1/Northumberland Fus: Korea GC
9309.19
Kinsey, T., Lt USS *St Louis*: Spanish Campaign Medal
group (mp) 9509.08
Kinta: damaged (1942) 9504.12-13
Kitchener, Frederick, Lt Col (p) 9404.22
Kitchener Battalions: Berkshire (cri) 9510.06
Knight, Henry RCS: IGS (1908) 9206.19
Knight's Batchelor badge 9311.20
Koh-i-Noor diamond, and 53/Foot 8910.20
Kojuhosho (Japan) 9002.26-27
Konigsberg, action (1914-15) (mr) 9205.18-19
Koosh-ab (Persia 1857) 9004.26
Kooshab (Persian Gulf) (1856): 3rd Bombay Light
Cavalry 9502.13
Korea (1950-53): Australian VCs 9102.21
Korea (1953-57): clasp to Australian Service Medal
(1945-75) 9511.11
Korea Medal (1950-53): ribbon 8909.26
Korn Spruit *see* Sanna's Post
'k' reports in PRO 9410.15-17
Krikly, Ivan, Capt: Ord of Patriotic War (USSR)
9409.17-18
Kroomen rating titles RN 9106.17
Krygger, A., Pte. Western Australians: Slingersfontein
(1900) 8909.19-20
Ku Lang Su police: badge 9303.26
Kulm Cross (Russia/Prussia) 9110.20
Kut (1916): RFA, RGA, RHA (nr) 9406.15-19
Kutuzov, Order of(USSR) 9409.17-19
Kuwait: clasp to Australia Service Medal (1975)
9403.11
Kuwaiti Liberation Medal 9304.10
(p) 9305.06
Kwai Bridge: Buddhist temple 9210.20-21
Kyle, Sgt RA: MSM 9303.28
Kyle, Sgt R.A. MSM 9503.21

L

Lady Brassey: *Glatton* (1918) 8909.15-17
Laffin, J. 'A Western Front Companion' (br) 9504.22
28th Lahore Mountain Battery: Somaliland (1903-04)
9006.15
Lake George (Australia) (1956): Boating disaster
9512.10-11
Lake Superior Scottish: badge 9106.27
Lally, S., Pte Connaught Rangers 9305.20-21
Lanark & Renfrew Scottish: badge 9106.27
Lanarkshire Yeomanry: badge 9209.24
Lancashire Fusiliers
badges 9611.21-22
cap 9202.24
Musician 9403.24
Haspres War Memorial (nr) 9512.13
Salford Battalion badge WWI 9012.22
Spion Kop (1900) (cr) 9408.14-17
Lancashire Regt: badges 9612.28
Lancastrian Brigade: badges 9612.28

Lancers
badges
1st Duke of York's 9409.22-23
2nd 9306.22-23, 9409.22-23
4th 9409.22-23
5th 9304.24-24
6th Duke of Connaught's 9410.22-23
7th Hariana 9409.22-23
9th/12th 9306.22-23
11th Prince of Wales' Own 9409.22-23
12th 9304.24-25
13th Duke of Connaught's 9409.22-23
14th Murray's Jat 9409.22-23
15th 9410.22-23
16th/5th 9306.22-23
16th 9305.24-25
17th/21st 9306.22-23
17th 9305.24-25
18th Tiwana 9409.22-23
19th 9409.22-23
19th King George's Own 9410.22-23
20th 9410.22-23
21st 9305.24-25
24th 9306.22-23
27th 9306.22-23
29th 9410.22-23
30th 9410.22-23
31st Duke of Connaught's 9410.22-23
32nd 9410.22-23
37th 9410.22-23
arm 9004.24, 9008.28
harness 9408.22-23
tropical helmet 9405.22-23
Campaign Service medal (1962) 9006.18
Gemaizah (1885) 9308.17-18
Wagon Hill (1900) (cr) 9306.14-18
Langford, George 19/Foot: Hazara (1868) 9310.13-14
Langley, Marcus L., Flt Sgt RNZAF: CGM(F) WWII
9609.15
Lapwing: Persian Gulf (1909-14) (mr) 9309.13-17
Larpool: sinking (1941) 9403.14-15
Larut: sunk (1942) 9504.12-13
Lascelles, John F., 2nd Lt RFC (p) 9210.08
Lashly, William, ldg Stoker: Antarctic Expeditions
9402.17-19
Lavery, B. 'Nelson's Navy' (br) 9010.20
Lawrence, T.E.: as AC Shaw 9111.21
Lawrenson, E., SPR RE 9208.13
Lawson, Richard G., Royal Tank Regt: Congo DSO
9408.10-11
LCI *see* Landing Craft, Infantry
Leach, Edgar, 2nd lt 2/Manchester 9309.26
Leander: Albania (1946) 9008.16-17
le Chene, Evelyn 'Silent Heroes: Bravery & Devotion
of Animals in War 9503.20
Lee, Joseph, Surgeon (mp) 9402.09
Leeds Pals: badge WWI 9012.22
Le Geyt, Alice Bell: RNLI Medal 8905.21
Legion of Honour Star (France) (p) 9512.07
Legion of Merit (USA): Australian awards (Vietnam)
9602.13
Legion Wallonie (German Army WWII) 9502.16-17
Leicestershire Regt: Musician badges 9403.24
Leitch, W.: *Britannia* 8906.21-22, 8909.25
Lenin, Order of (USSR) 9409.15-16
Leros Island WWII 9109.24-25
Lewis, H.W., pte Welch Regt: VC group (mp) 9402.08
Liberation of France Medal (France) 9011.23
Liddle, P.H. '1916 Battle of the Somme: a reappraisal'
(br) 9303.22

McGuigan, Sgt 1/ Argyll & Sutherland Highlanders: Palestine 9506.25

Machine Gun Corps
1st Bttn Sambre-Oise (1918) 8909.10-11
badges 9204.24-25
33rd Battn Musician 9403.25

McHugh, Stephen, Sgt Parachute Regt: MC (1994) 9602.17

McIntosh, G., Pte 6/Gordon High: Ypres VC 9411.15

McIntosh, John Cowe, Lt AIAF: London to Australia flight (1919-20) 9509.17, 22

McIntyre, C. 'Monuments of War' (br) 9012.23

McIntyre, William: 4 with that name (1806-1933) 9405.21

McKay, Robert 42/Highlanders 9109.20-21

Mackinlay, G 'True Courage: The DCM to Australians' (br) 9302.23

McKinley, PO: CGM group (p) 9006.08

Mackinnon, W.H., Gen Sir (p) 9302.09

McLauchlan, Don, Lt Cdr: notice of death 9602.05

McLean, N.L.D., Lt Col Royal Scots Greys/SOE 9102.20

McPhail, H. 'Wilfred Owen Poet and Soldier' (br) 9405.24-25

MacPherson, A, FO 228 Squad: DFC *Kensington Court* (1939) 9410.12-13

McVicar, William, 3rd Officer: *Britannia* 8906.21-22, 8909.25

McWilliams, G.F., Maj West Aust: Slingersfontein (1900) 8909.19-20

Maddocks, G. 'Liverpool Pals' (br) 9110.28

Madura: WWII 9504.18-19

Maigumeri, Chari, RWAFF
MM, BEM 9008.20
MM/Iron Cross 9105.28

Mailly: raid on (1944) 9410.15-16

Majorca Division, Cross of the (Spain) (p) 9510.08

Malaun Regiment: badge 9502.22

Malaya (1948-60): Australian VCs 9102.21

Malaya
clasp to GSM 9510.10-11, 9512.26
medal statistics 9510.10-11, 9602.25

Malay Peninsula: clasp to Australian Service Medal (1945-75) 9511.11

Malone, W.G., Lt Col Wellington Regt: Gallipoli 9202.15-18

Malta WWII 9008.18-19
counterfeit George Crosses 9603.06
George Cross 50th Anniversary Medal 9204.07

Manchester & Liverpool Regt: Musician badge 9403.25

Manchester (WWII) 8912.24-25

Manchester Regt
badges 9009.22-23, 9612.27-28
Manchester Pals 9012.22
Oldham Battn 9012.22
Elandslaagte (1899)(mr) 9510.14-18
Wagon Hill (1900) (cr) 9306.14-18

Manley, William G.N.: VC/Iron Cross 9103.24

Mannock, E., Maj RAF WWI (p) 9208.10, 9210.09

Mansfield, W.H.C., Lt Shropshire LI/RFC 9005.21

Manx Active Service Co: badge WWI 9012.22

Maori Wars (1861) 9010.12

Marie Cross (Germany) (WWI) 8908.09

Marien, Kerry F., Midshpmn, *Voyager*: Albert Medal 9404.17

Maritime Royal Artillery: WWII 9510.12-13, 9512.26

Maritz, Gen: Boer War 9108.21

Markham, C.R. 'Navy Arctic List 1773-1873) 9309.25

Marling, Percival, Sir: VC group (mp) 9410.07

Marshall, William, QMS: El Teb (1884) 8906.19

Martin, H. S/Ldr 617 Squad 9002.15-16

Mason, Dudley, Capt *Ohio*, 9402.14, 9510.12-13, 9602.25

Mason, Fred, Cpl RAAF (Timor WWII) 9502.18-19

Matanikau: Guadalcanal 9209.20-21

Mather, Michael V., 11 Squad RAAF 9409.11

Matschulat, G., Oberleutnant U-247 WWII 9012.11-12

Matthews, Len, RN WWII (p) 9112.06

Maund, Capt RN: Ord of Red Star (USSR) 9409.16

Mauritius: Albania (1946) 9008.16-17

Maxwell, Eugene P., CPO (RAN): CSC Iraq (1991) 9608.14-15

Maxwell, John G., Sir (mp) 9402.10

May, H., Pte 1/Cameronians 9408.05

Mayes, Charles, Col Sgt: CGM citation 9109.23

May Island (WWI) 8911.17

Mbilini (African Gen.): Zulu wars (1879) 8906.15-18

Mechanised Transport Corps: badge 9212.25

Medaille d'Honneur (France): 10/R Fus (Intelligence) (mr) 9004.16

Médaille Militaire (France)
6/Gordon Highlanders WWI (mr) 9411.17
10/R Fus (Intelligence) (mr) 9004.16
RN/RNR/RM (mr) 9109.22-23

Medal of Bravery (Canada) 9503.05

Medal for Bravery (Germany) 8911.21

Medal of Honor (USA)
Mogadishu award 9406.06
sale of now illegal 9508.05

Medal of Honour (Japan) 9311.19

medallions 9005.22
Lusitania 9006.10
Waterloo (1815) 9006.06

Medal for Merit (Montenegro): 10/R Fus (Intelligence) (mr) 9004.16

Medal of Merit (Ord of Merit of German Federal Republic) 8903.09

Medal for Military Merit (Germany) 8909.13

medals
MM location register 9108.28
abbreviations
Africa General Service Medal 8905.26, 8906.24
Army 9105.26, 9106.25
Navy 9010.18, 9106.25
attribution of 8911.22-23
brooches 9202.27, 9204.28
cigarette cards 9411.18-21
citations WWI, location of 9103.07
collectors & Regimental Museums 9212.21-22
collectors interests (statistics) 9503.16-18, 9506.25
Commanders' commendations 9610.12-13
common names on 9109.20-21
designers 9102.24
disposing of collections 9103.13-15
engraving gallantry decorations 9210.06
fakes 9109.21
WWII Australian 9503.24, 9508.07
fakes in circulation 9408.05
false insurance claims USA 9403.13
gallantry awards
citations publication policy 9502.11, 9509.11-12
posthomous 9206.09-12
recent changes 9311.05
single-service awards 9511.16-17
generalist v specialist collections 9506.20-21, 9509.23
guages 9302.27
Hong Kong Plague Medal location register 9108.28
licensing reproductions 9502.03
meaning of impressed indented etc. 9102.25

Plunkett: J.F., Lt Col Royal Irish Regt (p) (mp) 9403.07
Plymouth (1982) 9003.26
Plymouth Volunteer Training Corps: badges 8912.21-22
PNG: clasp to Australian Service Medal (1945-75) 9511.11
Polar Medal 9003.11-14
  Eliz. II inscriptions on 9408.04
  George VI 8904.11-13, 8906.24, 8910.23 (mr) 8905.15-18
  naming 8905.18
  silver medal with bronze and silver bars 8905.18
'Police Gallantry' (br) 9603.22
Police Overseas Service Medal (Australia): Haiti clasp 9511.11
Polish airmen: memorial plaques 8908.23
Polish militaria, rarity of 9206.21-22
Ponsonby, G.C., Gen Bengal Army: India Campaign group (mp) 9509.08
Poona Horse: badge 9410.23
Poplar & Stepney Rifles: badge 9111.26
Popski's Private Army 9611.05
Port Natal (1842) (cr) 8912.15-17, 9004.26-27
Port Said (1952): GSM (1918-28) 8905.28
Postcards, medal 9203.20-21
Post Office Rifles badge 9110.27
Potts, E.A., Lt Royal Fus WWI (p) 9409.08
Potts, Lt 80/Foot: Ntombe River (1879) 8906.18
Pouch badges 9411.22-23
Poulsen Mast (Portsmouth): seaplane crash (p) 9103.21
Poulton, J.H.T., AB *Beryl*: DSM WWII 9609.23
Pour le Mérite (Prussia)
  Military Air Service WWI 9411.12-13
  photo correction 9412.24
Pour le Mérite for Science and Art, Order (Germany) 8903.09
Powell, M.E., Nursing Sister: Royal Red Cross group (p) 9304.08
Powell, M.E., Sister (p) 9306.09
Powerful Naval Brigade: Wagon Hill (1900) (cr) 9306.14-18
Poziers 1916: Anzac forces 8903.15-17
Presidential Life Saving Medal (USA): Colman, C. *Othello* 9605.15
Preston Volunteers: shoulder-belt plates 9109.26-27
Prevost, George, Gen Sir (p) 9108.09
Prideaux-Brune, Beatrice May: RNLI Medal 8905.21
Prideaux-Brune, Ellen Francis: RNLI Medal 8905.21
Prideaux-Brune, Gertrude Rose: RNLI Medal 8905.21
Prideaux-Brune, Mary Katherine: RNLI Medal 8905.21
Prien, Gunther, U-47 WWII 9009.15-17
06/ Prince of Wales Cavalry: badge 9409.22
11/ Prince Albert Victor's Own Cavalry (FF): badge 9410.23
11/ Prince of Wales Own Lancers: badge 9409.23
14/ Prince of Wales's Own Scinde Horse: badge 9410.23
21/ Prince Albert Victor's Own Cavalry: badge 9409.23
34/ Prince Albert Victor's Own Poona Horse: badge 9410.22
Prince Edward Island Highlanders: badge 9106.27
10th Princess Mary's Own Gurkha Rifles: badge 9504.20-21
Prince of Wales Loyal Volunteers: pouch & valise badge 9411.23
Prince of Wales's Own Regiment of Yorkshire: badges 9602.21

Prince of Wales's Volunteers
  badges 9609.20
  tropical helmet badge 9405.23
Prince of Wales Visit to India Medal (mp) 9406.09
Prisoners of War, Allied: SE Asia (1945-46) 9005.15-17
Prisoner of War interrogation Section WWII 9303.15
Prisoner of War Medal (Belgium) 9011.23
prize money rolls (i) 9003.20
Probyn's Horse: badge 9409.23, 9410.23
PRO Dog National Charity Lifesaver Award
  'Murphy' 9504.05
  'Penny' 9504.05
  'Wotsit' 9504.05
professional researchers 9009.24
Projector, Infantry, Anti-Tank (mr VC) 9112.23
propoganda, danger of repeating 9108.13-14
Public Record Office
  George V Silver Jubilee roll 9112.27
  George VI Coronation Medal roll 9112.27
  rankers info available 9112.27
  research guide 8905.22
  World War I index 9002.10
  WWI/II records 9206.14-15
Public Service Medal (australia): increased no. of awards 9511.11
Puller, Lewis B., Lt Col US Marines: Guadalcanal 9209.20
Punjab Infantry
  27th Somaliland (1903-04) 9006.15
  Bhutan War (1864-65) 8910.16
  Hazara (1868) 9310.13-14
Punjab Medal (1848-49): naming 9003.22-23
Purdon, Corran, Maj Gen ' List the Bugle' (br) 9511.19
Purple Heart Medal (USA) 9011.23
  policy on awards to Australians (Vietnam) 9602.12
Purton, W.B., Flt Lt 11 Squad RAAF 9409.11
Purves, A.A. 'Medals Dec. & Orders of Great War' (br) 8911.16-18
Purves, Alec: obituary 9208.07

Q

Qantas Empire Airways
  WWII (cr) (mr) 9409.11-12
  WWII (mr Commend for brave condct) 9408.19-20
Q ships WWII 9112.27
2/ Quebec Rifles: Red River (1870) 9012.18-20
Queeen's Royal Irish Hussars: (mri) 9406.26
10/ Queen Victoria's Own Corps of Guides Cavalry (FF): badge 9410.23
17/ Queen Victoria's Own Poona Horse: badge 9410.23
Queen Alexandra's Royal Army Nursing Corps: badge 9212.24
Queen Alexandra Woman of the Bedchamber badge (mp) 8905.09
Queen Mary's Army Auxiliary Corps
  badge 9212.25
  OBE WWI (mr) 9302.15-17
33/ Queen's Own Light Cavalry: badge 9410.22
Queen's Commendation for Valuable Service in the Air: development 9402.13
Queen's Commendation for Valuable Services 9410.20-21
Queen's Dragoon Guards
  badge 9309.23
  Campaign Service Medal (1962) 9009.27
Queen's Gallantry Medal
  development 9402.14-15
  register (i) 9004.05

Sir Harry Smith Medal for Gallantry 8904.20
Sirmoor Rifles: badge 9502.22-23
Sita Ram Pande, 26 BNI: Kalanga (1814) 9405.10
Skinner's Horse: badge 9409.22, 9410.22
Slane, Edward, Merchant Navy: NZ Memorial Cross 9403.14-15
Slessor, Stewart, Surgeon Lt/Cmdr (Antarctic) 9003.11-14
Slingersfontein (1900)
 (cr) (nr) 8909.19-20
 New Zealand Hill (cr) 9011.15-17
Smith, H.G., Sir: Fort Cox private medal 9303.27
Smith, Keith, Lt Australian Flying Corps: London to Australia flight (1919-20) 9509.16-17, 22
Smith, Ross, Capt Australian Flying Corps: London to Australia flight (1919-20) 9509.16-17, 22
Smith, Rupert A., Lt Gen Sir: bar to DSO UNPROFOR (Yugoslavia) 9608.10
Smith, T.C., Capt 27/Foot 8912.15-17
Smith, T.M.W., Flt Lt 228 Squad: DFC *Kensington Court* (1939) 9410.12-13
Smith, Vernon, S/Ldr 144 Squad 8909.23-24, 9002.23
Smitham, James J.G. *Dunera* & *Madura* WWII 9504.18-19
Smith-Dorrien, Lt: Isandlwana 9102.14
Smith,Harry, Sir, medal for Gallantry 8904.20
Smithies, E. & Bruce, C. 'War at Sea 1939-45' (br) 9512.18
Snelling, Stephen, 'VCs of the First World War - Gallipoli' (br) 9510.20
Snowball, John, Lt Cmdr: Air Force Cross (Bosnia) 9602.16
Soldier's Medal of Merit (Germany) (WWI) 8908.09
Solon mutiny (1920): Connaught Rangers (mr) 9305.19-21
Somalia: clasp to Australia Service Medal (1975) 9403.11
Somaliland (1903-04) (mr) 9006.14-17
Somaliland (1920): RAF (mr) 9110.13-14
Somali Mounted Infantry: Somaliland (1903-04) 9006.15
Somerset Light Infantry
 badges
  Musician 9403.24
  Territorial Battn 9108.25
 Wagon Hill (1900) (cr) 9306.14-18
South Africa Medal: naming 9003.23
Southampton (Port Natal) 8912.16
South Atlantic Medal (1982): ribbon 8909.26
South Atlantic WWII 9003.11-12
South Australian Scottish: badge 9005.25
South-East Asia (1945-46) 9005.15-17
 post-surrender 9203.22-23
South Lancashire Regt
 badges 9609.20
  Musician 9403.24
  tropical helmet 9405.23
 Spion Kop (1900) (cr) 9408.14-17
South Wales Borderers
 badges 9606.20-21
  Territorial Battn 9108.25
  WWI 9012.22
Soviet Awards: WWII 9409.15-19
Sowar Ditto Ram, Indian Armoured Corps: George Cross (1944) 9402.14
Spanish/American War (Philipines) 9104.12
Special Air Service: WWII 9508.12-13
Special Air Service (Australian) (nr) (i) 8904.05
Special Constabulary: Defence Medal 8908.28

Special Operations Executive
 DSO (mr) 9108.15-17
 Dutch West Borneo 9104.21
Speke, John: Nile exploratons 9312.21-22
sphinx badges 9002.24-25
Spion Kop (Spioenkop) (1900) (cr) 9408.14-17
Sportsmen's Battalions: badges WWI 9012.21-22
11 Squadron RAAF 9409.11-12
10 Squadron RAF: Crete 1942 9402.22
35 Squadron RAF: & *Scharnhorst* 9304.16-17
76 Squadron RAF: & *Scharnhorst* 9304.16-17
152 Squadron RAF: Burma (1942-45) 9006.18
178 Squadron RAF WWII 9110.21-22
263 Squadron RAF: Norway WWII 9402.20-21
605 Squadron RAF WWII 9310.19-20
617 Squadron RAF 9004.28
 (cr) 9002.15-17
5140 Squadron RAF: Bomb Disposal Germany (1946) 9412.19
423 Squadron RCAF 9003.17-18, 9009.11
SS-Freiwillingen Sturmbrigade Wallonien (WWII 9502.17
Stacey, Arthur, Flt Lt RAF: Air Force Cross (1995) 9602.16
Staffordshire Volunteers: helmet plate 9006.22
Stamp, John, PO RNVR: heroism aboard *Dasher* 9606.04
stamps depicting military decorations 9506.16-17
Stanbridge, David, Col Sgt Parachute Regt: Queen's Gallantry Medal(1994) 9602.17
Stanhope Medal 8911.09-10
Stanton, James E., *Shannon*: Indian Muttiny 9302.12-14
Stanton, James W.W., Surgeon RN 9302.13-14
Staples, George E., Able Seaman RAN 9104.19-20
1914 Star 9109.19
 naming 9004.18
 ribbon 8908.26
 RN eligibility 9203.27
 rosette with 8906.27
1914-15 Star 9109.19
 naming 9004.18
Stars (WWII): fakes 9012.26
Steel, N. 'Battlefields of Gallipoli Then & Now' (br) 9106.24
Stephens, D.M., WO 550 Squad (1944) 9410.15-16
Steward, Gilbert D., Ch/Eng *Madura*: OBE WWII 9504.19
Stirling, J. 'Colonials in South Africa (1899-1902)' (br) 9010.21
Stirling, John 'British Regts in South Africa 1899-1902' (br) 9409.24
Stirling, W., Lt Col (p) 8905.09
Stoker, Albert E., P.O. RN: *Glatton* (1918) 8909.16-17
Stoker, H.H.G.D., Lt Cmdr *AE-2* 9306.12-13
Stone, T., Sgt, Royal Canadian Rifles (mp) 9602.08
Stormont Dundas & Glengarry Highlanders: badge 9106.27
'Story of the India General Service Medal 1908-1935' (br) 9610.22
Strathspey Fencibles (1793-99): shoulder-belt plate 9011.20
Strawbridge, R.M.B., Aus. Military Forces WWII (p) 8906.08
Stubby the bull terrier (p) 9503.20
submarines (Royal Navy) 8911.16-17, 24-25
Sudan Campaign (1898): Cameron Highlanders (mr Khedives Sudan Medal) 9504.14-17
Sudan Medal, (1896-97): naming 9004.18
Sudlow, Anthony: Burma WWII 9004.11-12
Suez (1882) 9308.14

Ulster Defence Regiment
  long Service Medal ribbon 8909.26
  part-time awards review 9603.10-11
Ulster Defence Regiment Medal: ribbon 8909.26
Ulster Home Guard: badge 9105.24-25
'Under the Guns of the Red Baron' (br) 9602.22
8th United States Army Air Force WWII 9208.14-15
United Nations Peace Keeping Medal (Ireland)
  9208.28
United States Awards
  fakes 9011.26
  to British WWI 9112.14
United States Marine Corps: Guadalcanal 9209.19-22
University & Public Schools Brigade: badge WWI
  9012.21-22
Upper Thames Patrol: badge 9105.24
Urban, Matt, Lt Col (US): death 9504.05
Urquhart, B.C., Maj 1/ Cameron Highlanders: Sudan
  (1898) 9504.14-17
Ushakov, Order of (USSR) 9409.17-19

V

Valentine: Heligoland (1917) (mr) 9303.17
Valise badges 9411.22-23
Valour awards, Ancient Rome 8903.23-25
Van Praag, Lionel Maurice, Sgt RAAF, GM (Timor
  WWII) 9502.18-19
Varyag (Russia): Chemulpo (1904) 9405.14-15
Vendetta: Heligoland (1917) (mr) 9303.17
Vernon, S.B. ' Vernon's Collectors Guide to Orders
  Medals & Decorations' (br) 9011.28
Vickers, Hugo 'Royal Orders - the Honours and the
  Honoured' (br) 9412.20
Vickers, Sgt Maj 55/Foot: Dewangiri 8910.15-19
Victoria Cross
  6/Gordon Highlanders WWI (mr) 9411.16-17
  Anzac forces WWI(mr) 8905.24-25
  Austalian Forces WWII (mr) 8911.26-27
  Australian Vietnam (mr) 9112.23
  development 9402.12-15
  files by Revd Canon Lummis (i) 8908.28
  location register 9108.28
  locations book 9110.05
  market for 9604.03
  miniature 9505.09
  Projector, Infantry, Anti-Tank (mr) 9112.23
  register (i) 9012.05
'Victoria Cross recipients of Manchester Regt &
  King's (Liverpool) Regt' (br) 9610.06
Victorian Military Society 8903.27
Victoria Volunteer Force: Long & Efficient Service
  Medal 9610.16-17
Victory, Order of (USSR) 9409.17-19
Victory Medal (1914-18)
  naming 9004.18
  ribbon 8908.26
Vietnam 1975: clasp to Australian Service Medal
  (1975) 9403.11
Vietnam
  Australian VCs (mr) 9102.21
  award of Honours to Australian Soldiers 9506.06
  US awards to Australians 9602.11-13
Vietnam Logistic and Support Medal (Australia)
  9410.11
Vietnam Medal (Australia): extended eligibility
  9511.11
Vigur, Edward T., 2/Yorks: Givenchy (1915) 9204.18
Vindictive: Zeebruge/Ostend (1918) 9005.13-14,
  9009.27

Vittoria 8906.11, 13
  15/Hussars 9003.16
Vivian, Sgt: MM WWII 9402.21
Volage: Albania (1946) (cr) 9008.16-17
Voltaire: sunk (1941) 8906.22
Voluntary Aid Detachment (VADs): memorial
  plaques 8905.11
Voluntary Sick Nursing Cross of Merit (Germany):
  1914 bar 8908.10
Voluntary War Assistance Cross (Germany) (WWI)
  8908.09
Volunteer Engineers: badge 9312.24-25
Volunteer Force
  (1914-18) badges 8912.21-22
  shoulder-belt plates 9109.26-27
Volunteer Long Service Medal: County of Devon (mr)
  9311.13
Volunteer Militia Medals (mp) 9509.08
Volunteer Service Company: Boer War (mr QSA)
  9104.15-17
Volunteer Training Corps (1914-18): badges 8912.21-
  22
Voorham, John A., PO (RAN): CSM Iraq (1991)
  9608.14-15
Voyage (HMAS): loss 1964 (cr) (mr) 9404.16-17
Vyner Brooke: sunk Feb (1942) 9504.12-13

W

Waddell, L.A., Lt Col: Gyantse Fort (1904) 9404.21
Wagon Hill (1900) (cr) 9306.14-18
Wake, Nancy: George Medal sold 9406.04
Walker, D.N.R., Pte Glos Regt (p) 9010.09
Walker, Joseph, 82/Foot 9109.21
Wallace, Leslie B., Flt Sgt RNZAF: CGM(F) WWII
  9609.14
Wallace, Mrs: RNLI Medal 8905.20-21
Walland, Beryl: obituary 9005.06
Walsh, ?: Tayleur Fund Medal 9403.19
Walsh, R.S., Capt.: Tank Corps DSO 9012.09
Walton, Eric W.K.: Albert Medal 9103.20
Walton, Kevin: AM Antarctic 9003.12
Wanderer: and Lusitania 9006.10-12
Wanderer (p) 9003.11-13
Wandsworth Battalion: badge WWI 9012.22
War Aid Cross of Merit (Germany) (WWI) 8908.09
War Commemorative Cross (Germany) 8911.21
War Cross of Honour for Heroic Deeds (Germany)
  8909.13
Ward, K. 'Courage Remembered' (br) 8912.06
War Decoration of Honour (Germany) 8909.12
Warden, Arthur, Lt Cdr: Albert Medal(WWI) 9602.06
Wark, Sarah Jane, L/Cpl: MM Northern Ireland
  9611.03
War Medal (1939-45): ribbon 8908.26
War Medal of Honour (Germany) 8909.13
war memorials as a resource 9105.20-21
War Merit Cross (Germany) 8909.13, 8911.20
  WWI 8908.10
War Merit Medal (German Empire) 8908.09
Warrant Officers class III WWII 9112.23
Warsaw raid: 205 group RAF 9212.18-20
War Welfare Work, Decoration of Honour for
  (Germany) 8909.12
Warwickshire Regt: tropical helmet badge 9405.22
Waterhouse, Darren, L/Sgt Coldstream Grds MC
  (1994) 9502.11
Waterloo (1815) 8906.11, 13, 9006.06
  15/Hussars 9003.16

INDEX OF MEDALS

NOTES

Printed in England at the Friary Press, Bridport Road, Dorchester, Dorset DT1 1JL